THE WILEY BICENTENNIAL—KNOWLEDGE FOR GENERATIONS

*E*ach generation has its unique needs and aspirations. When Charles Wiley first opened his small printing shop in lower Manhattan in 1807, it was a generation of boundless potential searching for an identity. And we were there, helping to define a new American literary tradition. Over half a century later, in the midst of the Second Industrial Revolution, it was a generation focused on building the future. Once again, we were there, supplying the critical scientific, technical, and engineering knowledge that helped frame the world. Throughout the 20th Century, and into the new millennium, nations began to reach out beyond their own borders and a new international community was born. Wiley was there, expanding its operations around the world to enable a global exchange of ideas, opinions, and know-how.

For 200 years, Wiley has been an integral part of each generation's journey, enabling the flow of information and understanding necessary to meet their needs and fulfill their aspirations. Today, bold new technologies are changing the way we live and learn. Wiley will be there, providing you the must-have knowledge you need to imagine new worlds, new possibilities, and new opportunities.

Generations come and go, but you can always count on Wiley to provide you the knowledge you need, when and where you need it!

PRESIDENT AND CHIEF EXECUTIVE OFFICER

CHAIRMAN OF THE BOARD

Finance

Ronald W. Melicher

Professor of Finance
University of Colorado at Boulder

and

Edgar A. Norton

Professor of Finance
Illinois State University

with Laura Town

BICENTENNIAL
1807
WILEY
2007
BICENTENNIAL

PUBLISHER   Anne Smith

ASSOCIATE EDITOR   Beth Tripmacher

MARKETING MANAGER   Jennifer Slomack

SENIOR EDITORIAL ASSISTANT   Tiara Kelly

PRODUCTION MANAGER   Kelly Tavares

PRODUCTION ASSISTANT   Courtney Leshko

CREATIVE DIRECTOR   Harry Nolan

COVER DESIGNER   Hope Miller

This book was set in Times New Roman, printed and bound by R.R. Donnelley. The cover was printed by Phoenix Color.

To order books or for customer service please, call 1-800-CALL WILEY (225-5945).

ISBN-13 978-0-470-39214-0
ISBN-10 0-470-39214-2

Printed in the United States of America

10   9   8   7   6   5   4   3   2   1

Library of Congress Cataloging-in-Publication Data
Melicher, Ronald W.
    Finance/Ronald W. Melicher, Edgar A. Norton with Laura Town.
      p.   cm.
    ISBN-13: 978-0-470-39214-0 (pbk.)
    ISBN-10: 0-470-39214-2 (pbk.)
    1. Finance.   I. Norton, Edgar, 1957-   II. Town, Laura.   III. Title.
    HG173.M3978 2007
    332—dc22   2006023043

College classrooms bring together learners from many backgrounds with a variety of aspirations. Although the students are in the same course, they are not necessarily on the same path. This diversity, coupled with the reality that these learners often have jobs, families, and other commitments, requires a flexibility that our nation's higher education system is addressing. Distance learning, shorter course terms, new disciplines, evening courses, and certification programs are some of the approaches that colleges employ to reach as many students as possible and help them clarify and achieve their goals.

Wiley Pathways books, a new line of texts from John Wiley & Sons, Inc., are designed to help you address this diversity and the need for flexibility. These books focus on the fundamentals, identify core competencies and skills, and promote independent learning. The focus on the fundamentals helps students grasp the subject, bringing them all to the same basic understanding. These books use clear, everyday language, presented in an uncluttered format, making the reading experience more pleasurable. The core competencies and skills help students succeed in the classroom and beyond, whether in another course or in a professional setting. A variety of built-in learning resources promote independent learning and help instructors and students gauge students' understanding of the content. These resources enable students to think critically about their new knowledge, and apply their skills in any situation.

Our goal with *Wiley Pathways* books—with its brief, inviting format, clear language, and core competencies and skills focus—is to celebrate the many students in your courses, respect their needs, and help you guide them on their way.

CASE Learning System

To meet the needs of working college students, *Finance* a four-step process: The CASE Learning System. Based on Bloom's Taxonomy of Learning, CASE presents key financial topics in easy-to-follow chapters. The text then prompts analysis, synthesis, and evaluation with a variety of learning aids and assessment tools. Students move efficiently from reviewing what they have learned, to acquiring new information and skills, to applying their new knowledge and skills to real-life scenarios:

- ▲ Content
- ▲ Analysis
- ▲ Synthesis
- ▲ Evaluation

Using the CASE Learning System, students not only achieve academic mastery of financial *topics*, but they master real-world finance *skills*. The CASE Learning System also helps students become independent learners, giving them a distinct advantage whether they are starting out or seek to advance in their careers.

Organization, Depth and Breadth of the Text

Finance offers the following features:

- ▲ **Modular format.** Research on college students shows that they access information from textbooks in a non-linear way. Instructors also often wish to reorder textbook content to suit the needs of a particular class. Therefore, although *Finance* progresses logically from the basics to increasingly more challenging material, chapters are further organized into sections that are self-contained for maximum teaching and learning flexibility.

- ▲ **Numeric system of headings.** *Finance* uses a numeric system for headings (for example, 2.3.4 identifies the fourth sub-section of section 3 of chapter 2). With this system, students and teachers can quickly and easily pinpoint topics in the table of contents and the text, keeping class time and study sessions focused.

- ▲ **Core content.** In today's competitive international economy, students need to not only understand the concepts of business and finance, but students also need to be able to apply them in your professional and personal life. In writing *Finance*, we worked to balance explanations of financial principles with their real-world applications. For the student who does not plan to take additional courses in finance, this book provides a valuable overview of major concepts of the discipline. For the student who wants to take additional courses in finance, the overview presented in this text provides a solid foundation upon which future courses can build. When we do introduce equations and mathematical concepts that are applicable to finance, we show step-by-step solutions.

Part I: Basic Financial Principles

Chapter 1, Introduction to Finance, presents an overview of the four principles of finance. This initial chapter lays a foundation for a discussion on institutions and markets, investments, and financial management.

Chapter 2, Money and Interest Rates, pays special attention to the definition of money, the inner workings on the U.S. monetary system, and the role of the Federal Reserve System. This chapter also discusses the cost of money and the structure of interest rates.

Chapter 3, Time Value of Money, continues with the discussion on interest rates with solutions on how to determine the time value of money.

Chapter 4, Financial Statements, Cash Flow, and Taxes, discusses how to apply this knowledge when reading financial statements, determining cash flow, and working with taxes.

Chapter 5, Analysis of Financial Statements, teaches the student how to read financial statements. Financial ratios, which assist in the process of analyzing a firm's strengths and weaknesses, are also examined. We also review their use as a means to help managers plan ahead for future asset and financing needs.

Part II: Using Financial Principles in Business

Chapter 6, The Basics of Capital Budgeting, reviews budgeting techniques for working with capital, including how to determine the profitability of such decisions.

Chapter 7, Cash Flow Estimation and Risk Analysis, further assesses how to analyze risk in capital budgeting projects and also takes a detailed look at cash flow from operations, cash flow from investment activities, cash flow from financing activities, and cash flow from financing activities.

Chapter 8, Managing Working Capital, discusses how to manage working capital and current assets which both reflect cash flow. This chapter also pays special attention to inventory management, which has a big impact on cash flow.

Chapter 9, Short-Term Business Financing, discusses how to secure additional capital through short-term business financing and what types of securities are needed to secure loans.

Chapter 10, Risk and Rate of Return, continues the discussion of securities by looking at the risk and rate of return on different assets.

Chapter 11, Capital Structure and the Cost of Capital, introduces different capital structures. Trends in the use of debt by corporations and differences in the use of debt by smaller and larger corporations are also examined.

Part III: Stocks, Bonds, and the International Market

Chapter 12, Stocks and the Markets, assesses the role of the New York Stock Exchange and how stocks are bought and sold.

Chapter 13, Distributions to Stockholders, examines the role of shareholders in a company and how distributions are made to shareholders.

Chapter 14, Annuities, Bonds, Futures, and Options, looks at these other investment vehicles.

Chapter 15, International Trade and Finance, offers a detailed discussion of the international monetary system and the effect of international trade and finance on U.S. companies.

It is our belief and hope that students will find that the mastery of the skills presented in this text will provide immeasurable support for their careers and also help them manage their personal finances as well.

Pre-reading Learning Aids

Each chapter of *Finance* features the following learning and study aids to activate students' prior knowledge of the topics and orient them to the material.

- ▲ **Pre-test.** This pre-reading assessment tool in multiple-choice format not only introduces chapter material, but it also helps students anticipate the chapter's learning outcomes. By focusing students' attention on what they do not know, the self-test provides students with a benchmark against which they can measure their own progress. The pre-test is available online at *www.wiley.com/college/Melicher.*

- ▲ **What You'll Learn in This Chapter and After Studying This Chapter.** These bulleted lists tell students what they will be learning in the chapter and why it is significant for their careers. They also explain why the chapter is important and how it relates to other chapters in the text. "What You'll Learn…" lists focus on the *subject matter* that will be taught (e.g. why a financial manager needs to analyze a company's profit-and-loss statement). Each bullet in the list corresponds to a chapter section. "After Studying This Chapter…" lists emphasize *capabilities and skills* students will learn (e.g. how to analyze a company's profit-and-loss statement).

- ▲ **Goals and Outcomes.** These lists identify specific student capabilities that will result from reading the chapter. They set students up to synthesize and evaluate the chapter material, and relate it to the real world.

▲ **Figures and tables.** Line art and photos have been carefully chosen to be truly instructional rather than filler. Tables distill and present information in a way that is easy to identify, access, and understand, enhancing the focus of the text on essential ideas.

Within-text Learning Aids

The following learning aids are designed to encourage analysis and synthesis of the material, and to support the learning process and ensure success during the evaluation phase:

▲ **Introduction.** This section orients the student by introducing the chapter and explaining its practical value and relevance to the book as a whole. Short summaries of chapter sections preview the topics to follow.

▲ **"For Example" Boxes.** Found within each section, these boxes tie section content to real-world organizations, scenarios, and applications.

▲ **Self-Check.** Related to the "What You'll Learn" bullets and found at the end of each section, this battery of short answer questions emphasizes student understanding of concepts and mastery of section content. Though the questions may either be discussed in class or studied by students outside of class, students should not go on before they can answer all questions correctly. Each *Self-Check* question set includes a link to a section of the pre-test for further review and practice.

▲ **Summary.** Each chapter concludes with a summary paragraph that reviews the major concepts in the chapter and links back to the "What you'll learn" list.

▲ **Key Terms and Glossary.** To help students develop a professional vocabulary, key terms are bolded in the introduction, summary and when they first appear in the chapter. A complete list of key terms with brief definitions appears at the end of each chapter and again in a glossary at the end of the book. Knowledge of key terms is assessed by all assessment tools.

Evaluation and Assessment Tools

The evaluation phase of the CASE Learning System consists of a variety of within-chapter and end-of-chapter assessment tools that test how well students have learned the material. These tools also encourage students to extend their learning into different scenarios and higher levels of understanding and thinking. The following assessment tools appear in every chapter of *Finance*.

▲ **Summary Questions** help students summarize the chapter's main points by asking a series of multiple choice and true/false questions that emphasize student understanding of concepts and mastery of chapter content. Students should be able to answer all of the Summary Questions correctly before moving on.

▲ **Review Questions** in short answer format review the major points in each chapter, prompting analysis while reinforcing and confirming student understanding of concepts, and encouraging mastery of chapter content. They are somewhat more difficult than the *Self-Check* and *Summary Questions,* and students should be able to answer most of them correctly before moving on.

▲ **Applying This Chapter Questions** drive home key ideas by asking students to synthesize and apply chapter concepts to new, real-life situations and scenarios.

▲ **You Try It Questions** are designed to extend students' thinking, and so are ideal for discussion or writing assignments. Using an open-ended format and sometimes based on Web sources, they encourage students to draw conclusions using chapter material applied to real-world situations, which fosters both mastery and independent learning.

▲ **Post-test** should be taken after students have completed the chapter. It includes all of the questions in the pre-test, so that students can see how their learning has progressed and improved.

Instructor and Student Package

Finance is available with the following teaching and learning supplements. All supplements are available online at the text's Book Companion Website, located at *www.wiley.com/college/Melicher.*

▲ **Instructor's Resource Guide.** Provides the following aids and supplements for teaching:

- *Diagnostic Evaluation of Grammar, Mechanics, and Spelling.* A useful tool that instructors may administer to the class at the beginning of the course to determine each student's basic writing skills. The Evaluation is accompanied by an Answer Key and a Marking Key. Instructors are encouraged to use the Marking key when grading students' Evaluations, and to duplicate and distribute it to students with their graded evaluations.

- *Sample syllabus.* A convenient template that instructors may use for creating their own course syllabi.

- *Teaching suggestions.* For each chapter, these include a chapter summary, learning objectives, definitions of key terms, lecture notes, answers to select text question sets, and at least 3 suggestions for classroom activities, such as ideas for speakers to invite, videos to show, and other projects.

▲ **Test Bank.** One test per chapter. Each includes true/false, multiple choice, and open-ended questions. Answers and page references are provided for the true/false and multiple choice questions, and page references for the open-ended questions. Available in Microsoft Word and computerized formats.

▲ **PowerPoints.** Key information is summarized in 10 to 15 PowerPoints per chapter. Instructors may use these in class or choose to share them with students for class presentations or to provide additional study support.

Taken together, the content, pedagogy, and assessment elements of *Finance* offer the career-oriented student the most important aspects of finance as well as ways to develop the skills and capabilities that current and future employers seek in the individuals they hire and promote. Instructors will appreciate its practical focus, conciseness, and real-world emphasis. We would like to thank the following reviewers for their feedback and suggestions during the text's development. Their advice on how to shape *Finance* into a solid learning tool that meets both their needs and those of their busy students is deeply appreciated.

William Cahaney, Jefferson Community and Technical College
Wayne Gawlick, Joliet Junior College
Lyle Hicks, Danville Area Community College
David Jones, Johnson County Community College
Janice Karlan, LaGuardia Community College
Jeffrey Keil, J Sargeant Reynolds Community College
Chow Lee, DeVry University
Jerrold Miller, Chaparral Career College
Joseph Nicassio, Westmoreland County Community College
Tom Thompson, Savannah Technical College

BRIEF CONTENTS

CONTENTS

1

INTRODUCTION TO FINANCE
The Basic Structure of Our Financial System

Starting Point

Go to www.wiley.com/college/Melicher to assess your knowledge of the basic structure of the financial system.
Determine where you need to concentrate your effort.

What You'll Learn in This Chapter

▲ The importance of a basic understanding of finance
▲ What finance is and its three primary areas of study
▲ The four principles of what serve as the foundation of finance
▲ The essential components of a financial system

After Studying This Chapter, You'll Be Able To

▲ Examine how a basic understanding of finance is essential even for non-business students
▲ Assess what is meant by *finance* and identify its three primary areas of study
▲ Examine the four principles of finance
▲ Examine the basic requirements of an effective financial system
▲ Compare the major types of securities traded in the securities markets

Goals and Outcomes

▲ Assess financial decisions in both your business and personal life
▲ Assess an organization's reputation as an investment criterion
▲ Evaluate risk versus return for various investments
▲ Select the appropriate category of investment for a particular application
▲ Compare the financial functions of each organization within the financial system
▲ Assess the use and application of specific financial markets
▲ Select international securities that are appropriate for specific investments
▲ Compare the relationship between savings and investments

INTRODUCTION

Most people associate the word *finance* with money, and in today's world, it's a natural and necessary connection. Finance encompasses all the forms that money becomes and all the ways that money is accumulated, managed, and spent. In this chapter, we will explore the basic elements of finance, the rules that govern it, and the institutions and organizations that facilitate it and keep our economy running smoothly.

1.1 Why Study Finance?

There are many varied and interesting career choices within the financial environment, but understanding finance is important to everyone regardless of where their goals and interests lie. Wherever you go, whatever you do in life, there will always be financial decisions to consider.

Money matters. It affects many of the personal decisions in life. Whether you're thinking about what shampoo to purchase, what car to buy, or where to go on your next vacation, you need to be aware of the economy and how the dollars you spend or save are affected by it.

Let's look at the facts. As the American economy moved from the industrial age to the information age, dramatic changes occurred in the importance of small businesses. While large firms with 500 or more employees continued to downsize and restructure throughout the 1990s and into the twenty-first century, small firms provided the momentum for economic growth.

Between the mid-1970s and the beginning of the 1990s, firms with fewer than 500 employees provided over half of total employment and nearly two-thirds of the net new jobs in the United States. Since the decade of the 1990s began, small firms have provided most of the net new jobs.

Why have small firms been so successful in creating new jobs? A Small Business Administration white paper suggests two reasons. First, small firms provide

FOR EXAMPLE

Professional Reasons to Study Finance

Even if you do not plan to have a career in finance, it is still in your professional interest to study finance. You will interact with finance professionals both within and outside your firm. This interaction will only be effective if you have a basic knowledge of the concepts, tools, and applications of financial management. For example, you may want to launch a new product at your firm. To do this, you will need to be able to demonstrate the costs, the profit, and the return on investment to the decision makers.

a crucial role in technological change and productivity growth. Market economies change rapidly, and small firms are able to adjust quickly. Second, small firms provide the mechanism and incentive for millions of individuals to pursue the opportunity for economic success.

Others may argue that it is the entrepreneurial spirit and activity that account for the importance of small firms in the U.S. economy. Whatever the reason(s), the ongoing growth of small businesses continues to be an important stimulus to the economy in the twenty-first century.

Understanding the financial environment will also help you to make wise personal and business investment decisions and allow you to manage your personal resources in a way that is likely to accumulate wealth over time.

SELF-CHECK

- List three reasons why the study of finance is important.

1.2 What Is Finance?

Finance is the study of how individuals, institutions, governments, and businesses acquire, spend, and manage money and other financial assets.

Notice that the definition of *finance* you have just read puts individuals first. That's because first and foremost, people are the financial system.

The main participants are not the large institutions or corporations you will learn about, but rather are people like you. For example, households, families, and individuals provide up to 80% of the savings flow in the U.S. economy.

The origins of finance are in economics and accounting. Economists use a supply-and-demand framework to explain how the prices and quantities of goods and services are determined in a free-market economic system.

Accountants play a pivotal role in every aspect of the business world. They are the record-keepers, providing a constant flow of information vital to the institutions, markets, investment firms, and managers. Accountants also record assets and liabilities, revenues and expenses, in order to determine the profitability of organizations that produce and exchange goods and services.

The financial environment consists of three areas called the *pillars of finance,* as demonstrated in Figure 1-1:

- ▲ Institutions and markets
- ▲ Investments
- ▲ Financial management

Figure 1-1

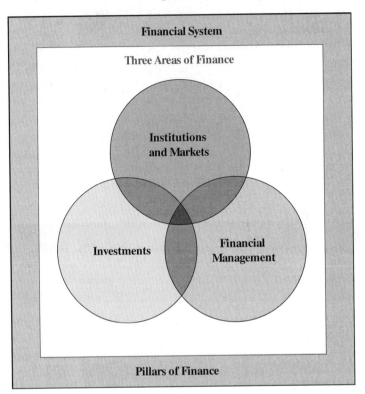

The financial environment.

1.2.1 Financial Institutions and Markets

Financial institutions and **financial markets** help the financial system operate efficiently. They act as intermediaries to transfer funds from savers and investors to individuals, businesses, and governments that seek to spend or invest the funds in physical assets like inventory, real estate, and equipment. Physical locations or electronic forums exist that facilitate the flow of funds.

Included in this category are banks, insurance companies, and investment firms. They are crucial elements of the financial environment and have a direct effect on the stability and interests of the economic system.

Efficient methods of production and specialization of labor can exist only if there is an effective means of paying for raw materials and final products.

Businesses can obtain the money needed to buy capital goods such as machinery and equipment because institutions and markets have established a policy and a method to make savings available for investment. Similarly, federal, state, and local governments and tax districts can carry out their wide range of activities only because effective means exist for raising money, for making payments, and for borrowing.

FOR EXAMPLE

Role of the Financial Manager

The goal of the financial manager in a profit-seeking organization is to maximize the owners' wealth. This is accomplished through effective financial planning and analysis, asset management, and the acquisition of financial capital. In a not-for-profit organization, the financial manager's goal is to provide a desired level of services at acceptable costs and perform the same financial management functions as their for-profit counterparts.

1.2.2 Investments

Investments include the sale or marketing of stocks, bonds, and securities; the analysis of securities; and the management of investment risk through portfolio diversification.

Portfolio diversification is a common term in the investment world and sounds more complicated than it is. There is an old adage that instructs you not to put all your eggs in one basket. This is the theory behind portfolio diversification. In other words, spread your investments around rather than putting all your funds into one stock. That way, if one of your stocks does poorly, you still have a number of others that continue to make money for you.

1.2.3 Financial Management

Financial management encompasses the people and companies who are responsible for financial planning, asset management, and fund-raising decisions. The goal of the management professional is to protect and increase the value of investments and businesses.

SELF-CHECK

- What role do accountants play in the financial environment?
- Define **finance**.
- List the three pillars of finance and describe each one.

1.3 Four Principles of Finance

Finance is founded on four important principles. The first three relate to the economic behavior of individuals, and the fourth one focuses on ethical behavior. Reviewing these principles will help you understand how managers, investors, and others incorporate "time" and "risk" in their decisions.

The following are the four principles that serve as the foundation of finance:

▲ Money has a time value.
▲ Higher returns are expected for taking on more risk.
▲ Financial markets are efficient in pricing securities.
▲ Reputation matters.

These four principles will be reviewed and explained in more detail in other chapters of this book. For now, we will take a brief look at them one by one.

1.3.1 Money Has a Time Value

Money in hand today is worth more than the promise of receiving the same amount in the future. The "time value" of money exists because a sum of money today could be invested and grow over time. Let's assume that you have $1,000 today and it could earn $60 (6%) interest at the end of 1 year from now. Thus, $1,000 today would be worth $1,060 at the end of one year ($1,000 plus interest of $60). So, it follows that a dollar today is worth more than a dollar received a year from now.

Understanding the time value of money should also help you to understand the economic behavior of individuals and the economic decisions of the institutions and businesses that they operate.

The time value of money is apparent in many of our own day-to-day activities. Buying a new car just before the next year's models are introduced gives you the same benefits of new-car ownership at a reduced price. Often there are several sides of a purchase that should be considered when making major expenditures and in determining how much of your paycheck should be saved rather than spent.

1.3.2 Higher Returns Are Expected for Taking on More Risk

The second principle of finance is a simple fact of life. Higher returns are expected for taking on greater risk. Risk is the uncertainty about the outcome or proceeds from an investment in the future.

Let's say you have $1,000 to invest. You have a choice between investing your money in a new business venture or using it to purchase a U.S. government bond. Many new businesses fail within the first year, so obviously that investment carries a higher risk than purchasing the government bond. If the business fails, your money will be lost. However, if the business succeeds, your investment could double or triple in a year's time. On the other hand, there is not much chance that you will lose money on the bond. It will earn interest during the year so you will retain your initial $1,000 and realize a small profit at the end of the year.

Rational investors would consider the business venture investment to be riskier and would choose this investment only if they felt the expected return would be high enough to make it worth the greater risk.

Investors and business managers make these trade-off decisions every day. Understanding the risk/return trade-off principle may also help you understand how individuals make the economic decisions that will be covered in future chapters.

1.3.3 Financial Markets Are Efficient in Pricing Securities

Financial markets must be efficient in evaluating and pricing securities and investment opportunities. Individuals are always looking for smart and lucrative investment opportunities. It is human nature. Like the horseplayer who is always looking for that long shot to cross the finish line first. And people involved in real estate want to buy low and sell high.

This desire to win or "beat the market" means we must be information efficient. Real estate investors always study the markets and locations before making a buying or selling decision to ensure that they are getting the best deal.

A financial market is said to be **information efficient** if at any point the prices of securities reflect all the information available to the public. When new information becomes available, prices can change quickly to reflect that information. Let's assume that a firm's stock is currently trading at $20 per share. If the market information is efficient, both potential buyers and sellers of the stock know that $20 per share is a "fair" price. Trades should be at $20, or near to it, if the demand (potential buyers) and supply (potential sellers) are in reasonable balance. Now, if that company announces the production of a new product that is expected to increase sales and profits, the price of the stock will most likely rise. This informational efficiency of financial markets exists because a large number of professionals are continually searching and studying and providing new information to the public. Information-efficient financial markets play an important role in the marketing and transferring of financial assets between investors by providing liquidity and fair prices.

1.3.4 Reputation Matters

An individual's reputation reflects his/her ethical standards or behavior. Ethical behavior dictates that an individual or organization treats others legally, fairly, and

---

FOR EXAMPLE

Information and Stock Prices

When the automotive giant General Motors experienced large financial losses beginning in 2005, its stock price fluctuated wildly. Daily stories in the press about GM's financial obligations and sales performance had investors interpreting the information as buying or selling opportunities. Favorable information drove up the stock price, but new data released the next day, viewed by investors as negative, caused the price to plummet. As GM's management sold off business units to bolster their cash reserves, the stock would climb. When news of a potential labor union strike at GM's primary supplier was released, the stock price again dropped.

honestly. Of course, the ethical behavior of organizations reflects the ethical behavior of their directors, officers, and managers. For institutions or businesses to be successful, they must have the trust and confidence of their customers, employees, and owners, as well as the community and society within which they operate.

Everyone agrees that firms have a responsibility to provide safe products and services and to afford safe working conditions for employees. We also expect them to protect the environment and not pollute it. Laws and regulations exist to ensure minimum levels of compliance. When a company meets and exceeds our expectations, we deem them to be ethical.

Unfortunately, because of the greed for more profits and returns, such as higher salaries, bonuses, and more valuable stock options, business managers have been known to reduce the quality of their products, ignore safety regulations, and in general engage in fraudulent or illegal activities.

In the long run, reputations are destroyed, criminal activities are prosecuted, and involved individuals may receive jail sentences. Unethical behavior usually damages a company's reputation and can totally destroy it.

Many examples of fraudulent and illegal behavior have been cited in the financial press over the past few decades. Most cases seem to be tied to greed and the desire for personal gain. Confidential information has been used for personal benefit, illegal payments or bribes have been made to gain business, accounting information has been fraudulently reported, and business assets have been converted to personal use.

In the early 1980s, a number of savings and loan association managers were found to have engaged in fraudulent and unethical practices. This resulted in some managers being prosecuted and sent to prison and their institutions being dissolved or merged with other institutions.

In the late 1980s and early 1990s, fraudulent activities and unethical behavior by investment banking firms resulted in several high-profile financial "wheeler-dealers" going to prison. This resulted in the collapse of Drexel, Burnham, Lambert and the near collapse of Salomon Brothers.

By the early part of the new century, major firms such as Enron, its auditor, Arthur Andersen, and WorldCom ceased to exist because of fraudulent and unethical behavior on the part of their managers and officers. In addition, key officials of Tyco and Adelphia were charged with illegal actions and fraud. Even more recently, managers and officers of mutual funds have been indicted for fraudulent and unethical business practices.

The list of improprieties seems to be endless and disheartening. However, while the news media chooses to sensationalize examples of unethical behavior, it does not give a true picture of the financial industry. On the contrary, most individuals are very ethical and professional in both their personal and business dealings.

Most financial managers believe that reputation matters. They know that an organization or business must maintain the trust and confidence of its customers, employees, owners, and the community in general to be successful.

Ethical behavior goes beyond meeting legal and regulatory requirements. Its importance has prompted many companies to develop and follow their own "code of ethics." A good reputation is priceless and essential for those who work in the financial environment.

Note that the Figure 1-2 depicts a simplified view of the U.S. financial system. A good financial system must have several sets of policy makers who pass laws and make decisions relating to fiscal and monetary policies. These policy makers include the president, Congress, the U.S. Treasury, and the Federal Reserve Board. Since the United States operates within a global economy, political and economic actions of foreign policy makers may also influence, although indirectly, the U.S. financial system and its operations.

In subsequent chapters, you will learn more about the Federal Reserve System and how policy makers here and abroad influence the economy and the financial system.

Financial institutions must exist that support capital formation either by channeling savings into investment in physical assets or by fostering direct investments by individuals in financial institutions and businesses.

Working in conjunction with the institutions, the financial system must also have markets that facilitate the transfer of financial assets among individuals, institutions, businesses, and governments.

SELF-CHECK

- Identify and briefly describe the four principles of finance.
- Name the principle of finance that explains the fact that a dollar today is worth more than a dollar received a year from now.
- Name the principle of finance that explains why investing in a start-up business has the potential of earning higher returns than investing in U.S. treasury bonds.
- Describe the characteristics of an information-efficient market.
- List one reason why reputation matters in finance.
- Name a firm publicly accused of unethical behavior.

1.4 The Financial System

An effective **financial system** is a complex mix of government and policy makers, a **monetary system**, financial institutions, and financial markets that interact to expedite the flow of financial capital from savings into investment. This process is called *capital formation*. **Capital formation** is the expansion of capital or capital goods through savings, which leads to investment. In a simple economy, such as a self-sufficient, one-person farm, this process takes place directly. The farmer creates capital by building a barn.

In a highly developed economy, productive capital formation typically takes place indirectly. If individuals, businesses, or government units do not need to spend all of their current income, they save some of it. These savings are placed with a financial institution and will be made available as loans to others who will then use them to purchase buildings, machinery, or equipment.

Keep in mind the indirect process of productive capital formation can work only if the proper legal instruments and financial institutions exist. Only then will people feel secure when transferring their savings to businesses and other institutions within the financial system.

Let's look at the process of capital formation by examining the U.S. financial system. Figure 1-2 depicts a simplified view of the U.S. financial system. A good financial system must have several sets of policy makers. These are the

Figure 1-2

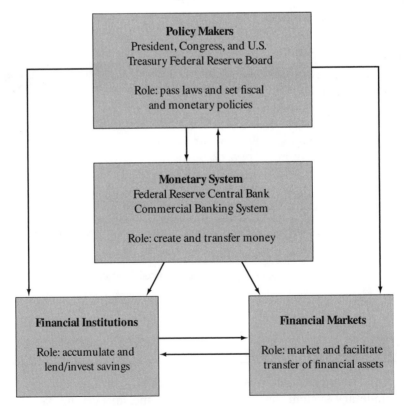

Overview of the U.S. financial system.

people who pass laws and make decisions relating to fiscal and monetary policies. Policy makers include the president, Congress, the U.S. Treasury, and the Federal Reserve Board. A financial system must make the creation of productive capital possible on a scale large enough to meet the demands of the economy. Productive capital formation takes place whenever resources are used to produce buildings, machinery, or other equipment used to produce goods for consumers or producers.

Because the United States operates within a global economy, political and economic actions of foreign policy makers may also influence, although indirectly, the U.S. financial system and its operations. It is important to remember that in the United States, we have financial institutions, financial markets, and a monetary system.

▲ **Financial institutions** must exist that support capital formation either by channeling savings into investment in physical assets or by fostering direct investments by individuals in financial institutions and businesses.

▲ **Financial markets,** working in conjunction with the institutions, must exist to facilitate the transfer of financial assets among individuals, institutions, businesses, and governments.

Financial markets are also necessary for productive capital formation needed to transfer financial assets, such as stocks and bonds, and to convert such assets into cash. They encourage investment by providing the means for savers to convert their financial assets quickly and easily into cash. For example, people are willing to invest billions of dollars in IBM, General Electric, and other companies because the New York Stock Exchange makes it possible to sell their shares to other investors quickly and easily when the need for cash arises.

FOR EXAMPLE

Federal Reserve Board

The Federal Reserve Board is the central banking system in the United States. The board has a central board of governors and includes 12 Federal Reserve banks, member banks, and other entities. The responsibilities of the Federal Reserve Board are to

- supervise and regulate banks;
- implement monetary policy;
- control the amount of currency that is produced and destroyed on a daily basis.

A monetary system is essential for any government. There must also be a convenient means to pay for goods and services purchased. A business worth millions of dollars should be as easy to purchase as a pack of chewing gum.

In addition to establishing money as the medium of exchange in the United States, the monetary system must also be able to create and transfer checks and electronic funds in various amounts easily and efficiently.

SELF-CHECK

- List the four components of an effective financial system.
- Explain the role of policy makers in the financial system.
- Explain the role of a monetary system in the financial system.
- Explain the role of financial institutions in the financial system.
- Explain the role of financial markets in the financial system.

1.5 Financial Functions

The main components shown in Figure 1-3 each have a particular financial function within the system. These components house different types of organizations and procedures under their main titles.

Figure 1-3

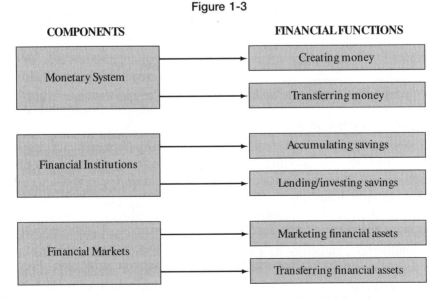

Three financial system components and their financial functions.

To give you a better understanding of each branch of the system, we will examine the various entities that are part of each one and their underlying functions.

1.5.1 Creating Money

The monetary system must also provide a practical means to exchange goods and services. A way to measure prices, called a **unit of account,** is a basic requirement. The unit of account in the United States is the U.S. dollar. The unit of account must be universally accepted if exchange is to function smoothly. Ideally, the value of the dollar should remain stable if it is to be widely used.

Money in the form of coins and currency has become the easiest way to pay for goods, services, and debts. The true value of money is said to lie in its purchasing power. Money is also the easiest way to measure a person's wealth because it can be exchanged for almost anything else.

Most transactions in today's economy involve money and would not take place if money were not available. Therefore, one of the most significant functions of the monetary system within the financial network is creating money, which serves as a medium of exchange.

In the United States, the Federal Reserve System is primarily responsible for the amount of money that is created, although most of the money is actually created by depository institutions.

Economic activity relies on a sufficient amount of money to run smoothly. Too little money restricts economic growth. Too much money often results in increases in the prices of goods and services.

1.5.2 Transferring Money

When money is placed in a checking account, payments can be easily made by check. The check is an order to the depository institution to transfer money to the party who received the check. This is a great convenience, since checks can be written for the exact amount of payments, can be safely sent in the mail, and can provide a record of payment.

Institutions can also transfer funds between accounts electronically, making payments without paper checks. Transfers can be made by telephone, at automated teller machines (ATMs) connected to a bank's computer, and via the Internet.

For the bank, the net result from all this money flowing back and forth is the accumulation of funds from many depositors or customers. This enables the bank to use those funds for loans and investments in amounts much larger than any individual depositor could supply. That's why depository institutions regularly conduct advertising campaigns and other promotional activities to attract new customers.

FOR EXAMPLE

Electronic Transfers

The most common form of electronic transfers today is through automated teller machines (ATMs) that most people use on a daily basis. Armed with an ATM card, you can withdraw money from your accounts from almost anywhere in the world. Even if you're in a foreign country, you receive the funds in the proper currency for that country, and the exchange rate is automatically calculated by your bank.

1.5.3 Savings

A function performed by financial institutions is the accumulation or gathering of individual savings. Most individuals, businesses, and organizations avoid the risks of keeping too much cash on hand by depositing their funds in a bank for safekeeping.

Money deposited in savings accounts is expected to remain in the bank and earn interest for longer periods of time than money deposited in checking accounts. The checking account is for funds that will be needed in a fairly short amount of time to pay the debts and expenses of the individual or business.

1.5.4 Lending and Investing Savings

For the bank, the net result from all this money flowing back and forth is the accumulation of funds from many depositors or customers. This enables the bank to use those funds for loans and investments in amounts much larger than any individual depositor could supply. That's why depository institutions regularly conduct advertising campaigns and other promotional activities to attract new customers. Financial institutions are responsible for the depositors' funds so there are rules in place for making loans. Borrowers must meet certain requirements as far as credit is concerned and must prove that they have the means to repay the loans. Basically, money is lent to individuals, businesses, other institutions, and governments.

The terms of a particular loan often depend on the amount of the loan, what it is going to be used for, and whether or not there is sufficient collateral to guarantee that loan will be repaid.

Some financial institutions make loans of all types, such as personal loans (to individuals) and commercial loans (to businesses). Others specialize in one or the other. Then there are those financial institutions that invest all or part of their accumulated savings in the stock of a business or in debt obligations of businesses or other institutions.

There are two basic types of loans that should be mentioned here: secured and unsecured. Most loans obtained through banks are **secured loans.** A mortgage is a secured loan because the property you are purchasing must be appraised and valued at the amount you are borrowing. The same is true of an auto loan. This is a safety net for the lending institution as the property that secures a loan can be confiscated if the borrower defaults (doesn't repay) the loan.

1.5.5 Marketing Financial Assets

New financial instruments and securities are created and sold in the primary securities market. For example, a business may want to sell shares of ownership, called *stock*, to the general public. It can do so directly, but the process of finding individuals interested in investing funds in that business is likely to be difficult, costly, and time consuming.

1.5.6 Transferring Financial Assets

Several types of financial institutions facilitate or assist in the processes of lending and selling securities. If shares of stock are to be sold to the general public, it is desirable to have a ready market in which such stocks can be resold when the investor desires. Organized stock exchanges provide active secondary markets for existing securities. The ability to buy and sell securities both quickly and at "fair market values" is important in a well-organized financial system. An in-depth look at the New York Stock Exchange is presented in Chapter 12.

SELF-CHECK

- List two financial functions of the monetary system.
- List two financial functions of financial institutions.
- List two financial functions of financial markets.
- Name two types of bank accounts.
- What is a secured loan?

1.6 Types of Financial Institutions

The system of financial institutions in the United States, like the monetary system, evolved to meet the needs of the country's citizens and to facilitate the savings-investment process.

Figure 1-4

FINANCIAL INSTITUTIONS CATEGORIES	PRIMARY SOURCES OF FUNDS
DEPOSITORY INSTITUTIONS	
Commercial banks	Individual savings
Savings and loan associations	Individual savings
Savings banks	Individual savings
Credit unions	Individual savings
CONTRACTUAL SAVINGS ORGANIZATIONS	
Insurance companies	Premiums paid on policies
Pension funds	Employee/employer contributions
SECURITIES FIRMS	
Investment companies (mutual funds)	Individual savings (investments)
Investment banking firms	Other financial institutions
Brokerage firms	Other financial institutions
FINANCE FIRMS	
Finance companies	Other financial institutions
Mortgage banking firms	Other financial institutions

Types of financial institutions.

Individuals may save and grow their savings with the assistance of financial institutions, as illustrated in Figure 1-4. While some individuals invest directly in the securities of business firms and government units, most prefer to invest indirectly through financial institutions that do the lending and investing for them.

Depository institutions accept deposits or savings from individuals and then lend these pooled savings to businesses, governments, and individuals. Depository institutions include commercial banks and thrift institutions.

▲ **Commercial banks** play an important financial role in the system by collecting deposits from individuals and lending those funds to businesses and individuals.

▲ **Thrift institutions,** including savings and loan associations, savings banks, and credit unions, accumulate individual savings and provide credit primarily to individuals.

Like commercial banks, **savings and loans** also lend to both businesses and individuals. **Savings banks** and **credit unions** focus on working with consumers and provide loans to individuals seeking to purchase items such as automobiles and houses.

▲ **Contractual savings organizations** collect premiums and contributions from participants and provide retirement benefits and insurance against major financial losses.

Insurance companies provide financial protection to individuals and businesses for life, property, liability, and health. Policyholders pay premiums to insurance companies that are then invested or withdrawn to pay claims.

Pension funds receive contributions from employees and/or their employers and invest the proceeds on behalf of the employees. Many business organizations provide private plans for their employees. State and some local governments also provide pension (retirement) funds for employees.

Like depository institutions, insurance companies and pension funds are actively involved in the financial intermediation process of gathering the funds of individuals (premium payments and employee contributions) and investing these collective funds so that businesses can grow and government units can provide more benefits for citizens.

▲ **Securities firms** accept and invest individual savings and also facilitate the sale and transfer of securities between investors.

Investment companies sell shares in their firms to individuals and others and invest the proceeds in corporate and government securities. One type of security investment, mutual funds, is dominant in size and investor popularity. Mutual funds are open-end funds because they can issue an unlimited number of their shares to their investors and use the pooled proceeds to purchase corporate and government securities. Mutual funds grow by investing the funds of their existing investors in securities that will pay or distribute cash and will appreciate in value. Successful mutual funds are able to attract more investor funds and, in turn, invest in more securities. Like depository institutions and contractual savings organizations, investment companies (particularly mutual funds) perform an important financial intermediation function.

Investment banking firms sell or market new securities issued by businesses to individual and institutional investors. **Brokerage firms** assist individuals who want to purchase new stock issues or who want to sell previously purchased securities. Investment banking and brokerage activities are often combined in the same firms. However, unlike mutual funds, investment banking and brokerage firms are not actively involved in financial intermediation. Rather than gathering the savings of individuals, these firms obtain their financial capital from their own resources or from other financial institutions.

▲ **Finance firms** provide loans directly to consumers and businesses, as well as help borrowers obtain mortgage loans on real property. Real property is land and/or the structures that are built on that land. Some finance companies offer consumers installment loans to purchase automobiles and other durable goods, while others provide small personal loans to individuals and households.

FOR EXAMPLE

Mortgage Loans

Mortgage loans are usually long-term loans backed by real property and typically are repaid in monthly installments of interest and a partial repayment of the loan amount that was borrowed. If a mortgage loan is not repaid by the borrower, the lender can seize and sell the pledged real property under foreclosure laws.

Individuals and businesses that are unable to obtain financing from commercial banks often turn to **finance companies** because their loan requirements are not as stringent. However, finance companies traditionally charge higher interest rates on the loans they make.

Mortgage banking firms, sometimes just called *mortgage companies*, originate real estate mortgages by bringing together borrowers and investors. Mortgage loan companies are usually not intermediaries in the financial system because they obtain their own financing from other financial institutions rather than from individual savers.

SELF-CHECK

- List the four major categories of financial institutions.
- Describe depository institutions and list three examples of such institutions.
- Describe contractual savings organizations and list two examples of such organizations.
- Describe securities firms and list two examples of such firms.
- Describe finance firms and list two examples of such firms.

1.7 Types of Financial Markets

There are three types of financial markets: securities markets, derivative markets, and currency exchange markets.

▲ **Securities markets** are physical locations or electronic forums where debt and equity securities are sold and traded.

▲ **Debt securities** are obligations to repay borrowed funds. Federal, state, and local governments can issue debt securities, while business corporations and financial institutions can issue both debt and equity securities.

▲ **Equity securities** are ownership rights in businesses and institutions.

Corporations can raise funds either through a private placement, which involves issuing new securities directly to specific investors, or through a public offering, which involves selling new securities to the general public.

There are primary and secondary markets for debt and equity securities.

▲ **Primary securities markets** facilitate the sales of initial offerings of debt and equity securities to the public.

Proceeds, after issuing costs, from the sale of new securities go to the issuing business or government entity. The primary market is the only place where the security issuer directly benefits (receives funds) from the sale of its securities.

▲ **Secondary securities markets** facilitate the transfer of previously issued securities from existing investors to new investors. Security transactions or transfers typically take place on organized security exchanges or in the electronic over-the-counter market.

Individuals and other investors can actively buy and sell existing securities in the secondary market. While these secondary market investors may make gains or losses on their security investments, the issuer of the securities does not benefit (nor does it lose) from these activities. The secondary market for securities is typically divided into short-term (money) and long-term (capital) market categories.

▲ **Derivatives markets** facilitate the purchase and sale of derivative securities.

▲ **Derivative securities** are financial contracts that derive their values from underlying securities or from other related financial assets.

A familiar form of derivative security is the opportunity to buy or sell a corporation's equity securities for a specified price and within a certain amount of time. Derivative securities may be used to speculate on the future price direction of the underlying financial assets, or to reduce price risk associated with holding the underlying financial assets. Organized exchanges handle standardized derivative security contracts, while negotiated contracts are handled in electronic markets often involving commercial banks or other financial institutions.

FOR EXAMPLE

Mortgage Markets

There are also mortgage markets. Mortgage markets are markets in which mortgage loans, backed by real property in the form of buildings and houses, are originated and sometimes traded. While it is difficult to buy and sell individual home mortgages in a secondary market, standardized high-quality mortgages have been "pooled" together in recent years into mortgage-backed securities that have active secondary markets.

▲ **Currency exchange markets** (also called *foreign exchange* or *FOREX markets*) are electronic markets in which banks and institutional traders buy and sell various currencies on behalf of businesses and other clients.

In the global economy, consumers may want to purchase goods produced, or services provided, in other countries. Likewise, an investor residing in one country may wish to hold securities issued in another country.

Businesses that sell their products in foreign countries usually receive payment in the foreign currencies. However, because the relative values of currency is subject to change, firms often use the currency exchange markets to reduce the risk of holding too much of certain currencies.

SELF-CHECK

- List the three types of financial markets.
- Explain what securities markets are and list two types.
- Explain the difference between debt securities and equity securities.
- Define **derivative securities** and name where they are they traded.
- Explain what currency exchange markets are.

1.8 Types of Securities

Money is the fundamental measure of wealth. In addition to money, an individual or a business also measures its wealth in terms of the real and financial assets or claims that it holds.

Figure 1-5

SECURITIES MARKETS CATEGORIES	ISSUERS
MONEY MARKETS	
Treasury bills	U.S. government
Negotiable certificates of deposit (CDs)	Commercial banks
Commercial paper	Corporations
CAPITAL MARKETS	
Treasury bonds	U.S. government
Municipal bonds	State/local governments
Corporate bonds	Corporations
Corporate stocks	Corporations

Types of debt and equity securities.

▲ **Real assets** include the direct ownership of land, buildings or homes, equipment, inventories, durable goods, and even precious metals.

▲ **Financial assets** or claims are debt instruments, equity securities, and other financial contracts that are backed by real assets. Examples include mortgages and auto loans.

Long-term debt issued by a corporation may represent a claim against specific assets, such as buildings and equipment. Checkable deposits, such as checking accounts and share drafts, and time deposits, such as savings accounts held in depository institutions, are also examples of financial assets. In fact, all kinds of promissory notes or IOUs represent financial assets to their holders.

When the public holds currency issued by the U.S. government, the currency is a financial asset. At the same time, it is a financial liability to the government.

Debt and equity securities are the primary types of financial claims that are actively traded in secondary markets.

▲ **Money markets** are the markets where debt securities with maturities of 1 year or less are traded.

▲ **Capital markets** include debt securities with maturities longer than 1 year and equity securities.

Figure 1-5 indicates the major types of securities that are issued in primary securities markets and are traded in secondary securities markets.

1.8.1 Money Market Securities

Debt securities with maturities of 1 year or less are considered to be major money market securities.

▲ **Treasury bills** are short-term debt obligations issued by the U.S. federal government to meet its short-term borrowing needs when imbalances exist between tax revenues and government expenditures.

Treasury bills are generally issued with maturities between 3 months and 1 year. Investors buy treasury bills for safety and liquidity reasons. They are considered a safe investment and there is an active secondary money market for Treasury bills, so investors can easily sell them at any time before maturity if cash needs arise.

▲ **Negotiable certificates of deposit,** or negotiable CDs, are short-term debt instrument issued by depository institutions to individual or institutional depositors.

Negotiable certificates of deposit are issued by commercial banks in denominations of $100,000 or more with typical maturities ranging from 1 month to 1 year. Negotiable CDs are money market securities with an active secondary market that allows short-term investors to easily match their cash or liquidity needs when they arise.

It is important to distinguish negotiable CDs from smaller-denomination CD time deposits offered by depository institutions to individual depositors. Small-deposit CDs are nonnegotiable—that is, they cannot be sold or used for collateral. They must be redeemed with the issuer, and thus no secondary securities market exists for them. In fact, owners of nonnegotiable CDs redeemed before maturity usually are charged an interest-deduction penalty.

Businesses often find it necessary to borrow short term to meet temporary imbalances between when cash is received from sales and when bills must be paid.

▲ **Commercial paper** is a short-term unsecured promissory note issued by a corporation with a high credit rating.

Maturities on commercial paper are generally 1 to 3 months in length. However, since there is an active secondary money market for commercial paper, purchasers can easily sell their commercial paper holdings at any time to meet their cash needs.

1.8.2 Capital Market Securities

Bonds and stocks are the principal securities traded in the capital markets. Bonds are debt securities with maturities greater than 1 year. Three major types of bonds, along with corporate stocks, are identified under the capital markets category in Figure 1-5.

▲ **Treasury bonds** are long-term debt securities issued by the U.S. federal government.

FOR EXAMPLE

Municipal Bonds

Some investors find municipal bonds to be attractive investments because the interest paid on these securities is exempt from federal income taxes and because these bonds can be sold in a secondary securities market.

Some investors find government bonds to be attractive investments because the interest paid on these securities is exempt from income taxes and because these bonds can be easily sold in a secondary securities market.

▲ **Municipal bonds** are long-term debt securities issued by state or local governments.

Maturities on these government bonds are often in the 5- to 20-year range. However, municipal bonds issued to build airports or bridges may have their maturities set to coincide with the expected lives of the assets being financed.

▲ **Corporate bonds** are issued by corporations and are typically issued with 5- to 20-year maturities.

The proceeds of corporate bonds are usually used for capital improvements such as new plants or equipment.

▲ **Common stocks** represent ownership shares in corporations.

Corporations issue new shares of their common stocks in the primary market to raise funds for capital expenditures and investments in inventories. Active secondary markets exist for trading common stocks after they are initially issued.

SELF-CHECK

- Define **real assets** and **financial assets** and give two examples of each.
- Explain the difference between money markets and capital markets.
- List the three major money market securities and explain each.
- List the three major types of bonds that comprise capital market securities and explain each.

1.9 International Securities and Markets

Debt and equity markets also are well developed in many foreign countries. Corporations based in foreign countries are able to issue bonds and stocks in their own home currencies and markets. Corporations also can sell their stocks in securities markets outside their home countries as a way of broadening investor recognition and raising more funds.

▲ **Foreign bonds** are bonds issued by a corporation or government that are valued in the currency of the country where it is sold.

For example, a U.S. corporation may issue a bond denominated in pounds to investors in Great Britain, or a German firm might issue a bond denominated in Australian dollars to Australians.

▲ **Eurobonds** are bonds denominated in U.S. dollars that are sold to investors located in a country outside the United States.

It is important to note that *euro* does not necessarily refer to Europe. For example, a German corporation may sell a $20 million Eurobond to either German or Australian investors. The fact that the bond will pay interest and repay the amount borrowed at maturity in U.S. dollars makes it a Eurobond.

International money markets also are important to business borrowers. For example, a U.S.-based corporation may have a foreign subsidiary that produces and sells products in European countries that have adopted the euro as their common currency. If the U.S. corporation's subsidiary is short of euros for conducting day-to-day operations, the subsidiary may borrow short-term by issuing commercial paper denominated in euros in Italy. Likewise, during periods when there are excess euros from operations, the U.S. foreign subsidiary may exchange its excess euros for a negotiable CD issued by a German bank.

FOR EXAMPLE

Eurobond

A Eurobond is also referred to as a *global bond*. A Eurobond is intended to be bought and sold during the period up to its maturity. It is usually launched through a public offering and is listed on a stock exchange. There is no central register where holders of the issue are named. So the Eurobond itself is a bearer instrument. Interests on the Eurobond are paid upon presentation of detachable coupons. The principal amount is paid on presentation of the Eurobond itself.

SELF-CHECK

- Explain what a foreign bond is.
- Explain what a Eurobond is.

SUMMARY

Finance is the study of how businesses and individuals acquire, spend, and manage money and other financial resources. Finance is composed of three areas: institutions and markets, investments, and management. However, these areas are not independent of one another, but connect, intersect, and often overlap. All of the activities under each of these areas operate together to create a smooth-running and efficient financial system.

KEY TERMS

Brokerage firms	Firms that assist individuals who want to purchase new stock issues or who want to sell previously purchased securities.
Capital formation	The expansion of capital or capital goods through savings, which leads to investment.
Capital markets	Markets that include debt securities with maturities longer than 1 year and equity securities.
Commercial banks	Financial institutions that collect deposits from individuals and lend those funds to businesses and individuals.
Commercial paper	A short-term unsecured promissory note issued by a corporation with a high credit rating.
Common stocks	Ownership shares in corporations.
Contractual savings organizations	Organizations that collect premiums and contributions from participants and provide retirement benefits and insurance against major financial losses.
Corporate bonds	Bonds issued by corporations and are typically issued with 5- to 20-year maturities.
Credit unions	Banks that focus on working with consumers and provide loans to individuals seeking to purchase items such as automobiles and houses.

Currency exchange markets   Electronic markets in which banks and institutional traders buy and sell various currencies on behalf of businesses and other clients. Also referred to as *foreign exchange* or *FOREX markets*.

Debt securities   Obligations to repay borrowed funds. Federal, state, and local governments can issue debt securities, while business corporations and financial institutions can issue both debt and equity securities.

Derivative securities   Financial contracts that derive their values from underlying securities or from other related financial assets.

Derivatives markets   Markets that facilitate the purchase and sale of derivative securities.

Equity securities   Ownership rights in businesses and institutions.

Eurobonds   Bonds denominated in U.S. dollars that are sold to investors located in a country outside the United States.

Finance   The study of how individuals, institutions, governments, and businesses acquire, spend, and manage money and other financial assets.

Finance companies   Companies that loan money to individuals and businesses. Their loan requirements are not as stringent. However, finance companies traditionally charge higher interest rates on the loans they make.

Finance firms   Institutions that provide loans directly to consumers and businesses, as well as help borrowers obtain mortgage loans on real property.

Financial assets   Debt instruments, equity securities, and other financial contracts that are backed by real assets. Examples include mortgages and auto loans.

Financial institutions   Institutions that support capital formation either by channeling savings into investment in physical assets or by fostering direct investments by individuals in financial institutions and businesses.

Financial management   Process that encompasses the people and companies who are responsible for financial planning, asset management, and fund-raising decisions. The goal of the management professional is to

	protect and increase the value of investments and businesses.
Financial markets	Markets that work with institutions to facilitate the transfer of financial assets among individuals, institutions, businesses, and governments.
Financial system	A network of financial institutions that match one person's savings with another person's investment.
Foreign bonds	Bonds issued by a corporation or government that are valued in the currency of the country where it is sold.
Information efficient	All information is available to the public; for example, when the prices of securities reflect all the information available to the public. When new information becomes available, prices can change quickly to reflect that information.
Insurance companies	Companies that provide financial protection to individuals and businesses for life, property, liability, and health. Policyholders pay premiums to insurance companies that are then invested or withdrawn to pay claims.
International money markets	The markets where debt securities with maturities of 1 year or less are traded in foreign currency.
Investment banking firms	Firms that sell or market new securities issued by businesses to individual and institutional investors.
Investment companies	Companies that sell shares in their firms to individuals and others and invest the proceeds in corporate and government securities.
Investments	The outlay of money for an income or a profit.
Monetary system	A network of institutions that regulate financial transaction types, the supply of money, and economic agents.
Money markets	The markets where debt securities with maturities of 1 year or less are traded.
Mortgage banking firms	Companies that originate real estate mortgages by bringing together borrowers and investors. Also referred to as *mortgage companies*.
Municipal bonds	Long-term debt securities issued by state or local governments.

Negotiable certificates of deposit

Short-term debt instrument issued by depository institutions to individual or institutional depositors. Also known as *negotiable CDs*.

Pension funds

Funds composed of contributions from employees and/or their employers who invest the proceeds on behalf of the employees.

Primary securities markets

Markets that facilitate the sales of initial offerings of debt and equity securities to the public.

Real assets

Property, including the direct ownership of land; buildings; or homes, equipment, inventories, durable goods, and even precious metals.

Savings and loans

Banks that lend to both businesses and individuals.

Savings banks

Banks that focus on working with consumers and provide loans to individuals seeking to purchase items such as automobiles and houses. Fulfill the same purpose as credit unions.

Secondary securities markets

They facilitate the transfer of previously issued securities from existing investors to new investors. Security transactions or transfers typically take place on organized security exchanges or in the electronic over-the-counter market.

Secured loan

Specific property is pledged as collateral for the loan.

Securities firms

Firms that accept and invest individual savings and also facilitate the sale and transfer of securities between investors.

Securities markets

Physical locations or electronic forums where debt and equity securities are sold and traded.

Thrift institutions

Institutions—including savings and loan associations, savings banks, and credit unions—accumulate individual savings and provide credit primarily to individuals.

Treasury bills

Short-term debt obligations issued by the U.S. federal government to meet its short-term borrowing needs when imbalances exist between tax revenues and government expenditures.

Treasury bonds

Long-term debt securities issued by the U.S. federal government.

Unit of account

A way to measure prices.

ASSESS YOUR UNDERSTANDING

Go to www.wiley.com/college/Melicher to evaluate your knowledge of the basic structure of the financial system.
Measure your learning by comparing pre-test and post-test results.

Summary Questions

1. The study of finance is important for which of the following reasons?
   (a) As a citizen (of the United States or another country), you should want to make informed economic decisions.
   (b) An understanding of various aspects of personal finance should help you better manage your existing financial resources, as well as provide the basis for making sound decisions for accumulating wealth over time.
   (c) To be successful in the business world, it is important to have a basic understanding of business finance in addition to an understanding of financial markets.
   (d) All of the above.
2. Finance is the study of how individuals, institutions, and businesses acquire, spend, and manage money and other financial resources. True or false?
3. Within the general field of finance, the three main areas of study are financial management, real estate, and pension fund management. True or false?
4. An effective financial system is a complex mix of government and policy makers, a monetary system, financial institutions, and financial markets that interact to expedite the flow of financial capital from savings into investment. True or false?
5. It is not necessary to have financial markets for a financial system to operate efficiently. True or false?
6. Financial markets are necessary for productive capital formation. True or false?
7. Financial institutions are physical locations or electronic forums that facilitate the flow of funds amongst investors, businesses, and governments. True or false?
8. _____ involve(s) financial planning, asset management, and fund-raising decisions to enhance the value of businesses.
   (a) Financial markets
   (b) Financial institutions
   (c) Finance
   (d) Financial management

9. A monetary system is a necessary part of a financial system for the efficient creation and transfer of money. True or false?

10. Financial markets are financial intermediaries that take deposits from suppliers of capital such as individual savers and investors and make loans to demanders of capital such as businesses. True or false?

11. The unit of account in the United States is which of the following?

   (a) Decimal system
   (b) Gold bars
   (c) U.S. dollar
   (d) U.S. treasury bonds

12. *Money* is most correctly defined as anything that

   (a) is generally accepted as payment of goods and services and for discharging debts.
   (b) has general value in exchange.
   (c) is designed by the government as a means of discharging obligations.
   (d) is accepted by the government as a means of paying taxes.

13. In the United States, most money is created by

   (a) depository institutions.
   (b) the United States Treasury.
   (c) the Federal Reserve System.
   (d) none of the above.

14. The transfer and marketing of financial assets is one of the requisites of an effective financial system. True or false?

15. Financial functions in the U.S. system include

   (a) transferring financial assets.
   (b) creating money.
   (c) accumulating savings.
   (d) all of the above.

16. Which of the following is not considered to be a depository institution?

   (a) Credit union
   (b) Money market fund
   (c) Savings and loan association
   (d) Savings bank

17. Finance is founded on which of the following principles?

   (a) Money has a time value.
   (b) Higher returns are expected for taking on more risk.
   (c) Financial markets are efficient in pricing securities.
   (d) Reputation matters
   (e) All of the above

18. Money in hand today is worth the same as the promise of receiving the same amount in the future. True or false?

19. Higher returns are expected for taking on greater risk. True or false?

20. Contractual savings organizations collect premiums and contributions from participants and provide insurance against major financial losses and retirement benefits. True or false?

21. Securities firms accept and invest individual savings and also facilitate the sale and transfer of securities between investors. True or false?

22. Finance firms collect premiums and contributions from participants and provide insurance against major financial losses and retirement benefits. True or false?

23. Contractual savings institutions include
    (a) money market funds.
    (b) mortgage banking companies.
    (c) credit unions.
    (d) none of the above.

24. Checks
    (a) are orders to depository institutions to transfer money to the party who received the check.
    (b) may be safely sent in the mail.
    (c) provide a record of payment.
    (d) All of the above
    (e) None of the above

25. What is the biggest source of loan funds?
    (a) Government bonds
    (b) Personal savings accounts
    (c) Business accounts

26. An investment-banking firm acts as an intermediary and can handle the stock sales. True or false?

27. Which of the following is a type of financial market?
    (a) Securities markets
    (b) Derivative markets
    (c) Currency exchange markets
    (d) All of the above

28. Equity securities are ownership rights in businesses and institutions. True or false?

29. Primary securities markets are markets where the initial offering of debt and equity securities to the public occurs. True or false?

30. Secondary securities markets are markets where the initial offering of debt and equity securities to the public occurs. True or false?

31. Secondary securities markets are markets where the transfer of existing debt and equity securities between investors occurs. True or false?

32. Currency exchange markets are electronic markets in which banks and institutional traders buy and sell various currencies on behalf of businesses and other clients. True or false?

33. _____ are obligations to repay borrowed funds.
    (a) Equity securities
    (b) Debt securities
    (c) Common stocks
    (d) Real assets

34. Derivative securities are financial contracts that derive their values from underlying securities or from other related financial assets. True or false?

35. Real assets include the direct ownership of land; buildings; or homes, equipment, inventories, durable goods, and precious metals. True or false?

36. Money markets are markets where debt instruments of 1 year or less are traded. True or false?

37. Capital markets are markets where equity securities and debt securities with maturities of greater than 1 year are traded. True or false?

38. Financial assets include debt and equity securities and other financial contracts that are backed by real assets. True or false?

39. A treasury bond is a long-term debt security issued by the U.S. federal government. True or false?

40. A municipal bond is a long-term debt security issued by the U.S. federal government. True or false?

41. Commercial paper is a short-term, unsecured promissory note issued by a high credit-quality corporation. True or false?

42. Which of the following claims to wealth would not be considered to be a capital market security?
    (a) Corporate stocks
    (b) Real estate mortgages
    (c) U.S. government agency bonds
    (d) Federal funds

43. Negotiable CDs
    (a) are securities backed by real assets.
    (b) are long-term debt instruments issued by commercial banks.
    (c) are issued in denominations of $1,000,000 or more.
    (d) have typical maturities ranging from 1 month to 1 year.

44. A Eurobond
    (a) is a bond issued by a corporation or government that is denominated in the currency of a foreign country where it is sold.

(b) is a bond denominated in U.S. dollars that is sold to investors located outside the United States.

(c) pays interest to investors only if the underlying company makes a profit.

(d) All of the above

45. A bond issued by a corporation or government that is denominated in the currency of a foreign country where it is sold is called a

(a) foreign bond.

(b) Eurobond.

(c) Yankee bond.

(d) euro note.

46. Why do investors buy treasury bills?

(a) Liquidity and security

(b) Interest rates

(c) Low cost

Review Questions

1. Complete the following statement: An understanding of various aspects of _____ should help you better manage your existing financial resources, as well as provide the basis for making sound decisions for accumulating wealth over time. To be successful in the business world, it is important to have a basic understanding of _____ in addition to an understanding of institutions, markets, and investments.

2. What are the goals of the financial manager of a nonprofit organization?

3. Financial institutions and markets help the financial system operate efficiently. Match the following financial functions of financial institutions and markets with the appropriate aspect of the financial system:

Aspect of Financial System	Financial Function
a. Efficient methods of production and specialization of labor	1. An effective means of paying for raw materials and final products
b. Businesses can obtain the money needed to buy capital goods such as machinery and equipment	2. Effective means exist for raising money, for making payments, and for borrowing
c. Federal, state, and local governments and tax districts can carry out their wide range of activities	3. Institutions and markets have established a policy and a method to make savings available for investment

4. When the prices of securities reflect all the information available to the public, the market is said to be what?

5. An effective financial system requires a monetary system, financial institutions, and financial markets. Financial markets encourage investment by doing what?

6. A basic requirement for an effective financial system is a monetary system that performs what financial functions?

7. Explain the term *productive capital* in a simple economy.

8. Match the following financial institutions with their primary source of funds.

Financial Institutions	Primary Source of Funds
a. Commercial banks	1. Premium paid on policies
b. Insurance companies	2. Employee/employer contributions
c. Pension funds	3. Other financial institutions
d. Finance companies	4. Individual savings

9. Name the three components of the financial system.

10. Who creates money in the United States?

11. Identify the ways money can be transferred electronically.

12. Explain the difference between a secured loan and an unsecured loan.

13. Describe the primary function of the investment-banking firm.

14. Match the following debt and equity securities with their issuers.

Securities	Issuers
a. Corporate stocks	1. Commercial banks
b. Treasury bonds	2. Corporations
c. Municipal bonds	3. U.S. government
d. Negotiable certificates of deposit	4. State/local governments

15. Identify the types of depository institutions.

16. What is meant by *intermediation*?

17. Identify the four types of financial markets.

18. What are the three measures of wealth?

19. Define the difference between money markets and capital markets securities.

20. How are treasury bills different from commercial paper?

21. Identify the three types of bonds.

22. Who would issue foreign bonds and in what currency would they be issued?

23. Are Eurobonds denominated in currencies other than the U.S. dollar?

24. Describe the importance of international money markets

Applying This Chapter

1. The three pillars of finance are financial institutions and markets, investments, and financial management. Although we identify three distinct areas, they do not operate in isolation of one another but rather closely interact with each other. Discuss how financial institutions and markets interact with the areas of investments and financial management.

2. A financial system must make the creation of productive capital possible on a scale large enough to meet the demands of the economy. General Motors buys land in Detroit on which to build a new plant to produce energy-efficient minivans. What part of GM's activity in this example involves productive capital formation?

3. The basic financial functions in an effective financial system include creation of money, transferring money, accumulating savings in financial institutions, lending and investing savings, marketing financial assets, and transferring financial assets. List five financial institutions and indicate which services you and your families receive from these institutions.

4. A company needs to raise $3,000,000 to create new products to increase its market share. What financial market might it turn to generate such cash?

5. You have $100,000 to invest and want to invest half for a period of less than 6 months and the other half for at least 16 months. List at least two types of securities you could invest in for each investment period.

6. A U.S.-based company with a subsidiary in Germany that has adopted the euro as its common currency is short of cash. What can it do to obtain more euros to conduct day-to-day operations?

YOU TRY IT

Running a Small Business

Visit the small business administration's Web site at www.sba.gov and look at what is involved in starting a new business. How much of what is suggested requires a knowledge of finance in some form or another?

Accountants Share the Blame

Review the Enron case and determine why their accountant, the respected firm Arthur Anderson, was also brought down and destroyed by the scandal.

Ethical Dilemmas

In business, ethical dilemmas or situations occur frequently. Laws and regulations exist to define what is unethical behavior. However, the practicing of high-quality ethical behavior often goes beyond just meeting laws and regulations. Indicate how you would respond to the following situations:

▲ Your boss has just told you that there will be an announcement tomorrow morning that the Federal Drug Administration has approved your firm's marketing of a new breakthrough drug. As a result of this information, you are considering purchasing shares of stock in your firm this afternoon. What would you do?

▲ In the past, your firm has been in compliance with regulatory standards relating to product safety. However, you have heard through the "company grapevine" that recently some of your firm's products have failed resulting in injuries to customers. You are considering quitting your job due to personal moral concerns. What would you do?

Foreign Exchange Rates

The Internet provides daily updates on the exchange rate of the U.S. dollar compared to foreign countries; a good Web site to try is www.xe.com. Run an Internet search and compare the dollar to the euro, which is widely used in European countries. Next, compare the U.S. dollar to the Canadian dollar. Which offers a better exchange rate?

2

MONEY AND INTEREST RATES
The U.S. Monetary System

Starting Point

Go to www.wiley.com/college/Melicher to assess your knowledge of the basics of the U.S. monetary system.
Determine where you need to concentrate your effort.

What You'll Learn in This Chapter

▲ The history of our monetary system
▲ How money is created and developed
▲ How the Federal Reserve sets interest rates
▲ How interest rates affect our economy

After Studying This Chapter, You'll Be Able To

▲ Examine the roles of major components of the financial system
▲ Differentiate between the three ways in which money is transferred from savers to businesses
▲ Examine why depository institutions are an important part of the monetary system
▲ Examine the functions of money
▲ Diagram the development of money in the United States
▲ Compare and contrast the M1, M2, and M3 definitions of the money supply
▲ Examine the possible relationships between money supply and economic activity

Goals and Outcomes

▲ Assess the role the Federal Reserve System plays in the United States economy
▲ Compare and contrast the three functions of money
▲ Assess the three requirements of the national banking system
▲ Assess the relationship between the money supply of the United States and the state of the economy
▲ Evaluate the effect inflation has on the economy
▲ Assess how investors are affected by interest rates
▲ Compare and contrast how different interest rates are determined
▲ Assess the relationship between yield curves and the economy

INTRODUCTION

Money in the world of finance takes a number of different forms, but the bottom line is that everything of value is measured by the amount of cash it would garner if sold. The Federal Reserve plays a crucial role in this process. Currency has been around since the 1600s and has a fascinating history that began when this country was nothing more than a handful of colonies populated by people seeking a new way of life. As you learn how money has evolved through the years, you will acquire a better understanding of how it is created and regulated in today's financial system. You will also learn about interest rates, how they are determined, and why they are so closely monitored by financial managers, business owners, and the general public.

2.1 Overview of the Monetary System

The monetary system is responsible for carrying out the financial functions of creating and transferring money. Money is needed to conduct day-to-day activities, facilitate the capital investment process, and support economic growth. To understand the monetary system requires a basic understanding of the savings-investment process involving the flow of funds from individual savers to businesses that want to invest in inventories, buildings, and equipment.

2.1.1 Savings-Investment Process

The savings involvement process involves the direct or indirect transfer of individual savings to business firms in exchange for their securities. Of course, a broader view of the savings-investment process would include the exchange of pooled individual savings for financial claims in the form or mortgage and other loans to individuals wanting to buy houses or make other purchases. A broader savings-investment process would include using pooled individual savings to purchase and hold debt securities issued by governmental units. However, our primary focus throughout this book is on the savings-investment process involving businesses. Savers can directly purchase the securities of a business firm by exchanging money for the firm's securities. No type of financial institution is used in this kind of savings-investment transaction since it involves only a saver and the business firm. There are two types of indirect transfers from savers to business firms as well. As discussed in the last chapter, one type of indirect transfer involves use of the primary securities market. Savers provide money to purchase the business firm's securities. Investment banking forms first purchase the securities from the issuing form and then resell the securities to the savers. The second type of indirect transfer is through a financial intermediary. Savers deposit or invest money with a financial institution such as a bank, insurance company, or mutual fund. The financial intermediary issues its own securities to the saver. For example, a saver invests in a certificate of deposit. The bank, in turn, lends this money to a business firm in exchange for that firm's IOU (I owe you) in the form of a loan.

2.1.2 Functions of Money

Money is anything commonly accepted as a means of paying for goods and services and for paying off debts. For something to serve successfully as money, it must be easily divisible, so that exchanges can take place in small or large quantities; relatively inexpensive to store and transfer; and reasonably stable in value over time. Money must perform three basic functions: it must serve as a medium of exchange, a store of value, and a standard of value.

Money was first developed to serve as a medium of exchange to facilitate transactions. Before currency, people would barter for belongings. For example, someone would exchange a table for a cow. The need for simpler means of exchange with assigned values led to the development of money.

Money also may be held as a **store of value**—that is, money may be spent immediately after it is received or after it has been held for some time. While money is held, it is a liquid asset and provides its owner with flexibility. But the owner pays for this flexibility by giving up the potential return that could be earned through investment or the satisfaction that could be gained from spending it for goods or services. Money can perform its function as a store of value only if its "purchasing power" is relatively stable over time. Under this condition, the spending decision is separated from the income decisions. Once income is received, the holder of the income can choose to spend it or save it. If the decision is to save, then that money can be made available through the savings-investment process to those who may want to invest now.

Any asset other than money can also serve as a store of value as long as that asset can be converted into money quickly and without significant loss of value. We refer to this quality, the ease with which an asset can be exchanged for money or other assets, as *liquidity*. Money is perfectly liquid since it is a generally accepted medium of exchange.

Money also serves as a **standard of value,** which means that prices and contracts for deferred payments are expressed in terms of the monetary unit. For example, in the United States, prices and debts are usually expressed in terms of dollars without stating whether the purchase will be cash or credit. Of course, if money is to perform its function as a standard of value, it is essential that the value of the monetary unit be relatively stable over time. For example, if one dollar can be used to purchase two ballpoint pens today but only one tomorrow, such money would not be very effective as either a store of value or standard of value.

FOR EXAMPLE

Your Net Worth

While money is the fundamental measure of wealth, an individual's net worth usually consists of more than just money. Individual net worth is the sum of an individual's money, real assets, and financial assets or claims against others less the individual's debt obligations. Real assets include your car, house, and all its contents. Any shares of stock you own are part of your net worth. However, you may have borrowed from a bank to purchase your auto, and you probably have a mortgage loan on the house you purchased. These are financial claims held by others against some of your real property. You must subtract debt obligations or financial claims against you or your real property to determine your net worth.

S E L F - C H E C K

- List three ways money is transferred from savers to business firms.
- Define the purpose of money.
- Define **store of value** and **standard of value**.

2.2 The Federal Reserve System

The **Federal Reserve System (Fed)** is the central bank of the United States and is responsible for setting monetary policy and regulating the banking system. The Federal Reserve System was created by the Federal Reserve Act in 1913 and began operating in 1914.

Banking acts passed in 1863 and 1864 provided for a national banking system. In addition to creating a system of national charters for banks, the laws established capital and reserve requirements on deposits and banknotes, and stipulated that banknotes could be issued only against U.S. government securities owned by the banks but held with the U.S. Treasury Department. These banknotes, backed by government securities, were supposed to provide citizens with a safe and stable national currency. Stability was further improved with the establishment of the Office of the Comptroller of the Currency, under the control of the U.S. Treasury.

Although the national banking system overcame many of the weaknesses of the prior systems involving state banks, it lacked the ability to carry out other central banking system activities essential to a smooth-running financial system. Those three requirements were

▲ **an efficient national payments system.** The payments system under the National Banking Acts was based on an extensive network of banks with correspondent banking relationships. It was costly to transfer funds from region to region, and the check-clearing and collection process was sometimes quite long. Checks written on little-known banks located in out-of-the-way places were often discounted or redeemed at less than face value. The amount of the discount was supposed to cover the cost of getting the check cleared and presented for collection to a bank located in another region;

▲ **a flexible money supply able to respond to changes in demand.** The money supply could not be easily increased or decreased to meet the needs of the ever-changing economic activity;

▲ **a borrowing program to help ease cash-flow problems when needed.** Instead of allowing the smaller banks to hold all of their reserve deposits, they were required to place most of their cash reserves with larger banks. The frequent inability of the large banks to meet the deposit withdrawal demands of their own customers combined with the withdrawal demands of the smaller banks pointed out the need for a system that could provide loans to help the smaller banks weather short-term liquidity problems.

However, the Fed did not replace the system that existed under the National Banking Acts. Instead, it superimposed the Federal Reserve System on the existing system. Certain provisions of the National Banking Acts were retained but modified to permit greater flexibility of its operations.

2.2.1 Central Banking Systems

A **central bank** is a government-established organization responsible for supervising and regulating the banking system and for creating and regulating the money supply. While central bank activities may differ somewhat from country to country, central banks typically play an important role in a country's payment system. It is also common for a central bank to lend money to its member banks, hold its own reserves, and be responsible for creating money.

The problems with our national banking system were widely known, yet in the 1800s there was much opposition in this country to the establishment of a central banking system. The vast western frontiers and the local independence of the southern areas during this time created distrust of centralized financial control.

The United States was one of the last major industrial nations to adopt a permanent system of central banking. The central banking system adopted by the United States was actually a compromise between the system of independently owned banks in this country and the single central bank systems of such countries as Canada, Great Britain, and Germany.

This compromise took the form of a series of central banks, each representing a specific region of the United States. The assumption was that each central bank would be more responsive to the particular financial problems of its region.

2.2.2 Structure of the Federal Reserve System

The Federal Reserve System (Fed) is an unusual mixture of public and private elements and is governed by a board of governors, located in Washington, D.C. Seven members appointed by the president and confirmed by the senate make up the board. Responsibilities of the board include

▲ overseeing monetary policy action;

▲ analyzing domestic and international economic and financial conditions;

▲ serving on committees that study current issues, such as consumer banking laws and electronic commerce;

▲ exercising control over the financial services industry;

▲ administering consumer protection regulations;

▲ monitoring the nation's payments system;

▲ setting the reserve requirements for depository institutions;

▲ approving discount rates recommended by member banks.

In addition to these responsibilities, the board of governors supervises the activities of the member banks, approving the appointments of their directors. However, the most important function of the board is participating in the **Federal Open Market Committee (FOMC).** Along with the five Reserve Bank presidents, the board manages our nation's money supply. FOMC meets eight times a year in Washington, D.C. to discuss the outlook for the U.S. economy and **monetary policy.**

▲ **Monetary policy** refers to the actions of the Federal Reserve that influence the amount of money and credit in the U.S. economy. That, in turn, largely determines interest rates and the performance of our economy. The goals of monetary policy are threefold: prolonged economic growth, full employment, and stable prices.

One of the most familiar words in the economic forecasts published and broadcasted is *inflation*. Literally speaking, it means increase, which doesn't sound like a bad thing. However, inflation does have a negative effect on the economy because it can hurt individuals and businesses.

▲ **Inflation** is a rise in the price of goods. Simply stated, it means that a dollar buys less. Inflation occurs when the supply of money and credit rises too rapidly over several months. Avoiding inflation is a primary consideration of the Federal Reserve when setting monetary policy.

The Federal Reserve has a number of tools at its disposal for maintaining a healthy economy:

▲ **Open market operations:** These involve the buying and selling of U.S. government securities. *Open market* refers to the fact that the Fed doesn't decide which security dealers to do business with on a specific day. The choice emerges from an open market, where the primary dealers the Fed does business with compete on the basis of price.

▲ **Change the reserve requirements:** The portions of deposits that banks must maintain either in their own vaults or on deposit at a Federal Reserve bank. Think of this as the cash on hand in our monetary system.

▲ **Change the discount rate:** The interest rate charged by Federal Reserve banks to depository institutions. This has a direct effect on the interest you may be charged when financing a major purchase, which is why the financial community and the public in general sit up and take notice whenever the chairman of the Federal Reserve Board announces whether the discount rate will rise, fall, or stay the same.

2.2.3 Member Banks

A network of 12 Federal Reserve banks and 25 branches make up the Federal Reserve System. Federal Reserve banks are located in the following major cities:

▲ San Francisco
▲ Dallas
▲ Kansas City
▲ St.Louis
▲ Minneapolis
▲ Chicago
▲ Cleveland
▲ Atlanta
▲ Richmond
▲ Philadelphia
▲ New York
▲ Boston

These reserve banks serve the U.S. Treasury, handling the Treasury's payments, selling government securities, and assisting with the Treasury's cash management and investment activities. Reserve banks also supervise commercial banks in their areas, store currency and coin, and process checks and electronic payments.

All member banks hold stock in Reserve banks and receive dividends. Unlike stockholders in a public company, the member banks cannot trade or sell their Fed stock.

An estimated 38% of the commercial banks in the United States are members of the Federal Reserve System. National banks must be members of the system, and state-chartered banks may join if they meet certain requirements. However, even if a bank is not formally a part of the system, it is still subject to Federal Reserve regulations.

2.2.4 Advisory Committees

The Federal Reserve System has three major advisory committees.

▲ **The Federal Advisory Council:** provides advice and general information on banking-related issues to the board of governors. Each of the 12 Federal Reserve districts elects one member to serve on the council.

▲ **The Consumer Advisory Council:** membership is composed of representatives from depository institutions and their customers. The council provides advice relating to consumer issues.

▲ **The Thrift Institutions Advisory Council:** consists of members from thrift institutions (savings and loans associations, savings banks, and credit unions). These members provide advice on issues that directly affect thrift institutions.

2.2.5 Fed Supervisory and Regulatory Functions

A strong and stable banking system is vital to the growth and the stability of the entire economy. The supervision of commercial banks and other depository institutions is primarily concerned with the safety and soundness of individual institutions. It involves oversight to ensure that depository institutions are operated carefully. Depository institution regulation relates to the issuance of specific rules or regulations that govern the structure and conduct of operations.

On-site examination of commercial banks is one of the Fed's most important responsibilities. This function is shared with the federal Office of the Comptroller of the Currency (OCC), the **Federal Deposit Insurance Corporation (FDIC)**, and state regulatory agencies.

The examination generally entails

▲ an appraisal of the soundness of the institution's assets;
▲ an evaluation of internal operations, policies, and management;
▲ an analysis of key financial factors, such as capital and earnings;

▲ a review for compliance with all banking laws and regulations;

▲ an overall determination of the institution's financial condition.

Although the Federal Reserve is authorized to examine all member banks, in practice it limits itself to state-chartered member banks and all bank holding companies. It cooperates with state examining agencies to avoid overlapping examining authority. The OCC directs its attention to nationally chartered banks, and the FDIC supervises insured nonmember commercial banks.

In addition to the three federal banking supervisory agencies, two federal agencies are primarily responsible for supervising and regulating depository institutions that are not commercial banks. The **National Credit Union Administration (NCUA)** supervises and regulates credit unions, and the **Office of Thrift Supervision (OTS)** oversees Savings & Loans and other savings institutions.

The Federal Reserve conducts on-site inspections of parent bank holding companies and their nonbank subsidiaries. These inspections include a review of nonbank assets and funding activities to ensure compliance with the Bank Holding Company Act.

The Federal Reserve has broad powers to regulate the overseas activities of member banks and bank holding companies. Its aim is to allow U.S. banks to be fully competitive with institutions of host countries in financing U.S. trade and investment overseas.

Along with the OCC and the FDIC, the Federal Reserve also has broad oversight authority to supervise all federal and state-licensed branches and agencies of foreign banks operating in the United States.

2.2.6 Financial Management and the Fed

Financial management activities are directly affected by Fed monetary policy actions. The Fed determines the amount of money in circulation. When they tighten monetary policy, this means that less money will be in circulation and there will be higher interest rates. They do this to prevent inflation. A tightening of monetary policy makes it more difficult and costly for businesses to borrow funds. Economic activity also declines because it is more difficult for financial managers to sell new stocks and bonds in the primary securities markets. On the other hand, an easing of monetary policy will make it easier for financial managers to raise financial capital, and they will be able to do so at lower interest rates.

2.2.7 The Fed and the Consumer

The Fed activities also affect personal finance in several ways. First, the Fed controls the money supply. Actions that severely restrict the supply of money may lead to an economic recession. Too rapid a growth in the money supply may result in inflation and a decrease in purchasing power.

Should the Fed act to slow down or reduce the growth rate of the money supply, there will be growing constraints on the ability of banks to lend as their excess reserves decline. This may result in higher interest rates as funds become scarcer. Sometimes this actually helps savers. As a way to attract more funds, banks may raise the interest they pay on saving accounts and CDs. Of particular interest to consumers is the fact that the board implemented several important credit control devices to protect them:

▲ The **Truth-in-Lending** section of the Consumer Credit Protection Act requires disclosure of the finance charges and the annual percentage rate of credit along with certain other costs and terms to allow consumers to compare the cost of credit from different sources. This act also limits the consumer's liability on lost or stolen credit cards.

▲ The **Fair Credit Billing Act** sets up a procedure for the prompt correction of errors on a revolving charge account and prevents damage to credit ratings while a dispute is being settled.

▲ The **Fair Credit Opportunity Act** prohibits discrimination in the granting of credit on the basis of sex, marital status, race, color, religion, national origin, age, or receipt of public assistance.

▲ The **Fair Credit Reporting Act** sets up a procedure for correcting mistakes on credit records and requires that records be used only for legitimate business purposes.

FOR EXAMPLE

Chairman of the Federal Reserve

The full title for the chair of the Federal Reserve is the Chairman of the Board of Governors of the United States Federal Reserve. The chairman is appointed by the president of the United States for a 4-year term and must be confirmed by Congress. In practice, the chair is reappointed several times. The chair must make two reports per year to Congress. The chair testifies in front of Congress on several monetary issues and meets with the secretary treasury. Many political commentators have commented that the chair of the Federal Reserve is more powerful than the president, as what the chair says affects the investors' perceptions and can lead to an increase or a decrease in the stock markets. The chair also influences monetary policy that affects all Americans. For example, when the Federal Reserve lowered interest rates in 2001, this affected mortgage rates, which led to many people buying homes for the first time. It also led many people to selling their homes and buying bigger homes.

SELF-CHECK

- Define **Federal Reserve System, central bank, discount rate, inflation,** and **monetary policy.**
- List the five steps of a Federal Reserve examination.
- Name and describe the Federal Reserve System's three advisory committees.
- Name and describe the four credit control devices the Federal Reserve Board implemented to help consumers.

2.3 The Development of Money in the United States

The two basic components of money supply in the United States are physical money and deposit money.

2.3.1 Physical Money

Physical money is the coin and paper currency used to pay debts and expenses and purchase goods and services. Despite predictions of a cashless society that depends on electronic payments, the public demand for currency continues to grow.

The U.S. Congress adopted the dollar as the standard monetary unit in 1785. Shortly thereafter, it created standards for the dollar in both grains of pure silver and grains of pure gold. All gold and silver coins were to be **full-bodied money,** meaning that the metal content was worth the same as the face values of the coins. After passage of the National Banking Act in 1863, paper money, fully backed by a precious metal, that would serve as an acceptable medium of exchange was finally issued and circulated successfully. The Federal Reserve System took over in 1914 and has been in charge of our coins and currency ever since.

Currency notes and coins are all produced by the United States Treasury Department. The U.S. Mints are responsible for producing coins while the Bureau of Engraving and Printing produces the currency notes. Both must create coins and currency in amounts sufficient to fill the needs of the public. The Treasury ships the money directly to Federal Reserve banks, which in turn release it to the commercial banking system in amounts that meet their current needs. While old and damaged currency and coins can be returned to the mints, there is no time limit on the value of our money.

2.3.2 Deposit Money

The use of physical money (coin and currency) to complete transactions can be costly, especially if large amounts and/or long distances are involved.

▲ **Credit money,** or money backed by the creditworthiness of the issuer, can be used instead of physical money.

A form of credit money called **deposit money** has grown readily in importance in the U.S. monetary system.

▲ **Deposit money** is a special type of credit money. It is backed by the good credit of the depository institution that issued the deposit.

Deposit money takes the form of **demand deposits** held at commercial banks or other checkable deposits held at S & Ls, savings banks, and credit unions.

▲ **A demand deposit** is a type of deposit money that gets its name from the fact that the owner of a deposit account may demand that all or a portion of the amount in his or her account be transferred to another individual or organization.

Checks, or drafts, have traditionally been used to transfer demand deposit or other checkable deposit amounts. However, the processing of paper checks is time consuming and costly. **Electronic funds transfers (EFTs)** can be used to transfer funds held in demand and other checkable deposit accounts electronically. For example, automatic transfer service (ATS) accounts are increasingly used to make direct deposits to and payments from checkable deposit accounts. Employers can have their employees' wages deposited directly in their checking accounts, rather than issuing payroll checks. Individuals can have regular payments such as mortgage payments or insurance premiums automatically deducted from their accounts.

Electronic funds transfers through the Internet for payment of utility bills, credit card balances, and other expenses are being done in ever increasing numbers. At the same time, debit cards provide for the immediate direct transfer of deposit amounts.

FOR EXAMPLE

Electronic Banking

When a debit card is used to purchase merchandise at a retailer's point-of-sale cash register, the cardholder's bank transfers the designated amount from the purchaser's account to the retailer's account. In a similar fashion, debit cards can be used to pay for purchases made using the Internet. Debit cards also can be used to make cash withdrawals from automated teller machines (ATMs). When cash is dispersed, the user's deposit account balance is immediately reduced by the amount of cash withdrawn.

SELF-CHECK

- Define **physical money, full-bodied money, credit money, and deposit money.**
- Why are electronic funds transfers used?
- How do banks receive physical money?

2.4 U.S. Money Supply Today

Economists try to count the money supply in the United States in order to help determine the state of the U.S. economy. Since this involves counting the money supply in the financial system at a particular point in time, this can also be viewed as the amount of money stock on a specific date. For purposes of counting the money supply, economists use three different definitions of *money supply*. Figure 2-1 shows several definitions of *money supply* in use today.

2.4.1 M1 Money Supply

The basic function of money is that it must be acceptable as a medium of exchange. The **M1 money supply** includes only types of money that meet this basic requirement. The M1 money supply consists of currency, travelers' checks, demand deposits, and other checkable deposits at depository institutions. All four components are types of credit money. Credit money is money that is worth more than what it is made of. For example, a dollar bill is credit money because the paper itself is not worth one dollar. It is also physical money. Figure 2-1 shows the components of M1.

- ▲ **Currency** is U.S. physical money in the form of coins and paper currency. Coins are token money, and paper currency is in the form of Federal Reserve notes. Currency comprises a little over half of the M1 money supply.
- ▲ **Travelers' checks,** offered by banks and other organizations, promise to pay on demand the face amounts of the checks. Once again, their acceptance is based on the creditworthiness of the issuer. Since travelers' checks are a widely accepted medium of exchange, they qualify as a component of the M1 money supply. Even so, their relative importance is small, as indicated by the fact that they represent less than 1% of the M1 total.
- ▲ **Demand deposits** (checking accounts) at commercial banks and other checkable deposits at savings and loan associations (S & Ls), savings

Figure 2-1

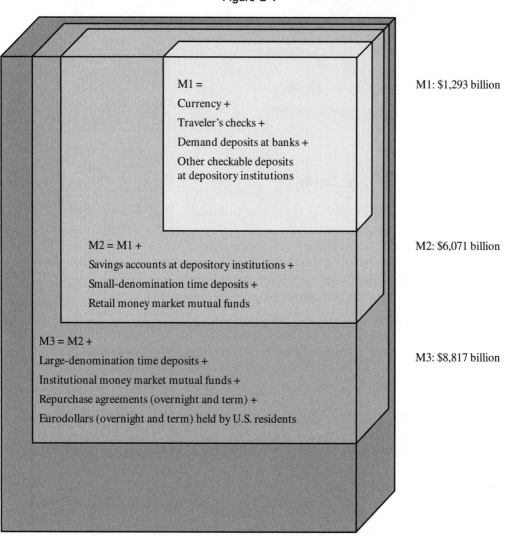

M1 =

Currency +

Traveler's checks +

Demand deposits at banks +

Other checkable deposits
at depository institutions

M1: $1,293 billion

M2 = M1 +

Savings accounts at depository institutions +

Small-denomination time deposits +

Retail money market mutual funds

M2: $6,071 billion

M3 = M2 +

Large-denomination time deposits +

Institutional money market mutual funds +

Repurchase agreements (overnight and term) +

Eurodollars (overnight and term) held by U.S. residents

M3: $8,817 billion

Definitions of money supply measures and seasonally adjusted totals for December 2003.

banks, and credit unions also are considered to be credit money and
account for 24% of the money supply.

▲ **Other checkable deposits,** which also represent 24% of M1, include
automatic transfer service (ATS) accounts and negotiable order of withdrawal (NOW) accounts at depository institutions.

Demand deposit and other checkable deposit accounts comprise a little less than
half of the M1 money supply. This high percentage shows the importance of

the banking system and its money-creating function within the U.S. financial system.

M1 measures transaction balances. These are sums of money that can be spent without first converting them to some other asset. These funds are mainly held for purchases or payments in the immediate future. Only those amounts that represent the purchasing power of dollars in the U.S. economy are counted.

Specifically excluded from M1 is currency in the vaults of depository institutions or cash held by the Fed and the U.S. Treasury. Demand deposits owed to depository institutions, the federal government, and foreign banks and governments also are excluded. Adjustment is also made to avoid double-counting checks being processed.

2.4.2 M2 Money Supply

The Fed's second definition of the money stock, M2, is a broader measure than M1 because it emphasizes money as a store of value in addition to its function as a medium of exchange.

The **M2 money supply** includes M1 plus financial assets that can be quickly turned into cash. This includes savings accounts, small denomination time deposits (under $100,000), and retail money market deposit accounts (MMDAs), plus balances in retail money market mutual funds (MMMFs) where initial investments are less than $50,000. Most of the financial assets added to M2 provide their owners with a higher rate of return than the components of the M1 category.

Figure 2-1 shows that M2, at $6,071 billion, is nearly five times the size of M1. Some of the owners of the assets included in M2 hold them as long-term savings instruments. Other individuals and firms hold these M2 assets even though they plan to spend the funds within a few days because the assets are very liquid.

M1 demonstrates the purchasing power of M2 minus the financial savings accounts that are included in M2. The types of accounts in M2 are still highly liquid, and this illustrates the difficulties the Fed has faced in drawing the boundaries of these definitions.

It can be argued that small-denomination time deposits should be excluded from M2 because they are not, in practice, very liquid. Small-time-deposit holders who wish to cash them in before maturity are penalized by having to forfeit some of the interest they have earned. However, these time deposits are included because they are considered to be close substitutes for some of the other savings accounts included in M2. Savings deposits alone, including money market deposit accounts are greater than the M1 total.

▲ **Money market mutual funds (MMMFs)** issue shares to customers and invest the proceeds in highly liquid, very-short-maturity, interest-bearing debt instruments called *money market investments*.

If we divide GDP by the money supply (MS), we get the number of times the money supply turns over to produce GDP. Economists refer to the turnover of money as the **velocity of money.**

▲ **The velocity of money** measures the rate of circulation of the money supply.

For example, if the annual GDP is $15 million and the MS is $5 million, the velocity of money (VM) is three times (15 [db] 5 = 3). In an alternative form, we can say that

$$MS \text{ [ts] } VM = GDP.$$

Economists also express nominal GDP as being equal to real output (RO) times the prices level (PL) of goods and services, or

$$RO \text{ [ts] } PL = GDP.$$

For example, if the real output in the economy is 150,000 products and the average price is $100, the GDP is $15 million (i.e., 150,000 [ts] $100). Putting these two equations together, we have

$$MS \text{ [ts] } VM = RO \text{ [ts] } PL.$$

An increase in the money supply and/or velocity causes nominal GDP to increase. And, for nominal GDP to increase, real output and/or price levels must increase. For example, let's assume the money supply increases by 10% or $500,000 to $5.5 million while the velocity stays at three times. Nominal GDP will increase to

$$\$5.5 \text{ million [ts] } 3 = \$16.5 \text{ million.}$$

And, since GDP equals RO [ts] PL, some change in real output or price level (or a combination of the two) needs to take place. One possibility is for real output to increase by 15,000 products or units to 165,000 with no change in prices. GDP then would be

$$165,000 \text{ units [ts] } \$100 = \$16.5 \text{ million.}$$

2.5.1 Monetarists and Inflation

Monetarists believe that when the money supply exceeds the amount of money demanded, the public will spend more rapidly, causing real economic activity or prices to rise. A too-rapid growth in the money supply will ultimately result in rising prices or inflation because excess money will be used to bid up the prices of existing goods. Inflation is a rise or increase in the prices of goods and services that is not offset by increases in their quality.

Because of the difficulty in measuring changes in quality, a more operational definition of inflation is a continuing rise in prices. For example, instead of the

$1.5 million increase in BDP from $15 million to $16.5 million, due to a 10% increase in the money supply, the increase might have been due solely to infla-tion. Let's assume that the quantity of products sold remains at the original 150,000-unit level but that the average price increases by 10% to $110. GDP would be calculated as

$$150,000 \text{ units [ts] } \$110 = \$16.5 \text{ million.}$$

Of course, there could be almost unlimited combinations of real outputs and price levels, including reducing one of the variables that could produce the same new GDP.

2.5.2 Keynesians and Inflation

Other economists, called *Keynesians* in honor of John Maynard Keynes, believe that a change in the money supply has a less direct relationship with the GDP. They argue that a change in money supply first causes a change in interest rate levels, which, in turn, alters the demand for goods and services. For example, an increase in the money supply might cause interest rates to fall (at least ini-tially) because more money is being supplied than is being demanded. Lower interest rates, in turn, will lead to an increase in consumption and/or investment spending, causing the GDP to grow. In contrast, a decrease in the money sup-ply will likely cause interest rates to rise. As a result, the GDP will grow more slowly or even decline, depending on how the higher interest rates affect con-sumption and spending decisions.

As you might guess, it is not possible to say that one group of economists (monetarists or Keynesians) is right and the other is wrong. The ability to identify relationships among GDP, money supply, and price levels has been complicated by the fact that the velocity of money has increased and the various measures of the money supply have grown at different rates. M1 velocity has increased as credit card usage has replaced the more traditional use of currency and deposit money when purchasing goods and services. The velocity of M1 money also has increased as the public has made more use of money market mutual funds and other liquid accounts that serve as stores of value relative to their usage of traditional deposit money in demand and other checkable accounts.

The M1 measure of the money supply grew at nearly a double-digit rate during the first part of the 1990s. Many economists thought that such growth might lead to higher inflation. However, over the same period, M2 and M3 grew much more slowly. The net result, along with other developments in the econ-omy, was a decline in inflation rates measured in terms of changes in consumer prices. Money supply growth remained moderate and inflation low during the last half of the 1990s and the first few years of the twenty-first century.

However, we must be careful in trying to interpret the near-term impact of changes in the money supply. Decreasing regulation and increasing competition

2.6.2 Loanable Funds Theory

The **loanable funds theory** holds that interest rates are a function of the supply and demand for funds earmarked for loans. How the supply of and the demand for funds interact determines both the interest rate and the quantity of funds that flows through the financial markets during any period. If the supply of funds increases, holding demand constant, interest rates will tend to fall. An increase in the demand for loans will usually cause interest rates to rise.

2.6.3 Volume of Savings

The volume of savings directly impacts the money supply and the funds available for loans. The major factor that determines the volume of savings, corporate and individual, is the level of national income. When income is high, savings are high; when it is low, savings are low.

The pattern of income taxes—both the level of the tax and the tax rates in various income brackets—also influences savings volume. Furthermore, the tax treatment of savings itself influences the amount of income saved.

The age of the population has an important effect on the volume of savings. Normally, little saving is done during the formative and education-building stage or during the family-creating stage. Therefore, an economy with a large number of young couples with children will have less total savings than an economy with more people in the older wealth-building stage.

The volume of savings also depends on the factors that affect indirect savings. Indirect savings are where someone does not put aside a certain amount of money for the express purpose of saving it but belongs to a contractual savings organization. A contractual savings organization collects premiums and contributions from participants and provides insurance against major financial losses and retirement benefits. For example, a pension is a program where a company contributes to an employee's retirement on a regular basis, and the employee may have the choice to contribute as well. This is a form of indirect savings. The more effectively the life insurance industry promotes the sale of whole life and endowment insurance policies, the larger the volume of savings. The greater the demand for private pension funds, the larger the volume of savings.

The effect of interest rates on such savings is often just the opposite of the normal effect of price on supply. As interest rates decrease, more money must be paid for insurance for the same amount of coverage, because a smaller amount of interest will be earned from the reinvestment of premiums and earnings.

As interest rates rise, less money needs be put into reserves to obtain the same objectives. The same is true of the amount of money that must be put into annuities and pension funds.

When savings result from the use of consumer credit, the effect of interest rates is delayed. For example, assume a car is bought with a 3-year loan. Savings, in the form of repaying the loan, must go on for 3 years regardless of changes in the interest rates. There may even be an opposite effect in the case of a mortgage because if interest rates drop substantially, the loan can be refinanced. At the lower interest rate the same dollar payments provide a larger amount for repayment of principal—that is, for saving.

Additions and reductions in the money supply cause the amount of the loan funds to rise and fall and the interest rates adjust accordingly. Available funds are either short-term funds or long-term funds. We can also group funds by (1) use, such as business credit, consumer credit, agricultural credit, and government credit; and (2) the institutions supplying each type.

One of the biggest borrowers historically has been the federal government, and Congress generally gives little consideration to interest rates in its spending programs.

Minor changes in interest rates do not affect short-term business borrowing. However, historical evidence shows that large increases in short-term interest rates do lead to a decrease in the demand for bank loans and other forms of short-term business borrowing.

Changes in long-term interest rates also affect long-term business borrowing. Most corporations put off long-term borrowing when rates are up if they expect rates to go down in the near future.

Minor changes in interest rates have little effect on consumer borrowing. For short-term installment loans, the monthly repayments of principal are so large compared to the interest cost that the total effect on the repayment schedule is small. However, larger interest rate changes have strongly influenced consumer borrowing in the past.

While the effect of interest rates on lending varies, both the supply of and the demand for funds are affected by the actions of the banking system and the government. When depository institutions expand credit by increasing the total volume of short-term loans, the supply of funds increases. When credit contracts, the supply of funds decreases.

The actions of the Federal Reserve in setting discount rates, buying securities in the open market, and changing reserve requirements also affect the supply of loan money.

Government borrowing has now become a major influence on demand for funds and will remain so for the foreseeable future. Government surpluses or deficits make funds available in the market or take them out of the market in substantial amounts. Treasury debt management policies also affect the supply-and-demand relationships for short-, intermediate-, and long-term funds.

2.6.4 Interest Rates and Business Decisions

Depository institutions make profits by achieving a spread between the interest rates they pay individuals on savings accounts and the interest rates they charge businesses and other individuals for loans.

> ## FOR EXAMPLE
>
> ### Personal Pension Plans
>
> The tax deferral (or postponement) on funds placed in individual retirement accounts (IRAs) increases the volume of savings.

Interest rates are also important to financial institutions, such as insurance companies and pension funds that accumulate premiums and contributions and invest these proceeds in government and corporate securities for the benefit of their policyholders and employees.

Interest rates are set in the financial markets based on the supply and demand for funds. The cost or price of home mortgage loans depends on the supply and demand for such loans in the mortgage markets.

Interest rates prevailing in the securities markets are also very important to borrowers and lenders or investors. Savings and investments in debt securities by institutions and individuals will accumulate more quickly when they earn high interest rates. On the other hand, business borrowers and individuals would prefer lower interest rates to help them run profitable enterprises.

Much depends on interest rates, and in a healthy economy, the cost of money should be affordable for all.

SELF-CHECK

- **Define interest rate.**
- **Explain the role of interest rates in the loanable funds theory.**
- **Identify three areas of business influenced by interest rates.**

2.7 Structure of Interest Rates

It's obvious that the financial markets are under the influence of the Treasury and the Federal Reserve when it comes to the supply and demand of funds. We must also consider that interest rates in the United States are also influenced by international factors.

2.7.1 Determinants of Market Interest Rates

The **prime interest rate** is the rate that banks charge each other. The prime interest rate is set by the Federal Reserve chairman. The chair can revise the rate when the Federal Reserve believes it is necessary. The rate charged consumers and businesses is always higher and is determined by various factors.

▲ **The nominal interest rate** is the rate that we observe in the marketplace.

The nominal interest rate includes a premium for expected inflation.

▲ **The inflation premium** is the average inflation rate expected over the life of the instrument.

A nominal interest rate that is not free from the risk of default by the borrower also will have a default risk premium.

▲ **The default risk premium** indicates compensation for the possibility that the borrower will not pay interest and/or repay principal according to the loan agreement.

It is quite common for mortgage loans to have default risk premiums. In such cases, the additional interest is called a *mortgage insurance premium* and is paid by the borrower until the principal on the loan is paid down.

▲ **The real rate of interest** is the interest rate on a risk-free financial debt instrument when no inflation is expected.

To cover both short-term and long-term debt instruments, two additional premiums—the maturity risk and liquidity premiums—are frequently added to the nominal interest rate.

▲ **The maturity risk premium** is the added return expected by lenders or investors because of interest rate risk on instruments with longer maturities.

Interest rate risk reflects the possibility of changes or fluctuations in market values of fixed-rate debt instruments as market interest rates change over time.

▲ **The liquidity premium** is the compensation for those financial debt instruments that cannot be easily converted to cash at prices close to their estimated fair market values.

Additional interest charges go along with the financial principle of higher returns for taking on greater risk.

2.7.2 Risk-Free Securities: U.S. Treasury Debt Obligations

By combining the real rate of interest and the inflation premium, we have the **risk-free rate of interest,** which in the United States is represented by U.S. Treasury debt instruments or securities.

> **FOR EXAMPLE**
>
> Mortgage Loans
>
> Foreclosures are rising in the United States. This is occurring for several reasons. First, many Americans do not have adequate savings to get them through a difficult financial time such as layoffs. Secondly, mass layoffs flood the job market with many applicants at once, which makes it more difficult to find a job. Third, many banks are authorizing very high loans for people who are not able to make the payments. Unfortunately, many Americans borrow close to the maximum without realizing how tight their cash flow will be with the large mortgage payments.

It is generally believed that even with the large national debt, the U.S. government is not going to renege on its obligations to pay interest and repay principal at maturity on its debt securities. Thus, we view U.S. Treasury securities as being default-risk-free. Technically, a truly risk-free financial instrument also has no liquidity risk or maturity risk. Treasury marketable securities are considered to have virtually no liquidity risk.

2.7.3 Home Mortgages

Interest rates on home mortgages are usually structured by the method outlined above. Also, keep in mind that in case of default, the mortgage company can take possession of the property and resell it to recoup the loan amount. This procedure is called *foreclosure*.

Another type of mortgage that you should be aware of is the **adjustable-rate mortgage (ARM)** or variable-rate mortgage. The interest rates on these home loans rise and fall in line with a specified government rate, usually a treasury security. While these mortgages may start with a lower payment, a rise in interest rates can cause the payment to be raised substantially and actually reduce the homeowner's equity in the property.

SELF-CHECK

- Define **nominal interest rate** and **inflation premium**.
- Explain when a lender might add a maturity risk premium or a liquidity risk premium to a loan.
- What represents the risk-free rate of interest in the United States?
- Explain how adjustable rate mortgages work.

2.8 The Yield Curve

The **yield** is the profit realized on investments. The term *structure of interest rates* indicates the relationship between interest rates or yields and the maturity of comparable debt instruments. This is typically depicted through the graphic presentation of a **yield curve.**

A properly constructed yield curve must

▲ reflect securities of similar default risk;

▲ represent a particular point in time, and the interest rates should reflect yields for the remaining time to maturity. That is, the yields should not only include stated interest rates but also consider that instruments and securities could be selling above or below their redemption values;

▲ show yields on a number of securities with differing lengths of time to maturity. U.S. government securities provide the best basis for constructing yield.

As you study Figure 2-2, notice that because of high inflation rates and monetary policy trying to constrain economic activity, the March 1980 yield curve was both downward sloping and at high overall interest rate levels. In contrast, the yield curve for November 2003 was upward sloping and much lower overall due to lower expected inflation rates and efforts by monetary policy to stimulate economic activity.

Figure 2-2

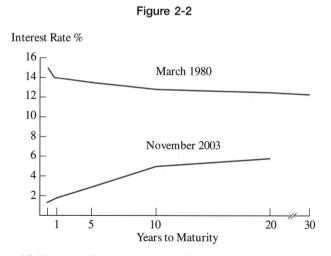

Yield curves for treasury securities at selected dates.
Source: Federal Reserve bulletin, various issues.

2.8.1 Relationship between Yield Curves and the Economy

Historical evidence suggests that interest rates generally rise during periods of economic expansion and fall during economic contraction. Therefore, the *structure of interest rates,* as depicted by yield curves, shifts upward or downward with changes in economic activity. Interest rate levels generally are the lowest at the bottom of a recession and are highest at the top of an expansion.

Also, when the economy is moving out of a recession, the yield curve slopes upward. The curve begins to flatten out during the latter stages of an expansion and typically starts sloping downward when economic activity peaks.

As the economy turns downward, interest rates begin falling and the yield curve again goes through a flattening-out phase to become upward-sloping when economic activity again reaches a low point.

2.8.2 Predicting Future Interest Rates Using the Yield Curve

Three theories are commonly used to explain the structure of interest rates. These are the expectations theory, the liquidity preference theory, and the market segmentation theory. We will focus on the expectations theory.

▲ **The expectations theory** contends that the shape of a yield curve reflects investor expectations about future inflation rates.

If the yield curve is flat, expectations are that the current short-term inflation rate will remain essentially unchanged over time. When the yield curve is downward-sloping, investors expect inflation rates to be lower in the future. Recall from Figure 2-2 that the shape of the yield curve in March 1980 was

---

⌐ FOR EXAMPLE ⌐

Market Segmentation Theory

An example of the premise of market segmentation theory can be seen in that commercial banks concentrate their activities on short-term securities because of their demand and other deposit liabilities. On the other hand, the nature of the insurance company and pension fund liabilities allows these firms to concentrate holdings in long-term securities. Thus, supply-and-demand factors in each market segment affect the shape of the yield curve. In some time periods, interest rates on intermediate-term treasury securities may be higher (or lower) than those for both short-and long-term treasuries.

downward-sloping. This led investors to believe that the double-digit inflation rates prevailing in 1980 would decline in the future. They did.

In contrast, the relatively low yield curve in November 2003 suggested that investors expected the low inflation rates in late 2003 to remain at low levels in the future and that the economy would continue to grow at a moderate rate.

The other two theories are as follows:

▲ The **liquidity preference theory** holds that investors or debt instrument holders prefer to invest short term so they have greater liquidity and less maturity or interest rate risk.

▲ The **market segmentation theory** holds that securities of different maturities are not perfect substitutes for each other.

SELF-CHECK

- Define **yield**.
- Explain what a yield curve is and list the three characteristics of a properly constructed yield curve.
- Describe the slope of yield curves when the economy is moving out of a recession, when it is in the latter stages of an expansion, and when economic activity is at its peak.
- Explain the expectations theory.

SUMMARY

You now have a working knowledge of the monetary system. This is essential to understanding the broader financial system and how businesses and financial institutions operate. The monetary system is responsible for creating and transferring money and is intertwined with the savings-investment process. Major participants in the monetary system include a central bank called the Federal Reserve and a banking system composed of depository institutions. Money must provide several functions for a monetary system to be successful. Money must serve as a medium of exchange, as a store of value, and as a standard of value. Money supply is measured in terms of M1, M2, and M3. Interest rates are another component of the monetary system. In this chapter, you defined the structure of interest rates and depicted through a yield curve graph.

KEY TERMS

Adjustable-rate mortgage (ARM)	Interest rates on these home loans rise and fall in line with a specified government rate, usually a treasury security.
Central bank	A government-established organization responsible for supervising and regulating the banking system and for creating and regulating the money supply.
Discount rate	The interest rate charged by Federal Reserve banks to depository institutions.
Reserve requirements	The portions of deposits that banks must maintain either in their own vaults or on deposit at a Federal Reserve bank.
Checks	Document used to withdraw, deposit, or transfer money from a bank account. Also referred to as *drafts*.
Consumer Advisory Council	Group composed of representatives from depository institutions and their customers. The council provides advice relating to consumer issues.
Credit money	Money backed by the creditworthiness of the issuer; can be used instead of physical money.
Currency	U.S. physical money in the form of coins and paper currency.
Default risk premium	Indicates compensation for the possibility that the borrower will not pay interest and/or repay principal according to the loan agreement.
Demand deposit	A type of deposit money that gets its name from the fact that the owner of a deposit account may demand that all or a portion of the amount in his or her account be transferred to another individual or organization.
Deposit money	A special type of credit money. It is backed by the good credit of the depository institution that issued the deposit.
Electronic funds transfers (EFTs)	Money that is transferred through the Internet.
Expectations theory	Belief that the shape of a yield curve reflects investor expectations about future inflation rates.

Fair Credit Billing Act	Sets up a procedure for the prompt correction of errors on a revolving charge account and prevents damage to credit ratings while a dispute is being settled.
Fair Credit Opportunity Act	Act that prohibits discrimination in the granting of credit on the basis of sex, marital status, race, color, religion, national origin, age, or receipt of public assistance.
Fair Credit Reporting Act	Act that sets a procedure for correcting mistakes on credit records and requires that records be used only for legitimate business purposes.
Federal Advisory Council	Group that provides advice and general information on banking-related issues to the board of governors.
Federal Deposit Insurance Corporation (FDIC)	Organization set up in 1933 to protect deposits in banks.
Federal Open Market Committee (FOMC)	Along with the five Reserve bank presidents, the board manages our nation's money supply. FOMC meets eight times a year in Washington, D.C., to discuss the outlook for the U.S. economy and monetary policy.
Federal Reserve System (Fed)	The central bank of the United States and is responsible for setting monetary policy and regulating the banking system.
Full-bodied money	The metal content in gold and silver coins is worth the same as the face values of the coins.
Gross domestic product (GDP)	The measure of the output of goods and services in the economy.
Inflation	A rise in the price of goods. Simply stated, it means that a dollar buys less.
Inflation premium	The average inflation rate expected over the life of the instrument.
Interest	The cost of money. For banks and other financial institutions, the cost of money is the interest they pay on savings accounts. For consumers, the cost of money is the interest they pay on loans and credit card accounts.
Interest rate	A price that equates the demand for and supply of loanable funds.

Liquidity preference theory   Belief that investors or debt instrument holders prefer to invest short term so they have greater liquidity and less maturity or interest rate risk.

Liquidity premium   The compensation for those financial debt instruments that cannot be easily converted to cash at prices close to their estimated fair market values.

Loanable funds theory   Belief that interest rates are a function of the supply and demand for funds earmarked for loans.

M1 money supply   Supply of currency, travelers' checks, demand deposits, and other checkable deposits at depository institutions.

M2 money supply   Includes M1 plus financial assets that can be quickly turned into cash.

M3 money supply   Includes M2 plus large time deposits (over $100,000) and institutional money market mutual funds (with minimal initial investments of $50,000).

Market segmentation theory   Belief that securities of different maturities are not perfect substitutes for each other.

Maturity risk premium   The added return expected by lenders or investors because of interest rate risk on instruments with longer maturities.

Monetary policy   Refers to the actions of the Federal Reserve that influence the amount of money and credit in the U.S. economy. That, in turn, largely determines interest rates and the performance of our economy.

Money   Anything that is commonly accepted as payment.

Money market mutual funds (MMMFs)   Issue shares to customers and invest the proceeds in highly liquid, very-short-maturity, interest-bearing debt instruments called *money market investments*.

National Credit Union Administration (NCUA)   Supervises and regulates credit unions.

Nominal interest rate   The rate that we observe in the marketplace. The nominal interest rate includes a premium for expected inflation.

Office of Thrift Supervision (OTS)	Oversees S & Ls and other savings institutions.
Open market operations	The buying and selling of U.S. government securities. *Open market* refers to the fact that the Fed doesn't decide which security dealers to do business with on a specific day.
Other checkable deposits	Twenty-four percent of M1 include automatic transfer service (ATS) accounts and negotiable order of withdrawal (NOW) accounts at depository institutions.
Physical money	The coin and paper currency used to pay debts and expenses and to purchase goods and services.
Prime interest rate	The rate that banks charge each other. The rate charged consumers and businesses is always higher and is determined by various factors.
Real rate of interest	The interest rate on a risk-free financial debt instrument when no inflation is expected.
Repurchase agreement	A way of making a loan. The lender buys an asset, usually securities, from the borrower, thus providing funds to the borrower. The borrower repays by buying back the asset at a prearranged time and price.
Risk-free rate of interest	Combines the real rate of interest and the inflation premium, which in the United States is represented by U.S. Treasury debt instruments or securities.
Store of value	Money held for some period of time before it is spent.
Standard of value	A function of money that occurs when prices and debts are stated in terms of the monetary value.
Thrift Institutions Advisory Council	Consists of members from savings and loans associations, savings banks, and credit unions and provides advice on issues that directly affect thrift institutions.
Travelers' checks	Offered by banks and other organizations, these are a promise to pay on demand the face amounts of the checks.
Truth-in-Lending	A section of the Consumer Credit Protection Act requires disclosure of the finance charges and the annual percentage rate of credit along with

certain other costs and terms to allow consumers to compare the cost of credit from different sources.

Velocity of money   The rate of circulation of the money supply.

Yield   The profit realized on investments.

Yield curve   Reflects the profits realized on securities of similar default risk. It represents a particular point in time, and the interest rates should reflect yields for the remaining time to maturity. U.S. government securities provide the best basis for constructing yield.

ASSESS YOUR UNDERSTANDING

Go to www.wiley.com/college/Melicher to evaluate your knowledge of the basics of the U.S. monetary system.
Measure your learning by comparing pre-test and post-test results.

Summary Questions

1. A central bank is a federal government agency that facilitates operation of the financial system and regulates growth of the money supply. True or false?
2. The primary function of the Federal Reserve System is to
   (a) issue currency to member banks.
   (b) regulate the growth of the money supply.
   (c) serve as a fiscal agent for the U.S. government.
   (d) regulate and conduct bank examinations.
3. The Federal Reserve System replaced the system that existed under the National Banking Act. True or false?
4. The Federal Reserve Advisory Council provides advice and general information to the secretary of the Treasury. True or false?
5. The members of the board of governors are also members of the Federal Open Market Committee. True or false?
6. The Federal Open Market Committee directs open market operations. True or false?
7. The three primary means that the Fed can use to exercise monetary policy includes open market operations, changing reserve requirements, and influencing the Federal Discount Rate. True or false?
8. Physical money includes coin and currency. True or false?
9. Representative full-bodied money consists of paper money fully backed by a precious metal. True or false?
10. Deposit money is backed by the creditworthiness of the depository institution that issued the deposit. True or false?
11. Demand deposits are issued by commercial banks and savings banks, and do not earn interest. True or false?
12. Credit money includes
    (a) checking accounts at commercial banks.
    (b) checkable deposits at savings and loan associations.
    (c) checking accounts at credit unions.
    (d) all of the above.
    (e) none of the above.

13. Which of the following describes the basic function of money?
    (a) Store of purchasing power
    (b) Standard of value
    (c) Medium of exchange
    (d) Liquidity

14. The only paper money of significance in the economy today is
    (a) silver certificates.
    (b) demand deposits.
    (c) greenbacks.
    (d) Federal Reserve notes.

15. The M1 definition of the money supply includes which of the following items?
    (a) Currency
    (b) Demand deposits and other checkable deposits at depository institutions
    (c) Travelers' checks
    (d) All of the above

16. Money market funds are not included in which of the following definitions of the money supply?
    (a) M1
    (b) M2
    (c) M3
    (d) M4 or L

17. In recent years, M2 is about twice as big as M1. True or false?

18. M2 excludes M1 money supply components. True or false?

19. Travelers' checks are included in which of the following money supply definitions?
    (a) M1
    (b) M2
    (c) M3
    (d) All of the above

20. M3 money supply includes M2 plus large time deposits and institutional MMMFs, repurchase agreements, and Eurodollar deposits. True or false?

21. A measure of the output of goods and services in an economy is called
    (a) output.
    (b) money supply.
    (c) gross domestic product.
    (d) velocity.

22. The faster the velocity of money, the greater an economy's GDP. True or false?

23. Inflation reflects a rise in prices not offset by increases in quality. True or false?

24. Monetarists believe that when the money supply exceeds the amount of money demanded, the public will spend more rapidly, causing inflation. True or false?

25. Keynesians believe that when the supply of money exceeds the quantity demanded, the public will spend more rapidly, causing inflation. True or false?

26. The interest rate is the basic price that equates the demand for supply of loanable funds in the financial markets. True or false?

27. Borrowers will demand funds from lenders as long as they can invest the funds and earn a satisfactory return above the cost of their loans. True or false?

28. The loanable funds theory states that interest rates are a function of the supply of and demand for loanable funds. True or false?

29. The more effectively the life insurance industry promotes the sale of whole life and endowment insurance policies, the larger the volume of savings. True or false?

30. When income is high, savings tend to increase. True or false?

31. Which of the following interest rates are not determined in the money market?
    (a) U.S. Treasury bill rate
    (b) Prime rate
    (c) Commercial paper rate
    (d) Federal funds rate

32. Interest rates in the United States are only influenced by domestic factors. True or false?

33. The interest rate that is observed in the marketplace is called a *real interest rate*. True or false?

34. The real rate of interest is the interest rate on a risk-free financial debt instrument with no inflation expected. True or false?

35. Which of the following is NOT a determinant of market interest rates?
    (a) The inflation premium
    (b) The maturity risk premium
    (c) The volatility risk premium
    (d) The real rate of interest

36. The maturity risk premium is the added return expected by lenders because of the expectation of inflation. True or false?

37. The liquidity premium is compensation for those financial debt instruments that cannot be easily converted to cash at prices close to their estimated fair market values. True or false?

38. Treasury marketable securities are considered to have no default risk but some liquidity risk. True or false?

39. As the economy begins moving out of a recessionary period, the yield curve is
    (a) upward-sloping.
    (b) flattened out.
    (c) downward-sloping.
    (d) discontinuous.

40. When referring to an "upward-sloping" yield curve, interest rates
    (a) are flat across all maturities.
    (b) decrease as maturity increases.
    (c) increase as maturity decreases.
    (d) increase as maturity increases.

41. When referring to a "downward-sloping" yield curve, interest rates
    (a) decline as maturities shorten.
    (b) rise as maturities shorten.
    (c) remain the same as maturities lengthen.
    (d) rise as maturities lengthen.

42. The expectations theory contends that the shape of the yield curve reflects investor expectations about future GDP growth rates. True or false?

Review Questions

1. The primary job of the Federal Reserve is to maintain a healthy economy. List three tools the Fed has at its disposal for carrying out this job.

2. *Monetary policy* refers to the actions of the Federal Reserve that influence the amount of money and credit in the U.S. economy. List the three goals of monetary policy.

3. The Fed's monetary policy can directly influence business activities. Compare the effects of tightening the monetary policy to that of loosening the monetary policy.

4. The Fed sometimes tries to tighten the money supply to slow the rate of inflation. How might such actions benefit people who want to save money?

5. The U.S. money supply is composed of physical and credit money. List one type of each.

6. A demand deposit is a type of deposit money that gets its name from the fact that the owner of a deposit account may demand that all or a portion of the amount in his or her account be transferred to another individual or organization. List two types of demand deposit and indicate when using them would be appropriate.

7. The M1 money supply measures only sums of money that can be spent without first converting them to some other asset. List the four components of the M1 supply and indicate whether they are physical or credit money.

8. How do some of the owners hold the assets included in M2?

 (a) As long-term savings instruments

 (b) As repurchase agreements

 (c) For purchases or payments in the immediate future

 (d) b and c

 (e) a and c

9. The use of credit cards can affect the rate of turnover of the money supply and may contribute to money supply expansion. What part of the money supply do credit card balances count as?

 (a) M1 money supply

 (b) M2 money supply

 (c) M3 money supply

 (d) None of the above

10. If the money supply for an economy is $3 trillion and the velocity of money is 4.5, then what is the GDP?

 (a) $0.67 trillion

 (b) $1.5 trillion

 (c) $7.5 trillion

 (d) $13.5 trillion

11. If the money supply for an economy is $3 trillion and GDP is $10 trillion, then what is the velocity of money?

 (a) $3.33 trillion

 (b) $13.0 trillion

 (c) $7.0 trillion

 (d) $30 trillion

12. Holding demand constant, an increase in the supply of loanable funds does what to interest rates?

 (a) Increase

 (b) Decrease

 (c) Increase or decrease

 (d) None of the above

13. Holding demand constant, a decrease in the supply of loanable funds does what to interest rates?

    (a) Increase
    (b) Decrease
    (c) Increase or decrease
    (d) None of the above

14. Holding supply constant, a decrease in the demand of loanable funds does what to interest rates?

    (a) Increase
    (b) Decrease
    (c) Increase or decrease
    (d) None of the above

15. If you expect the inflation premium to be 2%, the default risk premium to be 1%, and the real interest rate to be 4%, what interest would you expect to observe in the marketplace under the simplest form of market interest rates?

    (a) 4%
    (b) 7%
    (c) 2%
    (d) 1%

16. What is the real rate of interest if the nominal rate of interest is 15%, the inflation premium is 3%, the default risk premium is 3%, the maturity risk premium is 3%, and the liquidity premium is 2%?

    (a) 3%
    (b) 4%
    (c) 5%
    (d) None of the above

17. When investors expect _____ inflation rates, they will require _____ nominal interest rates so that a real rate of return will remain after the inflation.

    (a) higher, higher
    (b) higher, lower
    (c) lower, higher
    (d) None of the above

18. Assume that these current yields exist: long-term government securities yield 9%, 5-year treasury securities yield 8.5%, and 1-year treasury bills yield 8%. What type of yield curve is depicted?

    (a) Downward-sloping
    (b) Flat or level

(c) Upward-sloping

(d) U-shaped

19. What yield curve shape is depicted if intermediate-term treasury securities yield 10%, short-term treasuries yield 10.5%, and long-term treasuries yield 9.5%?

(a) Downward-sloping

(b) Flat or level

(c) Upward-sloping

(d) U-shaped

Applying This Chapter

1. Look at the content of your wallet or purse and identify all forms of physical and credit money.

2. Go to the Federal Reserve Board Web site, www.federalreserve.gov, and find information on the current money supply. Determine the current money supply of M1 and its four components, along with the size of M2 and M3.

3. Using the following information, determine the size of the demand deposits component of the M1 money supply.

Currency	$350 million
Traveler's checks	$10 million
Other checkable deposits	$200 million
Small time deposits	$100 million
M1 money supply	$800 million

4. Go to the St. Louis Federal Reserve Bank's Web site, www.stls.frb.org, and access the FRED database. Find the current size of the M1 money supply and the annual gross domestic product (GDP) and calculate the velocity of money.

5. A country's gross domestic product (GDP) is $20 billion and its money supply (MS) is $5 billion.

(a) What is the country's velocity of money (VM)?

(b) If the MS stays at the same level next year while the velocity of money "turns over" 4.5 times, what would be the level of GDP?

(c) Assume that the VM will turn over four times next year. If the country wants a GDP of $22 billion at the end of next year, what will have to be the size of the money supply? What percentage increase in the MS will be necessary to achieve the target GDP?

6. As an economist for a major bank, you are asked to explain the present substantial increase in the price level, notwithstanding the fact that neither the money supply nor the velocity of money has increased. How can this occur?

7. You are considering an investment in a 1-year government debt security with a yield of 5% or a highly liquid corporate debt security with a yield of 6.5%. The expected inflation rate for the next year is expected to be 2.5%.

   (a) What would be your real rate earned on either of the two investments?

   (b) What would be the default risk premium on the corporate debt security?

8. Inflation is expected to be 3% over the next year. You desire an annual real rate of return of 2.5% on your investments.

   (a) What nominal rate of interest would have to be offered on a 1-year treasury security for you to consider making an investment?

   (b) A 1-year corporate debt security is being offered at 2 percentage points over the 1-year treasury security rate that meets your requirement in (a) above. What would be the nominal interest rate on the corporate security?

9. Go to the St. Louis Federal Reserve Bank's Web site, www.stls.frb.org, and access the FRED database. Find interest rates for different maturities of U.S. Treasury securities and construct the yield curve.

Weaknesses of the Central Banking System

What were the main weaknesses of our central banking system? Consider how the time it took to process payments affected businesses.

Inflation

Inflation is a rise in prices not offset by increases in quality. List some everyday products, like coffee, where the prices have risen dramatically while the product has stayed the same.

Business Week

Obtain access to several recent issues of *Business Week*. Review the "Economic Analysis" section for articles relating to development in the U.S. monetary system. Also examine the "International Business" section for possible developments occurring in terms of foreign monetary systems.

3

TIME VALUE OF MONEY
Present Value and Future Value

Starting Point

Go to www.wiley.com/college/Melicher to assess your knowledge of the basics of the time value of money.
Determine where you need to concentrate your effort.

What You'll Learn in This Chapter

▲ How time affects the value of money
▲ The effects of inflation on purchasing power
▲ The discounting process
▲ The different types of interest rates used in financing
▲ How annuities are used
▲ The cost of consumer credit

After Studying This Chapter, You'll Be Able To

▲ Compare and contrast the present value and future value of money
▲ Examine the concept of simple interest and the process of compounding interest
▲ Describe the effects of inflation on purchasing power
▲ Examine the discounting process and how different time intervals affect it
▲ Evaluate how interest rates are calculated
▲ Differentiate between annuity and ordinary annuity
▲ Differentiate between APR and EAR

Goals and Outcomes

▲ Estimate the future value of money
▲ Estimate interest rates and time requirements for problems involving compound interest
▲ Assess how high inflation affects the purchasing power of consumers
▲ Assess how interest rates affect the economy
▲ Assess and make discounting calculations using time intervals that are less than 1 year
▲ Evaluate how annuities are used
▲ Compare and contrast APR with EAR

INTRODUCTION

Although we have touched on the time value of money in other chapters, it is a subject that requires more in-depth study. Businesses and individuals must acquire the basic skills necessary to calculate interest on a variety of different financial instruments. They should also understand the different forms of interest and how they are applied to savings accounts, mortgages, and other types of loans. Remember that money always has a price tag and like any type of asset, it must be used wisely to get the most out of it.

3.1 The Math of Finance

We can all agree with the following concepts:

- ▲ More money is better than less money.
- ▲ Money today is worth more than the same amount of money received in the future.

Of course, the value of an additional dollar is not necessarily the same for all individuals. A person trying to survive at the poverty level would likely find an added dollar to be worth more in economic terms than a millionaire. While we are not going to delve into the psychic values of money to specific individuals, we are going to revisit the principle of finance presented in section 1.3 that taught us that money has a time value. Money can grow or increase over time, which means that money has a lower value today if we have to wait to receive the money sometime in the future. That's because we lose the opportunity of earning interest on the money by not being able to save or invest the money today.

Money is often transferred into bonds, stocks, and real asset investments, and therefore we must understand how these are priced and valued. The time value of money is the math of finance, and basic calculations allow us to estimate the future value of money that is being saved or invested.

Let's begin with a savings account illustration. Assume you have $1,000 to save or invest; this is your principal.

> ▲ **The present value of a savings or an investment** is its amount or value today.

This is your $1,000. A bank offers to accept your savings for 1 year and agrees to pay to you an 8% interest rate on this savings account. This amounts to $80 in interest (0.08 × $1,000). At the end of the year, your savings account balance has grown to $1,080 (principal plus interest). This $1,080 is referred to as the future value or value after 1 year.

▲ **The future value of a savings amount or investment** is its value at a specified time or date in the future.

Now let's assume that your $1,000 investment remains on deposit for 2 years but that the bank pays only simple interest.

▲ **Simple interest** is interest earned only on the principal amount of the investment.

The calculation to find the earnings at the end of 2 years is $1,000 × .08 × 2 = $160, making the value of your initial investment grow to a total of $1,160.

Another bank will pay you a 10% interest rate on your money. Thus, you would receive $100 in interest ($1,000 × 0.10) or a return at the end of 1 year of $1,100 ($1,000 × 1.10) from this second bank. While the $20 difference in return between the two banks ($1,100 versus $1,080) is not great, it has some importance to most of us. For a 2-year deposit where simple interest is paid annually, the difference increases to $40. The second bank would return $1,200 to you versus $1,160 from the first bank. If the funds were invested for 10 years, we would accumulate $1,000 × [1 + (0.08 × 10)] or $1,800 at the first bank. At the second bank we would have $1,000 × [1 + (0.10 × 10)] or $2,000, a $200 difference.

FOR EXAMPLE

Investment Choices

In the earlier examples, we have looked at ways investments can earn money on top of the original principal. Unfortunately, you can also lose money. Let's look at the value of $1,000 in two scenarios. If, for example, you were to have invested that $1,000 in Enron stock and not sold any of the shares and kept the money until Enron collapsed, then you would have lost your entire principal. In fact, you would have been better off sticking the money under your mattress. On the other hand, if you bought stock in a company such as General Electric and held it for a year, on an average year, you would have earned a 10 to 15% return. On the conservative side, your investment would be worth $1,100. The profit, however, would not be realized until you sold your stock. Before the sale of the stock, your investment is only worth that much "on paper."

SELF-CHECK

- What is the time value of money?
- What do we mean by **present value** and **future value**?
- What is simple interest?

3.2 Compounding to Determine Future Values

A difference in interest rates between the two banks will become even more important when the interest changes from simple interest to compounded interest.

▲ **Compounding** is an arithmetic process whereby an initial value increases or grows at a compound interest rate over time to reach a value in the future.

▲ **Compound interest** involves earning interest on interest in addition to interest on the principal or initial investment.

To understand compounding, let's assume that you leave the investment with a bank for more than 1 year. The first bank accepts your $1,000 deposit now, adds $80 at the end of 1 year, retains the $1,080 for the second year, and pays you interest at an 8% rate. The bank returns your initial deposit plus accumulated interest at the end of the second year. How much will you receive as a future value? The calculation is done as follows:

$$\text{Future value} = \text{present value} \times [(1 + \text{interest rate}) \times (1 + \text{interest rate})]$$

For our 2-year investment example, we have

$$
\begin{aligned}
\text{Future value} &= \$1,000 \times (1.08) \times (1.08) \\
&= \$1,000 \times 1.1664 \\
&= \$1,166.40 \\
&= \$1,166 \text{ (rounded)}.
\end{aligned}
$$

The compounding concept also can be expressed in equation form as

$$FV_n = PV(1 + r)n.$$

FV is the future value, PV is the present value, r is the interest rate, and n is the number of periods in years. For our $1,000 deposit, 8%, 2-year example, we have

$$
\begin{aligned}
FV_2 &= \$1,000(1 + 0.08)^2 \\
&= \$1,000(1.1164) \\
&= \$1,166.40 \\
&= \$1,166 \text{ (rounded)}
\end{aligned}
$$

3.2.1 Financial Calculators

Texas Instruments (TI) and Hewlett Packard (HP) make two popular types of financial calculators. However, they are programmed differently. Other available financial calculators are usually programmed like either the TI or HP calculators. What is important is that if you are going to use a financial calculator to solve time-value-of-money problems, you must understand how your particular calculator works.

Most financial calculators are programmed to readily find future values. Typically, financial calculators will have a Present Value key (PV), a Future Value key (FV), a Number of Time Periods key (N), an Interest Rate key (usually designated %i), and a Compute key (usually designated as CPT). If you have a financial calculator, you can compute the future value result for the preceding example.

First, clear any values stored in the calculator's memory. Next, enter 1000 and press the PV key (some financial calculators require that you enter the present value amount as a minus value because it is an investment or outflow. Then, enter 8 and press the %i key (most financial calculators are programmed so that you enter whole numbers rather than decimals for the interest rate). Next, enter 10 for the number of time periods (usually years) and press the N key. Finally, press the CPT key followed by the FV key to calculate the future value of $2,158.93, which rounds to $2,159. However, financial calculators are programmed to calculate answers to 12 significant digits.

3.2.2 Spreadsheet Solutions

Computer spreadsheet programs also are available for finding future values. The following instructions will guide you through the process.

Set up the spreadsheet with descriptive labels in cells A1 through A4. Then solve the compound interest problem by placing the interest rate in decimal form (0.08) in Cell B1. On Row 2 place the time periods beginning with period 0 (the current period) in Cell B2 and so forth. The cash flow of $-1,000$ (an outflow) is listed in cell B3. Since this is a simple problem, first replicate the basic "by hand" calculations in spreadsheet format and the future value calculations beginning in C4 and continuing to D4.

In Cell C4 place the formula $=-B3*(1+B1)$, which reflects compounding the 1,000 investment at 8% interest for 1 year. Cell D4 shows compounding the investment at 8% for a second year and can be calculated as $C4*(1+B1)$. So, compounding at an 8% interest rate results in a future value of 1,166.40 after 2 years. Of course, it is possible to have made the FV calculation in one step as $=-B3*(1+B1)^2$, which also produces 1,166.40.

3.2.3 Table-Based Solutions

Table 3-1 shows Future Values Interest Factor (FVIF) carried to three decimal places for a partial range of interest rates and time periods. (Table 1 in the Appendix is a more comprehensive FVIF table.) Let's use Table 3-1 to find the

Table 3-1: Future Value Interest Factor (FVIF) of $1

Year	5%	6%	7%	8%	9%	10%
1	1.050	1.060	1070	1.080	1.090	1.100
2	1.102	1.124	1.145	1.166	1.188	1.210
3	1.158	1.191	1.225	1.260	1.295	1.331
4	1.216	1.262	1.311	1.360	1.412	1.464
5	1.276	1.338	1.403	1.469	1.539	1.611
6	1.340	1.419	1.501	1.587	1.677	1.772
7	1.407	1.504	1.606	1.714	1.828	1.949
8	1.477	1.594	1.718	1.851	1.993	2.144
9	1.551	1.689	1.838	1.999	2.172	2.358
10	1.629	1.791	1.967	2.159	2.367	2.594

future value of $1,000 invested at an 8% compound interest rate for a 10-year period. Notice that at the intersection of the 8% column and 10 years, we find a FVIF of 2.159.

Further examination of the table shows how a $1 investment grows or increases with various combinations of interest rates and time periods. For example, if another bank offers to pay you a 10% interest rate compounded annually, notice that the FVIF at the intersection of 10% and 10 years would be 2.594, making your $1,000 investment worth $2,594 ($1,000 × 2.594). Now you can

FOR EXAMPLE

Certificates of Deposit and Compound Interest

Banks offer certificates of deposit to individual savers for various lengths of time, including 1 month, 3 months, 6 months, 1 year, 3 years, and even 30 years. To entice investors to save with them, the banks state annual percentage rates, but they compound more frequently than once a year. The result is that the effective annual rate (EAR) is higher than the annual percentage rate (APR). Certificates of deposit are a very safe investment and are guaranteed to appreciate according to the interest terms offered. You cannot, however, withdraw the money before the certificates of deposit mature or you will have to pay a hefty penalty.

Figure 3-1

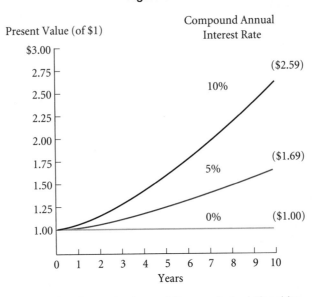

Future value, interest rate, and time period relationships.

readily see that the difference between the 8% and 10% rates is much more sig-nificant at $435 ($2,594 − $2,159) than the $200 difference that occurred with simple compounding over 10 years.

The compounding process can also be shown in graphic form. Figure 3-1 shows graphic relationships among future values, interest rates, and time peri-ods. Notice how $1 will grow differently over a 10-year period at 5% versus 10% interest rates. Of course, if there is no interest being earned, then the ini-tial $1 investment will remain at $1 no matter how long the investment is held. At a 10% interest rate, the initial $1 grows to $2.59 (rounded) after 10 years. This compares with $1.63 (rounded) after 10 years if the interest rate is only 5%. Notice that the future value increases at an increasing rate as the interest rate is increased and as the time period is lengthened.

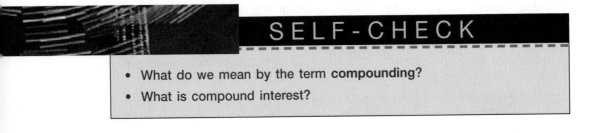

SELF-CHECK

- What do we mean by the term **compounding**?
- What is compound interest?

3.3 Inflation or Purchasing Power Implications

The compounding process described in section 3.2 does not say anything about the purchasing power of the initial $1 investment at some point in the future. As seen, $1 growing at a 10% interest rate would be worth $2.59 (rounded) at the end of 10 years. With zero inflation, you could purchase $2.59 of the same quality of goods after 10 years relative to what you could purchase now. However, if the stated or nominal interest rate is 10% and the inflation rate is 5%, then in terms of increased purchasing power, the "net" or differential compounding rate would be 5% (10% − 5%) and $1 would have an inflation-adjusted value of $1.63 after 10 years. This translates into an increased purchasing power of $0.63 ($1.63 − $1.00).

Also note that if the compound inflation rate is equal to the compound interest rate, the purchasing power would not change. For instance, if both the inflation and interest rates were 5%, the purchasing power of $1 would remain the same over time. To apply this concept, subtract the expected inflation rate from the stated interest rate and compound the remaining interest rate to determine the change in purchasing power over a stated time period. If the interest rate is 10% and the inflation rate is 3%, the savings or investment should be compounded at a differential 7% rate.

Financial contracts (e.g., savings deposits and bank loans) in countries that have experienced high and fluctuating inflation rates sometimes have been linked to a consumer price or similar inflation index. Such actions are designed to reduce the exposure to inflation risk for both savers and lenders.

Savers receive purchasing power protection, since the interest rate they receive on their savings deposits will vary with the rate of inflation. As inflation goes up, so will the rate of interest individuals receive on their savings deposits so that purchasing power will be maintained.

FOR EXAMPLE

Inflation and Purchasing Power

Many workers have experienced a time in their jobs in which they did not receive an annual raise or they received a very small raise. Inflation, however, never stops. Every year, there is inflation. For 2006, the government has calculated that inflation was at 4.1%. So if you made $30,000 in 2005 and did not have a raise in 2006, your real income actually decreased and you have less purchasing power. Inflation is automatically calculated for social security payments, and those payments are adjusted for the rate of inflation. In recent history, the early 1980s was the worst time for inflation. For example, in 1980 inflation was 14.3%.

Bank lenders are similarly protected against changing inflation rates, since the rates they charge on their loans will also vary with changes in inflation rates. At least in theory, banks will be able to maintain a profit spread between the interest rates they pay to savers and the higher interest rates they charge borrowers because inflation affects both financial contracts. Of course, if the borrowers are business firms, they need to be able to pass on higher prices for their products and services to consumers to be able to maintain profit margins when interest rates are rising along with increases in inflation.

SELF-CHECK

- Briefly explain how inflation affects the purchasing power of a future dollar amount.
- How is the differential interest rate calculated?

3.4 Discounting to Determine Present Values

Most financial management decisions involve present values rather than future values. A financial manager who is considering purchasing an asset wants to know what the asset is worth now rather than at the end of some future time period. The reason that an asset has value is because it will produce a stream of future cash benefits. To determine its value now in time period zero, we have to discount or reduce the future cash benefits to their present value.

▲ **Discounting** is an arithmetic process whereby a future value decreases at a compound interest rate over time to reach a present value.

Let's illustrate discounting with a simple example involving an investment. Assume that a bank or other borrower offers to pay you $1,000 at the end of 1 year in return for using $1,000 of your money now. If you are willing to accept a zero rate of return, you might make the investment. However, most people would require some return on the $1,000 investment. To receive a return of, say, 8%, you would invest less than $1,000 now. The amount to be invested would be determined by dividing the $1,000 that is due at the end of 1 year by one plus the interest rate of 8%. This results in an investment amount of $925.93 ($1,000 ÷ 1.08) or $926 rounded. This could also be calculated as follows: 1 ÷ 1.08, or 0.9259 (when carried to four decimal places) × $1,000, to get $925.90, or $926 when rounded.

To carry this one step further, assume that you will not receive the $1,000 for 2 years and the compound interest rate is 8%. This is computed as follows:

> ## FOR EXAMPLE
>
> ### Discount Bonds
>
> Discount bonds are an investment issued by an organization (usually a city, state, or country) that are sold for less than face value. The bond is held by the investor until maturity, which is a date in the future. Once the bond matures, the investor can redeem it for face value. Discount bonds are sometimes issued by cities to raise money for public works projects.

In our 2-year investment example, we get

$$\text{Present value} = \$1{,}000 \times \frac{1}{1.08} \times \frac{1}{1.08}$$
$$= \$1{,}000 \times .9259 \times .9259$$
$$= 1{,}000 \times 0.8573$$
$$= \$857.30$$

The discounted amount that would be invested is $857.30 in order to receive a return of $1,000 at the end of 2 years.

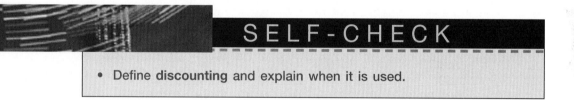

SELF-CHECK

- Define **discounting** and explain when it is used.

3.5 Finding Interest Rates and Time Requirements

Investors often dream about becoming millionaires. Let's look at how long it would take to reach the million-dollar level with an initial investment of $10,000 using the following interest rates:

Amount of Interest Rate (%)	Time (Years)
5	94.4
10	48.3
15	33.0
20	25.3

Notice that at a 5% compound rate it would take more than 94 years to accumulate $1 million. Even if we could compound our interest at a 20% annual rate, it would take a little more than 25 years to become a millionaire.

An alternative approach would be to create an investment annuity of $10,000 per year. The following chart shows the time required to become a millionaire under the assumptions of both an ordinary annuity (where the first investment will be made 1 year from now) and an annuity due (where the first investment is made now).

Interest Rate %	Ordinary Annuity	Annuity Due
5	36.7	35.9
10	25.2	24.3
15	19.8	18.9
20	16.7	15.8

With this approach, the time required, particularly at higher interest rates, is more feasible. Compounding at 5% would still require making annual investments for about 36 years to accumulate $1 million. At 10 percent, it would take you only 24 to 25 years.

Of course, the most crucial factor, which may be easier said than done, is coming up with $10,000 per year out of your disposable income.

3.5.1 Solving for Interest Rates

As mentioned earlier, there are four variables we can use to solve different calculations. The variables are

▲ PV = present value;
▲ FV = future value;
▲ r = interest rate;
▲ n = number of periods.

As long as we know the values for any three of these variables, we can solve for the fourth or unknown variable. We can do this by using a financial calculator, a spreadsheet program, or by using tables.

Let's use these variables to calculate compound interest rates. Assume we have a $1,000 investment, the future value is $1,403, and the time period is 5 years. What compound interest rate would be earned on this investment?

We can solve this with the help of a financial calculator. On the financial calculator, enter PV=1000, FV=1403, and press CPT followed by the %i key to find an r of 7.01, or 7% rounded. Some calculators may require either the PV or the FV to be negative.

We can also calculate this by using the following equation:

$$FVn = PV \, (FVIF \, r, n)$$

If we replace the variables with the numbers from our examples, it will look like the following:

$$\$1{,}403 = \$1{,}000 \, (FVIF \, r, 5)$$

$$FVIF \, r,5 = 1.403$$

Since we know that 5 is the number of periods, we can turn to Table 3-1 and read across the year-five role until we find FVIF of 1.403. This is under the 7% column. The interest rate r is 7%.

3.5.2 Solving for Time Periods

Taking the preceding example, let's assume the investment has a present value of $1,000, a future value of $1,403, and an interest rate of 7%. What length of time does the investment involve?

If a financial calculator is used, enter PV=1000, FV=1403, %i=7, and press the CPT key followed by the N key to find an n of 5.01, or 5 years.

We can also find the answer by using the following equation:

$$FVn = PV \, (FVIF \, 7\%, n)$$

$$\$1{,}403 = \$1{,}000 \, (FVIF \, 7\%, n)$$

$$FVIF \, 7\%,n = 1{,}403$$

Because we know the interest rate is 7%, we can turn to Table 3-1 and read down the 7% column until we find the FVIF of 1.403. This occurs in the 3-year row, which indicates that the time period is 5 years.

3.5.3 Rule of 72

Investors often ask, "How long will it take for my money to double in value at a particular interest rate?" We can look back at Table 3-1 (Future Value of Interest Factor) to illustrate the process for answering this question. We pick a particular interest rate and read down the table until we find an FVIF of 2.000. For example, at an 8% interest rate, it will take almost exactly 9 years (note the FVIF of 1.999) for an investment to double in value. At a 9% interest rate, the investment will double in about 8 years (FVIF of 1.993). An investment will double in a little over 7 years (FVIF of 1.949) if the interest rate is 10%.

A shortcut method, referred to as the **Rule of 72**, is used to approximate the time required for an investment to double in value. This method is applied by dividing the interest rate into the number 72 to determine the number of years it will take for an investment to double in value. For example, if the interest rate is 8%, 72 divided by 8 indicates that the investment will double in value in 9 years.

FOR EXAMPLE

Investments

Historically, the stock market has made gains of more than 10% per year. This is true even with taking the first 5 years of this century into account. With investing in stocks, you are likely to double your money more quickly than 7.2 years. If you invest in more guaranteed investments such as certificates of deposits with an average rate of return at 5%, then it will take you longer than 7.3 years to double your investment.

Notice that this is the same conclusion drawn from the table. At an interest rate of 10%, it will take approximately 7.2 years for an investment to double in value. However, be aware that if the interest rate is very low or very high, the Rule of 72 does not approximate the compounding process as well and thus a larger estimation error occurs in the time required for an investment to double in value.

SELF-CHECK

- How is the Rule of 72 used?

3.6 Future Value of an Annuity

Many cash payments or receipts are lump sum amounts that represent present and future values. However, annuities are widely used in the financial world. They provide a steady income, a series of equal payments that are received over a number of time periods.

- ▲ An **annuity** is a series of equal payments (receipts) that occur over a number of time periods.
- ▲ An **ordinary annuity** exists when the equal payments (receipts) occur at the end of each time period.

For example, suppose you want to invest $1,000 per year for 3 years at an 8% interest rate. However, since you will not make your first payment until the end of the first year, this will be an ordinary annuity.

Since the first payment is made at the end of the first year, it is compounded for 2 years, totaling $1,166. The second payment is compounded for 1 year for a total of $1,080. The third payment of $1,000 earns zero interest since the

Table 3-2: Future Value Interest Factor (FVIFA) for a $1 Ordinary Annuity

Year	5%	6%	7%	8%	9%	10%
1	1.000	1.000	1.000	1.000	1.000	1.000
2	2.050	2.060	2.070	2.080	2.090	2.100
3	3.152	3.184	3.215	3.246	3.278	3.310
4	4.310	4.375	4.440	4.506	4.573	4.641
5	5.526	5.637	5.751	5.867	5.985	6.105
6	6.802	6.975	7.153	7.336	7.523	7.716
7	8.142	8.394	8.654	8.923	9.200	9.487
8	9.549	9.897	10.260	10.637	11.028	11.436
9	11.027	11.491	11.978	12.488	13.021	13.579
10	12.578	13.181	13.816	14.487	15.193	15.937

payment is made at the end of the third year. This results in a future value of $3,246 ($1,166 + $1,080 + $1,000). We also can find the future value of this annuity by making the following computations:

$$\text{FV ordinary annuity} = \$1,000(1.08)2 + \$1,000(1.08)1 + \$1,000(1.08)$$
$$= \$1,000(1.166) + \$1,000(1.080) + \$1,000(1.000)$$
$$= \$1,000(3.246) = \$3,246$$

While the computational process was relatively easy for our 3-year ordinary annuity example, the required calculations become more difficult as the time period is lengthened. However, as you already know, most financial calculators are programmed to readily find future values of annuities. Spreadsheets and printed tables such as the ones in the appendix section of this book can also be used. Table 3-2 shows the future value interest factor of an annuity (FVIFA) for a partial range of interest rates and time periods. In other words, it shows how a $1 annuity grows or increases with various combinations of interest rates and time periods.

Let's use Table 3-2 in an example. If $1,000 is invested at the end of each year, beginning with year one, for 10 years at an 8% interest rate, the future value of the annuity would be $14,487 ($1,000 × 14.487). If the interest rate is 10% for 10 years, the future value of the annuity would be $15,936 ($1,000 × 15.937). These examples demonstrate the benefits of higher interest rates on the future values of annuities.

3.6.1 Present Value of an Annuity

Many present value problems also involve cash flow annuities. Usually these are ordinary annuities. Let's assume that we will receive $1,000 per year beginning 1 year from now for a period of 3 years at an 8% compound interest rate. How much would you be willing to pay now for this stream of future cash flows? Since we are concerned with the value now, this becomes a present value problem. We can find the present value of this annuity by making the following computations:

$$
\begin{aligned}
\text{PV ordinary annuity} &= \{\$1,000[1 \div (1.08)_1]\} + \{\$1,000[1 \div (1.08)_2]\} \\
&\quad + \{\$1,000[1 \div (1.08)_3]\} \\
&= [\$1,000(0.926)] + [\$1,000(0.857)] \\
&\quad + [\$1,000(0.794)] \\
&= \$1,000(2.577) \\
&= \$2,577
\end{aligned}
$$

Again, financial calculators, spreadsheet programs, and printed tables are available to calculate these values.

3.6.2 Interest Rates and Time Requirements for an Annuity

Earlier in this chapter, we discussed how to find or solve for interest rates or time periods for problems involving a lump sum present value or future value. Recall that we originally worked with four variables: PV = present value, FV = future value, r = interest rate, and n = number of periods. We now add a fifth variable to reflect payments (PMT) involving annuities.

Assume that the future value of an ordinary annuity is $5,751, the annual payment is $1,000, and the time period is 5 years. What is the interest rate for this annuity? Since we know that the number of time periods is five, we look back at Table 3-2 and read across the year-5 row until we find FVIFA of 5.751. This occurs under the 7% column, indicating that the interest rate r is 7%.

3.6.3 Determining Annual Annuity Payments

There are many instances for which we would want to determine the periodic equal payment required for an annuity. For example, you may wish to accumulate $10,000 at the end of 5 years from now by making equal annual payments beginning 1 year from now. If you can invest at a compound 6% interest rate, what will be the amount of each of your annual payments?

This is a future value of an ordinary annuity problem. Using a financial calculator, the annual payment (PMT) would be found as follows:

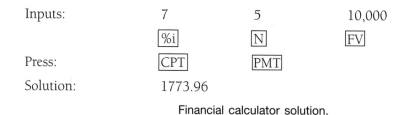

Inputs: 7   5   10,000

           %i   N   FV

Press: CPT   PMT

Solution: 1773.96

Financial calculator solution.

As another example, we might want to find the equal payment necessary to pay off, or amortize, a loan or real estate mortgage. An **amortized loan** is repaid in equal payments over a specified time period.

Let's assume that a lender offers you a $20,000, 10% interest rate, 3-year loan that is to be fully amortized with three annual payments. The first payment will be due 1 year from the loan date, making the loan an ordinary annuity. How much will you have to pay each year?

This is a present value problem because the $20,000 is the value or amount of the loan now. The annual payment can be found with a financial calculator, a financial function in a spreadsheet program, or by consulting Table 3-3.

Table 3-3: Present Value Interest Factor (PVIFA) for a $1 Ordinary Annuity

Year	5%	6%	7%	8%	9%	10%
1	0.952	0.943	0.935	0.926	0.917	0.909
2	1.859	1.833	1.808	1.783	1.759	1.736
3	2.273	2.673	2.624	2.577	2.531	2.487
4	3.546	3.465	3.387	3.312	3.240	3.170
5	4.329	4.212	4.100	3.993	3.890	3.791
6	5.076	4.917	4.767	4.623	4.486	4.355
7	5.786	5.582	5.389	5.206	5.033	4.868
8	6.463	6.210	5.971	5.747	5.535	5.335
9	7.108	6.802	6.515	6.247	5.995	5.759
10	7.722	7.360	7.024	6.710	6.418	6.145

Table 3-4: Sample Loan Amortization Schedule

Year	Annual Payment	Interest Payment	Principal Repayment	Loan Balance
0	—	—	—	$20,000
1	$8,042	$2,000	$6,042	13,958
2	$8,042	1,396	6,646	7,312
3	$8,042	731	7,311*	0

* Because of rounding, the final principal repayment is off by $1.

The present value interest factor (PVIFA) of 2.487 is taken from Table 3-3 at the intersection of the 10% column and the year-3 row. Dividing the loan amount by the factor results in an annual payment of $8,042.

Table 3-4 illustrates the repayment process with a loan amortization schedule.

▲ A **loan amortization schedule** shows the breakdown of each payment between interest and principal, as well as the remaining balance after each payment.

Since the interest rate is 10%, the first year you will pay interest of $2,000 ($20,000 × 0.10). Subsequent interest payments are based on the remaining loan balances, which are smaller each year (also referred to as the *declining balance*). Since $6,042 ($8,042 − $2,000) of the first year's $8,042 payment is used to repay part of the principal, the second year's interest payment will only be $1,396 ($13,958 × 0.10). The third and last payment covers the final year's interest of $731 plus the remaining principal balance.

FOR EXAMPLE

Home Mortgage Payment Schedules

The loan amortization process is the same as that used to determine monthly payments on home mortgages. However, because the discounting interval is very short, it would be difficult to calculate the monthly payment the long way for a typical 30-year loan. Therefore, a financial calculator or spreadsheet program is used.

SELF-CHECK

- What is an annuity?
- What is an ordinary annuity?
- How do we find the present value of an annuity?
- Explain what an amortized loan is.
- What is a loan amortization schedule?

3.7 Future Value of an Annuity Due

It is important to distinguish between an ordinary annuity and an annuity due. An **annuity due** exists when the equal periodic payments occur at the beginning of each period.

Let's return to the example used in section 3.7. Recall that the problem involved a 3-year annuity, $1,000 annual payments, and an 8% interest rate. However, let's assume that the first payment now is made at the beginning of the first year, namely at time zero. This will allow the first $1,000 payment to earn interest for 3 years, the second payment to earn interest for 2 years, and the third payment to earn interest for 1 year. The calculation process to find the future value of this annuity due problem is as follows:

$$FV \text{ annuity due} = \$1,000(1.08)_3 \ 1 \ \$1,000(1.08)_2 + \$1,000(1.08)_1$$
$$= \$1,000(1.260) + \$1,000(1.166) + \$1,000(1.080)$$
$$= \$1,000(1.260 + 1.166 \ 1 \ 1.080)$$
$$= \$1,000(3.506) = \$3,506$$

By making the first payment now, the future value of this annuity at the end of 3 years will be $3,506.

Annuity due problems also can be solved with financial calculators. In fact, most financial calculators have a DUE key for shifting payments from the end of time periods to the beginning of time periods.

3.7.1 Present Value of an Annuity Due

Occasionally there are present value annuity due problems. For example, leasing arrangements often require the person leasing equipment to make the first payment at the time the equipment is delivered. Let's illustrate by assuming that lease payments of $1,000 will be made at the beginning of each year for 3 years. If the appropriate interest rate is 8%, the following calculation will yield the present value of this annuity due leasing problem.

Inputs:
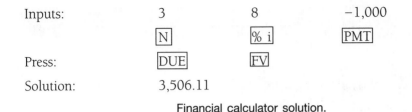
Press:

Solution: 3,506.11

Financial calculator solution.

By making the first payment up front, the present value of this annuity is $2,783. This contrasts with a present value of $2,577 if payments are delayed by 1 year, as would be the case with an ordinary annuity.

3.7.2 Interest Rates and Time Requirements for an Annuity Due

Tables containing FVIFA and PVIFA factors are not readily available for annuity due problems. Therefore, it is better to use a spreadsheet program or a financial calculator when trying to find the interest rate for an annuity due problem.

Let's assume that the future value of an annuity due problem is $6,153, each payment is $1,000, and the time period is 5 years. What is the interest rate on this problem? If you have a financial calculator, enter: FV = 6153, PMT = −1000, and N = 5. Press the DUE key and the %i key to find an r of 7%.

We can also solve for the n time periods involved in an annuity due problem with a financial calculator, as shown in Figure 3-2. The process is as follows:

Inputs: 7   −1000   6153
           %i   PMT   FV
Press: DUE   N
Solution: 5.00

Financial calculator solution.

Figure 3-2

Inputs:
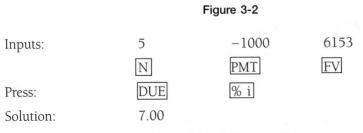
Press:

Solution: 7.00

Financial calculator solution.

We could use the same process for finding either interest rates or the number of time periods if we knew the present value of the annuity due instead of the future value. This would be done by substituting the PV value for the FV value in our financial calculator computation.

SELF-CHECK

- What is an annuity due?
- How do we find the future value of an annuity due?
- How do we find the present value of an annuity due?

3.8 Frequent Compounding or Discounting Intervals

There are many situations in which compounding or discounting may occur more often than annually. For example, recall from the beginning of this chapter the $1,000 that could be invested at one bank at an 8% annual interest rate for 2 years. Remember that the future value at the end of 2 years was $1,166. Now let's assume that another bank offers the same 8% interest rate but with semiannual (twice a year) compounding. We can find the future value of this investment by using this equation

$$FV_n = PV(1 + r \div m)^{n \times m}$$

where m is the number of compounding periods per year.

The financial calculator solution would be found as follows:

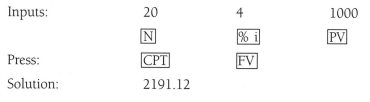

Inputs:	20	4	1000
	N	% i	PV
Press:	CPT	FV	
Solution:	2191.12		

Financial calculator solution.

FOR EXAMPLE

Borrowing Money

If a lender offers you a 12% interest rate with either monthly or semiannually compounding, you should take the semiannual option as it will cost you less money. Many mortgage loan interest rates are compounded more than once per year.

The future value interest factor (FVIF) can also be found in Table 1 in the Appendix. When a three-decimal-place table is used, the factor is 2.191 with a future value of $2,191 (rounded). Notice that semiannual compounding will result in $32 more than the $2,159 earned with annual compounding. It follows that more frequent compounding, such as quarterly or monthly, produces even higher earnings.

The process described also applies to discounting problems when discounting occurs more frequently than annually. The use of financial calculators and spreadsheet programs is more expedient, as the frequency of compounding or discounting within a year increases.

SELF-CHECK

- Briefly describe the process for compounding or discounting quarterly rather than annually.

3.9 APR versus EAR

Banks, finance companies, and other lenders are required by the Truth in Lending law to disclose their lending interest rates on credit extended to consumers. Such a rate is called a *contract* or *stated rate,* or more frequently, an *annual percentage rate* (APR).

The method of calculating the APR on a loan is set by law. The APR is the interest rate charged per period multiplied by the number of periods in a year, m:

$$APR = r \times m$$

This means a car loan that charges interest of 1% per month has an APR of 12% (i.e., 1% times 12 months). An unpaid credit card balance that incurs interest charges of 1.5% per month has an APR of 18% (1.5 × 12 months). However, the APR misstates the true interest rate. The effective annual rate (EAR), sometimes called the *annual effective yield,* is the true opportunity cost measure of the interest rate, as it considers the effects of periodic compounding.

For example, say an unpaid January balance of $100 on a credit card accumulates interest at the rate of 1.5% per month. The interest charge is added to the unpaid balance; if left unpaid, February's balance will be $101.50. If the bill remains unpaid through February, the 1.5% monthly charge is levied based on the total unpaid balance of $101.50. In other words, interest is also assessed on the previous months' unpaid interest charges. Since interest compounds, the APR formula will understate the true or effective interest cost. This will always be true except in the special case where the number of periods is one per year; that is, in annual compounding situations.

Since credit card charges are typically assessed monthly, m, the number of periods per year is 12. To find the true annual interest cost of a credit card that advertises an 18% APR, use the following calculation:

$$\frac{18\%}{12} = 1.5\%$$

If the periodic interest charge, r, is known, the EAR is found by using the following equation:

$$EAR = (1 + r)m - 1$$

where m is the number of periods per year. This is done as follows:

$$(1 + 0.015)^{12} - 1 = 1.1956 - 1 = 0.1956, \text{ or } 19.56\%$$

The true interest charge on a credit card with an 18% APR is really 19.56 percent.

When the annual stated rate stays the same, more frequent interest compounding helps savers earn more interest over the course of a year. Therefore, ask yourself if it is better to put your money in an account offering (1) 8% interest per year, compounded quarterly, or (2) 8% interest per year, compounded monthly?

Compounding interest quarterly means that the bank is paying interest four times a year to its depositors. Option (1) involved four periods per year and a periodic interest rate of 8% divided by 4, or 2%. Every dollar invested under option (1) will grow to $1.0824 [$1(1 + 0.02)^4] after 1 year's time. Another way of expressing this is that the effective annual rate of 8% compounded quarterly is 8.24%.

Under option (2), the relevant time period is 1 month, and the periodic interest rate is 8% divided by 12 or 0.67%. Every dollar invested under option (2) will grow to $1.0830 [$1(1 + 0.0067)^{12}]. Thus, the effective annual rate of 8% compounded monthly is 8.30%.

FOR EXAMPLE

Borrowing Options

If you have an option to invest $5,000 and earn a 10% interest rate annually or take the same amount of money and pay off a credit card with an 18% APR, which should you do? You should pay off the credit card. With the investment, you will make $500. By paying off the credit card, however, you would have saved 19.56% in interest payments, which is $978.

As option (2) gives the depositor more interest over the course of a year, depositors should choose it over the first option because more frequent compounding increases the future value of an investor's funds more quickly.

SELF-CHECK

- **What do we mean by the annual percentage rate (APR) on a loan?**
- **What is the effective annual rate (EAR) on a loan?**

3.10 Cost of Consumer Credit

Throughout history, there have been many examples of individuals being charged exorbitant interest rates on loans. The word for this is *usury*. **Usury** is the act of lending money at an excessively high interest rate.

Lenders who exhibited such unethical behavior were sometimes referred to as *loan sharks*. Lenders, of course, are in the business of making a rate of return on the money that they have to lend. Without question, lenders deserve to earn a fair rate of return to compensate them for their time and the risk that the borrower will not repay the interest and/or principal on time or in full. In Chapter 2 we called this added compensation a risk premium above the prevailing risk-free rate.

Good ethical behavior is consistent with treating borrowers honestly and fairly. However, because of the existence of unethical lenders, various laws have made usury illegal. Even so, there are still lenders who continue this practice. To counter these activities, Congress passed the Consumer Credit Protection Act of 1968, which prohibits excessively high-priced credit transactions. Regulation Z enacts the Truth in Lending section of the act, whereby the Federal Reserve has the responsibility of making consumers aware of the costs of alternative forms of credit. Lenders must disclose all loan costs (interest amounts, service

> ## FOR EXAMPLE
>
> ### Consumer Credit
>
> Americans are saving less than ever before; in fact, Americans are spending more than they make. This is because Americans are using credit cards to borrow money, they are using mortgages to get bigger houses than they could in the past, and they are not saving any money. With the average credit card company charging 18% interest, Americans are spending millions of dollars just paying the interest for the items they charged.

charges, loan and finder fees, etc.), as well as the annual percentage rate of interest. It is unfortunate, but a fact of life, that because of the unethical behavior of some lenders, laws must be enacted to protect consumers.

SELF-CHECK

- Define **usury.**

SUMMARY

Time does affect the value of money. Depending on how the money is invested, the amount of money you have could increase or it could decrease. Even if you do not invest your money, time affects the value of money. This is because inflation decreases the value of every dollar you have. In this chapter, you have applied the concept of simple interest. You have gone through the process of compounding interest. You have also learned about determining the future and the present value of money. These skills will serve you not only in your career, but with your personal finances as well.

KEY TERMS

Amortized loan	Loan that is repaid in equal payments over a specified time period.
Annuity	A series of equal payments (receipts) that occur over a number of time periods.
Annuity due	Exists when the equal periodic payments occur at the beginning of each period.

Compounding	An arithmetic process whereby an initial value increases or grows at a compound interest rate over time to reach a value in the future.
Compound interest	Process where an initial value earns interest on interest in addition to interest on the principal or initial investment.
Discounting	An arithmetic process whereby a future value decreases at a compound interest rate over time to reach a present value.
Future value of a savings amount or investment	Value of a savings amount or investment at a specified time or date in the future.
Loan amortization schedule	Worksheet that shows the breakdown of each payment between interest and principal, as well as the remaining balance after each payment.
Ordinary annuity	A series of equal payments (receipts) that occur at the end of each time period.
Present value of savings or investment	Current value or amount of savings or investment.
Rule of 72	Shortcut method used to approximate the time required for an investment to double in value. This method is applied by dividing the interest rate into the number 72 to determine the number of years it will take for an investment to double in value.
Simple interest	Interest earned only on the principal amount of the investment.
Usury	The act of lending money at an excessively high interest rate.

ASSESS YOUR UNDERSTANDING

Go to www.wiley.com/college/Melicher to evaluate your knowledge of the time value of money.

Measure your learning by comparing pre-test and post-test results.

Summary Questions

1. Money has a time value as long as interest is earned by saving or investing money. True or false?

2. As the interest rate increases, present value decreases. True or false?

3. Simple interest is interest earned on the investment's principal and interest. True or false?

4. Compound interest is interest earned on interest in addition to interest earned on the principal. True or false?

5. If the compound inflation rate were greater than the compound interest rate, the purchasing power would fall. True or false?

6. Discounting is an arithmetic process whereby a future value decreases at a compound interest rate over time to reach a present value. True or false?

7. The Rule of 72 is an estimate of how long it would take to double a sum of money at a given interest rate. True or false?

8. At a zero interest rate, the present value of $1 remains at $1 and is not affected by time. True or false?

9. An annuity is a series of equal payments that occur over a number of time periods. True or false?

10. An ordinary annuity exists when the equal payments occur at the beginning of each time period. True or false?

11. An annuity due may also be referred to as a *deferred annuity*. True or false?

12. For a given discount rate, an ordinary annuity and an annuity due have the same present value. True or false?

13. An amortized loan is repaid in equal payments over a specified time period. True or false?

14. A fixed-rate mortgage is an example of an annuity. True or false?

15. The effective annual rate is determined by multiplying the interest rate charged per period by the number of periods in a year. True or false?

16. The annual percentage rate is the true opportunity cost measure of the interest rate. True or false?

17. The method of calculating the annual percentage rate (APR) is set by law. True or false?

18. When the annual interest rate stays the same, more frequent interest compounding helps savers earn more interest over the course of the year. True or false?

19. The effective annual rate (EAR) is sometimes called the *annual effective yield.* True or false?

20. Usury is the act of lending money at an excessively low interest rate. True or false?

Review Questions

1. Briefly describe what is meant by the *time value of money.*
2. What is simple interest?
3. What is compound interest?
4. How does inflation affect interest rates?
5. What is the meaning of discounting?
6. How are present values and future values related?
7. Describe the process for solving for the interest rate in present and future value problems.
8. Describe the process for solving for the time period in present and future value problems.
9. How can the Rule of 72 be used to determine how long it will take for an investment to double in value?
10. What is an ordinary annuity?
11. Briefly describe how to solve for the interest rate or the time period in annuity problems.
12. Describe the process for determining the size of a constant periodic payment that is necessary to fully amortize a loan.
13. Determine the annual payment on a $500,000, 12% business loan from a commercial bank that is to be amortized over a 5-year period.
14. You have recently seen a credit card advertisement that states that the annual percentage rate is 12%. If the credit card requires monthly payments, what is the effective annual rate of interest on the loan?
15. Assume you are planning to invest $5,000 each year for 6 years and will earn 10% per year. Determine the future value of this annuity if your first $5,000 is invested at the end of the first year.
16. What does the abbreviation APR mean?
17. What does the abbreviation EAR mean?
18. If an individual invested $10,000 at 8% interest, how long would it take to accumulate $1 million?
19. What is discounting?

20. Why would a lender charge a premium on a loan's interest rate?

21. What is the word used for excessive interest rates?

22. What it the regulation that requires a Truth in Lending Disclosure to borrowers?

23. What is a cash due annuity?

24. What is purchasing power protection?

Applying This Chapter

1. A potential investment pays $10 per year indefinitely. The appropriate discount rate for the potential investor is 10%. How is the present value of this cash flow calculated?

2. Suppose you have a choice of two equally risky annuities, each paying $1,000 per year for 20 years. One is an annuity due, while the other is an ordinary annuity. Which annuity would you choose?

3. Your college has agreed to give you a $10,000 tuition loan. As part of the agreement, you must repay $12,600 at the end of the 3-year period. What interest rate is the college charging?

4. Tom Vu deposited $5,000 in a savings account that paid 8% interest compounded quarterly. What is the effective rate of interest?

5. Joseph has just accepted a job as a stockbroker. He estimates his gross pay each year for the next 3 years is $35,000 in year 1, $21,000 in year 2, and $32,000 in year 3. What is the present value of these cash flows if they are discounted at 4%?

6. Christine has just purchased a used Mercedes for $18,995. She plans to make a $2,500 down payment on the new car. What is the amount of her monthly payment on the remaining loan if she must pay 12% annual interest on a 24-month car loan?

7. Daniel deposits $2,000 per year at the end of the year for the next 15 years into an IRA account that currently pays 7%. How much will Daniel have on deposit at the end of the 15 years?

8. Cecilia bought 100 shares of Minnesota Mining and Manufacturing in June 1987 for $38 a share for a total investment of $3,800. She sold the shares in June 1996 for $8,960. What is Cecilia's annual rate of return on her investment?

9. You borrow $10,000 to pay for your college tuition. The loan is amortized over a 3-year period with an interest rate of 18%. What is your remaining balance at the end of year 2?

10. Jill Clinton puts $1,000 in a savings passbook that pays 4% compounded quarterly. How much will she have in her account after 5 years?

11. In 1966, the average tuition for 1 year in the MBA program at the University of Chicago was $3,600. Thirty years later, in 1996, the average tuition was $27,400. What is the compound annual growth rate in tuition (rounded to the nearest whole percentage) over the 30-year period?

12. You want to buy a Volvo in 7 years. The car is currently selling for $50,000, and the price will increase at a compound rate of 10% per year. You can presently invest in high-yield bonds earning a compound annual rate 14% per year. How much must you invest at the end of each of the next 7 years to be able to purchase your dream car in 7 years?

13. John deposits $2,000 per year at the end of the year for the next 20 years into an IRA account that pays 6%. How much will John have on deposit at the end of 20 years?

14. In 1976, the average price of a domestic car was $5,100. Twenty years later, in 1996, the average price was $16,600. What was the annual growth rate in the car price over the 20-year period?

15. Suppose you receive $3,000 a year in years 1 through 4, $4,000 a year in years 5 through 9, and $2,000 in year 10, with all the money to be received at the end of the year. If your discount rate is 12%, what is the present value of these cash flows?

16. Tracey deposits $5,000 in a 5-year certificate of deposit paying 6% compounded semiannually. How much will Tracey have at the end of the 5-year period?

17. Ken purchases a perpetual investment that pays $90 per year indefinitely, beginning 1 year from today. What is the price of this bond if the current discount rate is 7.6%?

18. What would be the future value of a loan of $1,000 for 2 years if the bank offered a 10% interest rate compounded semiannually?

Fuure Value of an Investment

You invest $10,000 today. What is the value of this investment after 5 years if the annual interest rate is 8%?

Maximizing Returns

Your current bank is paying a 6.25% simple interest rate. You can move your savings account to Harris Bank that pays 6.25% compounded annually or to First Chicago bank paying 6% compounded semiannually. To maximize your return, which bank should you choose?

Borrowing Money

Your company needs to borrow $100,000 for a capital improvement project. If the interest is 10% and it is compounded semiannually, how much will the loan cost the company in interest?

4

FINANCIAL STATEMENTS, CASH FLOW, AND TAXES
The Basics of Financial Reports

Starting Point

Go to www.wiley.com/college/Melicher to assess your knowledge of the basics of financial reports.
Determine where you need to concentrate your effort.

What You'll Learn in This Chapter

▲ The structure and organization of financial statements
▲ The different business structures and their relation to capitalization, liability, and tax issues
▲ The purpose of a mission statement
▲ The structure and organization of annual reports
▲ The tax rates for individual taxpayers and corporations

After Studying This Chapter, You'll Be Able To

▲ Interpret different financial statements
▲ Compare and contrast different business forms based on their relation to capitalization, liability, and tax issues
▲ Appraise a company's mission statement and compare it to other company's
▲ Analyze annual reports of different companies
▲ Examine the federal tax system as it pertains to individuals and corporations
▲ Examine depreciation and its effect on a company's financial health

Goals and Outcomes

▲ Assess a company's financial health by reading its financial statements
▲ Choose an appropriate business form for new ventures based on the company's relation to capitalization, liability, and tax issues
▲ Select and write an appropriate mission statement for a new company
▲ Assess the taxes for both individuals and corporations
▲ Assess depreciation and its impact on taxable income

INTRODUCTION

This is the study of how financial reports are structured and how the information they contain is used by investors, banks, and other markets and institutions. Becoming familiar with the reports issued by the many and varied companies that operate within our financial environment is vital to making good monetary decisions.

4.1 Overview of Financial Statements

Individual investors, financial managers, and anyone else who works within our financial system must learn how to read and interpret the data presented on a firm's financial statements. A company's **balance sheet, income statement,** and **statement of cash flows** provide an inside look at the overall stability and profits generated by its business operations and investment choices.

Financial statements are usually issued at the end of every month and can be structured to supply information in a number of different ways. When evaluating financial data, it is important to remember that it must be reviewed over a period of several months in order to get a clear picture of whether the company is moving forward or staying stagnant.

Changes in a firm's financial condition inform investors of a firm's strengthening or weakening position against its competitors. Investors and lending institutions often express concern if a firm begins to use much more debt financing than it has in the past. In addition, a drop in sales revenue or a sharp increase in expenses can also signal trouble. It is imperative that the company's managers heed the information that is imparted to them from the financial markets and institutions. A rise in the company's stock prices may reflect investor happiness, a positive reinforcement for managerial techniques and decisions. However, a drop in stock prices may reflect dissatisfaction with the company and its management. Managers should also use interest rate and stock price information from the financial markets to evaluate their company's investments. The level of short-term interest rates, the level of long-term interest rates, and stock prices should be taken into consideration when deciding how to raise funds to finance the firm's activities.

The way that financial data is presented depends in part on the structure and organization of the company that is issuing the statements. However, keep in mind that the basics of accounting do not change and are reflected in the data reported by every company regardless of how large or small or how their operations and goals may differ. Once you become familiar with the principles of accounting, you will be able to read and analyze the information presented by all types of profit-making entities as well as nonprofit corporations.

To begin, we look at the various ways a business can be organized and how IRS expects income and expenses on the businesses to be reported.

SELF-CHECK

- List three financial documents that together provide an inside look at the overall stability and profits generated by its business operations and investment choices.
- What does a rise in a company's stock price reflect?
- What does a drop in a company's stock price reflect?

4.2 U.S. Business Organizations

Three major forms of business ownership are used in the United States. The three categories have been formed for the most part by the tax structure that applies to it.

There is really no limit as to how many different types of businesses and enterprises can be encompassed under these three headings. Every day someone is coming up with a new product, a new business service, or a new way to present an old product or service.

4.2.1 Sole Proprietors

A sole proprietorship is generally a small business. About 72% of the business enterprises in our country are proprietorships. This includes all those millions of entrepreneurs who keep our economy moving with their originality and ambition. A **sole proprietorship** is a business venture that is owned by a single individual who personally receives all profits and assumes all responsibility for the debts and losses of the business.

Income and expenses from a proprietorship business are reported on the owner's personal tax return on Schedule C: Profit or Loss from a Business or Profession. The profit or loss from the business is then added to or subtracted from any other personal income and becomes the adjusted gross income of the proprietor. There are a number of deductions that are allowed, such as depreciation of business equipment and, with some restrictions, expenses for the business use of the home. With this type of business, the owner's Social Security number is also the tax identification number that IRS requires all businesses to have.

It follows that if Schedule C shows a profit, the proprietor is then required to file Schedule SE to calculate and report Social Security taxes on the business' earnings. Since the proprietor is self-employed, he/she pays both the employee and employer share of this tax, which is added into the overall tax liability and remitted with the personal return. To avoid a big tax payment with penalties at the end of the year, small business owners are advised to file estimated tax forms and pay their estimated tax on a quarterly basis.

One of the drawbacks of sole proprietorship is that the business owner is personally liable for anything that goes wrong with the business, including product failure. In other words, if someone sues the business, they are in effect suing the person who owns the business. Insurance can be purchased to eliminate some of this personal liability.

When estimating the value of a sole proprietor, it is important to look at the financial data as well as how much potential legal risk is involved in this particular business activity.

4.2.2 Partnerships

Two or more people can form a business partnership. A **partnership** is a form of business organization involving two or more people who own a business operated for profits.

Under a partnership agreement, the parties outline the duties and responsibilities of each partner in regard to the business and the percentage of ownership each has in the business. The business name can be a combination of the partners' names or can have a different name altogether. The partnership must be registered with the IRS with the names and Social Security numbers of all the partners. The IRS will assign a tax identification number to the partnership. An income tax return must be filed for the partnership at the end of the tax year. The same type of business deductions that are available to proprietors are afforded to partnerships. The tax return must include a schedule for each of the partners, and once the profit or loss has been determined, that amount is divided among the partners. If one partner owns 60% of the company and four other partners own 10% each, the profit or loss is assigned to each partner according to the percentage of ownership in the company.

Like the sole proprietor, each partner must then include the income or loss derived from the partnership on their personal tax returns and pay Social Security tax on their portion of the profits. Any liability associated with the business is also borne by the partners.

To protect the personal assets of business partners, they might choose to form what is called a limited liability company. A **limited liability company** is an organizational form whose owners have limited liability, the firm can have an unlimited number of shareholders, and income is taxed only once as personal income of the shareholders. The company still operates as a partnership, but it is afforded the liability protection enjoyed by corporations.

4.2.3 Corporations

There are various types of corporations, and only corporations can issue stock and have shareholders.

A sub-S corporation is for individuals or small businesses. It has a tax identification number and enjoys most of the benefits afforded to a regular corporation. The income of a sub-S corporation flows to the owner to include on his/her personal tax return. The person or persons who run the business are considered employees of the corporation and collect a salary from which Social Security taxes and other income taxes are deducted and then paid to IRS. The sub-S corporation is ideal for professional people like lawyers with small or specialized practices.

Within the corporation category are regular profit-seeking corporations and nonprofit corporations. The difference between these two entities is their tax structure:

▲ A **regular corporation** pays tax on its profits.

▲ A **nonprofit corporation** does not pay taxes unless their income rises above the level set by the IRS. Even then, the tax rate is reduced.

Both of these entities are very active in the financial system; therefore, financial managers, banks, institutions, stockbrokers, and dealers are constantly evaluating their financial data and business techniques.

Those firms organized as corporations must provide a summary of their financial performance in an annual report to their shareholders. Included in annual reports are three basic financial statements—the income statement, the balance sheet, and the statement of cash flows—that businesses need to prepare. Even individually owned or closely held firms need to prepare financial statements for tax purposes. Just as important, these financial statements contain much of the language of business, such as revenues, expenses, assets, liabilities, and **equity** or **retained earnings.**

FOR EXAMPLE

Which Business Organization to Use

Every business from the woman who sells Mary Kay part-time to a Fortune 400 company has a legal structure. The legal structure chosen depends on many factors such as the number of owners, the number of partners, the number of employees, taxation structure preferred, and benefits the business wants to provide to their employees. For example, a business run by one person is a sole proprietorship. A business that has thousands of employees can be a corporation and deduct the expenses of most employee benefits.

Table 4-1: Organization Forms and Financial Characteristics

Organizational Form	Number of Owners	Owner's Liability	Equity Capital Sources	Ease of Start-Up	Taxation	Liquidity of Ownership	Life Span
Proprietorship	1	Unlimited	Self, friends, relatives	Simple	Personal taxation	Difficult to sell	Linked to owner
Partnership (general)	>1	Unlimited, jointly and severally	Partners, friends, relatives	Not difficult	Personal taxation	Difficult to sell	Linked to owners
Limited partnership	at least 1 general, any number of limited partners	Limited partners' liability is limited to partners' investment	General and limited partners	More difficult	Personal taxation	Usually poor	Linked to general partner
Corporation	Unlimited	Limited to shareholders' investment	Common stock offerings	Difficult	Corporate taxation but dividends are taxed twice, both as corporate earnings and personal income	Can be very liquid	Unlimited
Subchapter S	<35	Limited to shareholders' investment	Sub S equity investors	Difficult	Income flows to shareholders for taxation at personal rates	Usually poor	Unlimited
Limited liability company (LLC)	Unlimited	Limited to owners' investment	Common stock offerings	Difficult	Income flows to shareholders for taxation at personal rates	Poor	Linked to current shareholders

SELF-CHECK

- In what ways does a sole proprietorship differ from a partnership?
- In what ways does a proprietorship differ from a corporation?
- What is the difference between a regular corporation and a nonprofit corporation?
- What is a limited liability company?

4.3 Starting a Business

A business should begin with a vision or *mission statement,* which indicates what the firm wants to produce, distribute, and sell or indicate what services it wants to provide. The statement helps declare the company's main reason for being; in times when new opportunities look attractive, the firm's managers should go back and read the mission statement to ensure their actions are consistent with it. Comments on quality objectives and customer and owner focus also are typically found in vision and mission statements. Some statements are idealistic in their views.

Wells Fargo, a nationwide diversified financial services company providing banking, insurance, investments, and other financial services, has the following vision statement:

> *We want to satisfy all of our customers' financial needs, help them succeed financially, be the premier provider of financial services in every one of our markets, and be known as one of America's great companies.*

Dell is a well-known computer company and its mission statement is short and to the point:

> *Dell's mission is to be the most successful computer company in the world at delivering the best customer experience in markets we serve.*

A guiding force behind top managements' decisions should be the mission statement. At the same time, the mission statement should not be carved in stone; it should be periodically reviewed to ensure it is up-to-date and reflects market needs in a dynamic, global economy. On the other hand, a business cannot chase every idea developed by its managers. Businesses need to stick to what they do best.

Businesses must support their visions and missions with business and financial goals or plans—sometimes referred to as *operating plans.* Such plans may include specific goals for customer satisfaction ratings, market share, and return

> **FOR EXAMPLE**
>
> **Google's Mission Statement**
>
> Google, the Web company, started with a simple mission statement of "do no evil." In 2006 when Google announced that it would do business with China despite their restrictions on information and human rights abuses, Google was the subject of investor and customer scorn. Google agreed to block the Chinese residents from Web sites that the Chinese government deemed "revolutionary." These Web sites included sites on democracy and English-speaking news organization sites.

to shareholders. Such plans allow managers to track their progress toward achieving the plan and mission of the firm.

Attracting and acquiring financing is necessary to obtain the **factors of production** (land, capital, and labor needed to operate a business) required to conduct business operations.

Allocation of these factors is largely automatic under the market system. Resources flow smoothly to those businesses that through their past operations and the promise of profitable future operations are able to pay for them. Investors, as providers of debt and equity capital, expect a return on their investment. The possibility of losing money is a risk faced by all investors. However, that risk can be minimized by gathering as much information as possible before investing money in a company. Financial data is obviously the most important thing to review, but examining the mission statement and then seeing if the management is actually working toward those goals is also a way to measure the potential profitability of an enterprise.

SELF-CHECK

- Define **mission statement**.
- Discuss why a mission statement is important to a firm.
- Provide an example of a mission statement.

4.4 Annual Reports

An important component of manager-owner communication is the firm's financial statements. Firms organized as proprietorships or partnerships are not required to prepare financial reports or statements except for tax purposes.

Of course, it is important for proprietors and partners to gather financial data so as to be able to evaluate their financial performance over time. Requests for bank loans will also need to be accompanied by recent financial statements.

In contrast, companies organized as corporations are required to prepare financial reports annually for the benefit of their shareholders. Public corporations also are required to file annual reports with the SEC. **Annual reports** contain descriptive information on operating and financial performance during the past year, a discussion of current and future business opportunities, and financial statements that provide a record of financial performance.

Usually financial highlights are provided on the first page or two followed by a letter to the stockholders by the firm's chairman of the board and chief executive officer (CEO). The CEO summarizes the financial results for the year and identifies the firm's strengths, such as employee talents and the size of its customer base. After the CEO's letter, most companies describe their current business areas, future opportunities, and financial goals, such as a target return on equity or earnings growth rate.

Three important financial statements are provided in the annual report. These are

▲ the balance sheet;

▲ income statement;

▲ the cash flow statement.

Financial data is gathered and reported on the financial statements using the accounting principles established by the Financial Accounting Standards Board (FASB). These rules are commonly known as **GAAP**, which stands for *generally accepted accounting principles*.

The FASB realizes that some flexibility is necessary because firms within certain industries operate much differently than those in other industries. On the negative side, this flexibility allows the possibility of deceptive accounting practices. It is the task of the financial manager to dig deep into the financial information to separate those firms that may appear attractive from those that are actually in good financial condition. To help analyze the financial reports, FASB requires that financial statements include footnotes. These footnotes inform analysts of which accounting principles were used by the firm.

The first step in reading and understanding financial reports is becoming familiar with the way the reports are structured. In other words, we need to take a look at the individual accounts where financial data is recorded and stored before it is transferred to the reports.

As we study these accounts, you will learn why most businesses use the accrual method of accounting rather than the cash accounting method. With the accrual method, income is reported in the fiscal quarter it is earned regardless

FOR EXAMPLE

Financial Statements

In several scandals from 2001 to 2004 where corrupt companies like Enron tanked, many CEOs blamed their CFO for hiding the truth from investors. The courts and public opinion has stated that when the CFO signs off on financial statements and annual reports, he or she is declaring them to be truthful.

of when it is received. With the cash method, income is only reported when it is received. You will also learn about debits and credits and how one must always offset the other.

SELF-CHECK

- Explain what the acronyms FASB and GAAP stand for.
- Define **annual report.**
- List three kinds of financial statements that are included in a company's annual report.

4.5 Balance Sheet

The balance sheet is a statement of a company's financial position as of a particular date, usually at the end of a quarter or a year. Whereas the income statement reflects the firm's operations over time, the balance sheet is a snapshot at a point in time. It reveals two broad categories of information: (1) the **assets,** which are the financial and physical items owned by a business; and (2) the claims of creditors and owners in the business assets. The creditors' claims, which are the financial obligations of the business, are referred to as *liabilities.* The company's equity is the funds supplied by the owners and represents their residual claim on the firm.

In addition to providing a snapshot of a firm's financial condition, the balance sheet also reveals much of the inner workings of the company's financial structure. The various types of assets indicate at once the results of recent business operations and the capacity for future operations. The creditors' claims and the owners' equity in the assets reveal the sources from which these assets have been derived. The term *balance sheet* itself indicates a relationship of equality

Table 4-2: Balance Sheet for Walgreens ($ in Millions)

	2003	2002
Cash & Marketable Securities	$1017.1	$449.9
Accounts Receivable	1017.8	954.8
Inventories	4,202.7	3,654.2
Other Current Assets	120.5	116.6
Total Current Assets	6358.1	5166.5
Net Fixed Assets	4940.0	4591.4
Other Long-Term Assets	107.8	120.9
TOTAL ASSETS	**11405.9**	**9878.8**
Accounts Payable	2077.0	1836.4
Notes Payable	0.0	0.0
Other Current Liabilities	1343.5	1118.8
Total Current Liabilities	3420.5	2955.2
Long-Term Debt	0.0	0.0
Other Liabilities	789.7	693.4
TOTAL LIABILITIES	**4210.2**	**3648.6**
Preferred Equity	0.0	0.0
Common Equity	777.9	828.5
Retained Earnings	6417.8	5401.7
Stockholders' Equity	7195.7	6230.2
TOTAL LIABILITIES & EQUITY	**11405.9**	**9878.8**

between the assets of the business and the sources of funds used to obtain them that may be expressed as follows:

$$\text{Assets} = \text{liabilities} + \text{owners' equity}$$

This "balance sheet equation" or "accounting identity" shows that every dollar of a firm's assets must be financed by a dollar of liabilities, a dollar of owner's equity, or some combination of the two. The firm's asset total shows what the firm owns; the total of liabilities and equity shows that the firm owes to its creditors and owners.

The balance sheet for the Walgreens Corporation shown in Table 4-2 reveals this equality of assets and the financial interests in the assets. Total assets were $11,405.9 million in 2003, a 15.5% increase over 2002's asset level of $9,878.8 million.

Total liabilities increased from $3,648.6 million to $4,210.2 million, which is a 15.4% increase. Owner's equity, which for Walgreens is stockholders equity, provided the balancing figure with $7,195.7 in 2003 and $6,203.2 in 2002. This was an increase of 15.5%.

4.5.1 Assets

Assets that are most liquid are typically listed first. By *liquidity* we are referring to the time it usually takes to convert the assets into cash. Two broad groups, current assets and fixed assets, are identified on the balance sheet.

The current assets of a business include cash and other assets that are expected to be converted into cash within 1 year. Current assets thus represent the working capital needed to carry out the normal operations of the business. The principal current assets of a business are typically its cash and marketable securities, accounts receivable, and inventories.

Cash and marketable securities include cash on hand and cash on deposit with banks; marketable securities, such as commercial paper issued by other firms; and U.S. government securities in the form of treasury bills, notes, and bonds.

Accounts receivable generally arise from the sale of products, merchandise, or services on credit. The buyer's debts to the business are generally paid according to the credit terms of the sale. Some firms also have notes receivable. A note receivable is a written promise by a debtor of the business to pay a specified sum of money on or before a stated date. Notes receivable may come into existence in several ways. For example, overdue accounts receivable may be converted to notes receivable at the insistence of the seller or upon special request by the buyer. Notes receivable may also occur as a result of short-term loans made by the business to its employees or to other persons or businesses.

The materials and products on hand that will be sold or transformed into a product are shown as inventories on the balance sheet. Generally, a manufacturing form categorizes its inventories in terms of raw materials, goods in the process of manufacture, and finished goods. Sometimes the balance sheet will reveal the amount of inventory in each of these categories.

Fixed assets are the physical facilities used in the production, storage, display, and distribution of the products of a firm. These assets normally provide many years of service. The principal fixed assets are plant and equipment and land.

In a manufacturing firm, a large investment in plant and equipment is usually required. As products are manufactured, some of the economic value of this plant and equipment lessens. This is called *depreciation,* and accountants reflect this use of real assets by charging off depreciation against the original cost of plant and equipment. The net fixed assets information at any point in time is supposed to reflect the their remaining useful lives. The net is calculated by subtracting the amount of depreciation that has accumulated over time from the gross plant and equipment.

Some firms own the land or real property on which their buildings or manufacturing plants are constructed. Other firms may own other land for expansion or investment purposes. The original cost of the land owned is reflected on the firm's balance sheet, under the tax code, and cannot be depreciated.

4.5.2 Liabilities

Liabilities are the debts of a business. The Liabilities section of the balance sheet holds the accounts that represent an ongoing expense to the company.

Liabilities come into existence through direct borrowing, purchases of foods and services on credit, and the accrual of obligations such as wages and income taxes. Liabilities are classified as current and long-term.

The current liabilities of a business may be defined as those obligations that must be paid within 1 year. They include accounts payable, notes payable, and accrued liabilities that are to be met out of current funds and operations. Although the cash on hand plus marketable securities of the Walgreens Company is $1,017.1 million compared with current liabilities of $3,420.5, it is expected that normal business operations will convert receivables and inventory into cash in time to meet current liabilities as they become due.

Accounts payable are debts that arise primarily from the purchase of goods and supplies on credit terms. Accounts payable arising from the purchase of inventory on credit terms represent trade credit financing as opposed to direct short-term borrowing from banks and other lenders. An account payable shown on one firm's balance sheet appears as an account receivable on the balance sheet of the firm from which goods were purchased.

A note payable is a written promise to pay a specified amount of money to a creditor on or before a certain date. The most common occurrence of a note payable takes place when a business borrows money from a bank on a short-term basis to purchase materials or for other current operating requirements.

Current liabilities that reflect amounts owed but not yet due as of the date of the balance sheet are called *accrued liabilities* or *accruals*. The most common form of accruals are wages payable and taxes payable. These accounts exist because wages are typically paid weekly, biweekly, or monthly, and income taxes are paid quarterly.

Business debts with maturities greater than 1 year are long-term liabilities. One of the common methods used by businesses for obtaining a long-term loan is to offer a mortgage to a lender as collateral for a corporate bond. In the event that the borrowing business fails to meet the obligations of the loan contract, the mortgage may be foreclosed—that is, the property may be seized through appropriate legal channels and sold to satisfy the indebtedness.

> ### FOR EXAMPLE
>
> ### Walgreens' Balance Sheet
>
> Notice that in the asset section of Table 4-2 there is an account labeled Net Fixed Assets. This means that the accumulated depreciation amount has been deducted from the original value of these assets, and the balance sheet account only shows the current value of the assets.

4.5.3 Owners' Equity

All businesses have owners' equity in one form or another. **Owners' equity** is the investment of the owners or owner in the business. It initially results from a cash outlay to purchase assets to operate the business. In some cases, the owners of a business may place their own assets, such as the machinery, real estate, or equipment, with the firm for its operation. In addition to the contributing cash or property, owners' equity may also be increased by allowing profits to remain with the business. On the balance sheet, the amount of owners' equity is always represented by the difference between total assets and total liabilities of the business. It reflects the owner's claims on the assets of the business as opposed to the creditors' claims.

In the case of a corporation, the owner's equity is usually broken down into three different accounts, as we showed for Walgreens in Table 4-2. Walgreens has no preferred stock outstanding, so the account balance is zero. The common stock account reflects the number of outstanding shares of common stock carried at a stated par value and the capital paid in excess of par. It is worth noting that the par value is an arbitrary value and thus is not related to a firm's stock price of market value. If we divide the common stock account amount by number of shares outstanding, $777.9 million/1,031,580,000 shares, the average selling price over time is about $.075 per share. The actual selling price of stock in Walgreens' equity offerings was undoubtedly higher than this, but the effects of stock splits and repurchases over time have changed the effective per-share price.

The third account is called the *retained earnings account,* and it shows the accumulated undistributed earnings within the corporation over time. These retained earnings do not represent cash. They have been invested in the firm's current and/or fixed assets. Together these three accounts comprise the corporation's equity.

SELF-CHECK

- Define **assets, liabilities, and equity.**
- Explain what a balance sheet is and list its three main sections.
- Provide an example of accounts payable.

4.6 Income Statement

An income statement reports the revenues generated and expenses incurred by the firm over an accounting period. This is also sometimes called a *profit and loss statement*.

It can be issued monthly, quarterly, or in the case of a very small business, annually. While corporations are required to provide annual reports to their stockholders, most companies issue internal financial statements on a monthly basis.

The income statement actually works in conjunction with the balance sheet, as one side of a transaction is often posted to a balance sheet account and the other side of it is posted to the income statement. How this works will become more clear as we review some of the accounts found on the income statement. An example of an income statement can be seen in Table 4-3.

4.6.1 Revenue

The first section of the income statement is the revenue section, so the first account listed in that section is usually sales or services. The amount of income realized from the primary business operation is posted as a credit to

Table 4-3: Income Statement from Walgreens ($ in Millions)

	2003	2002
Revenue	$32,505.40	$28,681.10
Cost of Goods Sold	$23,360.10	$20,768.80
GROSS PROFIT	**$9,145.30**	**$7,912.30**
Selling, General & Administrative Expense	$6,950.90	$5,980.80
Depreciation	$346.10	$307.30
OPERATING INCOME	**$1,848.30**	**$1,624.20**
Interest Expense	$0.00	$0.00
Other Expenses (Income)	($40.40)	($13.10)
INCOME BEFORE TAXES	**$1,888.70**	**$1,637.30**
Income Taxes	$713.00	$618.10
NET INCOME	**$1,175.70**	**$1,019.20**
EPS (as reported)	$1.14	$0.99
Weighted Avg. Shares Outstanding (000)	1,031,580	1,032,271

sales or services and as a debit to the cash account on the balance sheet; if the sale has been made on credit, the other side of the posting goes to accounts receivable. Both the cash account and accounts receivable should always carry a debit balance, and another debit posted to it increases the balance in it.

After income accounts come any accounts that are related to them, such as sales discounts and returns and allowances. These accounts reduce the revenue accounts.

Any other activities that produce income for the company accounts would also be listed in this section.

4.6.2 Cost of Sales

Cost of sales accounts are the next section of the income statement. These are costs that are directly related to the sales. In a retail business, you would see an account titled "purchases" in this area, representing merchandise purchased from vendors for resale. The difference between the income accounts and the cost of sales accounts is rolled into an account called "gross profit" or "gross income."

4.6.3 Expenses

The final section of the income statement contains the expense accounts. These are the day-to-day operating expenses of the business. In many accounting systems, these accounts are listed alphabetically.

The number of expense accounts depends on the size and type of business. Office expense, insurance, and utilities accounts are self-explanatory. Other accounts found in the expense section are directly linked to balance sheet accounts. Depreciation expense is the other side of accumulated depreciation, as many businesses write this amount off on a monthly basis. The entry would credit accumulated depreciation and debit depreciation expense.

Payroll tax expense is related to the payroll tax liability accounts. In the accrual accounting system, this would be posted at the time the payroll is prepared, and the entries would credit the payroll tax liability accounts and debit payroll tax expense for the employer's portion of the taxes. When the taxes are paid, the liabilities accounts are debited to erase the debt, and the cash account is credited to record the check that paid the taxes.

When all the expenses have been posted, the accounting system adds them up and deducts them from the gross profit; the difference is a net loss or a net profit for the company. In a computerized accounting system, the net profit is automatically transferred to the balance sheet as retained earnings.

▲ **Net loss:** Total expenses are greater than total revenue.
▲ **Net profit:** Total revenue is greater than total expenses.

> ## FOR EXAMPLE
>
> ### Net Losses
>
> There are times when a company will show a loss on their income state-ment that can be turned into a profit in the coming months. Consider whether a new product is being offered that requires extra expenses for advertising and promotion. With a good ad campaign, the new product can take off and make up the loss in no time.

The net profit shown on the income statement is subject to federal and state income taxes, which are estimated and subtracted from the profit. In some instances, corporations have both preferred and common stockholders. Divi-dends are paid to preferred stockholders out of net income. Corporations fre-quently pay cash dividends to their common stockholders. The percentage of net income or earnings paid out as dividends is referred to as the *dividend payout ratio*.

A net loss is where total expenses are greater than total revenue. Many new businesses have a net loss their first year. If a company has $20 million in revenue but has $30 million in expenses, then their net loss is $10 million.

SELF-CHECK

- Explain what an income statement is and discuss how it works in conjunction with a business's balance sheet.
- List the three sections of an income statement and describe each.
- Define **net loss** and **net profit**.

4.7 Cash Flow Statement

Obviously, financial managers, banks, and other lending institutions want to work with companies that are running profitable businesses, but the net profit is not the only thing that should be considered when reviewing a company's financial statements. It is all the reports together that give a true picture of a company's financial condition, and the cash flow statement should not be overlooked. Because of accrual accounting, it is important to note that a firm's net income over some periods is not necessarily the same as its cash flow. The amount of cash flowing into the firm can be higher or lower than the net income figure.

▲ **A statement of cash flows** provides a summary of the cash sources that come into the company and the cash that goes out of the company during a specified accounting period.

This statement consists of three sections: operating activities, investing activities, and financing activities. The primary approach to constructing a statement of cash flows begins with the net income from the income statement as a cash inflow. Then any noncash deductions, such as depreciation, that were deducted for tax purposes (although no actual cash outflow occurred) should be added back in.

The other cash flow adjustments are made by examining the differences in the accounts from two consecutive balance sheets. More specifically, cash flows are determined as follows:

▲ SOURCES (cash inflows)
  1. Amount of net income plus amount of depreciation
  2. Decrease in an asset account
  3. Increase in a liability account
  4. Increase in an equity account
▲ USES (cash outflows)
  1. Increase in an asset account
  2. Decrease in a liability account
  3. Decrease in an equity account
  4. Amount of cash dividends

Let's examine these more closely.

▲ **Assets:** The purchase of raw materials or fixed assets requires spending or investing cash. Thus, increases in assets are a use and are therefore subtracted in the statement of cash flows. In contrast, collection of accounts receivable or sale of an asset brings cash into the firm; reductions in asset accounts are a source and are added into the statement of cash flows.
▲ **Liabilities and equity:** Borrowing money from a bank increases liability, and receiving additional investment funds from a partner or stockholder increases equity. Both represent a new source of cash to the company. In contrast, using cash to pay off a bank loan decreases a liability; and using cash to repurchase shares of stocks results in a decrease in equity.

Changes in the cash account are not included. Rather, in the statement of cash flows, all of the firm's sources and uses of cash are added together. Their sum equals the change in the firm's cash account. If the statement of cash flows is constructed correctly, the sum of the items should equal the difference in the cash account between the two balance sheets used to generate it.

Table 4-4: Statement of Cash Flows Walgreen's ($ in Millions)

	2003
OPERATING ACTIVITIES	
Net Income (Loss)	$1,175.7
Depreciation	$346.1
Increase in Accounts Receivable	($63.0)
Increase in Inventories	($557.5)
Increase/Decrease in Other Current Assets	($3.9)
Increase in Accounts Payable	$240.6
Increase in Other Current Liabilities	$224.7
Other Adjustments, Net	($353.3)
CASH FROM OPERATIONS	$1,009.4
INVESTING ACTIVITIES	
Purchase of Property, Plant, and Equipment	($348.6)
Sale of Property, Plant & Equipment	$13.1
Cash In (Out) Flow	$96.3
CASH FROM INVESTMENTS	($239.2)
FINANCING ACTIVITIES	
Issuance of Capital Stock	
Repurchase of Capital Stock	($50.6)
Debt Increase (Decrease)	$0.0
Dividends	($152.4)
Other Cash In (Out) Flow	
CASH FROM FINANCING	($203.0)
Effect of Exchange Rates	
NET CHANGE IN CASH	$567.2

Table 4-4 shows the statement of cash flows for the Walgreens Company based on the 2003 income statement and the balance sheets for 2002 and 2003. Notice that cash flows are grouped on the basis of operating activities, investing activities, and financing activities. Sources of funds from operations begin with net income of $1,175.7 million plus depreciation of $346.10 million to reflect the fact that depreciation is a noncash charge against the firm's revenues. Walgreens also generated additional sources of cash from operations by increasing its accounts payable by $240.6 million and other current liabilities by $224.7 million. Uses of cash from operations were in the form of a $63-million increase in accounts receivable and a $557.5-million increase in inventories. Along with other operating activities, the overall result was a net cash inflow from operations during 2003 of $1,009.4 million. The cash from operations is an important figure for businesses. It may be negative for growing firms, but generally a firm cannot exist long if it continually creates net cash outflows from its operations.

From the financial manager's perspective, cash is what matters most. He or she knows that in an accrual accounting system, revenue is recognized in 1 month, but the actual cash may not come in for several months. This means that a firm may appear profitable and actually be cash poor and unable to pay their obligations. What matters to lenders is what cash inflows are expected in the near future so the firm can continue to stay in business and pay its bills in a timely manner.

SELF-CHECK

- Explain what a statement of cash flows is and list its three sections.
- Give examples of cash inflows and cash outflows.
- Define **assets** and **liabilities**.

4.8 Financial Statements of Different Companies

Financial statements reveal to investors the differences in how companies operate. Across industries, the composition of firms' assets and liabilities will differ. Similarly, how firms generate earnings will depend upon the characteristics of the industry in which they compete and the products or service they offer to consumers. It is difficult to directly compare the financial statements of a variety of firms. Because of size differences among firms, the dollar level of assets, liabilities, and expenses will be hard to compare. A means of addressing the size problem to aid firm comparisons is to use common-size financial statements. **Common-size financial statements** express balance sheet numbers as a percentage of total assets and income statement numbers as a percentage of revenue.

This way comparison between firms is based on relative numbers rather than absolute dollar figures.

Table 4-5 shows how common-size financial statements make it possible to compare three different companies. Walgreens is a leading firm in the retail drug

Table 4-5: Common-Size Financial Statements

BALANCE SHEET $ MILLIONS	WALGREENS 2003	PERCENT OF ASSETS	MICROSOFT 2003	PERCENT OF ASSETS	EXXONMOBIL 2003	PERCENT OF ASSETS
Cash & Marketable Securities	1,017.1	8.9%	49,048.0	61.6%	10,626.0	6.1%
Accounts Receivable	1,017.8	8.9%	5,196.0	6.5%	24,309.0	13.9%
Inventories	4,202.7	36.8%	640.0	0.8%	8,957.0	5.1%
Other Current Assets	120.5	1.1%	4,089.0	5.1%	2,068.0	1.2%
Total Current Assets	6,358.1	55.7%	58,973.0	74.1%	45,960.0	26.4%
Net Fixed Assets	4,940.0	43.3%	2,223.0	2.8%	104,965.0	60.2%
Other Long Term Assets	107.8	0.9%	18,375.0	23.1%	23,353.0	13.4%
TOTAL ASSETS	11,405.9	100.0%	79,571.0	100.0%	174,278.0	100.0%
Accounts Payable	2,077.0	18.2%	1,573.0	2.0%	15,334.0	8.8%
Short-Term Debt	0.0	0.0%	0.0	0.0%	4,789.0	2.7%
Other Current Liabilities	1,343.5	11.8%	12,401.0	15.6%	18,263.0	10.5%
Total Current Liabilities	3,420.5	30.0%	13,974.0	17.6%	38,386.0	22.0%
Long-Term Debt	0.0	0.0%	0.0	0.0%	4,756.0	2.7%
Other Liabilities	789.7	6.9%	4,577.0	5.8%	41,221.0	23.7%
TOTAL LIABILITIES	4,210.2	36.9%	18,551.0	23.3%	84,363.0	48.4%

	WALGREENS 2003	PERCENT REVENUE	MICROSOFT 2003	PERCENT OF REVENUE	EXXONMOBIL 2003	PERCENT OF REVENUE
Preferred Equity	0.0	0.0%	0.0	0.0%	0.0	0.0%
Common Stockholders' Equity	7,195.7	63.1%	61,020.0	76.7%	89,915.0	51.6%
TOTAL LIABILITIES & EQUITY	11,405.9	100.0%	79,571.0	100.0%	174,278.0	100.0%

INCOME STATEMENT $ MILLIONS	WALGREENS 2003	PERCENT REVENUE	MICROSOFT 2003	PERCENT OF REVENUE	EXXONMOBIL 2003	PERCENT OF REVENUE
Revenue	32,505.4	100.0%	32,187	100.0%	213,199	100.0%
Cost of Goods Sold	23,360.1	71.9%	4,247	13.2%	129,928	60.9%
GROSS PROFIT	**9,145.3**	**28.1%**	**27,940**	**86.8%**	**83,271**	**39.1%**
Selling, General & Admin.	6,950.9	21.4%	8,625	26.8%	51,041	23.9%
Depreciation	346.1	1.1%	1,439	4.5%	9,047	4.2%
Research & Development	0.0	0.0%	4,659	14.5%	0	0.0%
OPERATING INCOME	**1,848.3**	**5.7%**	**13,217**	**41.1%**	**23,183**	**10.9%**
Interest Expense	0.0	0.0%	0	0.0%	207	0.1%
Other Expenses (Income)	(40.4)	(0.1%)	(1,509)	(4.7%)	(8,990)	(4.2%)
INCOME BEFORE TAXES	**1,888.7**	**5.8%**	**14,726**	**45.8%**	**31,966**	**15.0%**
Income Taxes	713.0	2.2%	4,733	14.7%	11,006	5.2%
NET INCOME	**1,175.7**	**3.6%**	**9,993**	**31.0%**	**20,960**	**9.8%**

store industry; Microsoft is a major software and operating system provider; ExxonMobil is a leader in the oil industry. The differences among the industries in which these firms operate are apparent when looking at their common-size financial statements.

The balance sheets show the capital-intensive nature of oil exploration and refining as ExxonMobil only has 26% of its assets in current assets while the reminder are long-term assets. Walgreens and Microsoft have over half of their assets in the form of current assets. Noting differences in the composition of current assets, Walgreens has most of its current assets in inventory, which is expected for a retail establishment. ExxonMobil has more current assets in accounts receivable from its oil sales. Microsoft is cash-rich with over 60% of its total assets in the form of cash; this comprises over 80% of its current assets.

As a retail establishment, Walgreens has the largest percentage of accounts payable (18.2%) and the largest proportion of financing in the form of current liabilities (30%). Because of its large relative use of fixed assets, Exxon-Mobil has a large percentage of liability financing (its total liabilities are 48.4% of its assets). Microsoft has relatively few fixed assets; most of its capital is in the form of software code and organizational and human capital, of which lenders can't take possession in the event of financial difficulty. Thus, Microsoft's equity financing, almost 80%, is much larger than that of Walgreens and ExxonMobil.

The balance sheets provide insight into how a firm generates a product or service and how it finances itself. The income statement shows the effects of the firm's production operations, financing, competition, and industry characteristics. Microsoft by far had the most profitable year, with income after taxes equal to 31% of revenue. Microsoft's income statement shows the actual production of software (placing code on CDs or other media and packaging it) is rather low; its cost of goods sold is only 13.2% of sales and its gross profit is a huge 86.8%. Walgreens, operating in a mark-up retail environment, has a much higher cost of goods sold (71.9% of revenue) and lower gross profit (28.1%). Overhead in

FOR EXAMPLE

Common–Size Financial Statements Limitations

When using common-size financial statements, you have to be careful that both companies you are comparing use the same calendar year. For example, Microsoft may have a January through December calendar year for their numbers while Walgreen has a June 1 through July 31 fiscal year. Take this into account with any comparisons.

the form of selling, general, and administrative expenses is relatively higher for Microsoft. We see the need to invest in product and manufacturing to stay ahead of competitors in the size of Microsoft's research and development expense (14.5% of sales).

All three firms use little long-term debt financing; this is clear from the common-size balance sheet. It is also reflected in the common-size income statement with the low percentage of interest expense for each firm.

Common-size statements are easily computed using spreadsheet software.

SELF-CHECK

- Explain what a common-size financial statement is.
- Identify a situation in which a common-size financial statement would be useful.

4.9 Our Federal Tax System

Effective income tax rate is the tax rate that a company pays in all forms of taxes. It is computed by dividing the total tax paid by taxable income. It can vary substantially depending on whether the firm is organized as a proprietorship, partnership, or corporation. Income tax liabilities also may differ for each form of business organization selected. For instance, income from partnerships and proprietorships is combined with other personal income for tax purposes.

4.9.1 Personal Income Tax

Personal income tax rates are progressive, meaning that the higher the income, the larger the percentage of income that must be paid in taxes. A progressive tax rate is taxation that is dependent on income; the higher the income, the higher tax rate. See Table 4-6 as an illustration.

For example, let's assume that the taxable income from a proprietorship is $50,000 and that the owner does not have any additional income. If the owner is married and filing a joint return and the spouse has no reportable income, the income will be taxed as follows:

$$0.10 \times \$14,000 = \$1,400$$
$$\underline{0.15 \times \$36,000 = \$5,400}$$
$$\$50,000 \quad \$6,800$$

Table 4-6: 2006 Federal Personal Income Tax Brackets

Tax Bracket	Income if Single	Income if Married Filing Jointly
10%	Up to $7,550	Up to $15,100
15%	$7,551 to $30,650	$15,101 to $61,300
25%	$30,651–$74,200	$61,301 to $123,700
28%	$74,201–154,800	$123,701 to $188,450
33%	$154,801–336,550	$188,451 to $336,550
35%	All over $336,550	All over $336,550

FILING STATUS	TAXABLE INCOME	MARGINAL TAX RATE
Married Filing Jointly	$0–14,000	10%
	14,001–56,800	15
	56,801–114,650	25
	114,651–174,700	28
	174,701–311,950	33
	over $311,950	35
Single	$0–7,000	10%
	7,001–28,400	15
	28,401–68,800	25
	68,801–143,500	28
	143,501–311,950	33
	over $311,950	35

▲ **The marginal tax rate** is the rate paid on the last dollar of income.

In our example, the marginal tax rate is 15% and applies to that portion of the taxable income above $14,000.

▲ **The average tax rate** is determined by dividing the total tax amount by the total taxable income.

In our example, the total tax amount is $6,800 and the total taxable income is $50,000; $6,800 divided by $50,000 equals 13.6%. The marginal tax rate is the rate that is most important when making business decisions. It shows the percentage of new income that will be paid to the government, or alternatively, that will be lost to the firm because of tax obligations.

Personal taxable income as examined is considered to be ordinary taxable income and is taxed when it is received. Capital gains or losses arise from asset price changes on capital assets such as real estate, bonds, and stocks. Capital gains or losses are taxed only when the asset is sold and the gain or loss is realized. Unrealized capital gains reflect the price appreciation of currently held assets that have not been sold; the tax liability on unrealized capital gains can be deferred indefinitely. Capital gains become taxable only after the asset has been sold for a price higher than its cost or basis.

If appreciated assets are passed on to an heir upon the investor's death, the basis of the assets is considered to be their value on the date of the holder's death. The heirs can then sell the assets and not pay capital gains tax.

The top capital gain tax rate is 15% for assets held longer than 12 months. For taxpayers in the 15% tax bracket, the capital gains tax rate is only 5%.

4.9.2 Corporate Income Tax

Corporations, in contrast with proprietorships and partnerships, are taxed as separate entities. In 2006 the corporate tax rates on their taxable income were:

TAXABLE INCOME	TAX RATE
$0–50,000	15%
50,001–75,000	25%
75,001–100,000	34%
100,001–335,000	39%
335,001–10 million	34%
10 million–15 million	35%
15 million–18,333,333	38%
Over 18,333,333	35%

The 39% tax rate for income between $100,000 and $335,000 is designed to elicit the same percentage of money as the combined tax rates of the 15% and 25% rates. For example, if the company made $50,000, it would pay 15% in taxes. If the company made $75,000, the company would pay 25% in taxes. These two amounts combined are $125,000. That would push the company into a 39% tax bracket, which is just one less point than the combination of the two rates (40%). A similar recapture occurs for taxable income between $15 million and $18.3 million. Because of this, the average and marginal tax rates are both 35% for corporate incomes over $18,333,333.

A corporation with taxable income of $50,000 pays $7,500 (a 15% marginal and average rate), compared with $6,800 for a proprietor who is married and filing a joint return or $9,310 for a proprietor who is single. However, income distributed from after-tax corporate profits to owners is taxed again in the form of personal ordinary income. Thus, deciding whether there would be an income tax advantage associated with being taxed as a corporation rather than a proprietorship or partnership is a complex undertaking.

A corporation with taxable income of $200,000 would have the following tax obligation:

$$
\begin{array}{rcrcr}
0.15 & \times & \$50,000 & = & \$7,500.00 \\
0.25 & \times & 25,000 & = & 6,250.00 \\
0.34 & \times & 25,000 & = & 8,500.00 \\
0.39 & \times & 100,000 & = & 39,000.00 \\
\hline
 & & \$200,000 & & \$61,250.00
\end{array}
$$

The marginal tax rate would be 39%, and the average tax rate would be 30.6% ($61,250/$200,000).

A corporation pays taxes on its taxable income. Then, if cash from profits is distributed as dividends to stockholders, the stockholders must pay personal income taxes. This means that money paid out to the owners is taxed twice— once at the corporate level and once as personal income.

Small businesses can sometimes qualify as S corporations under the Internal Revenue Code. These organizations receive the limited liability of a corporation but are taxed as proprietorships or partnerships. Thus, the S corporation avoids double taxation because the business is taxed as a proprietorship or partnership. Whether or not this taxation option is selected depends on the level of the owner's personal tax bracket.

Businesses also have the opportunity of carrying operating losses backward for 2 years and forward for 20 years to offset taxable income. A new business corporation that loses, for example, $50,000 the first year can offset only taxable income earned in future years. However, initial losses by a new proprietorship or partnership can be first carried back against personal income taxes paid by owners, entitling them to tax refunds. This can be helpful for a new business that has limited funds.

4.9.3 Depreciation Basics

Depreciation write-offs are particularly important to businesses because depreciation is deductible from income before taxes and thus reduces the firm's income-tax liability. Table 4-7 illustrates the impact of deducting versus not deducting $20,000 in depreciation before computing income-tax liabilities.

The effects of the depreciation tax shield is seen in the operating cash flow calculation as well. Ignoring any changes in the current asset and current liability accounts, operating cash flow is net income plus depreciation.

Table 4-7: Depreciation Schedule

	WITH DEPRECIATION	WITHOUT DEPRECIATION
Income before depreciation and income taxes	$100,000	$100,000
Less: Depreciation	20,000	0
Income before taxes	80,000	100,000
Less: Income taxes (@ 30%)	24,000	30,000
Net income	$ 56,000	$ 70,000

IRS tax regulations allow two basic depreciation methods, straight-line depreciation and the modified accelerated cost recovery system (MACRS).

▲ **Annual straight-line depreciation** expense is computed by dividing the asset's cost by an estimate of its useful life.

The annual straight-line depreciation expense for an asset that costs $100,000 and is expected to be used for 8 years is $100,000/8 = $12,500.

▲ The **modified accelerated cost recovery system** (MACRS) depreciates assets by an accelerated method.

In essence, MACRS depreciates assets using the double-declining balance method until it becomes advantageous to use straight-line depreciation over the asset's remaining life. To ensure some uniformity, it assigns assets to depreciation classes:

3-year class	Designated tools and equipment used in research
5-year class	Cars, trucks, and some office equipment such as computers and copiers
7-year class	Other office equipment and industrial machinery
10-year class	Other long-lived equipment
27.5-year class	Residential real estate
31.5-year class	Commercial and industrial real estate

Assets in the 27.5- or 31.5-year classes must be depreciated with the straight-line method over the appropriate number of years. In addition, with some exceptions, MACRS follows a half-year convention. The asset receives a half-year's worth of

FOR EXAMPLE

Employee Benefits

Although the tax rates do seem high for businesses, businesses can take many expenses as tax deductions. Corporations can take all the same business tax deductions as other companies. In addition, they can deduct the following employee benefits:

▲ Disability insurance
▲ Medical expenses reimbursement
▲ Tuition reimbursement
▲ Meals and small gifts
▲ Cost of annual medical checkups
▲ Parking reimbursement
▲ Group term life insurance

Employees do not need to include these benefits on their income tax statements. Therefore, it's a win-win situation for both the company and the employee.

depreciation in the year it is acquired, regardless of when it is actually purchased. Thus, assets in the 3-year class are actually depreciated over 4 years. The owner writes off a half-year of depreciation in year 1, a full year of depreciation in each of years 2 and 3, and the remaining half-year of depreciation in year 4.

One important thing to remember about depreciation is that when the asset is sold, the proceeds from the sale could be taxable depending on how much depreciation was taken during the time the asset was in use.

Another tax benefit allows businesses to write off the entire cost of business property in the year it was purchased up to the current limit set by IRS. This could provide a nice tax savings in a year when profits are high.

SELF-CHECK

- Describe how the marginal tax rate and average tax rate are calculated.
- Explain the difference between personal income tax and corporate income tax.
- List the two kinds of depreciation and explain each.
- Define the **modified accelerated cost recovery system**.

SUMMARY

If you work within finance, you must be able to read and interpret financial statements. However, this skill is useful regardless of what your job is. Not only do financial statements give you a better sense for the strength of your company, but on a personal level they also shed some light on your investments. In this chapter, you learned the components of financial statements, including assets and liabilities. You can now differentiate between an annual report, balance sheet, and income statement. You also discovered what cash flow is and why it is so important to a company. You discovered the three major organizational forms for companies. You also calculated the tax rates of companies and individuals.

KEY TERMS

Annual reports	Contain descriptive information on operating and financial performance during the past year, a discussion of current and future business opportunities, and financial statements that provide a record of financial performance.
Annual straight-line depreciation	Expense is computed by dividing the asset's cost by an estimate of its useful life.
Assets	Cash, inventory, accounts receivable, fixed assets, and investments.
Average tax rate	Determined by dividing the total tax amount by the total taxable income.
Balance sheet	A statement of a company's financial position as of a particular date, usually at the end of the quarter or year.
Common-size financial statements	Express balance sheet numbers as a percentage of total assets and income statement numbers as a percentage of revenue.
Equity	Funds supplied by the owners and represents their residual claim on the firm.
Factors of production	Land, capital, and labor needed to operate a business.
Generally accepted accounting principles (GAAP)	A set of guidelines as to the form and manner in which accounting information should be presented.
Income statement	Reports the revenues generated and expenses incurred by the firm over an accounting period.

Liabilities	The debts of a business.
Marginal tax rate	The rate paid on the last dollar of income.
Modified accelerated cost recovery system (MACRS)	Depreciates assets by an accelerated method.
Net loss	Total expenses are greater than total revenue.
Net profit	Total revenue is greater than total expenses.
Nonprofit corporation	Does not pay taxes unless their income rises above the level set by the IRS. Even then, the tax rate is reduced.
Owners' equity	The investment of the owners or owner in the business.
Partnership	A form of business organization involving two or more people who own a business operated for profits.
Regular corporation	Pays tax on its profits.
Retained earnings	The amount that the company keeps to improve or expand business operations.
Sole proprietorship	A business venture that is owned by a single individual who personally receives all profits and assumes all responsibility for the debts and losses of the business.
Statement of cash flows	Provides a summary of the cash sources that come into the company and the cash that goes out of the company during a specified accounting period.

ASSESS YOUR UNDERSTANDING

Go to www.wiley.com/college/Melicher to evaluate your knowledge of the basics of financial reports.
Measure your learning by comparing pre-test and post-test results.

Summary Questions

1. A firm's financial statements include a(n)
   (a) balance sheet.
   (b) income statement.
   (c) statement of cash flows.
   (d) all of the above.

2. Profits from a proprietorship are taxed at the corporate income tax rates. True or false?

3. A partnership is a form of business organization when two or more people own a business operated for profit. True or false?

4. Limited partners face liability limited to their investment in the firm, but they can participate in the operations of the firm. True or false?

5. One of the important reasons corporations can accumulate large sums of capital is that they are allowed to sell capital stock. True or false?

6. Privately held corporations register shares with the Securities and Exchange Commission before selling them to shareholders. True or false?

7. A business should begin with a vision or mission statement that is consistent with the planned overall strategy. True or false?

8. The goal of any firm should be the maximization of sales. True or false?

9. With generally accepted accounting practices, there is one "right way" of accounting for business transactions. True or false?

10. Information about which accounting principles were used by the firm are included in the
    (a) balance sheet.
    (b) footnotes.
    (c) management discussion on annual report.
    (d) None of the above

11. Most of accounting practice is based upon the cash concept. True or false?

12. Assets are financial and physical items owed to the business. True or false?

13. The current liabilities of a business may include
    (a) notes payable resulting from borrowing from a bank on a short-term basis.
    (b) accounts receivable.

    (c) prepaid expenses.

    (d) depreciation reserves.

14. Equity is funds supplied by the owners that represent their residual claim on the firm. True or false?

15. A profit and loss statement is another name for

    (a) a statement of cash flow.

    (b) a balance sheet.

    (c) an income statement.

    (d) an annual report.

16. The three main sections of the statement of cash flows include all of the following *except*

    (a) cash from saving.

    (b) cash from investments.

    (c) cash from operations.

    (d) cash from financing.

    (e) All are included

17. A firm's net income over some period is the same as its cash flow. True or false?

18. Common-size financial statements express balance sheet and income statement numbers as a percent of sales. True or false?

19. A statement that expresses the income statement items as a percent of total sales is called

    (a) a percentage of sales income statement.

    (b) a cross-sectional income statement.

    (c) a common size income statement.

    (d) a ratio based income statement.

    (e) none of the above.

20. The marginal tax rate is determined by dividing the total tax amount by the total taxable income. True or false?

21. Annual straight-line depreciation expense is computed by dividing the asset's cost by an estimate of its useful life. True or false?

Review Questions

1. Identify two changes in a firm's financial condition that can be seen in its financial statements and that should be a cause of concern for investors.

2. What are the three major forms of business ownership in the United States?

3. Under which business organization do the owners have unlimited liability for all debts of the firm?

4. What are the differences in owner liability in proprietorships and partnerships versus corporations?

5. Briefly describe the differences between a subchapter S corporation and a limited liability company.

6. It has often been said that a business should begin with a vision or mission statement. Explain what this means.

7. What types of information are included in an annual report?

8. Who formulates the generally accepted accounting principles?

    (a) Securities and Exchange Commission

    (b) Financial Accounting Standards Board

    (c) Federal Trade Commission

    (d) General accounting office

9. What is the purpose of the balance sheet? Briefly identify and describe the major types of assets and the claims of creditors and owners shown on the typical balance sheet.

10. Describe the three different accounts that comprise the owners' equity section on a typical balance sheet.

11. What is the purpose of the income statement? Also briefly identify and describe the major types of expenses that are shown on the typical income statement.

12. What is a statement of cash flows? What are the three standard sections contained in a statement of cash flows?

13. What is included in cash flows from financing activities?

14. What is included in cash flows from operating activities?

15. Briefly explain how using relative numbers rather than absolute dollar figures makes it easier to compare the financial statements of firms in different industries.

16. Why is it said that the personal income tax rate in the United States is progressive?

17. Corporate tax rates vary with the amount of taxable income. What currently is the range (lowest and highest) of corporate tax rates in the United States?

18. If your business purchases a new factory, what depreciation method would you use for it, and over how long a period?

Applying This Chapter

1. Discuss why a firm that begins to use much more debt financing than it has in the past might still be considered a good investment by potential investors.

2. Identify the form of business organization of the following firms:
   (a) Target Corporation (www.target.com)
   (b) Zingerman's (www.zingermans.com)
   (c) Kohler Co. (www.kohler.com)
3. Identify a publicly owned retail firm and publicly owned manufacturing firm and find their mission statements on their Web sites. How do they differ? How are they similar?
4. Download a corporation's annual report and read the CEO letter. Based on the letter, what are the company's strengths?
5. Use your knowledge of balance sheets to fill in the amounts missing in the text.

ASSETS	
Cash	$10,000
Accounts receivable	100,000
Inventory	————
Total current assets	220,000
Gross plant and equipment	500,000
Less: accumulated depreciation	————
Net plant and equipment	375,000
Total assets	————

LIABILITIES	
Accounts payable	$12,000
Notes payable	50,000
Total current liabilities	————
Long-term debt	————
Total liabilities	190,000
Common stock ($1 par, 100,000 shares)	————
Paid-in capital	————
Retained earnings	150,000
Total stockholders' equity	————
Total liabilities and equity	————

6. Use your knowledge of balance sheets to fill in the amounts missing in the text.

ASSETS	
Cash	$50,000
Accounts receivable	80,000
Inventory	100,000
Total current assets	_____
Gross plant and equipment	_____
Less: accumulated depreciation	130,000
Net plant and equipment	600,000
Total assets	_____

LIABILITIES	
Accounts payable	$12,000
Notes payable	50,000
Total current liabilities	_____
Long-term debt	_____
Total liabilities	_____
Common stock ($1 par, 100,000 shares)	_____
Paid-in capital	250,000
Retained earnings	200,000
Total stockholders' equity	_____
Total liabilities and equity	$830,000

7. Use your knowledge of income statements to fill in the missing items:

Sales	_____
Cost of goods sold	$575,000
Gross profit	1,600,000
General and administrative expense	200,000
Selling and marketing expense	_____
Depreciation	50,000

Operating income	
Interest	100,000
Income before taxes	
Income taxes (30%)	
Net income	$700,000

8. Use the following information to construct an income statement:

Interest	$25,000
Sales	$950,000
Income tax rate	25%
Selling and marketing expenses	160,000
General and administrative expenses	$200,000
Gross profit	550,000
Depreciation	$30,000
Cost of goods sold	$400,000

9. Identify whether the following activities should be added to or subtracted from a statement of cash flow.
   (a) Purchase of raw materials
   (b) Sale of an asset
   (c) Receiving investment funds from stockholders
   (d) Paying off a bank loan

10. Use your knowledge of balance sheets and common-size statements to fill in the missing dollar amounts:

ASSETS		
Cash	$25,000	3.4%
Accounts receivable	$125,000	
Inventory		27.1%
Total current assets	$350,000	
Gross plant and equipment		95.0%
Less: accumulated depreciation	$313,000	42.5%
Net plant and equipment		
Total assets	$737,000	100.0%

LIABILITIES		
Accounts payable	————	15.7%
Notes payable	$29,000	3.9%
Total current liabilities	————	————
Long-term debt	$248,000	33.6%
Total liabilities	$393,000	————
Common stock ($.01 par, 450,000 shares)	$4,500	0.6%
Paid-in capital	$220,500	29.9%
Retained earnings	————	————
Total stockholders' equity	$344,000	46.7%
Total liabilities and equity	————	100.0%

11. Use your knowledge of income statements and common-size statements to fill in the missing dollar amounts:

Sales	$2,876,200	100.0%
Cost of goods sold	————	74.7%
Gross profit	————	25.3%
General and administrative expense	$250,000	8.7%
Selling and marketing expense	$140,000	4.9%
Depreciation	————	3.8%
Operating income	$229,000	8.0%
Interest	————	4.6%
Income before taxes	$97,000	3.4%
Income taxes (25%)	$24,250	0.8%
Net income	————	2.5%

12. Determine the marginal and average tax rates under the tax law for corporations with the following amounts of taxable income.
    (a) $60,000
    (b) $150,000
    (c) $500,000

13. Calculate the tax obligation for a corporation with pretax earnings of
    (a) $60,000.
    (b) $150,000.
    (c) $500,000.
14. What would be the personal tax obligation of a person filing her taxes under the "single" filing status if she had the above-pretax income levels?

Annual Reports

Locate the annual reports for Dell Computer and Apple on the Internet. Compare them. What similarities do you see? What differences? Which company is in a stronger financial position?

General Motors

Research the financial position of General Motors. For 2005 did they have a net loss or a net profit? Why?

Amazon

Research the financial position of the Internet retailer Amazon. List all their assets and liabilities. Based on this knowledge, what kind of financial position are they in? Will they make a profit?

China and Google

Reseach Google's relationship with China. Does their business relationship with the Chinese government contradict their mission? Why or why not?

5

ANALYSIS OF FINANCIAL STATEMENTS
Reviewing and Assessing Financial Information

Starting Point

Go to www.wiley.com/college/Melicher to assess your knowledge of the basics of financial statement analysis.
Determine where you need to concentrate your effort.

What You'll Learn in This Chapter

▲ The five basic types of financial ratios
▲ How to use financial ratios properly in order to achieve financial growth
▲ When to use specific ratios in different situations
▲ How internally generated financing occurs
▲ The effect of ratio analysis on long-term financial planning
▲ How to read a financial statement
▲ The application of the cost-volume-profit analysis concept

After Studying This Chapter, You'll Be Able To

▲ Distinguish the three categories of ratio analysis
▲ Compare and contrast financial statements from different companies
▲ Examine the link between asset investment and sales growth
▲ Apply the major components of Du Pont analysis
▲ Analyze the quality of financial reports
▲ Use analysis methods to evaluate profit levels

Goals and Outcomes

▲ Analyze and interpret financial statements
▲ Explain the categories of ratio analysis
▲ Perform the basic types of financial ratios
▲ Manage the application of ratios to evaluate business performance
▲ Prepare the requirements for external financing
▲ Evaluate the financial viability of particular business alternatives

INTRODUCTION

Now that you have studied the structure of business organizations and learned about financial data and how it is presented, it is time to move on to the next step in financial management. Analyzing financial statements is a skill shared by bankers, investors, bondholders, and stockholders as well as the firm's managers. Reviewing and assessing financial information helps us to recognize a company's strengths and weaknesses, which leads to good investment strategies and good financial planning.

5.1 Financial Statement Analysis

A countless number of financial market participants will use and analyze financial statement information, particularly bankers, other lenders, suppliers, investors, and even some of the firm's customers. Often firms make their financial data available to the public to show workers and investors how well the company is doing. For private firms, statement analysis and industry comparisons are done for internal use. A few simple ratio calculations can shed light on how well a company is doing and how it is making profits. Those same ratio calculations are done by lenders on personal financial data when individuals apply for a mortgage or an auto loan.

Successful financial analysis and planning require an understanding of a company's external and internal environments. External factors that affect a firm's profitability may be issues such as inflation, interest rates, exchange rates, and government policy. The firm's internal environment includes items that can be affected by management, such as organizational structure, employee motivation and productivity, cost control, and the company's plant and operations. Sales are affected one way or the other by the state of the economy, management's ability to handle growth, and the quality and marketing of the company's product. Pricing decisions are also influenced by the state of the economy, actions by competitors, and the firm's production costs. The joint impact of the external and internal environment on a firm should be reflected in its financial statements. These statements are a good way to assess the success or failure of the company's strategies and operations.

FOR EXAMPLE

Using Financial Statements

Different groups use financial statements for different purposes. Banks use financial statements to determine if they should loan money to a firm. Stock brokers use financial statements to determine if the stock of the company is going to be profitable and if the stock is a good buy. Manufacturers use financial statements to determine if they should work with a firm on a credit basis.

The information found on the financial statements is valuable to the company's managers, to stock and bond analysts, bank loan officers, and competitors. However, the way that investors view the results that come from analyzing financial statements often depends upon the current state of the economy. For example, a firm with high debt ratios may be an attractive investment at the end of a recession. That's because as economic growth begins, increased sales will generate cash to pay interest, leaving high levels of profits. Of course, the same debt ratios at the end of a period of economic growth, with a recession growing near, may make investors turn away.

Keep in mind that many individuals and organizations analyze financial statements. A company that seeks credit, either from a supplier or a bank, is usually required to submit financial statements for examination. Potential purchasers of a firm's stocks or bonds will analyze financial statements in order to judge the firm's ability to make timely payments of interest or dividends.

SELF-CHECK

- Describe how financial statements are used by a variety of different groups to discover information about a firm.
- Identify the external factors that affect a business's profitably.
- What are the internal factors that have an effect on the firm's profitably?
- How investors view the analysis of financial statements is affected by what current aspect?

5.2 Ratio Analysis

In this section we discuss ratio analysis as a means by which to gain insight into a firm's strengths and weaknesses.

▲ **Ratio analysis** is a financial technique that involves dividing various financial statement numbers into one another.

Ratios are computed by dividing one amount on the financial statements into another. They are percentages that are easily obtained by entering the numbers from financial data into a calculator. The ratios can then be examined to determine trends and reasons for changes in the financial statement from month to month. Ratios are valuable tools, as they standardize balance sheet and income statement

> ## FOR EXAMPLE
>
> ### Ratios
>
> Ratios are used in Chapter 2 to produce the common-size financial statements that made it possible for us to compare Walgreens, Microsoft, and ExxonMobil despite the differences in their sizes and business activities.

numbers. A firm with $10 billion in sales can be easily compared to a firm with $1 billion or $200 million in sales.

Three basic categories of ratio analysis are used.

▲ **Trend** or **time-series analysis** uses ratios to evaluate a firm's performance over time.

▲ **Cross-section analysis** uses ratios to compare different companies at the same point in time.

▲ **Industry-comparative analysis** is used to compare a firm's ratios against average ratios for other companies in the same industry.

Comparing a firm's ratios to average industry ratios requires a degree of caution. That's because some sources of industry data report the average for each ratio; others report the median; others report the interquartile range for each ratio, which is the range for the middle 50% of ratio values reported by firms in the industry.

The analyst must also be aware that industry ratios may be narrowly focused on a specific industry, but the operations of large firms such as GE, ExxonMobil, and IBM often cross many industry boundaries. Also, accounting standards often differ among firms in an industry. This can create confusion, particularly when some firms in the industry adopt new accounting standards set forth by the Financial Accounting Standards Board (FASB) before others. Adopting standards early can affect a firm's ratios by making them appear unusually high or low compared to the industry average.

Care also must be taken when comparing different types of firms in the same industry. In one industry there may be a mixture of very large and very small firms; multinational and domestic companies that operate nationally as opposed to those that focus only on limited geographic markets.

Analysts and sources of public information on ratios may compute ratios differently. Some may use after-tax earnings, some pre-tax earnings; others may assume *debt* refers only to long-term debt while others include all liabilities as debt. Therefore, when comparing ratios make sure you know how a resource defines its ratios before using it.

Sometimes how a ratio is interpreted depends on who has requested it—that is, whether a ratio appears favorable or unfavorable depends on the perspective

FOR EXAMPLE

Interpreting Ratios

If a short-term creditor such as a bank loan officer wants to see a high degree of liquidity, the analyst would be somewhat less concerned with a firm's profitability than if the user was an equity holder who would rather see less liquidity and more profitability.

of the user. Therefore, the analyst must keep in mind the viewpoint of the user in evaluating and interpreting the information contained in financial ratios.

SELF-CHECK

- Define **ratio analysis** and explain what it is used for.
- Explain why ratios are used for financial analysis.
- List and briefly explain the three basic categories of ratio analysis.
- Why must caution be used in comparing ratios of different companies?

5.3 Types of Financial Ratios

Many types of ratios can be calculated from financial statement data or stock market information. However, it is common practice to group ratios into five basic categories:

▲ Liquidity ratios

▲ Asset-management ratios

▲ Financial-leverage ratios

▲ Profitability ratios

▲ Market-value ratios

The first four categories are based on information taken from a firm's income statements and balance sheets. The fifth category relates stock market information to financial statement items. We will use the financial statements for Walgreens that were introduced in Chapter 2 to illustrate how financial statement analysis is conducted. Tables 5-1 and 5-2 contain the balance sheets and income statements for several years for Walgreens. For each ratio group, we present graphs of Walgreens's ratio as well as the average ratio for the retail drug store industry over the 1997–2003 time period.

Table 5-1: Balance Sheet for Walgreens ($ in Millions)

	2003	2002	2001	2000
ASSETS				
Cash & Marketable Securities	$1,017.10	$449.90	$16.90	$12.80
Accounts Receivable	$1,017.80	$954.80	$798.30	$614.50
Inventories $	$4,202.70	$3,645.20	$3,482.40	$2,830.80
Other Current Assets	$120.50	$116.60	$96.30	$92.00
Total Current Assets	$6,358.10	$5,166.50	$4,393.90	$3,550.10
Net Fixed Assets	$4,940.00	$4,591.40	$4,345.30	$3,428.20
Other Long-Term Assets	$107.80	$120.90	$94.60	$125.40
Total Fixed Assets	$5,047.80	$4,712.30	$4,439.90	$3,553.60
Total Assets	$11,405.90	$9,878.80	$8,833.80	$7,103.70
LIABILITIES AND EQUITY				
Accounts Payable	$2,077.00	$1,836.40	$1,546.80	$1,364.00
Notes Payable	$0.00	$0.00	$440.70	$0.00
Other Current Liabilities	$1,343.50	$1,118.80	$1,024.10	$939.70
Total Current Liabilities	$3,420.50	$2,955.20	$3,011.60	$2,303.70
Long-Term Debt	$0.00	$0.00	$0.00	$0.00
Other Liabilities	$789.70	$693.40	$615.00	$566.00
Total Liabilities	$4,210.20	$3,648.60	$3,626.60	$2,869.70
Common Equity	$777.90	$828.50	$676.30	$446.20
Retained Earnings	$6,417.80	$5,401.70	$4,530.90	$3,787.80
Total Stockholders' Equity	$7,195.70	$6,230.20	$5,207.20	$4,234.00
Total Liabilities and Equity	$11,405.90	$9,878.80	$8,833.80	$7,103.70

Table 5-2: Income Statement for Walgreens ($ in Millions)

	2003	2002	2001	2000
Revenue	$32,505.40	$28,681.10	$24,623.00	$21,206.90
Cost of Goods Sold	$23,360.10	$20,768.80	$17,779.70	$15,235.80
Gross Profit	$9,145.30	$7,912.30	$6,843.30	$5,971.10
Selling, General & Administrative	$6,950.90	$5,980.80	$5,175.80	$4,516.90
Depreciation	$346.10	$307.30	$269.20	$230.10
Operating Income	$1,848.30	$1,624.20	$1,398.30	$1,224.10
Interest Expense	$0.00	$0.00	$3.10	$0.40
Other Expenses (Income)	($40.40)	($13.10)	($27.50)	($39.60)
Income Before Taxes	$1,888.70	$1,637.30	$1,422.70	$1,263.30
Income	$713.00	$618.10	$537.10	$486.40
Net Income	$1,175.70	$1,019.20	$885.60	$776.90
Number of Shares Outstanding (000s)	1,031,580	1,032,271	1,028,947	1,019,889
Earnings Per Share	$1.14	$0.99	$0.86	$0.76

5.3.1 Liquidity Ratios

Liquidity refers to how quickly a firm can turn its assets into cash. A firm, for example, that has only cash assets is completely liquid. On the opposite extreme would be a firm whose only assets are real estate. Because real estate sales can take months, or even years, and may even take a loss on the transaction, the firm is illiquid. Liquidity is important because of the changing business climate. A firm must be able to pay its financial obligations when needed. If a firm cannot pay its financial obligations, it will go bankrupt.

The less liquid the firm, the greater the risk of insolvency or default. Because debt obligations are paid with cash, the firm's cash flows ultimately determine solvency.

We can estimate the firm's liquidity position by examining specific balance sheet items.

▲ **Liquidity ratios** indicate the ability to meet short-term obligations to creditors as they mature or come due.

This form of liquidity analysis focuses on the relationship between current assets and current liabilities, and the speed with which receivables and inventory turn into cash during normal business operations. This means that the immediate source of cash funds for paying bills must be cash on hand, proceeds from the sale of marketable securities, or the collection of accounts receivable. Additional liquidity also comes from inventory that can be sold and thus converted into cash either directly through cash sales or indirectly through credit sales (accounts receivable).

The dollar amount of a firm's net working capital is sometimes used as a measure of liquidity.

▲ **The net working capital** of a firm is its current assets minus current liabilities.

However, two popular ratios are also used to gauge a firm's liquidity position.

▲ **The current ratio** is a measure of a company's ability to pay off its short-term debt as it comes due.

The current ratio is computed by dividing the current assets by the current liabilities. Both assets and liabilities with maturities of 1 year or less are considered to be current for financial statement purposes.

A low current ratio (low relative to industry norms) may indicate that a company faces difficulty in paying its bills. A high value for the current ratio, however, does not necessarily imply greater liquidity. It may suggest that funds are not being efficiently employed within the firm. Excessive amounts of inventory, accounts receivable, or idle cash balances could contribute to a high current ratio.

The current ratio for 2003 and 2002 is calculated as follows:

CURRENT RATIO

2003: (Current assets/current liabilities) = $6,358.1/$3,420.5 = 1.86 times
2002: $5,166.5/$2,955.2 = 1.75 times

The balance sheet shows a large increase in Walgreens's cash account in 2003, and both accounts receivables and inventory rose. At first glance, analysts may think Walgreens has slow-paying accounts or sales slowdowns (because of the inventory rise). But the income statement in Table 5-2 shows that Walgreens had a healthy sales increase of over 13% in 2003.

▲ **The quick ratio**, or **acid-test ratio**, is computed by dividing the sum of cash, marketable securities, and accounts receivable by the current liabilities.

This comparison eliminates inventories from consideration since inventories are among the least liquid of the major current asset categories because they must first be converted to sales.

In general, a ratio of 1.0 indicates a reasonably liquid position in that an immediate liquidation of marketable securities at their current values and the collection of all accounts receivable, plus cash on hand, would be adequate to cover the firm's current liabilities. However, as this ratio declines, the firm must increasingly rely on converting inventories to sales in order to meet current liabilities as they come due. Walgreens's quick ratios for 2003 and 2002 are

QUICK RATIO

2003: (Cash + accounts receivable/current liabilities) = ($1,017.1
+ $1,017.8)/$3,420.5 = 0.59 times

2002: ($449.9 + $954.8)/$2,955.2 = 0.48 times

According to the financial statement data, Walgreens's quick ratio is well below 1.0. As we will soon see, this is not a major cause for concern in the retail drugstore industry. In this industry, we expect lower quick ratios, as much of their current assets are inventory items awaiting sale on their store shelves and warehouses.

When assessing the firm's liquidity position, financial managers also are interested in how trade credit from suppliers, which we call *accounts payable,* is being used and paid for. This analysis requires taking data from a firm's income statement in addition to the balance sheet.

▲ **The average payment period** is computed by dividing the year-end accounts payable amount by the firm's average cost of goods sold per day.

We calculate the average daily cost of goods sold by dividing the income statement's cost of goods sold amount by 365 days in a year. The average payment period is calculated as follows:

AVERAGE PAYMENT PERIOD

$$\frac{\text{Accounts Payable}}{\text{Cost of Goods Sold}/365} = \text{Accounts Payable/Cost of Goods Sold per Day:}$$

$$2003: \frac{\$2,077.0}{\$23,360.1/365} = \$2,077.0/\$64.00 = 32.5 \text{ days}$$

$$2002: \frac{\$1,836.4}{\$20,768.8/365} = \$1,836.4/\$56.90 = 32.3 \text{ days}$$

On average, it takes Walgreens a little over 1 month to pay its suppliers.

Figure 5-1 shows the liquidity ratios for Walgreens compared to the industry averages.

The industry's current and quick ratios rose slightly while the average payment period fell over the 1997–2003 period. Walgreens's current and quick ratios are above those of the industry in 1997 and 1998, but their relative positions reversed in 2000. Between 2000 and 2003, Walgreens's liquidity ratios recovered and moved closer to those of the industry.

Walgreens's average payment period remained constant, about 32 days, during this period. This is about 10 days quicker than the industry until 2000, when

Figure 5-1

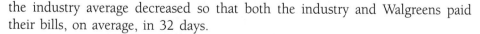

Liquidity ratios.

the industry average decreased so that both the industry and Walgreens paid their bills, on average, in 32 days.

5.3.2 Asset-Management Ratios

Asset-management ratios indicate the extent to which assets are used to support sales. These are sometimes referred to as *activity* or *utilization ratios,* and each ratio in this category relates financial performance on the income statement with items on the balance sheet. Once again, we will be using the information for Walgreens from Tables 5-1 and 5-2.

▲ **The total-assets-turnover ratio** is computed by dividing net sales by the company's total assets.

This ratio indicates how efficiently the firm is utilizing its assets to produce revenues or sales. It is a measure of the dollars of sales generated by $1 of the firm's assets. Generally, the more efficiently assets are used, the higher a firm's profits. The size of the ratio is significantly influenced by characteristics of the industry within which the firm operates.

Capital-intensive electric utilities might have asset turnover ratios as low as 0.33, indicating that they require $3 of investment in assets in order to produce $1 in revenues. In contrast, retail food chains with asset turnovers as high as 10 would require a $0.10 investment in assets to produce $1 in sales. A typical manufacturing firm has an asset turnover of about 1.5. Walgreens's 2002 and 2003 total-assets-turnover ratios are calculated as follows:

TOTAL ASSETS TURNOVER

2003: (Net sales/total assets) = $32,505.4/$11,405.9 = 2.85 times

2002: $28,681.1/$9,878.8 = 2.90 times

Asset utilization was consistent between 2002 and 2003, with each $1 in assets supporting slightly less than $3 in sales.

▲ **The fixed-assets-turnover ratio** is computed by dividing net sales by the fixed assets and indicates the extent to which long-term assets are being used to produce sales.

Similar to the interpretation given to the total asset turnover, the fixed assets turnover represents the dollars of sales generated by each dollar of fixed assets.

Investment in plant and equipment is usually quite expensive. Consequently unused or idle capacity is very costly and often represents a major factor in a firm's poor operating performance. On the other hand, a high (compared to competitors or the industry average) fixed-assets-turnover ratio is not necessarily a favorable sign. It may come about because of efficient use of assets (good), or it may come about because of the firm's use of obsolete equipment with reduced book values because of the effects of accumulated depreciation (poor). Therefore, it is usually necessary for an analyst to do some research to determine the true meaning of the ratio. The fixed-assets-turnover ratio is computed as follows:

FIXED ASSETS TURNOVER

2003: (Net sales/fixed assets) = $32,505.4/$4,940.0 = 6.58 times

2002: $28,681.1/$4,591.4 = 6.25 times

As you can see, Walgreens's fixed assets turnover increased from 6.25 to 6.58 between 2002 and 2003, indicating that sales increased more rapidly than fixed assets. In percentage terms, net fixed assets increased 7.6% [i.e., ($4,940.0 − $4,591.4)/$4,591.4] compared to 13.3% for sales [i.e., ($32,505.4 − $28,681.1)/$28,681.1]. In light of an increase in the fixed asset turnover, it may be surprising that total asset turnover fell slightly from 2002 to 2003. This is an indication that Walgreens used its working capital less efficiently.

▲ **The average collection period** is calculated by taking the year-end accounts receivable divided by the average net sales per day.

This indicates the average number of days that sales are outstanding. In other words, it reports the number of days it takes, on average, to collect credit sales. The average collection period measures the days of financing that a company extends to its customers. Obviously, a shorter average collection period is usually preferred to a longer one.

Another measure that can be used to provide this same information is the receivables turnover.

▲ **The receivables turnover** is computed by dividing annual sales, preferably credit sales, by the year-end accounts receivable.

If the receivables turnover is six, this means the average collection period is about 2 months (12 months divided by the turnover ratio of 6). If the turnover is four times, the firm has an average collection period of about 3 months (12 months divided by the turnover ratio of four). Walgreens's average collection periods for 2003 and 2002 were:

AVERAGE COLLECTION PERIOD

$$\frac{\text{Accounts Receivable}}{\text{Net Sales}/365} = (\text{Accounts Receivable}/\text{Net Sales per Day}):$$

$$2003: \frac{\$1,017.8}{\$32,505.4/365} = \$1,017.8/\$89.06 = 11.43 \text{ days}$$

$$2002: \frac{\$954.8}{\$28,681.1/365} = \$954.8/\$78.58 = 12.15 \text{ days}$$

Walgreens's average collection period fell slightly from 2002 to 2003. Comparing the average collection and payment periods, Walgreens is in a positive situation, as it collects from its customers about 20 days faster than it pays its suppliers. This has positive implications for Walgreens's asset efficiency and for its liquidity.

When comparing these figures to an industry average, an unusually low number of days required to collect sales may indicate that the company uses a rigid internal credit policy that might result in lost sales. On the other hand, a very high average collection period may indicate that the firm has too lax a credit

FOR EXAMPLE

Cash In/Cash Out

The ratios computed on accounts receivable and accounts payable give an analyst a good sense of how well a company is operating. A steady collection of receivables coupled with a steady stream of bill payments shows that the management has both under control.

policy and may be in danger of experiencing a larger number of credit accounts that cannot be collected. Remember that these ratios are only guides, and it is important to monitor trends over time in addition to comparing a company's ratio numbers to the industry averages.

The **inventory-turnover ratio** is computed by dividing the cost of goods sold by the year-end inventory. Here we are seeking to determine how efficiently the amount of inventory is being managed. With inventory management, it is prudent to have an adequate amount to avoid running out of products while avoiding the accumulation of too many products that may necessitate extra financing. The turnover ratio indicates whether the inventory is out of line in relation to the volume of sales when compared against industry norms or when tracked over time for a specific company.

Cost of goods sold is often used to compute this ratio instead of sales in order to remove the impact of profit margins on inventory turnover. Profit margins can vary over time, making it more difficult to interpret the relationship between volume and inventory.

The inventory-turnover ratio is computed as follows:

INVENTORY TURNOVER

2003: (Cost of goods sold/inventory) = $23,360.1/$4,202.7 = 5.56 times

2002: $20,768.8/3,645.2 = 5.70 times

Walgreens's annual inventory turnover decreased slightly from 5.70 in 2002 to 5.56 in 2003.

Inventory management also requires a delicate balance between having too low an inventory turnover, which increases the likelihood of holding obsolete inventory, and too high an inventory turnover, which could lead to stock-outs and lost sales.

When a firm is growing rapidly (or even shrinking rapidly), the use of year-end data may distort the comparison of ratios over time. To avoid such possible distortions, analysts can use the average inventory (beginning inventory balance plus ending inventory balance divided by two) to calculate inventory turnovers for comparison purposes. Likewise, average data for other balance sheet accounts should be used when rapid growth or contraction is taking place for a specific firm.

Figure 5-2 illustrates Walgreens's asset-management ratios in comparison to the industry average between 1997 and 2003. With the exception of the fixed-assets-turnover ratio, Walgreens had more favorable asset-management ratios than the industry.

5.3.3 Financial-Leverage Ratios

To assess the extent to which borrowed money or debt is used to finance assets, analysts use financial-leverage ratios.

▲ **Financial-leverage ratios** indicate the extent to which borrowed or debt funds are used to finance assets.

These ratios are also a good way to assess the ability of the firm to meet its debt payment obligations.

The total-debt-to-total-assets ratio is computed by dividing the total debt or total liabilities of the business by its total assets. This ratio shows the portion of the total assets financed by all creditors and debtors. Taking the relevant information from the Walgreens balance sheet (Table 5-1), the computation is done as follows:

TOTAL DEBT TO TOTAL ASSETS

2003: (Total debt/total assets) = $4,210.2/$11,405.9 = 0.369 = 36.9%

2002: $3,648.6/$9,878.8 = 0.369 = 36.9%

Walgreens's total debt ratio has not changed, meaning that the firm's debt load grew at approximately the same rate as its asset base. Compared to industry averages, a total-debt-to-asset ratio that is relatively high tells the financial manager that the opportunities for securing additional borrowed funds are limited. Additional debt funds may be more costly in terms of the rate of interest that will have to be paid. Lenders will want higher expected returns to compensate for their risk of lending to a firm that has a high proportion of debt to assets.

It is also possible to have too low a ratio of total debt to total assets. This can be quite costly to a corporation. Since interest expenses are deductible for income tax purposes, the government in effect pays a portion of the debt-financing costs.

Sometimes a debt ratio is calculated to show the total debt in relation to the dollars the owners have put in the firm. This is referred to as the *total-debt-to-equity ratio*.

▲ **The total-debt-to-equity ratio** shows a firm's total debt in relation to the total dollar amount owners have invested in the firm.

Figure 5-2

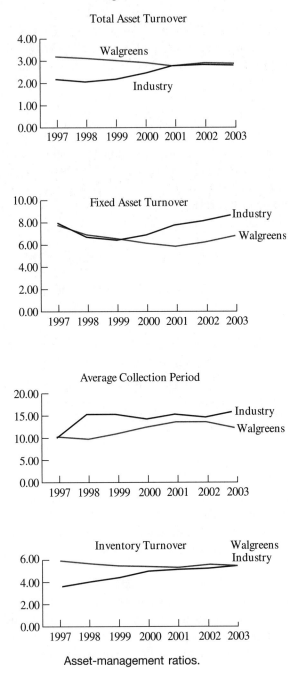

Asset-management ratios.

Walgreens's ratio for 2003 was 0.59 ($4,210.2/$7,195.7) and 0.59 ($3,648.6/$6,230.2) in 2002. This means for every dollar of equity, the firm has borrowed about 59 cents.

▲ **The equity multiplier ratio** provides another way of looking at the firm's debt burden.

The equity multiplier ratio is calculated by dividing total assets by the firm's total equity.

EQUITY MULTIPLIER

2003: (Total assets/total equity) = $11,405.9/$7,195.7 = 1.59

2002: $9,878.8/$6,230.2 = 1.59

Similar to the total-debt-to-total-assets ratio, the equity multiplier was unchanged between 2002 and 2003. Since Walgreens does not have long-term debt outstanding, these modest changes in the debt ratios occur because of changes in short-term debt or Walgreens's other liabilities, such as pension fund or health care benefits for workers.

At first glance, this last ratio appears to have little to do with leverage; it is simply the total assets divided by stockholders' equity. However, recall the concept behind the balance sheet. The concept is simple. In order to acquire assets, a firm must pay for them with either debt (liabilities) or with the owner's capital (shareholder's equity). Therefore the following equation must hold true: Assets = Liabilities + Equity. This is also known as the *accounting identity*. This formula shows that more assets relative to equity suggest greater use of debt. Thus, larger values of the equity multiplier imply a greater use of leverage by the firm. This can also be seen by rewriting the equity multiplier using the accounting identity:

$$(\text{Total assets/equity}) = [(\text{liabilities} + \text{equity})/\text{equity}] = (\text{liabilities/equity}) + 1$$

This is simply one plus the debt-to-equity ratio. Clearly, more reliance on debt results in a larger equity multiplier. While the equity multiplier does not add to the information derived from the other debt ratios, it is useful when financial analysis is conducted using certain financial models.

In addition to calculating debt ratios, the financial manager should be interested in the firm's ability to meet or service its interest and principal repayment obligations on the borrowed funds. This is accomplished through the calculation of interest coverage and fixed-charge-coverage ratios. These ratios make use of information directly from the income statement or from footnotes to a firm's financial statements.

▲ **The interest coverage,** or **times-interest-earned ratio,** is calculated by dividing the firm's operating income or earnings before interest and taxes (EBIT) by the annual interest expense.

Using data from Walgreens's 2000 and 2001 financial statements, we have:

INTEREST COVERAGE

2001: (Earnings before interest & taxes/interest expense) $1,398.3/$3.10 = 451.1 times

2000: $1,224.10/$0.40 = 3,060.3 times

Walgreens's interest coverage ratios are not defined for 2002 and 2003 since interest-paying notes payable and long-term debt are both zero on the firm's balance sheet in 2002 and 2003.

The interest coverage figure indicates the extent to which the operating income or EBIT level could decline before the ability to pay interest obligations would be impeded. Suppose a firm's interest coverage ratio is 5.0. This would mean that Walgreens's operating income could drop to 20%, or one-fifth of its current level, and interest payments still could be met.

In addition to interest payments, there may be other fixed charges, such as rental or lease payments and periodic bond principal repayments, the sinking fund payments that we learn about in Section 14.4.4.

▲ **The fixed-charge-coverage ratio** indicates the ability of a firm to meet its contractual obligations for interest, leases, and debt principal repayments out of its operating income.

Rental or lease payments are deductible on the income statement prior to the payment of income taxes just as is the case with interest expenses. In contrast, a sinking fund payment is a repayment of debt and thus is not a deductible expense for income tax purposes. However, to be consistent with the other data, we must adjust the sinking fund payment to a before-tax basis. We do this by dividing the after-tax amount by one minus the effective tax rate.

While footnotes to Walgreens's balance sheets are not provided, examination of the footnotes in Walgreens's annual reports shows property lease payments of $1,187.0 million in 2003 and $897.9 million in 2002. Walgreens has no interest-bearing liabilities, and it has no sinking fund obligations. We compute the fixed-charge-coverage ratio as follows: First, the numerator in the ratio must reflect earnings before interest, lease payments, and taxes, which we determine by adding the lease payment amount to the operating income or EBIT amount. Second, the denominator needs to show all relevant expenses on a before-tax basis.

Fixed Charge Coverage would be computed as follows:

FIXED-CHARGE COVERAGE

<u>Earnings before Interest, Lease Payments, and Taxes</u>

Interest + lease payments + (sinking fund payment)/(1 – tax rate)

2003: <u>$1,843.3 + $1,187.0</u>   = $3,035.3/$1,187.0 = 2.56

$0 + $1,187.0 + $0

2002: <u>$1,624.2 + $897.9</u>   = $2,522.1/$897.9 = 2.81

$0 + $897.9 + $0

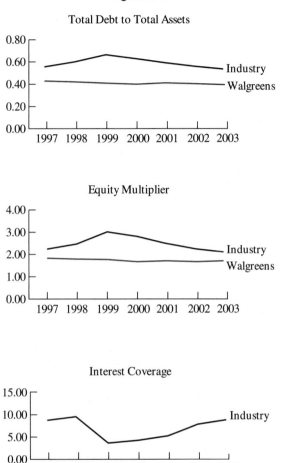

Figure 5-3

Financial-leverage ratios.

This is a marked difference from the interest coverage ratio. Information in Walgreens's annual report to shareholders tells us that the firm usually leases its store space rather than purchasing it. These long-term leases are a substitute for debt financing for Walgreens.

The graphs of Walgreens's financial-leverage ratios in Figure 5-3 show industry debt ratios declining slightly during the 1997–2003 time period. The deterioration in the industry's interest coverage, from about 9 in 1998 to about 3 in 2000, was a concern. Since the industry debt load rose only slightly until 2000, the decline in interest coverage was due to falling earnings. Since then, however, the industry's interest coverage ratio recovered.

In contrast to the retail drug store industry, Walgreens's debt ratio declined slightly while its interest-coverage ratio was either at extremely high levels or was undefined because of the absence of interest-bearing debt (thus, we don't show Walgreens's interest-coverage ratio in Figure 5-3).

From looking at Walgreens, we can come to three important conclusions. First, not all liabilities are contractual debt. Walgreens has a debt-to-assets ratio of about 40% but has no interest-bearing short-term (notes payable) or long-term (long-term debt) on its balance sheet. Second, not all liabilities require interest to be paid. Again, Walgreens has a debt ratio of 40% but virtually no interest payments. Third, to get a truer perspective of a company's financial situation, all contractual fixed charges, including interest, lease payments, and sinking fund payments, should be examined. This requires some reading of the footnotes and other information in the firm's financial statements. Walgreens's sky-high interest coverage ratio is brought back to earth when fixed charges are considered and a fixed charge-coverage ratio is computed.

5.3.4 Profitability Ratios

To determine a firm's ability to generate returns on its sales, assets, and equity, analysts use profitability ratios. **Profitability ratios** indicate the firm's ability to generate returns on its sales, assets, and equity.

Two basic profit margin ratios are important to the financial manager, the operating profit margin and the net profit margin.

▲ **The operating profit margin** is calculated on the firm's earnings before interest and taxes divided by net sales.

This ratio indicates the firm's ability to control operating expenses relative to sales. Table 5-2 contains income statement information for Walgreens and provides the necessary information for determining the operating profit margin.

OPERATING PROFIT MARGIN

2003: (Earnings before interest & taxes/net sales) = $1,848.3/$32,505.4
= 0.0569 = 5.69%

2002: $1,624.2/$28,681.1 = 0.0566 = 5.66%

These results indicate that Walgreens was able to slightly improve its operating profitability from 2002 to 2003. Whether it was because of higher selling prices or lower costs, operating profit (EBIT) rose about 13.8% on a sales increase of about 13.3%.

▲ **The net profit margin,** a widely used measure of a company's profitability, is calculated as the firm's net income after taxes divided by net sales.

In addition to considering operating expenses, this ratio also indicates the ability to earn a return after meeting interest and tax obligations. Walgreens's net profit margin shows a slight improvement in 2003 over 2002:

NET PROFIT MARGIN

2003: (Net income/net sales) = $1,175.7/$32,505.4 = 0.0362 = 3.62%

2002: $1,019.2/$28,681.1 = 0.0355 = 3.55%

Three basic rates-of-return measures on assets and equity are important to the financial manager.

▲ **The operating return on assets** is computed as the earnings before interest and taxes divided by total assets.

Notice that this ratio focuses on the firm's operating performance and ignores how the firm is financed and taxed. Relevant data for Walgreens must be taken from both the balance sheets and the income statement:

OPERATING RETURN ON ASSETS

2003: (Earnings before interest & taxes/total assets) = $1,848.3/$11,405.9
= 0.162 = 16.2%

2002: $1,624.2/$9,878.8 = 0.164 = 16.4%

Walgreens's operating return on assets was consistent in these 2 years.

▲ **The net return on total assets,** commonly referred to as the *return on total assets,* is measured as the firm's net income divided by total assets.

Here we measure the return on investment in assets after a firm has covered its operating expenses, interest costs, and tax obligations. Walgreens's return on total assets remained constant in 2002 and 2003:

RETURN ON TOTAL ASSETS

2003: (Net income/total assets) = $1,175.7/$11,405.9 = 0.103 = 10.3%

2002: $1,019.2/$9,878.8 = 0.103 = 10.3%

Since Walgreens leases many of its stores, this not only reduces its financing needs but also reduces its level of fixed and total assets. In turn, this can help to increase asset-based profitability ratios, such as the return on total assets, if indeed the firm is profitable.

A final profitability ratio is the return on equity.

▲ **The return on equity** measures the return that shareholders earned on their equity invested in the firm.

The return on equity is measured as the firm's net income divided by stock-holders' equity. This ratio reflects the fact that a portion of a firm's total assets

> **FOR EXAMPLE**
>
> **Cost Efficiency**
>
> Based on Figure 5-4, you can see that as of 2003, Walgreens is more cost-efficient (as seen in its higher operating and net profit margins) and generates more profit from its asset and equity base (as seen in the operating return on assets, return on total assets, and return on equity) than the retail drugstore industry as a whole.

are financed with borrowed funds. As with the return on assets, Walgreens's return on equity remained virtually the same from 2002 to 2003:

RETURN ON EQUITY

2003: (Net income/common equity) = $1,175.7/$7,195.7 = 0.163 = 16.3\%

2002: $1,019.2/$6,230.2 = 0.164 = 16.4\%

Figure 5-4 indicates that industry profitability ratios were below those of Walgreens during 1997–2003. Industry profitability fell sharply in 1999 and 2000 while Walgreens was able to maintain its profitability.

5.3.5 Market-Value Ratios

Market-value ratios indicate the willingness of investors to value a firm in the marketplace relative to financial statement values.

A firm's profitability, risk, quality of management, and many other factors are reflected in its stock and security prices by the efficient financial markets. Financial statements are historical in nature, but the financial markets look to the future.

We know that stock prices seem to reflect much of the known information about a company and are fairly good indicators of a company's true value. Hence, market-value ratios indicate the market's assessment of the value of the firm's securities.

▲ **The price/earnings ratio,** or **P/E ratio,** is simply the market price of the firm's common stock divided by its annual earnings per share.

Sometimes called the *earnings multiple,* the P/E ratio shows how much investors are willing to pay for each dollar of the firm's earnings per share. Earnings per share come from the income statement, so it is sensitive to the many factors that affect net income. Though earnings per share cannot reflect the value of the firm's patents or assets, human resources, culture, quality of management, or its risk, stock prices can and do reflect all these factors.

Comparing a firm's P/E relative to that of the stock market as a whole, or the firm's competitors, indicates the market's perceptions of the true value of the company.

Figure 5-4

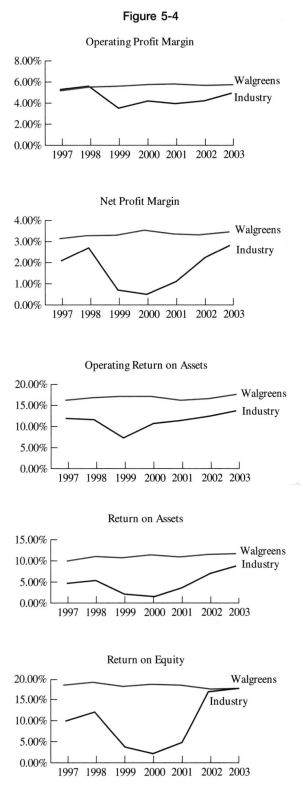

Profitability ratios.

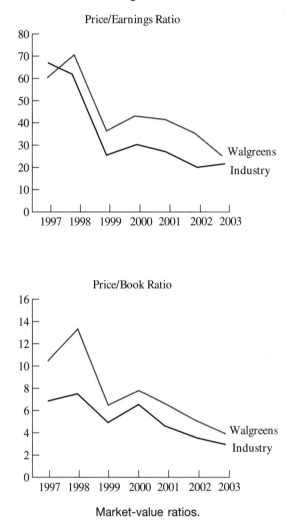

Figure 5-5

Price/Earnings Ratio

Price/Book Ratio

Market-value ratios.

▲ **The price-to-book-value ratio** measures the market's value of the firm relative to balance sheet equity.

The book value of equity is simply the difference between the book values of assets and liabilities appearing on the balance sheet. The price-to-book-value ratio is the market price per share divided by the book value of equity per share. A higher ratio suggests that investors are more optimistic about the market value of a firm's assets, its intangible assets, and its managers' abilities.

Figure 5-5 shows levels and trends in the P/E ratio and price/book ratio for Walgreens and the retail drugstore industry. Just as our analysis of financial statement ratios pointed out, Walgreens's higher profitability and consistency in its ratios over time has translated into higher relative market valuations.

The market is optimistic in its valuation of Walgreens's future prospects. Both the earnings multiple and price/book ratios have fallen for Walgreens and the industry, but Walgreens's ratios continue to exceed those of the industry.

Financial managers and analysts often talk about the quality of a firm's earnings or the quality of its balance sheet. This has nothing to do with the size of a company's earnings or assets or who audited the financial statements. Quality financial statements are those that accurately reflect the firm's true economic condition. In other words, accounting methods were not used to inflate its earnings or assets to make the firm look stronger than it really is. Therefore, based on a quality income statement, the company's sales revenues are likely to be repeated in the future. Earnings are not affected by one-time charges. A quality balance sheet will represent inventory that is marketable, not out of fashion or technologically obsolete. It will represent limited debt, indicating the firm could easily borrow money should the need arise. The firm's assets will have market values that exceed their accounting book values; in other words, the firm's assets will not be inflated by intangible assets such as "goodwill" or "patents."

All else constant, a firm with higher-quality financial statements will have higher market-value ratios. This occurs because the market will recognize and reward the economic reality of a firm's earnings and assets that are not temporarily bloated by accounting gimmicks.

Attempts to play accounting tricks will affect the firm's ratios. Overstating existing inventory can have the effect of making current cost of goods sold appear lower, thus inflating profits. Booking revenue in advance of true sales to customers will inflate both sales and profits. The effect of such actions will be to increase profitability and asset-management ratios. Unfortunately, watching for accounting tricks or outright fraud is necessary for investors, as problems with companies in different industries such as telecommunications equipment (Lucent), dot-com firms (many), and energy trading (Enron) have shown in recent years.

5.3.6 Summing up Ratios

Here's what we've learned about Walgreens by computing their ratios and comparing them to the industry averages. The liquidity ratios show consistency over time, but the favorable gap between Walgreens and its industry-average ratios has narrowed or been reversed. This is also true of the asset-management ratios. Walgreens's historical advantages have disappeared.

Should Walgreens need to raise money quickly, it should be able to issue debt, as Walgreens's debt ratios are lower than the industry averages (debt to assets, equity multiplier) and its interest coverage. But a truer picture would include fixed charges such as lease payments in the analysis. Walgreens's fixed-charge-coverage ratio shows that the firm does have an income cushion before it would have trouble meeting its stated lease payments.

Part of Walgreens's success can be traced to good control and, until recently, superior asset-management. The receivables collection period is shorter than average as well. The combination of good cost control and efficient asset management has resulted in good profitability compared to the industry averages. The stock market has recognized Walgreens's abilities, and Walgreens's market-value ratios are above those of the industry.

SELF-CHECK

- **What do liquidity ratios measure?**
- **Name three liquidity ratios and describe what they tell about a firm.**
- **What do asset-management ratios measure?**
- **List three asset-management ratios and describe what they tell analysts about a firm.**
- **What do financial-leverage ratios tell analysts about a firm?**
- **What do profitability ratios measure?**

5.4 Du Pont Method of Ratio Analysis

How does a supermarket generate profits? In general, supermarkets have very low profit margins. Many of its goods are sold for pennies above cost. Profits are generated by rapid turnover. The shelves are restocked daily with new items to take the place of items that were purchased. Thus, supermarkets generally have high asset-turnover ratios.

Jewelry stores generate their profits differently. They typically have very high profit margins but low turnover. Jewelry items may sit on the shelf for months at a time until they are sold.

This indicates there are two basic methods by which a firm can generate a return on its assets. It can offer low prices and low profit margins seeking high sales volumes on commodity products, like a supermarket, or it can sell its quality or differentiated goods at high prices and rely mainly on high profit margins to generate returns on low sales, like a jewelry store.

The return on total-assets ratio can be used to examine this relationship and to determine how a given firm generates profits. The return on assets can be broken into two components. It equals the product of the profit margin and total asset turnover ratio:

Return on total assets = profit margin × total asset turnover

(Net income/assets) = (net income/sales) × (sales/total assets)

A supermarket's profit margin may be 1%, but its total asset turnover may be 10. This would give it a return on total assets of 1% × 10 or 10%. A jewelry store may have a 25% profit margin and have a very low asset turnover of 0.40, also giving it a return on total assets of 10% (25% × 0.40). Year-to-year variations in a firm's return on total assets can be explained by changes in its profit margin, total asset turnover, or both.

Like the return on total assets, return on equity can be broken down into component parts to tell us why the level of return changes from year to year or why two firms' returns on equity differ. The return on equity is identical to return on total assets multiplied by the equity multiplier:

$$(\text{Net income/equity}) = (\text{net income/total assets}) \times (\text{total assets/equity})$$

We just saw how the return on total assets is itself comprised of two other ratios, so return on equity can be expanded to

$$\text{Return on equity} = \text{profit margin} \times \text{asset turnover} \times \text{equity multiplier}$$
$$(\text{Net income/equity}) = (\text{net income/sales}) \times (\text{sales/total assets})$$
$$\times (\text{total assets/equity})$$

Thus, a firm's return on equity may differ from one year to the next, or from a competitor's, as a result of differences in profit margin, asset turnover, or leverage. Unlike the other measures of profitability, return on equity directly reflects a firm's use of leverage or debt. If a firm uses relatively more liabilities to finance assets, the equity multiplier will rise, and, holding other factors constant, the firm's return on equity will increase. This leveraging of a firm's return on equity does not imply greater operating efficiency, only a greater use of debt financing.

This technique of breaking return on total assets, and return on equity into their component parts is called Du Pont analysis, named after the company that popularized it.

▲ **The Du Pont analysis** is the technique of breaking down return on total assets and return on equity into their component parts.

Figure 5-6 illustrates how Du Pont analysis can break return on equity and return on total assets into different components (profit margin, total asset turnover, and equity multiplier) and how these components can then be broken into their constituent parts for analysis. Therefore, an indication that a firm's return on equity has increased as a result of higher turnover can lead to study of the turnover ratio, using data from several years, to determine if the increase has resulted from higher sales volume, better management of assets, or some combination of the two.

Table 5-3 illustrates the use of Du Pont analysis to explain the changes in Walgreens's return on equity during 2000–2003. Between 2000 and 2001, the main reason for the decrease in Walgreens's return on equity was a decrease in

> ## FOR EXAMPLE
>
> ### General Motors Fails to Break Even
>
> In 2005, the automaker General Motors failed to break even. In fact, General Motors lost $8.6 billion. The losses were due to lower market share, higher labor costs, and higher health care costs. Due to the poor performance, General Motors was forced to lay off tens of thousands of workers worldwide and decrease benefits. General Motors hopes to break even or post a small profit in 2006.

This equals:

$$\frac{\$1,000}{\$4.00}$$

Dividing $1,000 by $4.00 gives us 250 units.

Walgreens must sell 250 units of the new product in order to break even. The break-even point occurs when total revenues equal total costs. The break-even point in sales dollars is equal to the selling price per unit times the break-even point in units. In our example, we have $10 times 250 units or $2,500.

Since a company's sales revenues are rarely constant, the variability of sales or revenues over time indicates a basic operating business risk that must be considered when developing financial plans. In addition, changes in the amount of income shown on the income statement are affected by both changes in sales and the use of fixed versus variable costs.

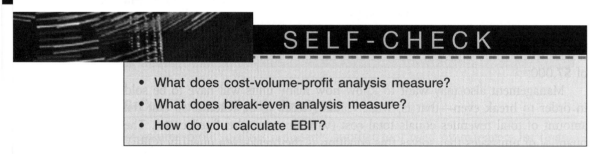

SELF-CHECK

- What does cost-volume-profit analysis measure?
- What does break-even analysis measure?
- How do you calculate EBIT?

SUMMARY

Good financial planning is essential to the success of any business. It requires an understanding of the financial statements and the ability to analyze them and interpret the ratios. As you have seen in this chapter, the ratios are helpful tools that can pinpoint problem areas that require deeper examination of the business entity.

KEY TERMS

Asset-management ratios	Measure that indicates the extent to which assets are used to support sales.
Average collection period	Measure that indicates how long it takes a company to collect its accounts receivables. It is calculated by taking the year-end accounts receivable divided by the average net sales per day.
Average payment period	Measure that includes all of a company's financial obligations and how long, in terms of days, it will take the company to fulfill their obligations. It is computed by dividing the year-end accounts payable amount by the firm's average cost of goods sold per day.
Break-even analysis	Financial technique used to estimate how many units of product must be sold in order for the firm to break even or have a zero profit.
Cost-volume-profit analysis	Financial technique used by managers for financial planning to estimate the firm's operating profits at different levels of unit sales.
Cross-section analysis	Financial technique that uses ratios to compare different companies at the same point in time.
Current ratio	Measure of a company's ability to pay off its short-term debt as it comes due.
Du Pont analysis	The technique of breaking down return on total assets and return on equity into their component parts.
Equity multiplier ratio	Measure of a company's financial leverage. Measure is determined by dividing total assets by total stockholders' equity. The higher the rate, the more the company is using debt to finance its asset base.
Financial-leverage ratios	Measure that indicates the extent to which borrowed or debt funds are used to finance assets.
Fixed-assets-turnover ratio	Measure of how efficiently a company uses its fixed assets to generate sales. It is computed by dividing net sales by the fixed assets.
Fixed-charge-coverage ratio	Measure that indicates the ability of a firm to meet its contractual obligations for interest, leases, and debt principal repayments out of its operating income.

Industry-comparative analysis Financial technique used to compare a firm's ratios against average ratios for other companies in the same industry.

Interest coverage Measures the ability of the firm to service all debts. It is calculated by dividing the firm's operating income or earnings before interest and taxes (EBIT) by the annual interest expense. It is commonly referred to as *times-interest-earned ratio*.

Inventory-turnover ratio Measures the number of times in a year that a company replaces its inventory. It is computed by dividing the cost of goods sold by total inventory.

Liquidity ratios Measures that indicate the ability to meet short-term obligations to creditors as they mature or come due.

Market-value ratios Measure that indicates the willingness of investors to value a firm in the marketplace relative to financial statement values.

Net profit margin A widely used measure of a company's profitability; it is calculated as the firm's net income after taxes divided by net sales.

Net return on total assets Firm's net income divided by total assets. Commonly referred to as the *return on total assets*.

Net working capital Measure of a firm's liquidity. The measure is the firm's current assets minus current liabilities.

Operating profit margin Indicates the profits of the company before interest and taxes are deducted from a firm's operations. It is calculated on the firm's earnings before interest and taxes divided by net sales.

Operating return on assets Earnings before interest and taxes divided by total assets.

Price/earnings ratio The market price of the firm's common stock divided by its annual earnings per share. Also referred to as the *P/E ratio*.

Price-to-book-value ratio Measures the market's value of the firm relative to balance sheet equity.

Profitability ratios Measure that indicates the firm's ability to generate returns on its sales, assets, and equity.

Quick ratio	Used to gauge a firm's liquidity. The measure is computed by dividing the sum of cash, marketable securities, and accounts receivable by the current liabilities. Also referred to as the *acid-test ratio*.
Ratio analysis	Financial technique that involves dividing various financial statement numbers into one another.
Receivables turnover	Measure of how effectively a firm extends credit and collects debts. It is computed by dividing annual sales, preferably credit sales, by the year-end accounts receivable.
Return on equity	Measures the return that shareholders earned on their equity invested in the firm.
Total-assets-turnover ratio	Measure of how efficiently a company uses its assets to generate sales. Measure that is computed by dividing net sales by the company's total assets.
Total-debt-to-equity ratio	Measure that shows a firm's total debt in relation to the total dollar amount owners have invested in the firm.
Trend analysis	Measure that uses ratios to evaluate a firm's performance over time. Also referred to as *time-series analysis*.

ASSESS YOUR UNDERSTANDING

Go to www.wiley.com/college/Melicher to evaluate your knowledge of the basics of financial statement analysis.
Measure your learning by comparing pre-test and post-test results.

Summary Questions

1. It would be possible for financial statement analysis to affect nonfinance operations of a firm. True or false?
2. Ratio analysis is a financial technique that involves dividing various financial statements numbers into one another. True or false?
3. Cross-sectional analysis is used to evaluate a firm's performance over time. True or false?
4. Ratios standardize balance sheet and income statement numbers, thus minimizing the effect of firm size. True or false?
5. Asset management ratios indicate the ability to meet short-term obligations to creditors as they come due. True or false?
6. Financial-leverage ratios indicate the extent to which borrowed funds are used to finance assets. True or false?
7. The market-value ratios indicate the willingness of investors to value a firm in the marketplace relative to financial statement values. True or false?
8. The net profit margin is an example of a market-value ratio. True or false?
9. Liquidity ratios indicate the extent to which assets are used to support sales. True or false?
10. The ability of a firm to meet its short-term debt obligations as they come due is indicated by which of the following ratios?
    (a) Liquidity ratios
    (b) Asset-utilization ratios
    (c) Financial-leverage ratios
    (d) Profitability ratios
11. The extent to which assets are used to support sales is indicated by which of the following ratios?
    (a) Liquidity ratios
    (b) Asset-utilization ratios
    (c) Financial-leverage ratios
    (d) Profitability ratios

12. Which item is not included in the calculation for both the quick ratio and the current ratio?

    (a) Accounts receivable

    (b) Current assets

    (c) Inventories

    (d) Current liabilities

13. Management of current assets does not involve which one of the following areas?

    (a) Cash and marketable securities

    (b) Accounts receivable

    (c) Inventory

    (d) Plant and equipment

14. The equity multiplier is calculated as

    (a) total assets divided by owners' equity.

    (b) net income divided by owners' equity.

    (c) net income divided by total assets.

    (d) net sales divided by total assets.

15. The extent to which assets are financed by borrowed funds and other liabilities is indicated by

    (a) liquidity ratios.

    (b) asset-utilization ratios.

    (c) financial-leverage ratios.

    (d) profitability ratios.

16. The price/earnings ratio (P/E) is calculated as

    (a) stock price divided by earnings per share.

    (b) stock price times earnings per share.

    (c) earnings per share divided by stock price.

    (d) stock price divided by the difference between earnings per share and cash dividends per share.

17. Financial analysis using ratios can assist managers in the firm's long-term financial-planning process. True or false?

18. The method of calculating return on assets, which highlights the importance of sales, profit margin, and asset turnover, is known as

    (a) the Gordon model.

    (b) cost-volume profit analysis.

    (c) Du Pont analysis.

    (d) break-even analysis.

19. In employing Du Pont analysis, the user would break the return on total assets into the profit margin, total asset turnover, and an equity multiplier. True or false?

20. Cost-volume-profit analysis can be used to estimate the firm's operating profits at different levels of

    (a) dollar sales.

    (b) unit sales.

    (c) dollar fixed costs.

    (d) unit variable costs.

21. The break-even quantity is inversely related to the level of a firm's variable costs. True or false?

Review Questions

1. List some reasons why financial statement analysis is conducted. Identify some of the participants that analyze firms' financial statements.

2. What is ratio analysis? Also, briefly describe the three basic categories or ways that ratio analysis is used.

3. Identify the types of ratios that are used to analyze a firm's financial performance based on its income statements and balance sheets. Which type or category of ratios relates stock market information to financial statement items?

4. What do liquidity ratios indicate? Identify some basic liquidity ratios.

5. What do asset-management ratios indicate? Identify some basic asset-management ratios.

6. What do financial-leverage ratios indicate? Identify some measures of financial leverage.

7. What do profitability ratios indicate? Identify some measures of profitability.

8. What do market-value ratios indicate? Identify some market-value ratios.

9. Describe the Du Pont method or system of ratio analysis. What are the two major components of the system? How is the system related to both the balance sheet and the income statement?

10. How is the process of financial planning used to estimate asset investment requirements?

11. What is cost-volume-profit analysis? How can it be used by a firm?

Applying This Chapter

1. Find the average payment period if accounts payable is $20,000, cost of goods sold is $200,000, and sales are $500,000.

2. Find the net profit if margin earnings before interest and taxes is $20,000, net income is $10,000, sales are $50,000, and total assets are $100,000.

3. What would be the return on total assets of a firm if net income is $50,000, total sales are $100,000, and total assets are $175,000?

4. If the total asset turnover of a firm is 1.5, total assets are $500,000, and net income is $50,000, what is the profit margin?

5. Assume a firm is developing, manufacturing, and selling a basic software package at $500 per copy. Raw materials and direct labor total $200 per copy. Fixed costs are $250,000. If the firm sells 5,000 units per year, what will be the operating profit?

6. Assume a firm is developing, manufacturing, and selling a basic software package at $300 per copy. Raw material and direct labor total $100 per unit. Fixed costs are $150,000. If unit sales are 3,000 per year, what will be the break-even point in units?

7. What is the current ratio of a firm with current assets of $300,000, current liabilities of $100,000, and inventory of $100,000?

8. What is the quick ratio of a firm with current assets of $300,000, current liabilities of $100,000 and inventory of $100,000?

9. If a firm's sales are $2,000,000, its cost of goods sold is $1,500,000, and its total assets are $1,000,000, what is total asset turnover?

10. If a firm's sales are $2,000,000, its cost of goods sold is $1,500,000, and its fixed assets are $1,000,000, what is fixed asset turnover?

11. If a firm's inventories on hand are $200,000, its cost of goods sold is $600,000, and its sales are $800,000, what is the inventory turnover using cost of goods sold?

12. If a firm has an after-tax profit margin of 5%, an asset turnover of 2.5 times, and no debt, what is the return on equity?

13. Given the following financial data—net income/sales = 6%; sales/total assets = 3.5; debt/total assets = 30%—what is the return on total assets?

14. What is the total asset turnover of a firm with total liabilities and owners' equity of $100,000 and net sales of $50,000?

15. If a firm has a receivables turnover of 12, on average, which of the following would be the firm's average collection period?

16. If a firm has sales of $100, total expenses (including interest and taxes) of $50, has a stock that is selling at $50 per share and has 10 share of stock outstanding, what is the firm's P/E ratio?

YOU TRY IT

Good Managers

Part of being a good manager is managing both people and assets well, and doing so often results in larger profits for a company. Review the companies listed on the New York Stock Exchange; based on the price of their stock, choose the companies that you think are managing assets and people well.

Average Inventory Calculation

Using the Walgreens's balance sheets that appear in this chapter, take the beginning inventory figure plus the ending inventory figure divided by two and use the result to calculate the inventory turnover ratio and see how it compares to the figures in the sample.

Leases versus Long-Term Debt

Consider whether long-term debt on buildings is a better option than leasing property for business operations. Long-term debt on a building results in interest charges, and the building must be maintained. Major repairs on leased properties are usually paid for by the owner, and the rental payments are a deductible business expense.

Stock Quotes for Walgreens's Competitors

Review the stock quotes in the *Wall Street Journal* for other companies in the retail drug industry like Osco and CVS and see which companies currently have the highest price per share of stock.

6

THE BASICS OF CAPITAL BUDGETING
Increasing Shareholder Wealth

Starting Point

Go to www.wiley.com/college/Melicher to assess your knowledge of the basics of capital budgeting.
Determine where you need to concentrate your effort.

What You'll Learn in This Chapter

▲ How the capital budgeting process is related to a firm's mission and strategies
▲ Five steps in the capital budgeting process
▲ The methods or techniques used to make proper capital budgeting decisions
▲ How a company determines its missions, objectives, goals, and strategies (MOGS)

After Studying This Chapter, You'll Be Able To

▲ Choose and evaluate projects that will enhance a firm's competitive advantage
▲ Analyze a business investment plan using the five stages of capital budgeting
▲ Calculate the market value and the net benefit of an investment
▲ Calculate the profitability index of a company
▲ Calculate the payback period for a company
▲ Use a company's missions, objectives, goals, and strategies (MOGS) to guide a company's decisions on what projects to pursue

Goals and Objectives

▲ Perform each of the four methods of capital budgeting to evaluate capital investment decisions
▲ Evaluate the relationship between shareholder wealth and the capital budgeting process
▲ Compare and contrast market value with net benefit of an investment
▲ Compare and contrast the cost of capital and the net present value of a project
▲ Compose the internal rate of return for a project

If future strategic moves by competitors are expected to damage or eliminate a firm's competitive advantage, the firm's base case cash flow forecast should reflect this situation. A project's incremental cash flows would then reflect expected changes from this declining trend.

For example, a firm such as Intel must consider competitors' responses when it invests in research and development to develop new computer chips. Intel's base case must include the impact on its sales if it does not develop the next generation of computer chips first. In the fast-moving technology market, being second to market could mean billions of lost sales. Intel has poured billions in factory improvement and expansion projects to increase its production capacity. The purpose: to maintain and increase Intel's competitive advantage over other chip manufacturers and to sustain cash flow growth. Greater capacity means greater economies of scale, lower costs, and better competitive position in the computer chip market. With forecasted chip demand experiencing double-digit growth rates each year, Intel needs additional capacity just to maintain its current market share of the chip market.

7.2.2 Irrelevant Cash Flows

There are also irrelevant cash flows that should be excluded from the stand-alone estimate. These include sunk costs and financing costs. A **sunk cost** is a project-related expense that does not depend on whether or not the project is undertaken.

For example, assume a firm commissioned and paid for a feasibility study for a project last year. The funds for the study are already spent; they represent a sunk cost. The study's cost is not an incremental cash flow, as it is not affected by the firm's future decision to either pursue or abandon the project. Therefore, the cost must be excluded from the project's cash flow estimates.

Although it may seem important to account for financing cash flows such as interest and loan repayments, there is a very good reason for excluding them from cash flow estimates. Capital budgeting analysis techniques explicitly consider the costs of financing a project when the analysis discounts project cash flows, so these costs should not be considered again.

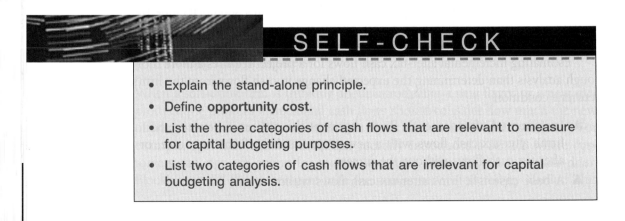

SELF-CHECK

- Explain the stand-alone principle.
- Define **opportunity cost**.
- List the three categories of cash flows that are relevant to measure for capital budgeting purposes.
- List two categories of cash flows that are irrelevant for capital budgeting analysis.

7.3 Approaches to Estimating Project Cash Flows

As an initial step of the financial analysis of a capital budgeting proposal, we should first construct year-by-year projected balance sheets and income statements for the project. Analysis of these forecasted statements tell us what the expected cash flows from the project will be. Changes over time in the project's working capital requirements or investment needs will represent cash inflows or outflows from the project. Similarly, the net income and non-cash expenses from the project are part of the project's periodic cash flows, too.

We learn in Chapter 4 that one of the financial statements that must be issued by public firms is the statement of cash flows. This section uses the format of the statement of cash flows to identify the periodic cash flows of a capital budgeting project.

As Section 4.7 notes, a firm's statement of cash flows has three sections. In the first section, cash flows from operations, reports on cash generated by the firm's day-to-day manufacturing and marketing activities. In the second section, cash flows from investments and usually involves data for investments in subsidiaries or the firm's plant and equipment. The third section lists the firm's financing cash flows, including sales and purchases of debt as well as dividend payments.

Using this format for a capital budgeting project, cash flows from operations summarize the sources of a project's operating cash flows. Cash flows from investing activities report a firm's fixed asset investments in the capital budgeting project. As section 7.2.2 explains, cash flows from financing activities are excluded from a project's cash flow analysis since their impact is measured in the discount rate or cost of capital used to discount a project's cash flow.

Table 7-1 summarizes the similarities between company and project cash flow statements.

7.3.1 Cash Flow from Operations

Cash flow from operations equals

$$\text{Net income} + \text{Depreciation} + \text{Current/asset/liability sources}$$
$$- \text{Current asset/liability uses}$$

A daily, weekly, or monthly project income statement can estimate the net income from a project, as shown in the following sample:

Project sales	(Generally a cash inflow)
−Project costs	(Generally a cash outflow)
−Depreciation	(A noncash expense)
EBIT = EBT	(Earnings before interest and taxes, which also equals earnings before taxes as financing costs are ignored in cash flow analysis)
−Taxes	(A cash outflow)
Net income	

Table 7-1: Firm versus Project Statement of Cash Flows

The Firm's Cash Flow Statement	A Project's Cash Flow Statement
Cash Flow from Operations	**Cash Flow from Operations**
Net Income	Net Income
+ Depreciation	+ Depreciation
+ Current asset/liability sources	+ Current asset/liability sources
− Current asset/liability uses	− Current asset/liability uses
Cash Flow from Investment Activities	**Cash Flow from Investment Activities**
− Change in gross fixed assets	− Funds invested in the project
− Change in investments	
Cash Flow from Financing Activities	**Cash Flow from Financing Activities**
− Dividends paid	Not applicable
+ Net new bond issues	
+ Net new stock issues	

All sales revenues may not be cash inflows. Some revenues may increase accounts receivable rather than cash. At the same time, not all costs reflect cash outflows; some may represent changes in accounts payable. Therefore, a project's operating cash flows are computed as

Cash flow from operations = net income + depreciation-change in net working capital

In most cases, in capital budgeting analysis, operating cash flow is calculated in part by using the traditional net working capital measure of current assets minus current liabilities. This occurs since typically a project's cash flows are immediately returned to the firm. The project's balance sheet cash account always will be zero. Thus, current sources and current uses can be summarized in the period-by-period change in a project's net working capital.

This means that a net cash inflow reduces net working capital; subtracting this negative change, in the preceding equation, results in an addition to operating cash flows. To illustrate this, assume that current assets are $700 and current liabilities are $400, so net working capital is $300. Customers pay $200 of their accounts receivable, thus decreasing current assets to $500 and net working capital to $100 ($500 − $400). Thus, a decrease in net working capital results from a net source or inflow of funds. Conversely, suppose with $700 in current assets and $400 in current liabilities we pay some bills so accounts payable falls by $150; the new value for net working capital will be $700 − $250 = $450. The change in net working capital is +$150. This illustrates that an increase in net working capital reflects a net use or outflow of funds, which reduces cash flows from operations.

7.3.2 Cash Flow from Investment Activities

Cash flow from investment activities will record the company's period-by-period investments in the capital project. In the typical capital budgeting project, cash flows from investments result from spending on fixed assets, namely the plant and equipment necessary to pursue the new project. Cash flow from investments is usually negative at the beginning of a project as the firm spends cash to acquire, build, modify, or replace assets. The cash flow from investments may be positive at the end of a project if it sells assets for salvage value.

7.3.3 Cash Flow from Financing Activities

Capital budgeting analysis excludes cash flows from financing activities. As section 5.2.2 discusses, capital budgeting analysis does account for relevant after-tax financing costs in the discount rate (interest rate being charged on the financing) used to discount estimated cash flows to the present. Here's an example of how that works.

Suppose you are considering opening a campus ice cream shop. Your initial investment in depreciating assets will be $10,000, and your initial investment in net working capital will be $3,500. This amount will include such inventory items as cones, ice cream, and toppings. You forecast no future changes in net working capital. You will depreciate the fixed assets on a straight-line basis over 4 years.

The shop's net income is estimated to be $0, $1,500, $2,500, and $4,000 over each of the next 4 years. At the end of 4 years, you expect to graduate with a bachelor's degree and some entrepreneurial work experience and will sell your ice cream shop to another student. You hope to be able to sell the business for $12,000. For simplicity, we'll ignore any tax consequences from the sale. What are the cash flows from this project?

It is sometimes easier to estimate cash flows if you construct a table or use a spreadsheet, such as the one shown on next page. It summarizes, by year and by cash flow category, the project's incremental after-tax cash flows. At year 0, the only expected cash flows are a $10,000 investment in fixed assets and a $3,500 outflow for net working capital. Depreciating the fixed assets of $10,000 over 4 years using the straight-line method results in a depreciation expense of $2,500 per year.

Year 1 net income is expected to be $0, along with the $2,500 depreciation expense and no change in net working capital. Year 1's operating cash flow is estimated at $2,500. Since you anticipate no investing cash flows, Year 1's cash flow should be $2,500.

The cash flows for years 2, 3, and 4 are computed in the same way. In year 4, the operating cash flows are supplemented by an investing cash flow of $12,000 for the sale of the business. Therefore, year 4's total cash flows total $18,500: $4,000 from net income, $2,500 from depreciation, and $12,000 from the sale of the business.

	Operating Cash Flows			Investing Cash Flows		
Year	Net Income	+ Depreciation	− Change in NWC	Change in Fixed Assets	=	Total Cash Flow
0	$0	$0	$−3,500	$−10,000		$−13,500
1	0	2,500	0	0		2,500
2	1,500	2,500	0	0		4,000
3	2,500	2,500	0	0		5,000
4	4,000	2,500	0	12,000		18,500

If 12% is your required rate of return, the net present value of this financial is slightly under $5,000. So, your personal wealth should rise from opening the ice cream shop.

Of course, in reality there would be tax consequences from selling the shop, and if the depreciation was actually used as a deduction on your personal tax return, it could result in a tax liability when the business was sold.

7.3.4 Depreciation as a Tax Shield

The term TDep, the tax rate multiplied by the depreciation expense, is called the *depreciation tax shield*. The **depreciation tax shield** represents the tax savings due to depreciation of fixed assets. It equals the amount of the depreciation expense multiplied by the firm's tax rate.

It represents the tax savings a company receives from its noncash depreciation expense. With a 34% tax rate, a depreciation expense of $1,000 saves a company $340 in income tax.

Despite political claims that tax incentives are needed to boost capital spending and investment, a healthy economy can do more for capital investment than the most generous of politicians. The United States enjoyed a capital spending boom in the 1990s despite not having favorable tax law changes, investment tax credits, or changes in depreciation rules. A good economy with sustained growth and low inflation is the best combination for corporate investment.

Economists do favor incentives, such as a capital gains tax cut, that would increase savings in the economy. Greater savings, all else being constant, would mean lower interest rates, higher stock prices, and lower financing costs for firms buying plants and equipment.

> ## FOR EXAMPLE
>
> ### Salvage
>
> Some firms sell old equipment on auction sites, such as www.ebay.com, in order to recover final or "salvage" cash flows at the end of a project's term. Another more business-oriented site is www.salvagesale.com

SELF-CHECK

- Explain how the format of a company's statement of cash flows is related to a project's cash flow estimate.
- Define the **depreciation tax shield.**
- How do you compute a project's operating cash flow?
- Provide two examples of cash flow from investments.

7.4 Risk-Related Considerations

The degree of risk associated with expected cash inflows may vary substantially among different investments. For example, a decision about whether to replace an existing machine with a new more efficient machine would not involve substantial cash inflow uncertainty because the firm already has some operating experience with the existing machine. Expansion in existing product lines allows the company to base cash inflow expectations on past operating results and marketing data. These capital budgeting decisions can be made by discounting cash flows at the firm's cost of capital because they are comparable in risk to the firm's other assets.

Expansion projects involving new areas, new product lines, and overseas development usually have more uncertainty as far as cash flow projections. To compensate for this greater risk, financial managers often apply risk-adjusted discount rates to these cash flows as a way to offset the risk/return trade-off. A higher-risk project needs to be evaluated using a higher required rate of return. To use a financial markets analogy, given the current return offered of safe, short-term treasury bills, investors will not want to invest in risky common stocks unless the expected returns are commensurate with the higher risk of stocks. The bottom line is that financial managers will not choose to undertake higher-risk capital budgeting projects unless their expected returns are in line with their risks.

▲ The **risk-adjusted discount rate (RADR)** approach adjusts the required rate of return at which the analyst discounts a project's cash flows.

Projects with higher (or lower) risk levels demand higher (or lower) discount rates. A project is expected to enhance shareholder wealth only if its net present value (NPV) based on a risk-adjusted discount rate is positive.

One way to determine project risk-adjusted discount rates is for the company's managers to use past experience to create risk classes or categories for different types of capital budgeting projects. Each risk category can be given a generic description to indicate the types of projects it should include and a required rate of return or "hurdle rate" to assign to these projects. An example is shown in the Table 7-2, which assigns projects of average risk or those that have risks about the same as the company's overall risk a discount rate equal to the firm's cost of capital—that is, projects of average risk must earn an average return as defined by the company's cost of financing. Projects with below-average risk levels are discounted at a rate below the cost of capital. Projects of above-average risk must earn premiums over

Table 7-2: Risk Categories, Sample Corporation

Below-average risk:

Replacement decisions that require no change, or only a minor change, in technology. No change in plant layout required.

Discount rate = Cost of capital − 2%

Average risk:

Replacement decisions involving significant changes in technology or plant layout; all cost-saving decisions; expansions and improvements in the firm's main product lines.

Discount rate = Cost of capital

Above-average risk:

Applied research and development; introduction of new products not related to major product lines; expansion of production or marketing efforts into developed economies in Europe and Asia.

Discount rate = Cost of capital + 2%

High risk:

Expansion of production or marketing efforts into less-developed and emerging economies; introduction of products not related to any of the firm's current product lines.

Discount rate = Cost of capital + 5%

> **FOR EXAMPLE**
>
> ### Categories
>
> It is sometimes difficult to get an agreement on how risky a project is. Differences of opinion or internal politics may lead to controversy in classifying a project, so clearly defined category descriptions can minimize such problems. For example, one person might see a risk as a great opportunity for growth, while another person will believe that the risk will ruin the company. Carly Fiorina, former CEO of Hewlett-Packard, wanted to take over Compaq in 2002. Bill Hewlett, the son of the cofounder of the company, led stockholders to vote against the merger. While Fiorina won the battle to merge the two companies, she ultimately lost her job as she was voted off the board in 2005.

the company's cost of capital to be acceptable. Management must decide the number of categories and the required rate of return to assign to each category. Differences of opinion or internal politics may lead to controversy in classifying a project, so clearly defined category descriptions can minimize such problems.

SELF-CHECK

- Explain why capital budgeting analysis should consider a project's risk.
- What is RADR?
- When is a project expected to enhance shareholder wealth?

7.5 Strategic Analysis

Proper analysis of a capital spending project must tie together the details of the firm's competitive and strategic analyses and the cash flow estimates of the proposed project. In the end, strategic analysis, marketing analysis, and financial analysis should agree. If they seem to conflict, which may happen when the corporate planners strongly favor a project with a negative NPV for "strategic" reasons, everyone involved in the decision must work together to discover the cause of the conflict. Some common problem areas are

▲ determining the correct base case;

▲ overvaluing strategy;

▲ using unrealistic economic assumptions.

FOR EXAMPLE

Capital Spending and Competition

Trying to stay competitive, Google's capital spending was $838 million in 2005. This spending was in new computers, networks, and data centers needed to stay competitive. In addition, Google hired overseas staff to help oversee their presence in other countries. Their staff increased by 88% in 2005.

Incremental cash flows were defined as the anticipated changes in cash flow from a base case. The firm's base case projection must assess what the firm's market share and cash flows would be if no new projects are implemented. The corporation's planners must recognize that if nothing is done, customers may start buying competitors' products in response to the marketing, new-product development, and/or quality efforts of the competitors. The base case estimate should reflect these potential declines in cash flow.

When business planners overvalue strategy, they may make projects look more attractive than they really are. This can happen, for instance, if the analysts ignore cannibalization effects. The project analysis must also consider the effects of competitor retaliation; should you introduce a new product or innovation, your competition will take action to try to blunt the effectiveness of your strategy.

Finally, analysts need to be careful not to lose sight of the assumptions behind the estimates. Too many analysts start changing a few numbers and playing "What if?" games with their computer spreadsheets to get a positive project NPV. The spreadsheet output may soon lose any relationship with valid economic assumptions.

Estimates of revenues and costs should take the corporate view, rather than the business unit view. A project may look attractive to business unit managers because, as either an intended or unintended consequence, it shifts revenues or costs from one part of the company to another. Such projects will most likely fail to enhance shareholder value when total corporate incremental cash flows are properly estimated.

SELF-CHECK

- List three common obstacles to accurate analysis of capital spending initiatives.
- When business planners overvalue strategy, how does this affect projects?

7.6 Real-Option Analysis

Real-option analysis is a new type of financial analysis that incorporates strategic thinking better than traditional discounted cash flow analysis. **Real-option analysis** evaluates investments by recognizing the sources of flexibility that can enhance a project's value.

Traditional discounted cash flow analysis develops a single set of cash flow estimates, applies a market-determined discount rate, and computes a net present value. To be sure, different sets of cash flow estimates can be used and compared by outlining two different scenarios. This gives managers a "feel" for potential variability of cash flows and NPVs, but the project's risk, if evaluated correctly, should be reflected in the project's discount rate.

Real options analysis incorporates managerial flexibility into analysis where the NPV stays the same and can incorporate the following five different considerations.

▲ The **waiting-to-invest option.** Rather than begin a project this year, there may be value in waiting until next year in order to better evaluate changing technology, input prices, or conditions in their own product market.

▲ The **learning option.** Successful introduction of a product may lead managers to expand a product or innovation more quickly than initially proposed to take advantage of consumer interest and to gain production experience, lock up distribution channels, and to shut competitors out of the market.

▲ The **exit or abandonment option.** If initial results from a multistage project are poor, managers can save the firm's value by reducing the size of the initial project, or pulling the plug and stopping the project completely to stop further value-diminishing investments.

▲ The **growth-opportunities option.** Investing may create as-yet-unforeseen opportunities that would not be available if the firm doesn't undertake the project. Investing now in a new technology may create options for future growth, market expansion, technology development, and other activities to enhance shareholder value.

▲ The **flexibility option.** Flexibility adds value; a work disruption in a plant in one country can allow the firm to shift production to another plant elsewhere. Furnaces that can operate with different fuel sources allow the owner to switch to whatever fuel source is less expensive.

Sophisticated real-options analysis attempts to evaluate future opportunities represented by these five options. The following example illustrates the value of the exit or abandonment option.

Suppose a mining firm is considering operating a copper mine for an additional year, but to do so will need to make additional investments of $1 million in equipment. The mine is almost depleted, and the price of copper is subject to large market fluctuations. Analysts estimate, based upon past movements in

Figure 7-1

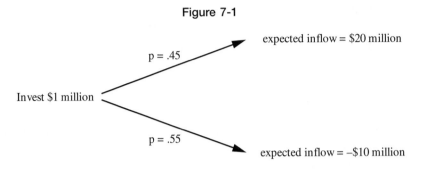

Payoff diagram for copper mining example.

copper prices, that there is a 45% chance that copper prices will be high and the cash inflow from operating the mine for an additional year will be $20 million. There is a 55% chance of low copper prices, in which case the cash flow is a negative $27 million. The expected cash inflow is

$$\text{E (inflow)} = .45 \ (\$20 \ \text{million}) + .55 \ (-\$27 \ \text{million}) = -\$5.85 \ \text{million}.$$

If the risk-adjusted discount rate for the mining project is 15%, the NPV of operating the mine for an additional year is

$$\text{NPV} = -\$1 \ \text{million} + (-\$5.85 \ \text{million})/(1 + .15) = -\$6.1 \ \text{million}.$$

Take a look at figure 7-1 that diagrams the mining project:

With a negative NPV, the decision is to not invest in another year's operations and to shut down the mine immediately. But consider the role of management if they invested in the operation but then walked away from it if copper prices remained low. In other words, they would invest the $1 million in new equipment and invest in fixed extraction costs. But if the variable costs of processing the ore do not exceed the market price of copper, they will abandon the project. In this case, the losses would be restricted to the cost of extraction, not the combined loss of extracting and processing the ore.

If the fixed cost of mining the ore is $10 million, we have the situation as diagramed in Figure 7-2.

Figure 7-2

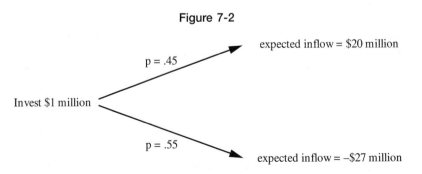

Payoff diagram for copper mining example with abandonment.

FOR EXAMPLE

The Abandonment Option

Every year there are more than 30,000 new products introduced in grocery stores. The vast majority of these are not successful. Retailers often test these products in selected markets with different demographics. If the products are not successful, they either pull the product and abandon the project so the company does not lose additional money or they work on redesigning the product for a later reintroduction.

There is a 45% chance of high copper prices with a subsequent cash inflow of $20 million and a 55% chance of low copper prices, in which case the mine would be abandoned; no refining of the mined ore will occur; and the cash flow would be −$10 million, the fixed cost of mining the ore. With the abandonment option, the expected cash inflow is

$$E \text{ (inflow)} = .45 \text{ ($20 million)} + .55 \text{ (−$10 million)} = \$3.5 \text{ million.}$$

Using the risk-adjusted discount rate of 15%, the NPV of operating the mine for an additional year is

$$\text{NPV} = -\$1 \text{ million} + (\$3.5 \text{ million})/(1 + .15) = \$2.0 \text{ million.}$$

Now we are able to see the value of the real option to abandon the project; having this option raised the NPV from −$6.1 million to $2 million. Real options have value, and real-option analysis is a new method to incorporate managerial flexibility into financial analysis.

SELF-CHECK

- Define **real-option analysis.**
- Explain the process of real-option analysis.
- List five different considerations that can be analyzed using real-option analysis.

SUMMARY

The way to maximize shareholder wealth is to identify and select projects that are expected to result in positive cash flows, which will lead to increased profits. Although selecting the right projects is always going to be a challenge, if managers make use of the estimation techniques outlined in this chapter and stay focused on the main goals of the corporation, they will have a better chance of success.

KEY TERMS

Base case	A firm's after-tax cash flows without a new project.
Cannibalization	Occurs when a project robs cash flow from the firm's existing lines of business.
Competitive advantage	The reason that customers are willing to purchase one company's products or services rather than another firm's.
Depreciation tax shield	Represents the tax savings due to depreciation of fixed assets. It equals the amount of the depreciation expense multiplied by the firm's tax rate.
Enhancement	Reflects an increase in the cash flows of the firm's other products that occur because of a new project.
Exit or abandonment option	If initial results from a multistage project are poor, managers can save the firm's value by reducing the size of the initial project or by pulling the plug and stopping the project completely to stop further value-diminishing investments.
Flexibility option	Flexibility adds value; a work disruption in a plant in one country can allow the firm to shift production to another plant elsewhere.
Growth opportunities option	Investing may create as-yet-unforeseen opportunities that would not be available if the firm doesn't undertake the project.
Incremental after-tax cash flows	Represent the difference between the firm's after-tax cash flows with a new project and the firm's base case, or after-tax cash flows without the project.
Learning option	Successful introduction of a product may lead managers to expand a product or innovation more quickly than initially proposed to take advantage of consumer interest and to gain

production experience, lock up distribution channels, and to shut competitors out of the market.

Opportunity cost

The cost of passing up the next best alternative.

Real-option analysis

Evaluates investments by recognizing the sources of flexibility that can enhance a project's value.

Risk-adjusted discount rate (RADR)

Adjusts the required rate of return at which the analyst discounts a project's cash flows.

Stand-alone principle

Ensures that analysis focuses on the project's own cash flows, without regard to the cash flows produced by the firm's other activities.

Sunk cost

A project-related expense that does not depend on whether or not the project is undertaken.

Waiting-to-invest option

Rather than begin a project this year, there may be value in waiting until next year in order to better evaluate changing technology, input prices, or conditions in their own product market.

ASSESS YOUR UNDERSTANDING

Go to www.wiley.com/college/Melicher to evaluate your knowledge of the basics of informed investment decisions.
Measure your learning by comparing pre-test and post-test results.

Summary Questions

1. The stand-alone principle suggests that a project must be viewed separately from the rest of the firm. True or false?
2. Incremental cash flows represents a project's cash flows summed together with the firm's other cash flows to get a total firm view of the project. True or false?
3. Enhancement occurs when a project robs cash flow from the firm's existing line of business. True or false?
4. Cannibalization occurs when a project robs cash flow from the firm's existing line of business. True or false?
5. The risk-adjusted discount rate (RADR) is the risk-adjustment factor that represents the percent of estimated cash inflows that investors would be satisfied to receive for certain rather than the cash inflows that are possible for each year. True or false?
6. The higher the risk of a project, the higher its risk-adjusted discount rate and thus the lower the net present value for a given stream of cash inflows. True or false?
7. Sunk costs are relevant in capital budgeting analysis and should be considered in calculating a project's initial investment. True or false?
8. Opportunity costs reflect the cost of passing up the next best alternative and are irrelevant in capital budgeting analysis. True or false?
9. The after-tax cash flows without the project are referred to as
   (a) the net investment.
   (b) incremental cash flows.
   (c) the base case.
   (d) none of the above.
10. The stand-alone principle means that
   (a) projects should not be evaluated against one another.
   (b) projects must operate independently of the firm's other projects.
   (c) analysts should focus on the project's cash flows, uncontaminated by cash flows from the firm's other activities.
   (d) None of the above

11. All of the groups of cash flows from the firm's statement of cash flows are also used in the analysis of project cash flows EXCEPT
    (a) cash flow from financing.
    (b) cash flow from investment.
    (c) cash flow from operations.
    (d) All are included
12. The relevant cash flows of a project do not include which one of the following?
    (a) Incremental after-tax cash flows
    (b) Cannibalization effects
    (c) Opportunity costs
    (d) Sunk costs

Review Questions

1. How is the stand-alone principle applied when evaluating whether to invest in projects?
2. Does an increase in net working capital increase or decrease operating cash flow? Explain.
3. How is a project's cash flow statement similar to that of a company?
4. When developing a project income statement, why does EBIT equal EBT?
5. How does depreciation affect a project's cash flow?
6. Why are cash flows, rather than cash earnings, used in capital budget analysis?
7. What is a risk-adjusted discount rate? How are risk-adjusted discount rates determined for individual projects?

Applying This Chapter

1. For a capital budgeting proposal, assume this year's cash sales are forecast to be $220, cash expenses $130, and depreciation $80. Assume the firm is in the 30% tax bracket. Using the methods discussed in the chapter, determine the project's after-tax cash flow.
2. The Brassy Fin Pet Shop is considering an expansion. Construction will cost $90,000 and will be depreciated to zero, using straight-line depreciation, over 5 years. Earnings before depreciation are expected to be $20,000 in each of the next 5 years. The firm's tax rate is 34%. What are the project's cash flows?

3. The following is a simplified project income statement for Ma & Pa Incorporated. The project is expected to last 8 years. Its up-front cost is $2,000. Its cost of capital is 12%.

Sales	$925.00
Less cash expenses	310.00
Less depreciation	250.00
Earnings before taxes	$365.00
Less taxes (at 35%)	127.75
Net income	$237.25

Compute the project's after-tax cash flow.

4. You are a financial analyst for an oil company. Due to recent political developments, there is an 80% chance of high oil prices with a subsequent cash inflow of $70 million and a 20% chance of low oil prices; wells would be shut down, and the cash flow would be –$5 million, the fixed cost. With the abandonment option, calculate the expected cash inflow.

Base Case

Explain the term *base case* as it applies to estimating cash flows on a new product.

No Free Lunch

If a restaurant that has only been open for dinner decides to start serving lunches, what new additional costs must be considered? Would the cannibalization or enhancement effect apply in this case?

EBIT equals EBT

Assume you are developing a project income statement and explain why EBIT would be the same as EBT in this statement.

8

MANAGING WORKING CAPITAL
Cash Budgets and Current Assets

Starting Point

Go to www.wiley.com/college/Melicher to assess your knowledge of managing capital.
Determine where you need to concentrate your effort.

What You'll Learn in This Chapter

▲ Different types of financial capital
▲ Cash budgets and how they are used
▲ Types of marketable securities
▲ The five Cs of credit analysis
▲ The definition of a just-in-time (JIT) inventory control system

After Studying This Chapter, You'll Be Able To

▲ Compare and contrast working and fixed capital
▲ Examine the impact of the operating cycle on the size of investment in accounts receivable and inventories
▲ Differentiate between the three motives
▲ Differentiate between float, collection float, and disbursement float
▲ Appraise a firm's credit worthiness
▲ Appraise the effectiveness of a firm's inventory management policies

Goals and Outcomes

▲ Assess the length of the operating cycle and cash conversion cycle
▲ Evaluate how a firm's levels of accounts receivable, inventory, and accounts payable are affected by an increase in sales
▲ Evaluate a firm's cash budget
▲ Evaluate how seasonal and cyclical trends affect the operating cycle, cash conversion cycle, and investments in current assets
▲ Assess the motives underlying the management of cash and marketable securities
▲ Evaluate how financial managers can shorten the cash conversion cycle
▲ Assess how a firm can improve its inventory management system

INTRODUCTION

A positive cash flow means the money coming into a business exceeds the money being paid out. The profit margin coupled with the company's current assets comprises what is known as *working capital*. Inventory must be sold and accounts receivable must be collected in order for operating expenses to be paid and for profits to increase. Therefore, one of the prime functions of financial managers is to carefully monitor and manage the working capital.

8.1 Identifying Working Capital

A firm can invest in both working capital and fixed capital.

▲ **Working capital** is a firm's current assets as shown on the balance sheet and includes cash in the bank accounts, marketable securities, inventory, and accounts receivable.

▲ **Fixed capital** is a firm's fixed assets, which include plant, equipment, and property.

In this chapter we focus on managing a firm's working capital. The financial manager must decide how much to invest in working capital or current assets and how to finance these current assets.

How important are working capital issues? In a word, very. Firms that cannot obtain needed short-term financing are candidates for bankruptcy.

Supplies and raw materials are converted to inventory that must be sold to generate income. Cash sales result in immediate income, while credit sales become the company's accounts receivable. Accounts receivable represents the cash that must be collected in a timely manner to keep the company's cash flow positive. Unexpected increases in inventory mean products are not being sold. Increases in accounts receivable mean customers are not paying for the products bought on credit. Financial managers are expected to keep these situations from occurring.

Current assets typically comprise from one-third to one-half of a firm's total assets and can be affected by day-to-day marketing, production, and human resource

---

FOR EXAMPLE

Importance of Working Capital in Small Business

For U.S. manufacturing firms, current assets represent about 40% of total assets, and current liabilities are about 25% of the total financing. A financial manager may spend over one-half of his or her time on the management of working capital.

issues. Short-term financing, which is covered in the Chapter 9, also figures prominently into the management process, as securing additional financing increases a company's working capital. However, for now we will concentrate on preparing cash budgets and managing securities, inventories, and accounts receivable.

The management of working capital is particularly important to the entrepreneurial or venture firm. The need for all types of financial capital is important as the firm moves from a start-up situation to rapid growth in revenues. To reduce financing needs, it is important for the small firm to keep only a necessary level of inventories on hand.

SELF-CHECK

- Define **working capital** and list three examples.
- Define **fixed capital** and list three examples.
- What type of firm relies heavily on working capital?

8.2 Operating Cash and Conversion Cycles

Two important concepts in managing working capital are the operating cycle and cash conversion cycle.

▲ The **operating cycle** measures the time between receiving raw materials and collecting the cash from credit sales posted to accounts receivables.

Figure 8-1 diagrams a typical operating cycle. Raw materials are purchased and products are manufactured from them to become finished goods. Effort then is made to sell the finished goods. A service firm would have a similar cycle except for the manufacturing stage—that is, finished goods would be purchased, consumed in the process of providing a service, and receivables collected. Of course, the operating cycles of both service and manufacturing firms are shorter when and if sales are made for cash instead of credit.

Figure 8-2 depicts a timeline reflecting the operating cycle for a manufacturing firm. The cycle begins with the receipt of raw materials. The inventory period involves manufacturing the finished goods and ends when those products are sold on credit. This leads to the accounts receivable period, which extends through the approximate month it takes to collect the receivable amounts. The inventory period and the accounts receivable period are the company's operating cycle.

The accounts payable period covers the period between when the order for raw materials is invoiced and when the invoice is paid. The accounts payable period is subtracted from the length of the operating cycle to get the cash

Figure 8-1

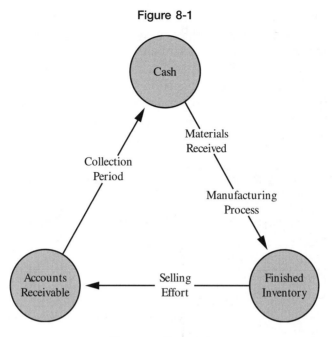

The operating cycle.

conversion cycle. The **cash conversion cycle** measures the time it takes to collect money from the company's customers and use those funds to pay its suppliers.

Of course, if no credit is extended by suppliers, then the operating cycle and the cash conversion cycle would be the same.

Increases in the cash conversion cycle mean the firm must finance itself for a longer time. If the company does not have a savings account or other liquid

Figure 8-2

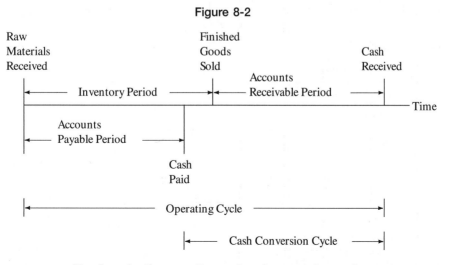

Timelines for the operating and cash conversion cycles.

assets to fall back on, it may have to borrow operating funds and incur financing costs. So, financial managers will want to monitor the cash conversion cycle and take action should it begin to lengthen.

It is possible to estimate the span of time for the company's operating and cash conversion cycles by using information from the income statement and balance sheet. Calculating three ratios will tell the manager the average length of these cycles. Tables 8-1 and 8-2 contain balance sheets and income statements, respectively, for Walgreens.

Table 8-1: Balance Sheet for Walgreens ($ in Millions)

	2003
ASSETS	
Cash & Marketable Securities	$1,017.10
Accounts Receivable	$1,017.80
Inventories	$4,202.70
Other Current Assets	$120.50
Total Current Assets	$6,389.10
Net Fixed Assets	$4,940.00
Other Long-Term Assets	$107.80
Total Fixed Assets	$5,047.80
Total Assets	$11,405.90
LIABILITIES AND EQUITY	
Accounts Payable	$2,077.00
Notes Payable	$0.00
Other Current Liabilities	$1,343.50
Total Current Liabilities	$3,420.50
Long-Term Debt	$0.00
Other Liabilities	$789.70
Total Liabilities	$4,210.20
Common Equity	$777.90
Retained Earnings	$6,417.80
Total Stockholders' Equity	$7,195.70
Total Liabilities and Equity	$11,405.90

Table 8-2: Income Statement for Walgreens ($ in Millions)

	2003
Revenue	$32,505.40
Cost of Goods Sold	$23,360.10
Gross Profit	$9,145.30
Selling, General & Administrative	$6,950.90
Depreciation	$346.10
Operating Income	$1,848.30
Interest Expense	$0.00
Other Expenses (Income)	($40.40)
Income before Taxes	$1,888.70
Income Taxes	$713.00
Net Income	$1,175.70
Number of Shares Outstanding (000s)	1,031,580
Earnings per Share	$1.14

8.2.1 Determining the Inventory Period

First, we would like to know how many days items were in inventory during 2003. That will tell us the time between when an order for raw materials was received and when the finished goods were sold. To determine the length of this period, we can use the inventory turnover ratio (cost of goods sold divided by inventories) from Chapter 5. Based on Walgreens's financial information, it is computed as follows:

$$\frac{23,360.10}{4,202.70} = 5.56 \text{ number of times a year inventory is turned over.}$$

The next step is determining the inventory conversion period by dividing the number of times per year by the number of days in a year.

$$\frac{365}{5.56} = 65.6 \text{ days}$$

As an alternative calculation, we can divide the 2003 year-end inventories amount by the 2003 cost of goods sold (COGS) per day, but the answer will be the same. By either method, it took about 65.6 days in 2003 for Walgreens to complete the inventory conversion period.

8.2.2 Determining the Accounts Receivable Period

The second step is to determine the average collection period in 2003 for Walgreens. This ratio is explained in Chapter 7. It measures the average time between when a product is sold on credit and when cash is received from the buyer. It is calculated as follows:

$$\text{Average collection period} = \frac{\text{Accounts Receivable}}{\text{Net Sales}/365}$$

$$= \frac{\$1,017.80}{\$32,505.40/365} = \frac{\$1,017.80}{\$89.10} = 11.4 \text{ days}$$

The $1,017.80 for accounts receivable is taken from the balance sheet in Table 8-1, and the $32,505.40 in net sales comes from the income statement in Table 8-2. Based on these calculations, it took Walgreens 11.4 days, on average, during 2003 from the time finished goods were sold on credit to when the resulting receivables were actually collected.

The operating cycle is determined as follows:

Operating cycle = Inventory conversion period + Average collection period

Walgreens's average 2003 operating cycle is 77.1 days (65.6 days plus 11.4 days).

8.2.3 Determining the Average Payment Period

The average payment period represents the time it takes Walgreens to pay its suppliers. We are introduced to this ratio in Chapter 7. The average payment period is calculated by dividing a company's accounts payable by its costs of good sold per day. Using the information from Tables 8-1 and 8-2, the average payment period is calculated as follows:

$$\text{Average payment period} = \frac{\text{Accounts Payable}}{\text{Cost of goods sold}/365}$$

$$= \frac{\$2,077.0}{\$23,360.10/365} = \frac{\$2077.00}{\$64.00} = 32.5 \text{ days}$$

Thus, Walgreens was able to get on average about 32.5 days of credit from its suppliers in 2003. The cash conversion cycle is the operating cycle less the average payment period:

Cash conversion cycle = Operating cycle – Average payment period

For Walgreens, we start with an operating cycle of 77.1 days and subtract the average payment period of 32.5 days to arrive at a cash conversion cycle of 44.6 days

> ## FOR EXAMPLE
>
> ### Repayment Periods
>
> A venture or entrepreneurial firm may find it advantageous to seek longer repayment terms from suppliers to help finance growth in sales. In fact, sometimes suppliers will negotiate converting accounts payable to notes payable. Such a conversion is usually not cost-free to the small business. Rather, to convert an accounts payable with 30-day terms to a notes payable due in 90 days usually requires the payment of interest on the amount of the notes payable in addition to the amount owed when the accounts payable comes due.

for 2003. The average time between when Walgreens received materials and when it received payment from its customers after their final sale was about 45 days. Managing the cash conversion cycle is a major task of a firm's financial manager. The shorter the cash conversion cycle, the smaller will be the firm's investment in inventory and receivables, and there will be no need for more financing to keep the company on an even keel.

SELF-CHECK

- What is the operating cycle?
- What is the cash conversion cycle?
- What is the difference between the accounts receivable period and the average repayment period?
- What is a firm's inventory period?

8.3 Working Capital Requirements

The length of the operating cycle affects the amount of funds invested in accounts receivable and inventories. Using the previous calculations, we can determine Walgreens's average investment in accounts receivable. This is done as follows:

Receivables investment amount = Net sales per day × Average collection period

Receivables investment amount = $89.10 × 11.4 days = $1,015.7

With this figure, the financial manager can now estimate what the investment in accounts receivable will be for the following year if sales increase by 10% to $35,756 and the average collection period remains at 11.4 days. If there is a constant relationship between sales and receivables, a 10% increase in sales should lead to a 10% increase in receivables. This would mean investment in receivables would rise to $1,119.6. However, if the relationship between sales and accounts receivable does not remain constant, the numbers will change by the same percentage. For example, as sales rise or fall over time, the accounts receivable period may change. If the economy goes into a recession, the accounts receivable period may rise as customers take longer to pay their bills. Or focusing marketing efforts on better credit-quality customers may allow the firm to increase sales and reduce its receivables balance because customers pay early.

Assume that credit sales increase by 10% to $35,756. Dividing $35,756 by 365 we get $97.96 sales per day. Now we should ask, What will the necessary investment in accounts receivable be if sales increase to $35,756 but Walgreens is able to decrease its average collection period to 11 days?

$$\text{Receivables investment amount} = \underline{\$35,756} = \$97.96 \times 11 \text{ days} = 1,077.6$$

So, even a half-day reduction in the average collection period would mean that the amount of increased investment required in accounts receivable to support a 10% increase in sales would be only $59.8 ($1077.6 − $1,017.8).

A similar analysis can be conducted in terms of inventories. The 2003 cost of goods sold was $23,360.10 for the year, or $64.00 on a per-day basis ($23,360.10/365). We know that in 2003 it took Walgreens on average 65.7 days between when raw materials were received and when the finished goods were sold. By multiplying the average cost of goods per day times the inventory conversion period, you can determine the investment required in inventories:

$$\text{Inventories investment amount} = \text{Average cost of goods sold per day} \times \text{inventory conversion period}$$

For Walgreens in 2003 we have:

$$\text{Inventories investment amount} = \$64.00 \times 65.7 \text{ days} = \$4,204.8$$

This is the same amount, within rounding error, shown for the inventories account in Table 8-1 for Walgreens's balance sheet. It should be clear that this required investment will change if the cost of goods sold, the inventory conversion period, or both change. However, Walgreens may be able to achieve a reduction in its inventory conversion period by managing inventories more efficiently. Some strategies for doing this will be presented later in this chapter.

The size of the accounts payable account is also affected by two basic factors: the level of the firm's cost of goods sold and the average payment period.

Walgreens's income statement shows that the cost of goods sold in 2003 was $23,360.10. On a per-day basis, the cost of goods sold was $64.00 ($23,360.10/365). We previously calculated that Walgreens's average payment period is 32.5 days. With this information, we can determine the required amount of accounts payable as follows:

Accounts payable = Cost of goods sold per day × average payment period

For Walgreens in 2003 we have

Accounts payable = $64.00 × 32.5 days = $2,080.

This amount is the same, within rounding error, as the accounts payable amount in Table 8-1, but keep in mind that as the cost of goods sold increases, its credit purchases and its accounts payable should also increase. Like accounts receivable and inventory and sales, if costs of goods rise by 10%, so will accounts payable provided that the payment period does not change

At the same time, consider that while an increase in sales and cost of goods should result in an increase in the investment in accounts receivable and inventories, these increases will be partially offset by an increase in accounts payable. This is why it is important for financial mangers to look at all sides of the operations and cash conversion cycles and recalculate their estimates often to incorporate changes

Table 8-3: Effect of a 10% Increase in Sales and Cost of Goods Sold on Receivables, Inventory, and Payables*

Account	2003 Results for Walgreens	10% Increase in Sales and Cost of Goods Sold
Investment		
Accounts Receivable	$1,017.80	$1,116.70
Inventories	$4,202.70	$4,625.30
Total	$5,220.50	$5,742.00
Financing		
Accounts Payable	$2,077.00	$2,288.00
Net Investment		
Investment – Financing	$3,143.50	$3,454.00

*Assumptions: Average collection period = 11.4 days; inventory period = 65.7 days; average payment period = 32.5 days.

Table 8-4: Effect of a 10% Increase in Sales and Cost of Goods Sold on Receivables, Inventory, and Payables*

Account	2003 Results for Walgreens	10% Increase in Sales and Cost of Goods Sold
Investment		
Accounts Receivable	$1,017.80	$1,077.60
Inventories	$4,202.70	$4,224.00
Total	$5,220.50	$5,301.60
Financing		
Accounts Payable	$2,077.00	$2,605.00
Net Investment		
Investment—Financing	$3,143.50	$2,696.60

*Assumptions: Average collection period = 11 days; inventory period = 60 days; average payment period = 37 days.

in sales, collection periods, payables, and payment periods to keep investments and financing needs in good balance.

Using Walgreens's financial data, the Table 8.3 and 8.4 demonstrate the changes that are affected by a 10% change in the accounts we have just reviewed.

Although investment in accounts receivable and inventories would be expected to increase by $521.5 from $5,220.5 to $5,742.0, the expected increase in accounts payable of $211 from $2,077 to $2,288 causes the impact to be only a 310.5 increase in needed financing. The financial manager will have to plan ahead to obtain the necessary funds to support this increase needed for the company's net working capital. Funds can be obtained from short-term financing or perhaps the company can draw funds from their long-term sources, such as stocks and bonds.

Table 8-4 summarizes our estimates of receivables, inventory, and payables if sales and cost of goods sold rise by 10% and changes occur in the operating and cash conversion cycles. Specifically, Table 8-4 shows the effects of an average collection period of 11 days, inventory period of 60 days, and a payables period of 37 days.

Although 10% seems like a small change, its effect on the company's working capital accounts is remarkable. The firm's net investment in these working capital accounts will fall to $2,696.6, nearly $447 less than the current (2003) situation and nearly $760 less than the scenario in Table 8-3. This means less debt and external equity financing is needed, saving the firm extra financing

> ### FOR EXAMPLE
>
> #### Accounts Receivable
>
> To be competitive, businesses often must offer credit to their customers, which results in the need to finance accounts receivable. However, the entrepreneurial or venture firm should not overlook the possibility that customers in some cases can actually provide financing help in the form of advance payments. For example, if you produce and sell an important component that is essential to a customer's own product that it markets and sells, your customer may actually be willing to provide partial payments in advance to help ensure that you will continue to manufacture the products on time and to maintain adequate quality.

expenses. Activities that decrease the cash conversion cycle will reduce the firm's need to obtain financing.

SELF-CHECK

- Explain how a firm's levels of accounts receivable, inventory, and accounts payable are expected to be affected by an increase in sales.
- Describe what happens to accounts receivable if both sales and the collection period rise.
- How does the length of the operating cycle affect the amount of funds invested in accounts receivable and inventories?

8.4 Cash Budgets

A company needs accurate information over the course of a business year to determine if it will have the funds needed to pay all the bills. Sometimes unforeseen expenses are incurred in addition to the normal operating costs.

A corporation must mail dividend checks to its shareholders. Other companies may not have shareholders to pay, but they will have suppliers to pay, salaries to cover, and a number of other typical expenses such as insurance, utilities, interest, and payments on loans used to finance growth and expansion. This means the firm's treasurer or accounting team will have to track and forecast daily, weekly, or monthly cash receipts and disbursements to ensure that the company can meet all its financial obligations.

If the bank balances become too low, the company may have to negotiate short-term financing or, if available, sell marketable securities. To avoid an unexpected cash shortage, the company's financial manager should prepare a cash budget. A **cash budget** details the cash inflows and cash outflows of a firm over a specific time frame.

Small- and medium-size firms may prepare annual or monthly cash budgets, while larger firms will forecast cash flows weekly or daily.

If cash surpluses are forecast, managers can plan how that excess money can be invested to earn interest or used to make improvements or initiate new projects. If a cash deficit is forecast, the manager can devise ways to raise the funds to cover it.

With this in mind, we'll study cash budgets prepared for Global Manufacturing. Global's sales pattern is seasonal, with strong sales the last few months of the year followed by a sharp decline at the beginning of the calendar year. We'll see how the decision to keep production levels the same all year long will affect its cash needs throughout the year.

To construct a cash budget, the following information is needed: the firm's minimum desired cash balance, estimated cash inflows, and estimated cash outflows.

8.4.1 Minimum Cash Balance

Most firms have a minimum desired cash balance. Cash will be needed to pay the month's bills, but extra cash may also be desired because the forecasts are never perfect. The minimum cash balance is intended to protect against lower-than-expected cash inflows and higher-than-expected cash outflows. The size of the desired bank balance depends on several influences, including the firm's ability to acquire financing easily on short notice, the predictability of cash inflows and outflows, and management's preferences.

8.4.2 Cash Inflows or Cash Receipts

The estimates of cash inflows are driven by two main factors: the sales forecast and customer payment patterns. Over any period, the main sources of cash inflows for the firm will be cash sales and collections of receivables. If we know the proportion of cash sales and the percentage of customers who pay their bills every month, we can use sales forecasts to estimate future cash inflows.

Sales forecasts will be affected by its seasonal patterns. Obviously, monthly sales figures will differ for swimsuit makers and snowblower manufacturers. Managers can determine seasonal patterns by merely tracking monthly or quarterly sales figures from the prior year's financial statements, as in Figure 8-3.

For example, Table 8-5 presents Global Manufacturing's actual November and December 2004 sales and forecasted sales for January, February, March, and

Figure 8-3

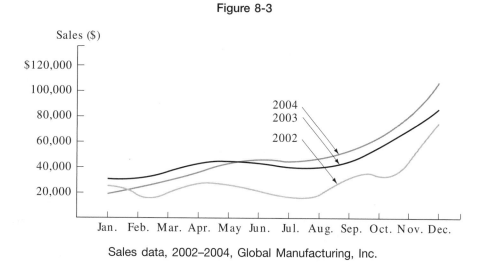

Sales data, 2002–2004, Global Manufacturing, Inc.

April 2005. As shown in Figure 8-3, Global knows that its sales volume is highly seasonal, with a large proportion of sales occurring in the last few months of the year.

All of Global's sales are credit sales and become accounts receivable. From reviewing past payment patterns, Global knows that receivables representing 50% of a month's sales are paid one month after purchase while the remaining 50% are paid 2 months later. For January through April, each month's cash inflows have two sources: cash receipts equal 50% of the sales from the previous month and 50% of the sales from 2 months prior. Thus, for January, receipts total 50% of December sales and 50% of November sales.

Table 8-5: Monthly Cash Inflows for Global Manufacturing, Inc.

	Nov	*Dec*	*Jan*	*Feb*	*Mar*	*Apr*
Sales	$80,000	$100,000	$30,000	$40,000	$50,000	$60,000
Collections:						
50% of sales of the previous month		40,000	50,000	15,000	20,000	25,000
50% of sales of the second previous month			40,000	50,000	15,000	20,000
Total cash receipts			$90,000	$65,000	$35,000	$45,000

8.4.3 Cash Outflows or Cash Disbursements

Every month, Global will have bills to pay, and these cash outflows need to appear in the cash budget. Suppliers of raw materials must be paid, as well as the firm's payroll, taxes, and other operating expenses. Any anticipated purchases of plant and equipment also must be listed in the budget. Production, over the course of the year, can be seasonal, rising and falling along with the sales forecast, or level, producing a constant amount of product every month. Here we assume Global uses seasonal production. Later, we will see the effect of a level production schedule on Global's cash budget.

Table 8-6 shows Global's expected cash disbursements, or cash outflows. Raw materials and supplies equal to 50% of each month's sales are purchased each month. Global pays its suppliers 2 months after the goods are purchased. Each month's estimated salary and overhead expenses are $20,000. Interest payments of $7,000 are due in February, and a quarterly dividend, expected to be $6,000, is to be paid in March. Quarterly taxes of $3,000 also need to be paid in March. In anticipation of growing sales, Global is planning to purchase $50,000 worth of capital equipment in February.

Table 8-6: Monthly Cash Outflows, Seasonal Production, Global Manufacturing, Inc.

	Nov.	Dec.	Jan.	Feb.	Mar.	Apr.
Sales	$80,000	$100,000	$30,000	$40,000	$50,000	$60,000
Materials and supplies purchases (50% of monthly sales)	40,000	50,000	15,000	20,000	25,000	30,000
Payments 100% of purchases of the second previous month			40,000	50,000	15,000	20,000
Salaries and overhead			20,000	20,000	20,000	20,000
Interest				7,000		
Dividends					6,000	
Taxes					3,000	
Capital expenditures				5,000		
Total cash payments			$6,000	$127,000	$44,000	$40,000

Table 8-7: Net Monthly Cash Flows, Seasonal Production, Global Manufacturing, Inc.

	Jan	Feb	Mar	Apr
Total cash receipts	$90,000	$65,000	$35,000	$45,000
Less: Total cash payments	$60,000	$127,000	$44,000	$40,000
Net cash flow	$30,000	($62,000)	($9,000)	$5,000

8.4.4 Constructing the Cash Budget

After listing all the expected cash inflows and cash outflows for each month, it is possible to estimate the net cash flow. As shown in Table 8-7, this is simply the difference between Global's cash receipts and cash disbursements from Tables 8-5 and 8-6.

From Table 8-7 we see that January will be a month with a large positive cash flow but that February and March are expected to have larger cash outflows than inflows. April is expected to have a positive cash flow of $5,000. To help Global determine its short-term financing needs, we need to put together a fully developed cash budget that indicates Global's minimum desired cash balance as well as its monthly loan (or loan repayment) needs. We'll assume Global's minimum desired cash balance is $25,000. Should the cash position in any month fall below $25,000, Global's treasurer will need to borrow sufficient funds so that the cash balance is restored to the $25,000 level.

From Table 8-7 we see that January's net cash flow is $30,000; adding this to Global's beginning-of-January cash balance of $25,000 gives Global a cumulative cash balance of $55,000. Adding the $55,000 cash balance to February's net cash flow of −$62,000 means that Global is forecasted to spend $7,000 more in cash than it is expected to have available. To meet the expected payments and to raise the cash balance to its minimum desired level of $25,000, Global's treasurer will need to borrow $32,000 ($7,000 + $25,000). After doing so, the ending cash balance of February will be $25,000.

When March's net cash flow of −$9,000 is added to March's beginning cash balance of $25,000, Global's available cash will be $16,000. To maintain the minimum desired cash balance of $25,000, Global should plan to borrow $9,000. When this is added to the already outstanding loans from February, Global's total loan balance at the end of March will be $32,000 + $9,000, or $41,000. The ending cash balance in March will be $25,000.

April's positive net cash flow, when added to the beginning cash balance, will give Global a positive cash balance of $30,000. This exceeds Global's minimum desired cash balance of $25,000, so in all likelihood the excess cash of $5,000 will be used to repay some of the funds it borrowed over the last 2 months.

FOR EXAMPLE

Cash Budget

The average firm has one-third or more of its assets in the form of current assets (cash, accounts receivable, and inventory). Financial managers spend a lot of their time and effort on short-term finance issues. Thus, managing working capital and maintaining short-term financing sources are main concerns to a financial manager and to the well-being of a firm. Efforts to cut operating expenses and to increase the firm's efficient use of its working capital can help increase a firm's profits, making it a potentially attractive investment. General Electric's efforts to manage its inventory more efficiently freed up an extra $1 billion in cash. This cash can be redirected to more productive investments to increase shareholder return.

The Global budgeting process illustrates the usefulness of looking ahead so that the company is prepared to deal with cash shortages before payments become delinquent. Forecasted sales are used to estimate future cash inflows and outflows based on expected payment patterns. The treasurer can plan ahead to invest excess cash or to borrow needed funds. In addition to its value as a planning tool, the cash budget will be a necessary part of any short-term loan request from a bank. The bank will not only want to see when and how much the firm may need to borrow, but also when the firm will be able to repay the loan.

SELF-CHECK

- Explain what influences affect the size of a firm's minimum desired cash buffer.
- Describe the factors that influence the size of a firm's periodic cash inflow.
- Explain what affects the size of a firm's periodic cash outflows.
- Describe how a cash budget is constructed.

8.5 Seasonal versus Level Production

The sample budget for Global assumes that the company uses seasonal production to meet its seasonal sales forecast. Raw materials purchases rise or fall in anticipation of higher or lower sales. Such a strategy can help minimize

Figure 8-4

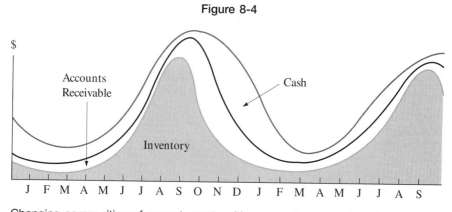

Changing composition of current assets with seasonal sales and level production.

the effect of seasonal sales on inventory, because goods are manufactured shortly before they are sold. However, seasonal production can lead to other problems, such as idle plant and laid-off workers during slow sales months and production bottlenecks and overtime wages during busy times. Consequently, for better production efficiency, some firms with seasonal sales use a level production plan. Under a **level production plan,** the same amount of raw material is purchased and the same amount of finished product is manufactured every month.

Inventory builds up in anticipation of the higher seasonal sales while cash and accounts receivable are quite low. When the selling season begins, inventories fall and receivables rise. After a time, inventories are nearly exhausted and the firm is collecting cash from its customers. The changing composition of current assets for a firm with a seasonal sales pattern is illustrated in Figure 8-4.

Now let's see how Global's cash budget will be affected if it switches to a level production plan. Table 8-5, the schedule of cash inflows, will not be affected. But Table 8-6, the schedule of outflows, will have to be redone to reflect the change in the amount of materials purchased each month. We will assume that the amount of materials and supplies over the course of a year is one-half of estimated sales. If forecasted sales are $700,000, this means Global purchases $350,000 of materials over the course of a year, or approximately $29,200 each month. Table 8-8 shows the revised cash outflow schedule assuming purchases, and subsequent payments, of a constant $29,200 each month.

With these new cash payments, Table 8-9 shows the monthly net cash flows and Table 8-10 shows the new cash budget.

Although the negative cash flows with level production continued into the month of April, the lower costs of level production meant that the company did not need to borrow as much to meet its expenditures. This lowered the loan amounts from $41,000 to $27,800 for the same 4-month period. Once again,

Table 8-8: Monthly Cash Outflows, Level Production

	Nov	Dec	Jan	Feb	Mar	Apr
Sales	$80,000	$100,000	$30,000	$40,000	$50,000	$60,000
Materials and supplies purchases (50% of average monthly sales)	29,200	29,200	29,200	29,200	29,200	29,200
Payments (100% of purchases of the second previous month)			29,200	29,200	29,200	29,200
Salaries and overhead			20,000	20,000	20,000	20,000
Interest				7,000		
Dividends					6,000	
Taxes					3,000	
Capital expenditures				$50,000		
Total cash payments			$49,200	$106,200	$58,200	$49,200

you can see that analyzing the financial data and forecasts in different ways is beneficial.

The projections on a cash budget will reflect the firm's marketing efforts as well as its credit policies, how it manages its receivables, and how it decides to manage its production and inventories. In general, firms with larger receivables balances and easier credit terms will have slower cash receipt inflows, but this must be balanced against the competitive impact of tightening up its receivables management policies.

Firms with larger inventories will face large accounts payable balances and larger cash payments than firms operating on leaner inventories and tighter production schedules.

Table 8-9: Net Monthly Cash Outflows, Level Production

	Jan	Feb	Mar	Apr
Total cash receipts	$90,000	$65,000	$35,000	$45,000
Less: Total cash payments	49,200	106,200	58,200	49,200
Net cash flow	$40,800	($41,200)	($23,200)	($ 4,200)

Table 8-10: Monthly Cash Budget, Level Production

	Jan	Feb	Mar	Apr
Net cash flow	$40,800	($41,200)	($23,200)	($4,200)
Beginning cash balance	25,000	65,800	25,000	25,000
Cumulative cash balance	65,800	24,600	1,800	20,800
Monthly loan (or repayment)	0	400	23,200	4,200
Cumulative loan balance	0	400	23,600	27,800
Ending cash balance	$65,800	$25,000	$25,000	$25,000

SELF-CHECK

- Define **level production** plan.
- Explain how the choice of season or level production affects a firm's monthly cash flows over the course of a year.

8.6 Management of Current Assets

Management of current assets involves the administration of cash, marketable securities, accounts receivable, and inventories. On the one hand, the financial manager should strive to minimize the investment in current assets because of the cost of financing them. On the other hand, adequate cash and marketable securities are necessary for liquidity purposes, acceptable credit terms

FOR EXAMPLE

Seasonal Sales

In addition to companies that have seasonal production, there are also firms that have seasonal sales. For example, Christmas sales, sales from the Thursday after Thanksgiving to Christmas Eve account for 25% of the retail industry's revenue. In addition, this period of time is the second largest grossing period for the movie industry as well, surpassed only by summer. The film industry releases their best films at this time not only to capture the holiday audiences, but also to position themselves for the Academy Awards.

are necessary to maintain sales, and appropriate inventory levels must be kept to avoid running out of stock and losing sales. Successful management requires a continual balancing of the costs and benefits associated with investment in current assets.

8.6.1 Cash and Marketable Securities

Business firms should strive to minimize their cash holdings since, under current law, businesses cannot earn interest on funds in their checking accounts. Some large firms exist with virtually no cash balances although others hold billions of dollars in cash and marketable securities. For firms that operate with little or no cash, whatever funds they need they obtain from short-term bank loans or overdrafts that are repaid the next day from cash inflows or from selling marketable securities. The greater the ability of a firm to tap into short-term sources of financing, which will be covered in the next chapter, the less the need to hold cash and marketable securities balances. Firms that do hold cash generally do so for specific reasons.

Some cash is necessary to carry on day-to-day operations. This is the transactions motive or demand for holding cash.

▲ The **transactions motives** are demands for holding cash is that cash is needed to conduct day-to-day operations.

If cash inflows and outflows could be projected with virtual certainty, the transactions demand for cash could theoretically be reduced to zero. Most businesses prepare cash flow forecasts or budgets, trying to predict the amount of cash holdings they will need. However, most firms are forced to hold some cash because of cash flow uncertainties and because minimum cash balances often are required on loans from commercial banks.

Marketable securities are held primarily for precautionary motives.

▲ **Precautionary motives** are demands for funds that may be caused by unpredictable events, such as delays in production or in the collection of receivables.

Marketable securities can be sold to satisfy such liquidity problems. In the event of strong seasonal sales patterns, marketable securities can also be used to reduce large fluctuations in short-term financing requirements. Funds may be held for precautionary reasons, so the firm can continue to invest in assets like plant, equipment, and technology, even if future sales and cash flows fall.

Marketable securities may also be held for speculative motives.

▲ **Speculative motives** are demands for funds to take advantage of unusual cash discounts for needed materials.

In certain instances, a company might be able to take advantage of unusual cash discounts or bargain prices on materials if it can pay quickly with cash. Marketable securities are easily converted into cash for such purposes.

To qualify as a marketable security, an investment must be highly liquid—that is, it must be readily convertible to cash without a losing its value. Generally, this requires that it have a short maturity and that an active secondary market exists so that it can be sold prior to maturity if necessary. The security must also be of high quality, with little chance that the borrower will default.

U.S. Treasury bills offer the highest quality, liquidity, and marketability. Other investments that serve well as marketable securities include negotiable certificates of deposit (CDs) and commercial paper, both of which offer higher rates but are more risky and less liquid than treasury bills. Business firms can also hold excess funds in money market accounts, or they can purchase bankers' acceptances or short-term notes of U.S. government agencies.

8.6.2 U.S. Treasury Bills

Treasury bills are sold at a discount through competitive bidding in a weekly auction. These bills are offered in all parts of the country but sell mostly in New York City. Treasury bills are actively traded in secondary money markets, again mostly in New York.

U.S. Treasury bills are considered to be essentially risk-free in that there is virtually no chance of default. Consequently, interest rates are higher for other money market instruments of similar maturity at the same point in time. Once again, this points out the fact that higher investment risk is expected to bring in higher returns.

Corporate financial managers who find themselves with excess cash receipts sometimes attempt to "ride the yield curve" (an example of the yield curve is shown in Figure 8-5). When the yield curve is sloping up, they use their excess cash to purchase longer-term securities rather than short-term ones. (In this case, longer-term securities mean investments that mature in a year, rather than short-term securities that often mature within 30 days.) This is because longer-term securities yield higher interest income when the yield curve is sloping upward. Also, as the security nears maturity with a rising yield curve, its market yield will fall, and a falling interest rate results in higher prices for fixed-income securities. Therefore, aggressive financial managers ride the curve to try to get higher returns on the investments made with excess cash inflows.

8.6.3 Federal Funds

Managing working capital is a necessary skill for managers regardless of the type or size of the business enterprise. Consider that as a result of normal operations,

Figure 8-5

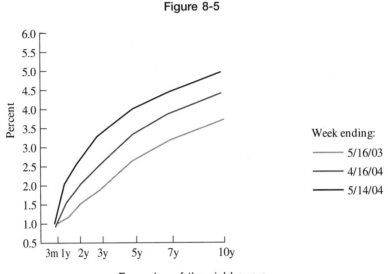

Examples of the yield curve.

some commercial banks and other depository institutions find their reserves are temporarily greater than their required reserves. These temporary excess reserves, *federal funds* as they are called when loaned, are lent on a day-to-day basis to other depository institutions that are temporarily short of reserves.

The lending for a 1-day period is generally done by an electronic funds transfer and can be illustrated with an example involving two commercial banks. The deal may be made by one or more telephone calls from the bank wanting to borrow funds, or it may be arranged through a federal funds broker. Funds are electronically transferred from the lending bank's reserve account to the borrowing bank's reserve account at the Federal Reserve Bank. Repayment of the loan plus interest occurs the next day. Many of these transactions are between New York City banks, but banks in other cities also enter the New York money market, usually as lenders. The most common trading unit for federal funds is $1 million, but this is often exceeded.

Federal funds rates usually parallel U.S. Treasury bill rates. Normally the spread, or difference, between the two rates is narrow. However, during periods of tight money and credit, federal funds can be bid up to very high levels. Banks and other depository institutions choose between borrowing at the discount rate from the Federal Reserve and borrowing federal funds to meet reserve requirements. If they could be freely substituted for each other, the discount rate set in accordance with monetary policy objectives would set an upper limit for the federal funds rate, since banks would borrow at the lower of the two rates. In practice, however, banks prefer to borrow federal funds, even at the high rates that occur when money is tight, rather than borrow too frequently from the Federal Reserve, which discourages continued use of this alternative.

8.6.4 Commercial Paper

Commercial paper is the short-term, unsecured notes of well-known business firms such as IBM or General Electric. Basically, these are unsecured promissory notes, but financially strong firms such as these are able to raise short-term funds virtually at will by selling "IOUs" to financial market participants who seek short-term investments for their funds. Both major finance companies and nonfinancial corporations have sold commercial paper through dealers or commercial paper houses for many years. More recently, many issuers, particularly finance companies, have begun to issue or sell their own commercial paper.

Of course, because of a great risk of default, commercial paper rates for similar maturities are higher than treasury bill rates at any point in time. However, since commercial paper rates are typically below bank prime rates, they are a valuable short-term financing source for high-quality business firms.

8.6.5 Negotiable Certificates of Deposit

A certificate of deposit is in essence a receipt issued by a bank in exchange for a deposit of funds. The bank agrees to pay the amount deposited plus interest to the bearer of the receipt on the date specified on the certificate. Many banks had issued such certificates as early as the turn of the century, but before 1960 they were rarely issued in negotiable form.

Negotiable CDs can be traded in the secondary market before maturity. The volume of negotiable CDs (usually issued in denominations of $100,000 or more) has increased dramatically. Interest rates on these CDs usually parallel rates on other money market instruments such as commercial paper and bankers' acceptances, which are promissory notes issued by a firm and guaranteed by a bank. The interest rates on these instruments are above the less-risky treasury bill rates.

8.6.6 Bankers' Acceptances

Bankers' acceptances are primarily used to finance exports and imports. Since it is the unconditional obligation of the accepting bank, these notes generally have a high-quality rating. Yields on bankers' acceptances closely follow yields on commercial paper.

8.6.7 Eurodollars

Eurodollars are deposits placed in foreign banks that remain denominated in U.S. dollars. A demand deposit in a U.S. bank becomes a Eurodollar when the holder of such a deposit transfers it to a foreign bank or an overseas branch of an American bank. After the transfer, the foreign bank holds a claim against the U.S. bank, while the original deposit holder (usually a business firm) now holds a

Eurodollar deposit. It is called a *Eurodollar deposit* because it is still denominated in U.S. dollars rather than in the currency of the country in which the foreign bank operates.

Large commercial banks have raised money by borrowing from the Eurodollar market through their overseas branches. Overseas branches of U.S. banks and banks outside the United States get funds in the Eurodollar market by accepting dollars in interest-bearing time deposit accounts. These dollar deposits are lent anywhere in the world, usually on a short-term basis. Banks generally transfer funds by telephone or electronically, lending large sums without collateral between banks. Banks that handle Eurodollars are located in Europe, with London as the center, and in other financial centers throughout the world, including such places as Singapore and the Bahamas.

Eurodollar deposit liabilities have arisen because the dollar is widely used as an international currency and because foreigners are holding more dollars as a result of the ongoing U.S. balance-of-payment problems. Eurodollars are supplied by national and international corporations, banks, insurance companies, wealthy individuals, and some foreign governments and agencies. Eurodollar loan recipients also are a diverse group, but commercial banks, multinational corporations, and national corporations are heavy users.

There are several major reasons why U.S. banks have entered the Eurodollar market through their overseas branches:

▲ To finance business activity abroad
▲ To switch Eurodollars into other currencies
▲ To lend to other Eurodollar banks

Other than those previously listed, the most important reason, and the one that has received the most publicity in the United States, is for banking offices in the United States to borrow Eurodollars from their overseas branches. In this way they get funds at lower costs and during periods of tight money.

A summary of short-term instruments and their interest rates, as of mid-2004, is shown in Figure 8-6.

FOR EXAMPLE

Preferred Parking

Where do firms invest their short-term cash holdings? U.S. government securities (mainly treasury bills) are the most popular place to "park" cash, followed by CDs (time deposits), commercial paper, and other short-term investments such as bankers' acceptances and Eurodollars.

Figure 8-6

Money Rates

Thursday, June 10, 2004

The key U. S. and foreign annual interest rates below are a guide to general levels but don't always represent actual transactions.

Commercial Paper

Yields paid by corporations for short-term financing, typically for daily operation

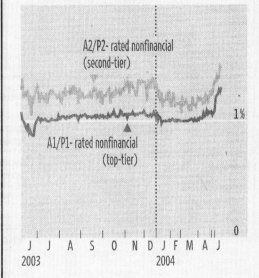

J J A S O N D J F M A J
2003   2004

Source: Federal Reserve

Prime Rate: 4.00% (effective 06/27/03). The base rate on corporate loans posted by at least 75% of the nation's 30 largest banks.
Discount Rate (Primary): 2.00% (effective 06/25/03).
Federal Funds: 1.063% high, 0.875% low, 0.875% near closing bid, 1.000% offered. Effective rate: 1.01%. Source: Prebon Yamane (USA) Inc. Federal-funds target rate: 1.000% (effective 06/25/03).
Call Money: 2.75% (effective 06/30/03).
Commercial Paper: Placed directly by General Electric Capital Corp.: 0.80% 30 to 34 days; 1.13% 35 to 59 days; 1.23% 60 to 90 days; 1.38% 91 to 105 days; 0.80% 106 to 117 days; 1.49% 118 to 145 days; 1.59% 146 to 178 days; 1.70% 179 to 209 days; 1.80% 210 to 238 days; 1.90% 239 to 270 days.
Euro Commercial Paper: Placed directly by General Electric

Capital Corp.: 2.04% 30 days; 2.05% two months; 2.07% three months; 2.09% four months; 2.11% five months; 2.14% six months.
Dealer Commercial Paper: High-grade unsecured notes sold through dealers by major corporations: 1.12% 30 days; 1.27% 60 days; 1.40% 90 days.
Certificates of Deposit: 1.15% one month; 1.43% three months; 1.75% six months.
Bankers Acceptances: 1.11% 30 days; 1.22% 60 days; 1.40% 90 days; 1.54% 120 days; 1.64% 150 days; 1.73% 180 days. Source: Prebon Yamane (USA) Inc.
Eurodollars: 1.12% - 1.10% one month; 1.25% - 1.22% two months; 1.40% - 1.37% three months; 1.58% - 1.54% four months; 1.67% - 1.64% five months; 1.76% - 1.73% six months. Source: Prebon Yamane (USA) Inc.
London Interbank Offered Rates (Libor): 1.21125% one month; 1.46875% three months; 1.7950% six months; 2.3650% one year. Effective rate for contracts entered into two days from date appearing at top of this column.
Euro Libor: 2.07588% one month; 2.10738% three months; 2.18350% six months; 2.40200% one year. Effective rate for contracts entered into two days from date appearing at top of this column.
Euro Interbank Offered Rates (Euribor): 2.077% one month; 2.109% three months; 2.178% six months; 2.386% one year. Source: Reuters.
Foreign Prime Rates: Canada 3.75%; European Central Bank 2.00%; Japan 1.375%; Switzerland 2.13%; Britain 4.50%.
Treasury Bills: Results of the Monday, June 7, 2004, auction of short-term U.S. government bills, sold at a discount from face value in units of $1,000 to $1 million: 1.230% 13 weeks; 1.505% 26 weeks. Tuesday, June 8, 2004 auction: 1.000% 4 weeks.
Overnight Repurchase Rate: 0.95%. Source: Garban Intercapital.
Freddie Mac: Posted yields on 30-year mortgage commitments. Delivery within 30 days 6.06%, 60 days 6.13%, standard conventional fixed-rate mortgages: 2.875%, 2% rate capped one-year adjustable rate mortgages.
Fannie Mae: Posted yields on 30 year mortgage commitments (priced at par) for delivery within 30 days 6.12%, 60 days 6.19%, standard conventional fixed-rate mortgages; 3.40%, 6/2 rate capped one-year adjustable rate mortgages. Constant Maturity Debt Index: 1.369% three months; 1.743% six months; 2.309% one year.
Merrill Lynch Ready Assets Trust: 0.52%.
Consumer Price Index: April, 188.0, up 2.3% from a year ago. Bureau of Labor Statistics.

Short-term interest rates.

SELF-CHECK

- Define **transactions motives**, **precautionary motives**, and **speculative motives**.
- Why do firms hold cash and marketable securities?
- What are Eurodollars and why would a firm use them?
- List at least four types of marketable securities a firm may use to invest excess cash to earn a short-term loan

8.7 Getting—and Keeping—the Cash

In addition to prudent investment of excess cash, there is another aspect of cash management that requires attention. Managers must monitor the cash conversion cycle and endeavor to speed up cash collections while slowing down the payment process. In effect they are then allowing the company to retain the funds for a longer period of time, which could reduce or eliminate the necessity of outside funding. Ethically there are concerns with lengthening the payables period by paying bills late, and it could damage the company's credit rating. However, there are tools that company's use to speed up collections and slow down disbursements. Most of them use the concept of float.

▲ **Float** is the time between sending out payments and having them actually be charged to the bank account.
▲ **Collection float** is the time between when a payer sends payment and the funds are credited to the payee's bank account.
▲ **Disbursement float** is the time between when a payer sends payment and when the funds are deducted from the payer's bank account.

Individuals can appreciate the concept of float just by comparing their checkbook balance to the bank's record of their checking account balance. The difference between the two amounts arises because of float. Float is the checks that have been written but have not yet been deducted from your account.

By taking steps to reduce collection float or to increase disbursement float, the firm's treasurer can reduce the cash conversion cycle. Reducing the cash conversion cycle benefits the firm. Besides reducing the need for external financing, it leads to increased profitability.

Extra cash can be invested in securities, used to reduce interest-bearing loans, invested productively in the firm, or distributed to shareholders.

Float, whether we are dealing with collections or disbursements, has three components.

1. Delivery or transmission float. This is the delay in transferring the means of payment from the payer (customer) to the payee (the provider of the goods or services). A payment placed in the mail may take several days before it reaches its destination.

2. Processing float. Once the payment reaches its destination, an envelope must be opened and its contents processed and entered into the firm's financial processing system.

3. Clearing float. This is the delay in transferring funds between payer and payee because of the banking system. You have probably seen this in your bank statements or in your bank's check availability policy; funds from a check deposited in your account may not be available to you for 1 to 3 days. This time is needed for the check to be routed back to the payer's bank and for the payer's bank to transfer funds to your bank.

Seeking ways to reduce the components of collection float is one of the practical issues facing a firm's treasurer. To speed up cash collections from customers, firms can use a lockbox system. If you pay your phone bill, utility bill, or credit card bill to a "P. O. box number" address, the firm receiving your payment is probably using a lockbox. Most lockboxes are managed by banks. Several times a day, bank personnel will empty the postal box and immediately begin processing and depositing payments from customers. You can readily see the benefits of this system as payments are processed almost immediately instead of sitting on someone's desk for a day or two.

Preauthorized checks are a means to reduce both delivery and processing delays.

▲ **Preauthorized checks** are regular (typically monthly) deductions by a vendor from a customer's checking account.

These represent instant withdrawals for the payer and instant receipts for the payee.

Processing delays (as well as some delivery delays) are reduced by the use of technology. Large incoming payments (say, over $1 million) can be automatically flagged by the lockbox bank and alerts sent to the firm's treasurer. Electronic check images and electronic payments (rather than the use of paper checks) reduce mail and processing delays. Forms recognition technology allows incoming payments and data to be read electronically and for data to be stored in a form usable to the vendor. Use of the Internet and other electronic means for making payments eliminates delivery float and speeds processing.

FOR EXAMPLE

Online Banking

Many companies pay their bills electronically. Also, many Americans are using online banking for their own personal finances. Over 22 million people pay bills online. Bank of America reports that half of their customers pay their bills online. Many banks are experiencing the same phenomena. Online banking offers many advantages, such as an easy way to search transactions, no postage costs, and you can enter in payments ahead of time before you want them sent. The main concern remains, and will probably always be, security. If someone hacked into your account or into the bank's mainframe, you could be robbed of your money. Banks heavily invest in security safeguards to prevent this from happening.

Clearing float is reduced by the Fed and the banking system. Under Check 21, a new law that went into effect in late 2004, payee banks can present electronic or digital images of checks to payer banks, rather than having to physically deliver paper checks for payment. As this technology is adopted, clearing delays will be greatly reduced as this law eliminates the need to physically transport, record, and reconcile billions of paper checks per year.

Fewer options are available for slowing disbursements because of fears of being considered a poor customer at best or unethical at worst. When credit gets tight, the slow-paying customers will be the first ones terminated. Most disbursement systems involve selected banks where funds to be disbursed are deposited to maximize float. Many firms use a zero-balance account in which just enough funds are transferred into an account to cover that day's checks presented for payment.

With the growing use of electronic payments, it's only a matter of time before float will totally disappear.

SELF-CHECK

- Define **float, collection float,** and **disbursement float.**
- List the components of float.
- Give an example of float in personal finance.
- What is the purpose of the Check 21 law?

8.8 Accounts Receivable Management and Credit Analysis

The management of receivables involves conducting credit analysis, setting credit terms, and carrying out collection efforts. Taken together, these decision areas determine the level of investment in accounts receivable. The selling of goods on credit is generally driven by industry norms and competitive pressures. The time it takes to collect accounts receivable depends on industry norms for credit terms, as well as the firm's policies for setting credit standards and carrying out collection efforts.

Credit analysis involves appraising the creditworthiness or quality of a potential customer. The decision to grant credit to an individual or another company is made on the basis of the applicant's character, capacity, capital, collateral, and conditions. These are the five Cs of credit analysis, and they can be broken down as follows:

▲ **Character** is the ethical quality of the applicant and his/her willingness to pay bills on time and is best judged by reviewing the past credit history of the company or person.

▲ **Capacity** is the ability to pay bills and often involves an examination of liquidity ratios.

▲ **Capital** indicates the adequacy of owners' equity relative to existing liabilities as the underlying support for creditworthiness.

▲ **Collateral** reflects whether assets are available to provide security for the potential credit.

▲ **Conditions** refer to the current economic climate and state of the business cycle. They are an important consideration in assessing whether the applicant can meet credit obligations.

Once a firm has established its credit quality standards, credit analysis is used to determine whether an applicant is granted credit or rejected, or falls into a marginal category. Whether or not credit should be extended to marginal applicants depends on such factors as the prevailing economic conditions and the extent to which the selling firm has excess production capacity. During periods of economic downturn and excess capacity, a firm may need to sell to lower-quality credit applicants who may be slow paying but are not likely to default.

An example of this comes from your local car dealership. To entice buyers when sales are sluggish, auto manufacturers may offer below-market financing rates, attractive refunds, and/or low (or no) down payment requirements. Sales can rise sharply as a result of aggressive marketing via credit terms, but there is a definite downside. In 2003–2004, Mitsubishi extended credit to some buyers who found themselves unable to repay the loans with the result of large losses accruing to the firm. When Mitsubishi tightened its credit standards, sales fell sharply. The success of a firm requires a product offering good value to customers more so than attractive credit terms.

8.8.1 Credit-Reporting Agencies

Several sources of credit information are available to help a firm decide whether or not to extend credit. **Credit bureaus** exist to obtain credit information about business firms and individuals. Credit bureaus are nonprofit institutions, established and supported by the businesses they serve.

The local mercantile, or business, credit bureau provides a central record for credit information on firms in the community. Bureau members submit lists of their customers to the bureau. The bureau determines the credit standing of these customers by contacting other bureau members who have extended credit to them. A member firm need only contact its credit bureau for information on prospective customers rather than deal with many individual creditors.

The exchange of mercantile credit information from bureau to bureau is accomplished through the National Credit Interchange System. Credit bureau reports are factual rather than analytical, and it is up to each credit analyst to interpret the facts.

Local retail credit bureaus have been established to consolidate and distribute credit information on individuals in the community. These organizations are generally owned and operated by participating members on a nonprofit basis. A central organization known as the Associated Credit Bureaus of America enables local retail credit bureaus in the United States to transmit credit information from bureau to bureau.

American businesses selling to foreign customers encounter all the problems involved in a domestic sale, such as credit checking, plus several others. Among these are increased distance, language differences, complicated shipping, government regulations, differences in legal systems, and political instability. To help exporters with these problems, the National Association of Credit Management established the Foreign Credit Interchange Bureau. Just as local credit bureaus increase their information on business credit risks by pooling credit and collection experience, so the members of the Foreign Credit Interchange Bureau have established a central file of information covering several decades of credit experience. The Bureau is located in New York to serve the numerous export and financial organizations there that do business overseas.

Some private firms also operate as credit-reporting agencies. The best known is Dun & Bradstreet, which has been in operation for well over a century and provides credit information on businesses of all kinds. The information that is assembled and evaluated is brought into the company through many channels. The company employs full- and part-time employees for direct investigation, communicates directly with business establishments by mail to supplement information files, and obtains the financial statements of companies being evaluated.

All information filed with public authorities and financial and trade papers is carefully gathered and analyzed to produce a credit analysis. The basic service supplied to the manufacturers, wholesalers, banks, and insurance companies who subscribe to Dun & Bradstreet is rendered in two ways: through written reports on individual businesses and through a reference book.

A Dun & Bradstreet report is typically divided into five sections: (1) rating and summary, (2) trade payments, (3) financial information, (4) operation and location, and (5) history. In addition, they publish a composite reference book of ratings on thousands of manufacturers, wholesalers, retailers, and other businesses six times per year.

When many customers want to apply for credit, in-depth credit analysis focusing on the five Cs is not practical. Companies that offer credit cards use a sophisticated statistical tool called *credit scoring*. Credit scoring takes information about thousands of customers and, through computer number-crunching, develops a formula that tries to predict who is a good credit risk (someone who will likely pay their bill in a timely manner) and who is a poor credit risk. Credit scoring models use quantitative items such as a person's income, past mortgage or credit card payment history, marital status, homeowner/renter status, and current debts to make this determination. However, such models will make errors. One person applied for a credit card and was rejected despite having a clean credit record. He earns $123,100 in salary at age 41 in a job with excellent security. The person was Lawrence B. Lindsey, who at the time was on the board of governors of the Federal Reserve System. A man who helps set interest rate and bank policy was rejected because the computer models could not handle the qualitative data that explained why his credit report appeared as it did.

8.8.2 Credit Terms and Collection Efforts

Businesses extend trade credit to their customers. **Trade credit** is extended on purchases to a firm's customers.

This credit appears as accounts payable on the balance sheet of the customer and as accounts receivables to the seller. The seller sets the terms of the credit. For example, the firm might require full payment in 60 days, expressed as net 60. If all customers pay promptly in 60 days, this would result in a receivables turnover of 365/60, or about six times a year. Based on that, annual net sales of $720,000 would require an average receivables investment of about $120,000. A change in credit terms or in the enforcement of the terms through the collection effort will alter the average investment in receivables. As you saw earlier, shortening the collection time for receivables results in the reduction of the average investment in receivable. The imposition of net 50-day terms would lead to an increase in the receivables turnover to 7.3 (365/50) times and the average investment in receivables would decline to about $100,000 ($720,000/7.3).

Table 8-11: Analysis of a Change in Credit Policy

Marginal or Additional Benefits:
Increased sales (estimate): $100,000
Additional bad debt expense from change in sales: 5%
0.05 × $100,000 = $5,000 in losses
Net estimated increase in sales: $95,000.
Expected profit margin: 10%
Net increase in profits = 0.10 × $95,000 = $9,500
Marginal or Additional Costs:
Increases in asset accounts:
Accounts receivables average increase: $14,000
Inventory average increase: $18,000
Total: $32,000 increase in current assets to be financed.
Cost of financing: 15%
Net increase in financing costs = 0.15 × $32,000 = $4,800

Assuming that interest rate on external funding was 15%, this would save the company $3,000 ($20,000 × 15%).

The financial manager must be very careful not to impose credit terms that will alienate customers and lower sales, as lost profits would more than offset any financing cost savings. Table 8-11 shows the effect that changing credit terms could have on a company's current assets.

8.8.3 Global Credit

In a global business, a concern with managing accounts from overseas is the effect of changing exchange rates on the funds received by the firm. For example, assume a firm sells an item for $50 to customers in the United States and for $57 to customers in France based upon an exchange rate of about $1 = 1.14 euros. Over the next 60 days when payment is due, should the dollar strengthen ($1 = 1.20 euros), only $47.50 will come in, which will hurt its profitability.

There are two ways for a firm to handle this issue. First, the firm can invoice customers in the firm's home currency. That is, a U.S. firm can request payment from a customer in France in terms of the U.S. dollar instead of the euro. This shifts the risk of changing exchange rates to the payer. Second, if a U.S. firm

> **FOR EXAMPLE**
>
> **Collections**
>
> Collecting money on past-due accounts is a tough job. Collectors use a variety of techniques to collect money for firms. Techniques include sending letters, making telephone calls, and even making personal visits for very large customers with past-due bills. One credit card company sent Hallmark greeting cards to delinquent customers to encourage them to contact the firm and arrange a repayment schedule. If the customer continues to fail to pay a bill, then the account may be turned over to a commercial collection firm. If this fails, the last resort is to take legal action.

allows customers to pay in their own currencies rather than in U.S. dollars, the firm can hedge, or reduce the risk, of changing exchange rates by using currency futures or options contracts.

SELF-CHECK

- List the five Cs of credit analysis.
- Explain the purpose of the following agencies: National Credit Interchange System, Associated Credit Bureaus of America, and the Foreign Credit Interchange Bureau.
- Define **credit bureaus** and **trade credit**.
- How can a firm manage accounts from overseas effectively?

8.9 Inventory Management

Inventory management is primarily a production management function. The length of the production process and the production manager's willingness to accept delays will influence the amount invested in raw materials and work in progress. The amount of finished goods available for sale may depend on the company's willingness to accept stockouts and lost sales. Ideally, the financial manager must also be involved in the inventory decisions. If the firm is able to increase its inventory turnover, then the investment in inventories could be reduced and some financing costs would be saved. However, if a tight inventory policy is imposed, lost sales due to stockouts could result in lost profits that more than offset financing cost savings. So reducing the inventory turnover could reduce the investment in inventory and some financing costs could be saved.

However, the financial manager must balance the possible savings against potential costs if a tight inventory policy results in lost sales.

The **just-in-time (JIT) inventory control system** is gaining increased acceptance by firms trying to reduce the amount of inventories they must carry. This is a system where there are enough materials in inventory to cover needs for a short time, but not more inventory than is needed for short-term needs. With this system, the vendor and the manufacturer work together to reduce lead time, setup time, and production time so when needs surpass the inventory, the manufacturer can get it to the company quickly or "just in time." Under this system, substantial coordination is required between the manufacturer and its suppliers so that materials needed for the manufacturing process are delivered just in time to avoid delays in production. For example, automobile manufacturers who used to keep a 2-week supply of certain parts now place orders on a daily basis and expect daily shipment and delivery.

The latest innovation in inventory control is JIT II, which moves the JIT relationship between vendor and purchaser one step closer. The position of the buyer's purchasers or materials planners is eliminated and replaced by a representative of the supplier. This person works closely with the buyer to, at times, manage inventories and issue purchase orders to supply additional materials. The advantages of this new system are increased efficiency by reducing inventory, eliminating duplicate positions and assistance in planning.

Tracking inventory also allows firms to reduce the inventory conversion period and the cash conversion cycle. Bar codes on boxes are scanned to track inventory in transit between vendor, warehouse, retail store, and checkout counter. RFID (radio frequency identification) tag sends out a radio signal to electronic readers that allow companies to know the location of inventory on a minute-by-minute basis. RFID tags for cargo containers can send alarms when a break-in has occurred; when it has been sitting in one location for too long; or when preset conditions relating to temperature, air pressure, motion, and so on, inside the container are violated. Tracking inventory with such detail can

FOR EXAMPLE

Just-in-Time Inventory and Dell

Dell Computers began with a simple proposition: They would have no inventory. When you order a Dell, parts are shipped to Dell from one of their four manufacturing facilities in the world. Dell receives these parts usually within 24 hours; they then put together your computer. For the majority of orders, they only have physical possession of those parts for 8 hours or less. They put together the computer and then ship it to your door. This is one of the qualities of Dell that has made it successful.

reduce theft and spoilage as well as inventory levels and the cost of carrying inventory.

Cutting working capital generates cash and can increase company earnings. Financing costs should decline as less financing is needed to support large receivable and inventory balances. Cost of warehousing and handling inventory will fall as inventory levels are reduced. Slimmed-down asset balances will lead to reduction in total assets. The results of cost savings and smaller asset bases will mean higher returns on assets and, in all likelihood, increases in shareholder wealth.

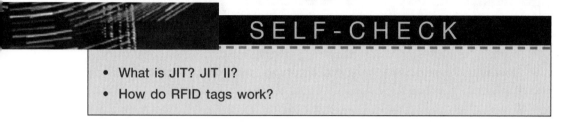

SELF-CHECK

- What is JIT? JIT II?
- How do RFID tags work?

8.10 Technology and Managing Working Capital

Technology is improving the ability of firms to manage cash and receivables, to control inventory, and to communicate with customers and suppliers more efficiently. Industries such as auto manufacturing, oil and gas, and retailing are initiating Internet-based systems or portals. **Portals** are specialized and secure Web sites through which clients can access order and account information.

B2B (business to business) portals have the promise of lowering procurement and supply-chain costs. They also provide a way for firms to sell excess inventory or assets.

The Internet also allows financial personnel to more closely track the company's cash flows and needs. Information on bank balances, incoming checks, and the status of disbursements are available online through bank portals. The use of the Web allows the transfer of funds between corporate accounts and the

FOR EXAMPLE

Helpful Web Site

Visit www.afponline.org, the Web site of the Treasury Management Association. The site is specifically oriented toward those working in cash collection, disbursement, management, and investment. Learn about the CTP (Certified Treasury Professional) professional designation while visiting this site.

initiation of electronic payments and preauthorized check transactions. Traveling executives can access financial information online from the company's bank and from all of its banking relationships. Access to such information allows the treasurer to forecast and estimate the firm's needs for cash on a day-to-day basis, thereby reducing the level of excess cash and keeping short-term borrowing at a minimum.

SELF-CHECK

- Define portals.
- How is technology improving cash management? Reducing float?
- How is technology helping to improve inventory management?

SUMMARY

As you have discovered, it is cash, not earnings, that keeps a company in business. Financial managers are therefore mainly interested in watching a firm's cash flows and forecasting future cash flows to ensure adequate cash is available when the firm's obligations are due. In this chapter, you examined several aspects of working capital management that will be of practical concern to those watching the firm's cash flow. You also determined the impact inventory has on a company. You assessed a cash budget and how it is used. You examined accounts receivable management and how it is best carried out. With these skills, you will help a firm not only stay in business but also be profitable.

KEY TERMS

Capacity	The ability to pay bills and often involves an examination of liquidity ratios.
Capital	The adequacy of owners' equity relative to existing liabilities as the underlying support for creditworthiness.
Cash budget	The cash inflows and cash outflows of a firm over a specific time frame.
Cash conversion cycle	The time it takes to collect money from the company's customers and use those funds to pay its suppliers.

Character	The ethical quality of the applicant and his/her willingness to pay bills on time and is best judged by reviewing the past credit history for the company or person.
Collateral	Assets that secure credit.
Collection float	The time between when a payer sends payment and the funds are credited to the payee's bank account.
Conditions	The current economic climate and state of the business cycle. They are an important consideration in assessing whether the applicant can meet credit obligations.
Credit bureaus	Firms that obtain credit information about business firms and individuals.
Disbursement float	The time between when a payer sends payment and when the funds are deducted from the payer's bank account.
Fixed capital	A firm's fixed assets, which include plant, equipment, and property.
Float	The time between sending out payments and having them actually be charged to the bank account.
Just-in-time (JIT) inventory control system	A system where there are enough materials in inventory to cover needs for a short time, but not more inventory than is needed for short-term needs.
Level production plan	Schedule where the same amount of raw material is purchased and the same amount of finished product is manufactured every month.
Operating cycle	The time between receiving raw materials and collecting the cash from credit sales posted to accounts receivables.
Portals	Specialized and secure Web sites through which clients can access order and account information.
Preauthorized checks	Regular (typically monthly) deductions by a vendor from a customer's checking account.
Precautionary motives	Demands for funds that may be caused by unpredictable events, such as delays in production or in the collection of receivables.

Speculative motives	Demands for funds to take advantage of unusual cash discounts for needed materials.
Trade credit	Credit that is extended on purchases to a firm's customers.
Transactions motives	Demands for holding cash is that cash is needed to conduct day-to-day operations.
Working capital	A firm's current assets as shown on the balance sheet and includes cash in the bank accounts, marketable securities, inventory, and accounts receivable.

ASSESS YOUR UNDERSTANDING

Go to www.wiley.com/college/Melicher to evaluate your knowledge of the basics of managing capital.

Measure your learning by comparing pre-test and post-test results.

Summary Questions

1. Working capital is essentially a firm's current assets and consists of cash, accounts receivable, inventories, plant, and equipment. True or false?

2. Fixed capital would be defined as the firm's fixed assets, which include plant, equipment, and property. True or false?

3. The operating cycle measures the time it takes between ordering materials and collecting cash from receivables. True or false?

4. If a firm has $50,000 in profit and pays out about one-half to the owners of the company, the amount of profit retained in the firm would show up as

   (a) an increase in owners' equity.

   (b) a decrease in owners' equity.

   (c) a decrease in retained earnings.

   (d) a decrease in long-term debt.

5. The accounts payable period is the time between a firm's paying its suppliers for inventory and collecting cash from inventories. True or false?

6. Increases in the cash conversion cycle will lower the firm's short-term financing needs. True or false?

7. The inventory conversion period is calculated by inventory divided by costs of goods sold. True or false?

8. Activities that decrease the cash conversion cycle will increase the firm's need to obtain financing. True or false?

9. More efficient management of working capital assets will lessen the firm's needs for financing. True or false?

10. A cash budget is a tool the treasurer uses to forecast future cash flows and estimate future short-term borrowing needs. True or false?

11. To construct a cash budget, two sets of information are needed: estimated cash inflows and estimated cash outflows. True or false?

12. The estimated cash inflows are affected by the sales forecast and customer payment patterns. True or false?

13. Assume a firm's production process requires an average of 80 days to go from raw materials to finished products and another 40 days before the

finished goods are sold. If the accounts receivable cycle is 70 days and the accounts payable cycle is 80 days, what would the short-term operating cycle be?

(a) 110 days

(b) 130 days

(c) 190 days

(d) 270 days

14. If a firm has net sales of $400,000, annual cost of goods sold of $315,000, an inventory turnover of 4.5 times a year, and an accounts receivable turnover of five times a year, the combined investment in inventories and accounts receivable would be

(a) $64,500.

(b) $92,000.

(c) $122,500.

(d) $150,000.

15. Calculation of a firm's average collection period is the same as calculating the

(a) accounts receivable cycle.

(b) inventory cycle.

(c) accounts payable cycle.

(d) short-term operating cycle.

16. Which one of the following activities is not a major component of the short-term cash operating cycle?

(a) Manufacturing process

(b) Selling effort

(c) Collection period

(d) Asset investment decisions

17. A level production plan has problems, such as idle plant and laid-off workers during slow sales months and production bottlenecks during busy times. True or false?

18. The accounts receivable period may be calculated as accounts receivable divided by daily sales. True or false?

19. The transactions motive is the demand for holding cash. True or false?

20. Firms may not sell marketable securities to cover cash shortfalls. True or false?

21. The federal funds rate is normally several points lower than the treasury bill rate. True or false?

22. The five Cs of credit analysis is a popular concept used by inventory managers. True or false?

23. A mercantile credit bureau serves primarily as a(n)

   (a) collection agency for delinquent accounts.

   (b) common meeting place where credit managers may exchange information.

   (c) organization through which accounts receivable may be sold to other businesses.

   (d) central record-keeping organization for credit information on business firms.

24. The objective of just-in-time (JIT) inventory control is to carry a minimum level of inventories. True or false?

25. The delivery or transmission float is the delay in transferring the means of payment from the payer (customer) to the payee (the provider of goods or services). True or false?

26. The disbursement float is the delay in transferring the means of payment from the payer (customer) to the payee (the provider of goods or services). True or false?

Review Questions

1. What is meant by *working capital?*

2. Briefly describe a manufacturing firm's operating cycle.

3. Explain how the cash conversion cycle differs from the operating cycle.

4. Describe how the length of the cash conversion cycle is determined.

5. Explain how the length of the operating cycle affects the amount of funds invested in accounts receivable and inventories.

6. What affects the amount of financing provided by accounts payable as viewed in terms of the cash conversion cycle?

7. What is a cash budget? How does the treasurer use forecasts of cash surpluses and cash deficits?

8. Three sets of information are needed to construct a cash budget. Explain what they are.

9. Why might firms want to maintain minimum desired cash balances?

10. What are the sources of cash inflows to a firm over any time frame?

11. What are the sources of cash outflows from a firm over any time frame?

12. How does the choice of level or seasonal production affect a firm's cash over the course of a year?

13. Describe what happens to a firm's current asset accounts if the firm has seasonal sales and they use (a) level production or (b) seasonal production.

14. Describe the three motives or reasons for holding cash.

15. What characteristics should an investment have to qualify as an acceptable marketable security?

16. Identify and briefly describe several financial instruments used as marketable securities.

17. What is float? Why is it important to cash management?

18. What are the three components of float? Which are under the control of the firm seeking to reduce collection float?

19. What are some strategies a firm can use to speed up its collections by reducing float?

20. How can processing float be reduced?

21. How can a firm use float to slow down its disbursements?

22. Why can't a firm that wants to increase disbursement float simply make payments after the stated due date?

23. What is credit analysis? Identify the five Cs of credit analysis.

24. Describe various credit-reporting agencies that provide information on business credit applicants.

25. How can a firm control the risk of changing exchange rates when billing an overseas customer?

26. What risks arise when a firm lowers its credit standards to try to increase sales volume?

27. How do credit terms and collection efforts affect the investment in accounts receivable?

28. How is the financial manager involved in the management of inventories?

Applying This Chapter

1. Pretty Lady Cosmetic Products has an average production process time of 40 days. Finished goods are kept on hand for an average of 15 days before they are sold. Accounts receivable are outstanding an average of 35 days, and the firm receives 40 days of credit on its purchases from suppliers.

   (a) Estimate the average length of the firm's short-term operating cycle. How often would the cycle turn over in a year?

   (b) Assume net sales of $1,200,000 and cost of goods sold of $900,000. Determine the average investment in accounts receivable, inventories, and accounts payable. What would be the net financing need considering only these three accounts?

2. The Robinson Company has the following current assets and current liabilities for these 2 years:

	2004	2005
Cash and marketable securities	$50,000	$50,000
Accounts receivable	300,000	350,000
Inventories	350,000	500,000
Total current assets	$700,000	$900,000
Accounts payable	$200,000	$250,000
Bank loan	0	$150,000
Accruals	$150,000	$200,000
Total current liabilities	$350,000	$600,000

3. If sales in 2004 were $1.2 million and sales in 2005 were $1.3 million, and cost of goods sold was 70% of sales, how long were Robinson's operating cycles and cash conversion cycles in each of these years? What caused them to change during this time?

4. The Robinson Company from Problem 2 had net sales of $1,200,000 in 2004 and $1,300,000 in 2005.

   (a) Determine the receivables turnover in each year.

   (b) Calculate the average collection period for each year.

   (c) Based on the receivables turnover for 2004, estimate the investment in receivables if net sales were $1,300,000 in 2005.

   (d) How much of a change in the 2005 receivables occurred?

5. Suppose the Robinson Company had a cost of goods sold of $1,000,000 in 2004 and $1,200,000 in 2005.

   (a) Calculate the inventory turnover for each year. Comment on your findings.

   (b) What would have been the amount of inventories in 2005 if the 2004 turnover ratio had been maintained?

6. Given Robinson's 2004 and 2005 financial information presented in problems 2 and 4,

   (a) compute its operating and cash conversion cycle in each year.

   (b) what was Robinson's net investment in working capital each year?

7. Robinson expects its 2006 sales and cost of goods sold to grow by 5% over their 2005 levels.

   (a) What will be the effect on its levels of receivables, inventories, and payments if the components of its cash conversion cycle remain at their 2005 levels? What will be its net investment in working capital?

(b) What will be the impact on its net investment in working capital in 2006 if Robinson is able to reduce its collection period by 5 days, its inventory period by 6 days, and increase its payment period by 2 days?

8. Robinson expects its 2006 sales and cost of goods sold to grow by 20% over their 2005 levels.

(a) What will be the effect on its levels of receivables, inventories, and payments if the components of its cash conversion cycle remain at their 2005 levels? What will be its net investment in working capital?

(b) What will be the impact on its net investment in working capital in 2006 if Robinson is able to reduce its inventory period by 10 days?

9. Following are financial statements for the Genatron Manufacturing Corporation for the years 2004 and 2005:

Selected Balance Sheet Information	2004	2005
Cash	$50,000	$40,000
Accounts receivable	$200,000	$260,000
Inventory	$450,000	$500,000
Total current assets	$700,000	$800,000
Bank loan, 10%	$90,000	$90,000
Accounts payable	$130,000	$170,000
Accruals	$50,000	$70,000
Total current liabilities	$270,000	$330,000
Long-term debt, 12%	$300,000	$400,000

Selected Income Statement Information	2004	2005
Net sales	$1,300,000	$1,500,000
Cost of goods sold	$780,000	$900,000
Gross profit	$520,000	$600,000
Net income	$93,000	$114,000

10. Calculate Genatron's operating cycle and cash conversion cycle for 2004 and 2005. Why did they change between these years?

11. Genatron Manufacturing expects its sales to increase by 10% in 2006. Estimate the firm's investment in accounts receivable, inventory, and accounts payable in 2006.

12. With concerns of increased competition, Genatron is planning in case its 2006 sales fall by 5% from their 2005 levels. If cost of goods sold and the current asset and liability accounts decrease proportionately,

    (a) calculate the 2006 cash conversion cycle.

    (b) calculate the 2006 net investment in working capital.

13. In Problem 10, we assumed the current asset and liability accounts decrease proportionately with Genatron's sales. This is probably unrealistic following a decline in sales. What will be the impact on the working capital accounts if its collection period lengthens by 5 days, its inventory period lengthens by 7 days, and its payment period lengthens by 3 days if Genatron's sales and COGS fall 5% from their 2005 levels?

14. Suppose Global Manufacturing is planning to change its credit policies next year. It anticipates that 10% of each month's sales will be for cash; two-thirds of each month's receivables will be collected in the following month, and one-third will be collected 2 months following their sale. Assuming the Global's sales forecast in Table 8-5 remains the same and the expected cash outflows in Table 8-6 remain the same, determine Global's revised cash budget.

15. Global's suppliers are upset that Global takes 2 months to pay their accounts payable; they demand that in the following year Global pay its bills within 30 days, or 1 month after purchase.

    (a) Using this new information, update Global's cash outflow forecast shown in Table 8-6.

    (b) Using the cash inflows given in Table 8-5, construct a revised cash budget for Global.

16. Of its monthly sales, the Kingsman Company historically has had 25% cash sales with the remainder paid within 1 month. Each month's purchases are equal to 75% of the next month's sales forecast; suppliers are paid 1 month after the purchase. Salary expenses are $50,000 a month, except in January when bonuses equal to 1% of the previous year's sales are paid out. Interest on a bond issue of $10,000 is due in March. Overhead and utilities are expected to be $25,000 monthly. Dividends of $45,000 are to be paid in March. Kingsman's 2005 sales totaled $2 million; December sales were $200,000. Kingsman's estimated sales for January are $100,000; February, $200,000; March, $250,000, and April, $300,000.

    (a) What are Kingsman's expected monthly cash inflows during January through April?

(b) What are Kingsman's expected monthly cash outflows during January through April?

(c) Determine Kingsman's monthly cash budget for January through April. Assume a minimum desired cash balance of $40,000 and an ending December cash balance of $50,000.

17. Redo Problem 14 using the following monthly sales estimates:

(a) January $300,000

(b) February $250,000

(c) March $200,000

(d) April $100,000

YOU TRY IT

Just-In-Time Inventory

You are the financial manager for a company that makes popular teddy bears. How do you explain the pros and cons to just-in-time inventory to the management team?

Trade Credit

Your company supplies the automakers with different types of parts for their cars. What are the pros and cons of offering your customers, the automakers, with trade credit?

Managing Working Capital

What are the essential skills that financial managers must have to manage working capital?

9

SHORT-TERM BUSINESS FINANCING
Types of Funding and Strategies

Starting Point

Go to www.wiley.com/college/Melicher to assess your knowledge of the basics of short-term business funding.
Determine where you need to concentrate your effort.

What You'll Learn in This Chapter

▲ The relationship between risk and return
▲ The role of the Small Business Administration
▲ The charge for factoring
▲ How life insurance can be used as security or a loan
▲ The cost of short-term financing

After Studying This Chapter, You'll Be Able To

▲ Compare the various approaches in financing working capital
▲ Examine the major influences on a firm's short-term financing mix decision
▲ Compare and contrast short-term financing sources
▲ Calculate the cost of a loan
▲ Compare and contrast maturity and advance factoring
▲ Distinguish between different types of collateral

Goals and Outcomes

▲ Evaluate what approach a firm should use when financing different working capital projects
▲ Assess a firm's approach to short-term financing
▲ Select the appropriate source of short-term financing for a firm
▲ Evaluate what happens to a borrower's effective interest rate when a loan is discounted
▲ Select the type of security that a firm should use as collateral in trying to secure a short-term loan

INTRODUCTION

Managing working capital often means that a financial manager needs to find short-term financing to keep a company operating. This financing can be obtained in a number of different ways using several different financial instruments. In this chapter, we will focus on finding the funds that will fit in with the financial plans and forecasts of companies and individual business owners.

9.1 Strategies for Financing Working Capital

Working capital includes a firm's current assets, including cash, marketable securities, accounts receivable, and inventories. Current assets are cash and securities, which are expected to be turned into cash within 1 year. Fixed assets, also known as *capital assets,* are properties that are not consumed in the normal course of business. Examples of fixed assets include office buildings and equipment. Fixed assets are often financed. Current liabilities generally include accounts payable (trade credit), notes payable (short-term loans), and accrued liabilities. Net working capital is the difference between the current assets and the current liabilities. Ideally, that difference results in a positive cash flow, but for many businesses that is not always the case. When the bank balance dips below the required minimum to pay salaries, taxes, and other operating expenses, the financial manager must find a way to meet the company's obligations. Unless the company owns securities or other assets that can be sold quickly to raise funds, the manager must arrange for short-term financing. Figure 9-1 depicts the various strategies used in financing.

9.1.1 Maturity-Matching Approach

Panel A of Figure 9-1 illustrates the maturity matching approach for financing a firm's assets. Fixed assets like buildings and major equipment secure mortgages and loans on their value. This is generally long-term financing. With current assets or an unexpected cash shortage, the company tries to obtain short-term financing that can be repaid as soon as the crisis is over. In the **maturity-matching approach** to financing, the financial manager tries to match the term of the loan to the life of the asset it is financing.

This is also sometimes referred to as the *balanced approach* to financing. Fixed assets and the level of permanent current assets have long maturities, so they should be financed with long-term financing sources. Temporary current assets are short-lived, so they should be financed with short-term financing. An example would be using a bank loan to finance inventory buildup in anticipation of heavy seasonal sales. After the inventory is sold and cash is received, the loan is repaid. With maturity matching, the amount of current assets is greater than that of current liabilities, so net working capital will be positive.

Figure 9-1

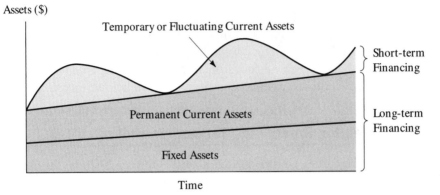

Panel A: Maturity Matching

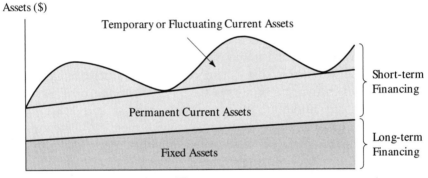

Panel B: Aggressive Financing

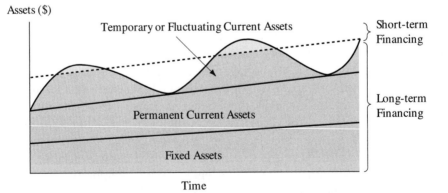

Panel C: Conservative Financing

Financing strategies.

9.1.2 Aggressive Approach

Panel B in Figure 9-1 depicts an aggressive approach to the financing of a firm's current assets. An **aggressive approach** to additional funding is when all current assets, both temporary and permanent, are financed with short-term financing.

Only fixed assets are financed with long-term debt and equity funds. Such an approach could result in liquidity problems in the event that future sales decline. Since all current assets are financed with current liabilities, the current ratio would be equal to 1.0 under this aggressive scenario. An even more aggressive approach would be for the firm to rely on short-term funds to finance all the current assets as well as some of the fixed assets. In such a case, the company's net working capital on its balance sheet would be negative and its current ratio would be less than 1.0.

9.1.3 Conservative Approach

Panel C in Figure 9-1 depicts a very conservative approach to the financing of a firm's assets. In this case, except for automatic or "spontaneous" financing provided by accounts payable and accrued liabilities, all the financing is done through long-term debt and equity funds.

At times the firm will have excess liquidity, when available funds exceed necessary current asset levels. During these periods, the company will have large cash balances and will probably seek to invest the excess cash in marketable securities. As the amount of current assets is much greater than that of current liabilities, net working capital will be positive and the current ratio will comfortably exceed 1.0.

9.1.4 Risk versus Return

Like many other aspects of finance, deciding how much short-term financing the firm should use has risk/return implications. As you know from studying the yield curve in Chapter 8, short-term securities generally have lower yields than long-term securities. From the borrower's perspective, that means the cost of paying short-term financing charges (interest rates) will be less than the cost of paying long-term interest rates and equity holders' required rates of return.

Compared to a conservative financing plan that relies more on long-term financing, an aggressive financing plan using more short-term financing will generally have lower financing costs and will be more profitable. As it comes due, short-term debt is replaced by new short-term debt. This replacement is called *rolling over the debt*. However, with the expectation of higher return comes higher risk. Short-term interest rates are more unstable than long-term rates, and in periods of tight money or in periods of pending inflation, short-term rates can

FOR EXAMPLE

Problems with Financing Strategies

Following the high-growth 1990s, the economy cooled during 2000–2001. Some firms began to have trouble meeting sales and earnings targets. A credit crisis occurred as some formerly top-quality firms had difficulty arranging new short-term financing. Aggressive financing strategies, with their reliance on large amounts of short-term funds and the constant rollover of short-term debt, resulted in problems for many companies. Wary lenders demanded higher interest rates for their short-term loans. Companies such as AT&T, Lucent, and Daimler-Chrysler experienced sharp increases in commercial paper rates. As the economy weakened and corporate balance sheets deteriorated, some firms, including Xerox, Lucent, Daimler-Chrysler, and Goodyear, were not able to roll over their commercial paper. Some of these firms maintained an aggressive financing policy by tapping into bank borrowing (Xerox, Tyco) to replace the funds they could not raise in the commercial paper market; others, such as Daimler-Chrysler, Sprint, and GE Capital, switched to a less aggressive stance by issuing bonds to raise long-term funds. Analysts predicted that Sprint's long-term bond issues would increase its interest expenses by almost $200 million annually, while others estimated GE Capital's interest costs would rise $100 million because of the shift from short-term borrowing to long-term borrowing. These examples show the impact that borrowing choices can have on the firm's expenses and profits.

rise quickly, increasing the cost of using short-term money. Sources of short-term credit also may disappear. In such a credit crunch, banks may not have enough funds to lend to satisfy demand and investors may not be willing to purchase the firm's short-term debt. A conservative financing plan has a higher financing cost but a lower risk of not being able to borrow when short-term funds are needed.

SELF-CHECK

- What is the relationship between risk and reward?
- List and define the three approaches to financing a firm's working capital.
- Explain the risk/return implications for each of the three strategies.

9.2 Factors Affecting Short-Term Financing

Whether a company uses an aggressive approach, a conservative approach, or maturity matching depends on an evaluation of many factors. The company's operating characteristics will affect a firm's financing strategy. Other factors having an impact include cost, flexibility, the ease of future financing, and other influences specific to the type of business enterprise.

9.2.1 Operating Characteristics

Often the demand for funds depends in part on the industry in which a business operates and on the characteristics of the business itself. It is influenced by such factors as seasonal variations in sales and the growth of the company. The need for funds also depends on fluctuations of the business cycle.

Some industries, such as utilities and oil refineries, have a larger amount of fixed assets than current assets and will prefer to use long-term financing. Others, such as service industries, have more current assets than fixed assets and will prefer short-term financing. Within each industry, some firms will choose different operating structures with different levels of operating leverage. Some examples of ratios of current liabilities to total assets are presented in Table 9-1.

The composition of the asset structure, or current assets versus fixed assets, of an industry and of a firm within that industry is a significant factor in determining the relative proportions of their long-term and short-term financing. An industry that needs large amounts of fixed capital can do more long-term financing than one that has a relatively small investment in fixed assets.

While manufacturing companies often require substantial investments in fixed assets for manufacturing purposes, they also have significant investments

Table 9-1: Short-Term Financing: Amount of Short-Term Financing Relative to Total Assets for Selected Firms (2003)

AT&T	18.5%
Consolidated Edison	9.1
ExxonMobil	22.0
General Motors	16.8
Microsoft	17.6
Sears	49.6
Walgreens	30.0
Wal-Mart	35.7

in inventories and receivables. Manufacturers generally have a more equal balance between current and fixed assets than electric utility and telephone companies and will use relatively more short-term financing than utilities.

The same is true for large retail stores. They often lease their business quarters and hold substantial assets in the form of inventories and receivables. They are characterized by relatively high current assets to fixed assets ratios and so will have a greater tendency than utilities to use short-term debt.

The size and age of a company and the stage of its financial life cycle may also influence management's short-term/long-term financing decisions. A new company's only source of funds may be the owner and possibly his or her friends. Some long-term funds may be raised by mortgaging real estate and buying equipment on credit, while some current borrowing may be possible to meet seasonal needs. As a business grows, it has more access to short-term capital from finance companies and banks. Further along, its growth and good record of profitability may enable a business to arrange better financing with banks or other financial agencies such as insurance companies. At this stage in its financial development, it may also expand its group of owners by issuing stock to people other than the owner and a few friends.

The growth prospects of a company also have an effect on financing decisions. If a company is growing faster than it can generate funds from internal sources, it must give careful consideration to a long-term financing plan. Even if it can finance its needs in the current situation from short-term sources, it may not be wise to do so. Sound financial planning calls for raising long-term funds at appropriate times. Patterns of short-term and long-term financing needs are depicted in Figure 9-2.

9.2.2 Seasonal Variations

Seasonal variations in sales affect the demand for current assets. Inventories are built up to meet seasonal needs, and receivables rise as sales increase. The peak of receivables will come after the peak in sales; the time in between depends on the credit terms and payment practices of customers.

Accounts payable will also increase as inventories are purchased. The difference between the increase in current assets and accounts payable should be financed by short-term borrowing because the need for funds will disappear as inventories are sold and accounts receivable are collected. When a need for additional funds is financed by a short-term loan, such a loan is said to be self-liquidating since funds are made available to repay it as inventories and receivables are reduced.

9.2.3 Sales Trends

A company's sales trend also affects the financing mix. As sales grow, fixed assets and current assets also must grow to support the sales growth. This need for funds is ongoing unless the upward trend of sales is reversed.

Figure 9-2

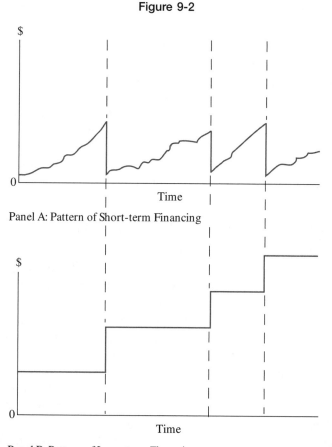

Panel A: Pattern of Short-term Financing

Panel B: Pattern of Long-term Financing

Patterns of short-term and long-term financing needs over time for a growing firm.

If asset growth is initially financed by short-term borrowing, the outstanding loans will continue to rise as sales rise. The amount of debt may rise year by year as the growth trend continues upward. After a while, the current ratio will drop to such a level that no financing institution will provide additional funds. The only alternative then is long-term financing.

9.2.4 Cyclical Variations

The need for current funds increases when there is an upswing in the business cycle or in the sales cycle of an industry. Since the cycle is not regular in timing or degree, it is hard to predict exactly how much, or for how long, added funds will be needed. The need should be estimated for a year ahead in the budget and checked quarterly. When the sales volume of business decreases, the need for funds to finance accounts receivable and inventory will decrease as well.

It is possible, however, that for a time during the downturn, the need for financing will increase temporarily. This will occur if the cash conversion cycle lengthens as receivables are collected more slowly and inventories move more slowly and drop in value.

If cyclical needs for funds are met by current borrowing, the loan may not be self-liquidating in a year. There are hazards in financing these needs on a short-term basis. The lending institution may demand payment of all or part of the loan just as profits fall. Funds may be needed more than ever at this stage of the cycle, and the need may last until receivables can be collected and inventory can be reduced. Firms in cyclical industries should use a more conservative approach that makes use of long-term financing.

9.2.5 Other Influences in Short-Term Financing

There are other advantages to using short-term borrowing rather than other forms of financing. Short-term borrowing offers more flexibility than long-term loans, since a business can borrow only those sums needed currently and pay them off if the need for financing diminishes. Long-term financing cannot be retired so easily, and it may include a prepayment penalty, as is the case with the call premium for callable bonds. If an enterprise finances its growing current asset requirements entirely through long-term financing during a period of general business expansion, it may be burdened with excess funds and financing costs during a subsequent period of general business reduction. Using short-term financing along with long-term financing creates a financial flexibility that is not possible with long-term financing alone.

Short-term financing has advantages that result from continuing relationships with a bank or other financial institution. A record of frequent borrowing and prompt repayment to a bank is an extremely important factor in sound financial management. A bank will make every effort to accommodate regular business customers who do this. The enterprise that has not established this type of working relationship with its bank will scarcely be in a position to seek special loans when it has emergency needs. The credit experience of a business with short-term financing may be the only basis on which its potential long-term lenders will be able to judge it. Hence, the business that intends to seek long-term loans may wish to establish a good credit reputation based on its short-term financing.

Offsetting these advantages of short-term financing is the need for frequent renewals. Even though short-term credit is usually easy to obtain, time and effort must be spent at frequent intervals because of the short duration of these loans. In the event that sales revenues decline, a great deal of negotiation may be required to receive needed credit.

Frequent maturities also create an added element of risk. The bank or finance company can call the loan whenever it is due. The bank may not want to roll

---
FOR EXAMPLE

Cyclical Business and Auto Manufacturing

Major U.S automobile firms, in a highly cyclical business, have been preparing for the next recession. Ford Motor Company, for example, went through $10 billion in cash during the 1990–1991 recession and $8.5 billion during 1999–2001. During 2003, Ford and its car financing subsidiary had over $33 billion in cash and short-term marketable securities as a cushion. In 2006, Ford projected that it would invest $7 billion in its automotive plans, which would leave $20 billion in cash in its core automotive operations.

---

over a loan. Borrowing costs may also rise if short-term interest rates increase. A company in a temporary slump due to the business cycle or some internal problem could possibly work out its problems in time with adequate financing. If the company had acquired funds on a long-term basis, it might have a better chance of resolving its problems. On the other hand, if it relies heavily on short-term financing, its loans may be reduced or not renewed, which may make it nearly impossible to recover and might even lead to liquidation.

SELF-CHECK

- List the major influences on a firm's short-term financing mix decision.
- What other influences can affect a firm's level of short-term financing?
- Give two examples of the types of firms that have a large amount of fixed assets.
- Name two benefits that short-term financing has over long-term financing.

9.3 Short-Term Financing Sources

Short-term financing sources include bank loans, trade credit or accounts payable, and commercial paper, among others. The ability to obtain short-term financing is made easier for firms with acknowledged character (ethics), the capacity to pay bills, a strong capital base, collateral to act as security for loans, and favorable conditions in the economy and the firm's industry.

Businesses can attempt to obtain short-term financing from a number of different providers and methods. Some are financial institutions, such as banks, that lend to firms for both working capital and long-term purposes, such as equipment loans. Other sources of financing include the firm's suppliers (trade credit); other corporations (commercial finance companies); the financial markets (commercial paper); and, when a small business is deemed "too risky" for a bank loan, they may be able to obtain financing by way of a government loan guarantee through the U.S. Small Business Administration.

9.3.1 Commercial Banks

Although many banks require a pledge of specific assets, the unsecured loan still remains the primary type of loan arrangement. The stated rate on such loans is based on the bank's prime rate, or, the interest rate the bank charges its most creditworthy customers.

Interest rates on loans typically are stated in terms of the prime rate plus a risk differential, such as prime + 2%. Loan papers will call this prime plus 2 or simply P + 2. Higher-risk borrowers will have higher differentials to compensate the bank for lending to riskier customers.

9.3.2 Bank Lines of Credit

A business and a bank often have an agreement regarding the amount of credit that the business will have at its disposal. A **line of credit** is the loan limit that the bank establishes for each of its business customers.

Lines of credit cost the business only the normal interest for the period during which money is actually borrowed. Under this arrangement, the business does not wait until money is needed to negotiate the loan. Rather, it files the necessary financial statements and other evidences of financial condition with the bank prior to the need for credit.

The banker is interested in how well the business has fared in the past and its probable future because the line of credit generally is extended for a year at a time. The banker may require that other debts of the business be subordinated to the claim of the bank. Banks may also require their business customers to "clean up" their lines of credit for a specified period of time each year—that is, to have no outstanding borrowing against the credit line, usually for a minimum of 2 weeks. This ensures that the credit line is being used for short-term financing purposes rather than for long-term needs.

Continued access to a line of credit may be subject to the approval of the bank if there are major changes in the operation of a business. A major shift or change in management personnel or in the manufacture or sale of particular products can greatly influence the future success of a company. Therefore, the bank, having contributed substantially to the financial resources of the business, is necessarily interested in these activities. The bank may also seek information on the business through organized credit bureaus, through contact with other businesses having dealings with the firm, and through other banks.

In the event that the business needs more money than was anticipated at the time the line of credit was set up, it may request the bank to increase the limit on its line of credit. It must be prepared, however, to offer very sound evidence of the need for additional funds and the ability of the business to repay the increased loan from business operations. A request for an increased line of credit frequently occurs when a business is growing and needs more capital to make its growth possible. Banks, following the principal of maturity matching discussed previously, generally insist that expansion be financed with long-term funds, but they may assist growth by temporarily providing a part of the additional money.

The business that is unable to obtain additional unsecured credit from its bank may seek a loan secured with collateral from the bank or other lenders.

Banks are a major participant in the commercial paper market, as they frequently support this market by offering paper issuers a line of credit or an arrangement similar to the revolving credit agreement. Some mutual funds are willing to lend to firms and to take the place of the traditional banking relationship.

Although the practice is diminishing, some banks require a compensating balance. A **compensating balance** requires that 10 to 20% of outstanding unsecured loans be kept on deposit by the business.

The most frequently cited justification for this requirement is that banks cannot lend without deposits and bank borrowers should be required to be depositors. These compensating balances are also a means of increasing the effective cost of borrowing by increasing the amount on which interest is computed.

9.3.3 Revolving Credit Agreements

The officers of a business may feel rather certain that an agreed-upon line of credit will provide the necessary capital requirements for the coming year. However, the bank is not obligated to continue to offer the credit line if the firm's financial condition worsens. Line-of-credit agreements usually allow the bank to reduce or withdraw its extension of credit to the company.

The well-established business with an excellent credit rating may be able to obtain a revolving credit agreement. A **revolving credit agreement** is a commitment in the form of a standby agreement for a guaranteed line of credit.

Unlike a line of credit, a revolving credit agreement is a legal obligation of the bank to provide funds up to the agreed-upon borrowing limit during the time the agreement is in effect. In addition to paying interest on borrowed funds for the period of the loan, the business must pay a commission or fee to the bank based on the unused portion of the credit line, or the money it has "on call" during the agreement period. This fee is usually between 0.25 and 0.50% of the unused amount of the line.

To compute the effective cost of a revolving agreement, the joint effect of interest on borrowed funds and the commitment fee on the unused portion of credit must be considered. Assume Global has a 1-year $1 million revolving credit agreement with a local bank. The annual interest rate on the agreement is 9% with a commitment fee of 0.40% on the unused credit amount. Global expects to have average outstanding borrowings against the revolver of $300,000. Over the year, the interest cost on the average amount borrowed is 0.09 × $300,000 or $27,000. The commitment fee on the average unused credit portion is 0.0040 × $700,000, or $2,800. With total interest and fees of $29,800 ($27,000 + $2,800) on average borrowings of $300,000, the expected annual cost of the revolving credit is $29,800/$300,000, or 9.93%.

9.3.4 Small Business Administration

Another source of short-term financing is the Small Business Administration (SBA). The **Small Business Administration** was established by the federal government to provide financial assistance to small firms that are unable to obtain loans through private channels on reasonable terms.

Created in 1953, the Small Business Administration provides a wide variety of services in addition to loan guarantees through its more than 100 field offices. It is important to note that the Small Business Administration does not make loans. Instead, it guarantees them. Under their 7(a) loan program, the SBA will guarantee up to 85% of the loan amount for loans of $150,000 or less. Loans larger than $150,000 up to $2 million can obtain a guarantee of up to 75%.

The loan guarantee means a bank can lend a sum to a small business owner and only have a small portion of the funds at risk. In case of default, the SBA will repay the loan. For example, a bank lending $100,000 under the SBA loan guarantee program has 85% of the loan guaranteed by the SBA. This means only 15%, or $15,000, of their funds are at risk. In case the borrower cannot repay the loan, the SBA will reimburse the bank for up to $85,000.

If a firm is able to obtain financing elsewhere, its loan application to the SBA is rejected. An applicant for a loan must prove that funds needed are not available from any bank, that no other private lending sources are available, that issuing securities is not practicable, that financing cannot be arranged by disposing of business assets, and that the personal credit of the owners cannot be used. These loans may not be used for paying existing creditors or for speculative purposes.

In addition to its business-lending activities, the SBA is responsible for several related financial activities. These include loans to development companies, disaster loans, lease guarantees, surety bond support, minority enterprise programs, procurement assistance, and support for investment companies that service small businesses.

SBA working capital loans are limited to 7 years, while regular business loans have a maximum maturity of 25 years. It also sets a maximum allowable rate that banks can charge on guaranteed loans. These rates are adjusted periodically by the SBA to reflect changes in market conditions.

9.3.5 Trade Credit from Suppliers

The most important single form of short-term business financing is the credit extended by one business organization to another. **Trade credit** is accounts receivable together with longer-term notes receivable taken by manufacturers, wholesalers, jobbers, and other businesses that sell products or services to businesses.

The establishment of trade credit is the least formal of all forms of financing. It involves only an order for goods or services by one business and the delivery of goods or performance of service by the selling business. The purchasing business receives an invoice stating the terms of the transaction and the time period within which payment is to be made. The purchaser adds this liability to accounts payable. The seller adds this credit sale to accounts receivable. In some instances, the seller may insist on written evidence of liability on the part of the purchaser. Such written evidence is usually in the form of a note that is payable by the purchaser and is considered as a note receivable by the seller.

Before a business organization delivers goods or performs a service for another business, it must determine the ability and willingness of the purchaser to pay for the order. The responsibility of such credit analysis in most businesses belongs to the credit manager.

Sales may be made on a variety of terms, including the following:

▲ Cash: payment due upon receipt of invoice
▲ EOM: payment due at the end of the month
▲ MOM: payment due at the middle of month
▲ ROG: payment due upon receipt of goods

Or such terms as 2/10, net 30 may be offered, which means the purchaser may deduct 2% from the invoice amount if payment is made within 10 days of shipment; if not paid within 10 days, the net amount is due within 30 days. Such trade discounts to purchasers for early payment are common and are designed to provide incentive for prompt payment of bills. Occasionally, sellers offer only net terms such as net 30 or net 60.

Even a cash sale usually involves credit. This is because the purchaser is often allowed a certain number of days to pay the invoice. For example, a sale of merchandise in which the purchaser is permitted up to 10 days to pay may be considered a cash transaction, but credit is extended to the purchaser for that time. Even for the firm that purchases products entirely on a cash basis, the volume of accounts payable outstanding on its books at any one time may be large.

When trade credit terms do not provide a discount for early payment of obligations, there is no cost to the buyer for such financing. Even when discounts are available, it may seem that there is no cost for trade credit since failing to take the early payment discount simply requires the purchaser to pay the net price. However, there is a cost involved when the discount is not taken. The cost is, of course, the amount of the lost discount that was offered for making the payment within 10 days.

To compare the cost of trade credit and bank credit, the cost of the trade credit must be placed on an annual interest rate basis. The lost discount of 2% is the cost of trade credit for those 20 days that the payment time was extended. If we also consider that it is the discounted price (invoice price minus the percentage discount) that is being financed, the approximate effective cost (EC) is computed as follows:

$$EC = \frac{\% \text{ discount}}{100\% - \% \text{discount}} \times \frac{365 \text{ days}}{\text{Credit period} - \text{discount days}}$$

For our 2/10, net 30 example:

$$EC = \frac{2\%}{100\% - 2\%} \times \frac{365}{30 - 10} = 2.04\% \times 18.25 = 37.2\%$$

This shows that the cost of trade credit typically is far in excess of bank rates. So, it is usually worthwhile to borrow funds to take advantage of cash discounts on trade credit. Failure to take advantage of the trade discount is the same as borrowing from the vendor at the effective cost.

The cost of trade credit in most lines of business activity is high when discounts are missed. However, it should not be assumed that high cost necessarily makes trade credit an undesirable source of short-term financing. It can be the most important form of financing for small and growing businesses that are unable to qualify for short-term credit through customary financial channels.

The firm in a weak financial condition will find trade credit more readily available than bank credit. The bank stands to gain only the interest on the loan if repayment is made, but it will lose the entire sum loaned if the borrower's obligation is not met. The manufacturer or merchant, on the other hand, has a profit margin on the goods sold. If the purchaser fails to meet the obligation, the seller loses, at most, the cost of the goods delivered to the purchaser.

9.3.6 Commercial Finance Companies

The first commercial finance company in the United States was chartered about 100 years ago. Since that time, the number of these institutions has increased to more than 500. Some of these organizations are small, offering limited financial services to their customers, while others have vast resources and engage in broadly diversified programs of business lending. A **commercial finance company** is an organization without a bank charter that advances funds to businesses by

(1) discounting accounts receivable, (2) making loans secured by chattel mortgages on machinery or liens on inventory, or (3) financing deferred-payment sales of commercial and industrial equipment.

These companies also are known as *commercial credit companies, commercial receivables companies,* and *discount companies.* Commercial finance companies, such as CIT Group, Celtic Capital, GE Capital, and Heller Financial, offer many of the same services as commercial banks for financing accounts receivable and inventory. Lending funds based upon the amount of a firm's accounts receivable balances was, in fact, originated by commercial finance companies and only later was adopted by commercial banks.

Both consumer and business financing can be obtained from firms such as General Electric Capital Corporation and Ford Motor Credit Company. Commercial finance companies grew to their present number for the following reasons:

▲ They were completely free to experiment with new and highly specialized types of credit arrangements.
▲ State laws concerning lending on the basis of accounts receivable were generally more favorable to these non-banking organizations.
▲ They were able to charge high enough rates to make a profitable return on high-risk loans. Frequently these rates were far above rates bankers were permitted to charge.

In addition to financing accounts receivable and inventories, commercial finance companies provide large credit limits for businesses by financing assets such as commercial vehicles and industrial and farm equipment. The Commercial Finance Association estimates the total volume of business credit outstanding by the commercial finance companies to be more than $325 billion.

The equity position of commercial finance companies is considerably greater than that of banks. However, these organizations do not operate on equity capital alone. Additional long-term capital is acquired by selling their loans or unsecured bonds. Commercial banks actually lend a large volume of money at wholesale rates to commercial finance companies, which in turn lend it to business borrowers at retail rates.

Based on the high interest rates (sometimes as high as 15 to 20%) for commercial finance company loans, a business that has ample current assets and is in a highly liquid position may be well advised to rely on other sources of short-term financing. However, a business that has been rejected by a bank and has only inventory or accounts receivables as collateral often finds it necessary to deal with a commercial finance company for their funding needs.

Commercial finance companies are able to operate through a system of branches on a regional or national basis, unhampered by restrictions on bank branch operations. Therefore, they can acquire the volume of business necessary to cover overhead and provide the needed diversification of risks for high-risk financing. Several bank holding companies have purchased or established commercial finance companies to take advantage of their special operating characteristics.

9.3.7 Commercial Paper

A final source of short-term financing is the financial markets. Large U.S. corporations of high credit quality can issue or sell commercial paper. **Commercial paper** is a short-term promissory note backed solely by the credit quality of the issuer; there is no security or collateral behind them.

Commercial paper may be sold directly by the issuer to financial institutions or other investors. It can also be sold to commercial paper houses or dealers who purchase the promissory notes to resell them to individuals or businesses. A fee based on the amount of notes purchased, charged to the issuer of the notes, provides the basic income of commercial paper dealers. In the early 2000s, over $1.4 trillion of commercial paper was traded annually.

A firm that wishes to obtain funds from a commercial paper house must have an unquestioned reputation for sound operation. First the commercial paper house makes a thorough investigation of the firm's financial position. If it appears that the notes of the firm can be sold with little difficulty, an agreement is made for the outright sale of a block of the firm's promissory notes to the commercial paper house. They, in turn, will resell these notes as quickly as possible to banks, managers of pension funds, business corporations that have surplus funds, or other investors. The notes are usually prepared in denominations of $100,000 or more with maturities ranging from a few days to 270 days. The size of the notes and the maturities, however, can be adjusted to suit individual investor requirements.

Commercial paper is sold on a discount basis. Dealers will pay the borrower the face amount of the notes minus the interest charge and a fee that is usually between 0.02 and 0.05%. The interest charge is determined by the general level of prevailing rates in the money market and the strength of the borrowing company. When these notes are resold to banks and other lenders, only the prevailing interest charge is deducted from the face value of the notes. The commercial paper dealer receives the fee as compensation for the negotiation and intermediation.

Commercial paper is no longer sold only through dealers or brokers. Investors can now buy commercial paper online through an electronic trading system. The first firm to offer its paper online was Ford Motor Company on a commercial paper trading system designed by CS First Boston. Since then, others have developed online commercial paper systems to facilitate the direct issue of paper to investors. In recent years the most successful of them has been Sungard's Transaction Network. Online issuance of paper allows issuers to reduce the fees to half of what is usually collected by dealers.

Commercial paper is issued by large, well-known, and financially stable firms; only they have the ability to raise large sums of short-term financing quickly and with a bank's backing. Many of the borrowers of commercial paper are financial firms such as commercial finance companies. They seek to finance their own lending and leasing operations by raising short-term funds through commercial paper. They will borrow at the commercial paper rate and then lend the funds to others at higher interest rates.

Assume that Global Manufacturing wants to issue $100,000 of commercial paper that will mature in 9 months (270 days). The placement fee is 1% and the interest charge will be 7.5% over the 9-month period. Global's net proceeds from the commercial paper are computed as follows:

Principal amount ($100,000) × interest rate (7.5%) = $7,500 interest

Principal amount ($100,000) × placement fee (1%) = $100 fee

Total cost   = $ 7,600

Net Proceeds = $100,000 − $7,600 = $92,400

The 9-month financing cost for the commercial paper issue is $7,600/$92,400 = 0.0823, or 8.23%. The annual (yearly) cost of the commercial paper issue will be $(1 + 0.0823)^{12/9} - 1 = 0.1111$ or 11.11%.

The most important reason for a company to issue commercial paper is that the cost of borrowing is generally less than regular bank rates. The reason for the lower rates is that only the largest, most financially stable firms can issue commercial paper. And unlike banks, which typically service a geographic region, commercial paper is sold by dealers to investors worldwide, so international short-term rates help determine commercial paper rates rather than bank loan committees. Also, the need for compensating bank balances that increase interest costs on short-term bank loans is avoided. Loan restrictions on the amount that can be borrowed from a single bank may also favor the issuance of commercial paper by large corporations.

Like bonds, commercial paper is rated. The rating is important to the issuer, as the higher the rating, the lower the interest expense. Industrial firms and other nonbank lenders often purchase commercial paper as a more profitable alternative to treasury bills for investing excess cash. Commercial paper provides a yield slightly above that of short-term government securities. Although commercial banks were historically the main purchasers of commercial paper, it is now actively held by industrial corporations, money market mutual funds, and other lenders.

Many top-rated U.S. commercial paper issuers can also issue paper overseas. The **European commercial paper (Euro CP) market** offers advantages to commercial paper issuers just as the Eurodollar bond market offers advantages over the U.S. bond market. There is no SEC regulation of the Euro CP market, so commercial paper maturities are generally a little longer and interest costs lower. In addition, Euro CP is available only to the "cream" of the commercial paper

> ## FOR EXAMPLE
>
> ### Bank Financing for Small Business
>
> Getting a small business bank loan is much harder than it was in the 1980s. Bankers are making greater demands on entrepreneurial or venture firms. More comprehensive financial statements must be provided and more collateral must be pledged. Banks lend at the **prime rate**, which is their best rate, to larger businesses. In contrast, small businesses are asked to pay two or more points above prime. For example, if the prime rate is 8%, small businesses will have to pay 10% or more to obtain bank loans.

issuers, so no ratings are needed. Investors already know who the safest issuers are. So not having to pay for a rating also makes the Euro CP market attractive to those firms that are able to use it.

SELF-CHECK

- List seven sources of short-term financing
- Explain how a bank line of credit differs from a revolving credit agreement.
- Explain how the SBA can help a company obtain short-term financing.
- Define **trade credit** and indicate whether it is usually more or less expensive than bank financing.
- Explain what a commercial finance company is.
- Define **commercial paper** and explain how it is sold.

9.4 Computing Interest Rates

In the world of finance, it is necessary to know how to calculate the cost of a loan. Let's take Global Manufacturing's loans as an example: Global Manufacturing can borrow $10,000 for 6 months at 8% APR (annual percentage rate). The 6-month interest cost will be 8% × $10,000 divided by 2, or $400. Note that the interest is divided by 2 because Global is repaying the loan in 6 months rather than 1 year. If the term of the loan was 1 year, the cost of it would simply be $10,000. (Principal) × 8%, or $800.

At times, banks will discount a loan. A **discounted loan** is one in which the borrower receives the principal less the interest at the time the loan is made.

At maturity, the principal is repaid. Discounting has the effect of reducing the available funds received by the borrower while raising the effective interest rate. If Global's loan is discounted, Global will receive $9,600 ($10,000 less $400) and will repay $10,000, in essence paying $400 interest on the $9,600 funds received. This is a periodic rate of $400/$9,600, or 4.17%. The effective annual rate is $(1 + 0.0417)2 - 1$, or 8.51%, an increase of 0.35 percentage points over the undiscounted loan.

When a loan is discounted, a firm has to borrow more money than the amount it really needs. To counteract the effect of discounting, to acquire $10,000 in usable funds they will have to borrow $10,000/(1 − 0.04) or $10,416.67.

Also, when a loan of $10,416.67 is discounted at a 6-month rate of 4%, the net proceeds to Global will be $10,000 (that is, $10,416.67 − [0.04][10,416.67] = $10,000). In general, to receive the desired usable funds, the loan request must equal

Loan request = desired usable funds/(1 − discount).

9.5 Asset-Based Lending For Short-Term Financing

In this section we examine the use of secured, or asset-based, lending for short-term financing purposes. **Secured lending,** also called **asset-based lending,** means that there is some collateral or security backing the loan that can be claimed or sold by the lender if the borrower defaults.

9.5.1 Accounts Receivable Financing

The business that does not qualify for an unsecured bank loan or that has emergency needs for funds in excess of its line of credit may offer a pledge of its accounts receivable as collateral for a loan. A **pledge** is a means of obtaining a short-term loan by using accounts receivable as collateral.

In this case, the lender gives close attention to the borrower's collection experience on its receivables and to certain characteristics of its accounts receivable.

The bank may spot-check the receivables of the firm and may analyze each account to determine how quickly the firm's customers make payments. It is also important for the bank to know something about these customers. The customers' ability to pay their debts will strongly influence how well the business applying for the loan will be able to collect payment. In addition, the bank studies the type and quality of goods that are sold. If the merchandise is inferior, there may be objections from the customers that could result in slower payment of bills or sales returns. Accounts receivable are of little value as security for a loan if large quantities of merchandise are returned and the amount of accounts receivable is reduced accordingly.

The Bank Management Commission of the American Bankers Association recommends that a loan based on the security of accounts receivable generally be no more than 80% of the gross receivables. It also recommends that this amount be reduced by any discounts allowed to customers for quick payment and by the normal percentage of merchandise returns. If there is reason to believe that many of the loan applicant's customers are not suitable risks, or if adequate credit ratings are not available, the bank may decide to lend a lower percentage of the face value of the receivables.

Under the pledged receivables arrangement, there is, in addition to the basic interest charge, a fee to cover the extra work needed for such a loan. The bank must periodically check the books of the business to see that it is, in fact, living up to the terms of the agreement. At the time the loan is made, individual accounts on the ledger of the business are designated clearly as having been pledged for the bank loan. Only those accounts suitable for collateral purposes for the bank are designated. When these accounts are paid in full or become unsatisfactory, they are replaced by other accounts. The bank also receives copies of all shipping invoices to show that the goods have been shipped and an account receivable is valid.

As customers pay their bill on the accounts that have been assigned as security for the loan, the proceeds must be turned over to the bank. The bank also reserves the right to have an outside accounting firm examine the books. Checking the accounts in this routine manner leaves customers of the business unaware that their accounts have been pledged as collateral for a loan. Businesses that pledge their receivables as collateral for bank loans often prefer to keep this knowledge from their customers as it could be viewed as an indication of instability.

Although businesses using this form of loan arrangement frequently are in a financially weak condition, this is not always the case. Some financially sound firms use accounts receivable financing because they feel it has advantages for them over other loan arrangements.

Manufacturing companies appear to be the largest users of accounts receivable financing. In particular, this is true of manufacturers of food products, textiles, leather products, furniture, paper, iron, steel, and machinery.

Another type of accounts receivable financing is called *factoring*. A **factor** purchases the accounts receivable outright and assumes all credit risks.

Factoring takes two forms:

▲ Under **maturity factoring,** the firm selling its accounts receivable is paid on the normal collection date or net due date of the account.

▲ Under **advance factoring,** the factor pays the firm for its receivables before the account due date.

Under a factoring arrangement, customers whose accounts are sold are notified that their bills are payable to the factor. The task of collecting on the accounts is then shifted from the seller of the accounts to the factor.

To use a factor, a contract is drawn establishing the duties and obligations of the seller and the factor. This contract includes the conditions under which accounts may be sold to the factor, the responsibility for the payment of these accounts, the collection procedures to be followed, and the method of reporting balances due. The contract also provides that the accounts so established be assigned to the factor and that invoices for sales to these customers, together with the original shipping documents, be delivered daily to the factor. All sales must be approved by the factor before goods are delivered. Sales are subject to rejection if the credit rating of the customer does not meet the factor's standards. Daily reports must be given to the factor on all credits, allowances, and returns of merchandise. The contract also stipulates the charges for the factoring service.

The credit analysis department is the heart of the factoring organization since it must conserve the factor's assets and be in constant contact with its clients. Members of the factor's credit department must be extremely prompt and accurate in their credit analyses. Also, because they work closely with the firm's clients, they must retain the goodwill of the companies that use its services.

The charge for factoring has two components:

▲ Interest is charged on the money advanced.

▲ A factoring commission or service charge is figured as a percentage of the face amount of the receivables. This charge typically ranges from 1.5% to 2% of the face amount of the accounts financed.

The commission charge is determined after considering such things as the volume of the client's sales, the general credit status of the accounts being factored, and the average size of individual accounts. As further financial protection, the factor will exclude late receivables, such as those 90 days or more overdue. Factors will typically lend 85% of the remainder, although they may reduce the amount of the loan anywhere from 5 to 15% of the total amount of receivables factored to make adjustments for merchandise that may be returned to the seller.

This portion of the receivables is returned to the seller if it is not needed for adjustment purposes.

Factors obtain their operating funds through a combination of equity capital, long-term borrowing, short-term borrowing, and profits from operations. Although a factor's services may be used by a firm that is unable to secure financing through customary channels, financially strong companies also use these services to good advantage. In fact, factors are of greatest benefit to companies that enjoy very strong sales and growth. Sometimes during such periods, companies experience extreme shortages of working capital. The sale of receivables without recourse (that is, sellers do not have to repay any funds received from the factor in the case of a bad debt) has the effect of substituting cash for accounts receivable. This may make even greater growth and profitability possible in the long run.

Some firms factor their receivables for other reasons. First, the cost of doing business through credit sales is definite and can be determined in advance because the factor assumes all risks of collection. This is, in effect, a form of credit insurance. Second, factoring eliminates expenses, including bookkeeping costs, the maintenance of a credit department, and the expenses of collecting delinquent accounts. A less tangible advantage is that factoring frees the management of a business from concern with financial matters and permits it to concentrate on production and distribution. Factoring has become increasingly important in supporting export sales. The company that is unfamiliar with the problems of financing international shipments of goods is relieved of such details by factoring foreign receivables.

Although factoring services are regarded highly by some businesses, others object to their use. The two reasons cited most frequently are the cost and the implication of financial weakness. The cost of factoring is unquestionably higher than the cost of borrowing from a bank on the basis of an unsecured loan. However, it is difficult to conclude that the net cost is higher. The elimination of overhead costs that would otherwise be necessary plus the reality that management need not concern itself with financial matters may completely offset the additional cost involved in factoring.

9.5.2 Inventory Loans

A business may use its inventory as collateral for a loan in much the same manner that it may borrow on its receivables. The bank evaluates the physical condition of the firm's inventory and the inventory's general composition. Staple items that are in constant demand serve well as collateral for a loan. Style and fashion items such as designer clothes are not as acceptable as collateral except for brief periods. Firms that use inventory as collateral usually do so because they are not in a position to obtain unsecured loans.

The bank may protect itself when lending to a business by having a blanket inventory lien. A **blanket inventory lien** is a claim against a customer's inventory

> ## FOR EXAMPLE
>
> ### Factoring in the Retail Industry
>
> Few industries are affected by factors as much as retailing. Factors guarantee payment to suppliers of many large retail firms. With such guarantees, suppliers ship goods to the retailers, confident that they will get paid. Should factors refuse to guarantee payments to suppliers because the factors believe a retailer to be on shaky financial ground, a retailing firm can find itself with no merchandise to sell. If one factor hesitates to stand behind a retailer's credit, all factors turn their backs on the retailer since no one factor wants to be left alone supporting a financially troubled firm. Often, factors act as an early warning signal of a retailer's financial deterioration.

when individual items are indistinguishable, as may be the case with grain or clothing items.

For such loans, a borrower may receive only 60 to 80% of the inventory's value in a loan. A manufacturer's work-in-process inventory may receive only 20 to 30% of its value.

In other cases, when goods can be clearly identified, a trust receipt may be used.

▲ A **trust receipt** is a lien against specific items in inventory.

This method of financing, sometimes called *floor-plan financing,* is used by car dealerships and appliance stores, where inventory items financed by trust receipts can be identified by serial number. Under a trust receipt arrangement, the bank retains ownership of the goods until they are actually sold in the regular course of business. Audits are simply a matter of checking serial numbers of inventory items to determine if items held against a trust receipt have been sold.

Sometimes when inventory is used as collateral, the bank may insist that the inventory be placed in a warehouse.

▲ **Warehouse receipt** involves placing inventory in a bonded warehouse for safekeeping; items are removed as they are paid for.

The warehouse receipt issued by the warehouse is then turned over to the bank, which holds it until the loan is repaid.

It is frequently inconvenient for a business to deliver large bulky items of inventory to a warehouse for storage. This problem is solved by using a field warehouse.

▲ A **field warehouse** is an enterprise that has the means to establish a warehouse on the grounds of the borrowing business establishment.

Field warehouses differ from the typical public warehouse in that (1) they serve a single customer—that customer on whose property the field warehouse is established—and (2) they exist only until the loan is repaid.

In setting up a field warehouse, the warehouse operator usually must first obtain a lease on that portion of the property to be used for warehousing purposes. Then he or she must establish fences, barriers, walks, and other postings to indicate clear possession of the property. This is done to avoid accidental or deliberate removal of stored items during the general course of business operations. A guard may be posted to check on the safety of the warehoused goods, or a room may be sealed and the seal inspected periodically to make sure the company is honoring its agreement.

There also must be a complete statement of the commodities or items that are to be warehoused, and agreements must be made about the maintenance of the property, proper fire precautions, insurance, and other necessary physical requirements. Under certain circumstances, the warehouse operator is authorized to release a certain quantity of goods by the day, week, or month to make possible a rotation of merchandise. Under this arrangement, physical inventories must be taken from time to time.

Field warehouses are in operation throughout the United States but are concentrated in the Central and Pacific Coast regions. Canned goods, miscellaneous groceries, lumber, timber, and building supplies fill about two-fifths of all field warehouses in this country. Those banks that make loans involving commodities will generally accept field warehouse receipts as collateral.

Inventory loans are somewhat more expensive than unsecured loans to business borrowers. The higher cost is due in part to the cost of warehousing operations and also because the borrower's credit rating may be low. Bank interest rates for warehouse loans ordinarily are somewhat higher than for unsecured loans. In addition, a warehouse fee of 1 to 2% of the loan, depending on size and other factors, must be paid.

9.5.3 Loans Secured by Stocks and Bonds

Stocks and bonds are often used as collateral for short-term loans. These securities are welcomed as collateral primarily because of their marketability and their value. If the securities are highly marketable and if their value is high enough to cover the amount of the loan requested, even if the stock's price goes down somewhat, a banker will not hesitate to extend a loan. Securities listed on one of the national exchanges are preferred because frequent price quotations are available. Banks usually will loan from 60 to 70% of the market value of listed stocks and from 70 to 80% of the market value of high-grade bonds.

Only assignable stocks and bonds are eligible for this type of collateral financing, with the exception of nonassignable U.S. savings bonds. When assignable securities are placed with a bank, a stock or bond power is executed that authorizes the bank to sell the securities should it become necessary to protect the loan.

SELF-CHECK

- List two types of accounts receivable financing.
- What is meant by **pledging** receivables and how does it differ from factoring?
- Define **blanket inventory lien, trust receipt, warehouse receipt,** and **field warehouse.**
- What is the difference between advance factoring and maturity factoring?

9.6 Other Forms of Security

Security for short-term bank loans may include such things as the cash surrender value of a life insurance policy, guarantee of a loan by co-signer, and acceptances.

9.6.1 Life Insurance Loans

The cash surrender value of insurance polices or the amount a business will receive upon cancellation of a policy are sometimes pledged as collateral for a short-term loan. The policies must be assignable, and many insurance companies insist that their own forms be used for such purposes.

Since this collateral is considered safe, loans secured by insurance usually have lower interest rates. The banks also take into consideration the fact that the borrower could obtain a loan directly from the insurance company that issued the policy. Even with the reduction, bank interest rates are often higher than the rates charged by the insurance company. As a result, there has been an increase in the number of these loans made by insurance companies.

9.6.2 Comaker Loans

Many small businesses find it necessary to provide the bank with a guarantor in the form of a cosigner on their loans. It is expected that the cosigner has a credit

FOR EXAMPLE

Life Insurance Loans

Life insurance loans are attractive to many people who need cash for personal reasons as well as for their business. Once you have money built up in your life insurance policy, you can borrow against the cash value that you have accumulated. You can get the money quickly, within days. You can borrow up to 95% of the policy's cash balance. You do not even have to pay the money back directly to the life insurance company; it is important to remember, however, that the unpaid portion of the loan is deducted from the face value of the policy.

rating superior to the borrower. If the original borrower should default on the loan, the lending institution will look to the comaker for repayment.

9.6.3 Acceptances

Another type of collateral for a short-term loan is the acceptance. As explained in Section 10.6.6, an acceptance is a receivable from the sale of merchandise on the basis of a draft or bill of exchange drawn against the buyer or buyer's bank. The seller of the merchandise holds the accepted draft or bill until the date payment is due. During this period, the business may discount the note to use as security to obtain a bank loan.

SELF-CHECK

- Briefly explain how businesses can use life insurance policies to get short-term financing.
- What is a loan comaker?
- How can acceptances be used as a source of short-term financing?

9.7 The Cost of Short-Term Financing

For most asset-based and unsecured loans, a simple method can be used to determine the cost of the short-term financing. It is the same process used in computing the interest, fees, and net proceeds of commercial paper:

1. Determine the amount to be borrowed, or the principal of the loan.
2. Determine the interest rate and the term of the loan.

FOR EXAMPLE

Short-Term Financing and Personal Financial Planning

Money market mutual funds are a link between an individual's savings and investment needs and a firm's needs for short-term financing. These funds invest in market securities, which are securities that mature, or come due, in less than 1 year. The typical fund invests in securities that mature much sooner. The average maturity of the securities held by some funds is 1 week or less.

Money market securities exist because of the short-term financing needs of governments, banks, and businesses. The funds pool the savings of many investors. The funds use the savings to invest in T-bills, short-term state and local government debt, negotiable certificates of deposit (CDs), and commercial paper.

---

3. Multiply the principal by the interest rate to get the interest for 1 year.

4. Divide the interest by 365 days or 12 months to get the daily or monthly rate.

5. Multiply the daily or monthly rate by the term of the loan and add any fees associated with the loan.

For example, a company borrows $10,000 for 14 months and is charged a fee of $200 for servicing the loan. The interest rate is 8% per annum. The computation is as follows:

$$\$10,000 \text{ (principal)} \times .08 \text{ (interest)} = \$800.00 \text{ (interest for 1 year)}$$

$$\frac{\$800}{12 \text{ months}} = 66.67 \text{ (interest per month)} \times 14 \text{ months}$$

$$= 933.38 \text{ interest cost} + \underline{200.00 \text{ servicing fee}}$$

$$\text{Cost of the short-term financing} \quad \$1,133.38$$

The preceding example is for loans with simple interest. In the case of long-term loans with compounded interest, there are printed tables available that calculate interest and payments.

SELF-CHECK

- How do you calculate the cost of short-term financing?
- If you are given the annual rate of interest for a loan, how do you get the daily rate of interest?

SUMMARY

Working capital is the grease that keeps the wheels turning in a company. Inventories are needed to meet customer demands for a firm's products. When they are sold, accounts receivable are created that will one day be converted into cash. A firm without working capital is a firm unlikely to remain in business. In this chapter, you learned about financing strategies and which one to use. You examined the different types of loans and the requirements for each. You defined the role of the Small Business Administration and how it aids businesses in meeting short-term financing needs. All of these strategies will enable you to help your employer to secure financing for short-term needs.

KEY TERMS

Advance factoring	Form of factoring where the factor pays the firm for its receivables before the account due date.
Aggressive approach	When all current assets, both temporary and permanent, are financed with short-term financing.
Blanket inventory lien	A claim against a customer's inventory when individual items are indistinguishable, as may be the case with grain or clothing items.
Commercial finance company	An organization without a bank charter that advances funds to businesses by (1) discounting accounts receivable, (2) making loans secured by chattel mortgages on machinery or liens on inventory, or (3) financing deferred-payment sales of commercial and industrial equipment.
Commercial paper	A short-term promissory note backed solely by the credit quality of the issuer; there is no security or collateral behind them.
Compensating balance	Ten to 20% of outstanding unsecured loans be kept on deposit by the business.
Discounted loan	Loan in which the borrower receives the principal less the interest at the time the loan is made.
European commercial paper (Euro CP) market	A market that offers advantages to commercial paper issuers just as the Eurodollar bond market offers advantages over the U.S. bond market. There is no SEC regulation of the Euro CP market, so commercial paper maturities are generally a little longer and interest costs lower.

Factor	Engages in accounts-receivable financing for business; purchases the accounts receivable outright and assumes all credit risks.
Field warehouse	An enterprise that has the means to establish a warehouse on the grounds of the borrowing business establishment.
Line of credit	The loan limit that the bank establishes for each of its business customers.
Maturity factoring	A form of factoring where the firm selling its accounts receivable is paid on the normal collection date or net due date of the account.
Maturity-matching approach	The financial manager tries to match the term of the loan to the life of the asset it is financing.
Pledge	A way of obtaining a short-term loan by using accounts receivable as collateral.
Prime rate	The interest rate the bank charges its most creditworthy customers.
Revolving credit agreement	A commitment in the form of a standby agreement for a guaranteed line of credit.
Secured lending	Lending with some collateral or security backing the loan that can be claimed or sold by the lender if the borrower defaults. Also called **asset-based lending.**
Small Business Administration	Organization that was established by the federal government to provide financial assistance to small firms that are unable to obtain loans through private channels on reasonable terms.
Trade credit	Accounts receivable together with longer-term notes receivable taken by manufacturers, wholesalers, jobbers, and other businesses that sell products or services to businesses.
Trust receipt	A lien against specific items in inventory.
Warehouse receipt	Placing inventory in a bonded warehouse for safekeeping; items are removed as they are paid for.

ASSESS YOUR UNDERSTANDING

Go to www.wiley.com/college/Melicher to evaluate your knowledge of the basics of short-term business funding.
Measure your learning by comparing pre-test and post-test results.

Summary Questions

1. Working capital includes a firm's marketable securities, accounts receivable, inventories, and mortgage debt. True or false?

2. If net working capital is negative, current assets are partially financed by the firm's long-term debt. True or false?

3. The maturity matching approach is a financing strategy that attempts to match the maturities of assets with the maturities of the liabilities by which they are financed. True or false?

4. An aggressive financing plan has a higher financing cost, but with lower risk of not being able to borrow when short-term funds are needed. True or false?

5. An advantage of short-term borrowing is the need for frequent renewals. True or false?

6. Short-term financing sources include bank loans, trade credit, and commercial paper. True or false?

7. A line of credit costs the firm only the normal interest for the period during which money is actually borrowed. True or false?

8. A compensating balance requirement means that a lending institution will require a borrowing company to keep a certain percentage of the loaned amount on deposit with that institution. True or false?

9. Discounting has the effect of reducing the available funds received by the borrower while raising the effective interest rate. True or false?

10. Manufacturing companies tend to be the largest users of accounts receivable financing. True or false?

11. Inventory loans are less expensive than unsecured loans to business borrowers. True or false?

12. An acceptance is a receivable from the sale of merchandise on the basis of a draft or bill of exchange drawn against the buyer or the buyer's bank. True or false?

13. Short-term financing may come in the form of trade credit extended between businesses. True or false?

14. A commercial finance company is an organization without a bank charter that advances funds to businesses. True or false?

15. A revolving credit agreement is a commitment in the form of a standby agreement for a guaranteed line of credit. True or false?

16. If a borrowing firm does not qualify for an unsecured bank loan and pledges its accounts receivable as security, it eliminates the need for a credit investigation. True or false?

17. An owner of a business may not assign life insurance as collateral for a short-term loan. True or false?

18. Trade credit may be considered the least formal of all forms of financing. True or false?

19. Using the conservative approach for financing a firm's assets, long-term financing would be used only to finance fixed assets, while short-term financing would be used to finance current assets, including seasonal fluctuations. True or false?

20. The choice of financing strategy involves a trade-off between return and risk. True or false?

21. The requirement that 10 to 20% of a loan be kept on deposit at the bank is called a *line of credit.* True or false?

22. A discounted loan is one in which the borrower receives the principal plus the interest at the time the loan is made. True or false?

Review Questions

1. What is meant by *net working capital*?

2. What is meant by "permanent" current assets? How do "temporary" current assets differ from permanent current assets?

3. Explain the strategies businesses can use to finance their assets with short-term and long-term funds.

4. What influences affect the nature of the demand for short-term versus long-term funds?

5. Explain how a conservative approach to financing a firm's assets is a low-risk/low-expected-return strategy, whereas an aggressive approach to financing is a high-risk/high-expected-return strategy.

6. Prepare a list of advantages and disadvantages of short-term bank borrowing relative to other short-term financing sources.

7. What is meant by an unsecured loan? Are these loans an important form of bank lending?

8. Explain what a bank line of credit is.

9. Explain how discounting and compensating balances affect the effective cost of financing.

10. Describe the revolving credit agreement and compare it with the bank line of credit.

11. When might a business seek accounts receivable financing?

12. What safeguards may a bank establish to protect itself when it lends on the basis of a customer's receivables pledged as collateral for a loan?

13. When a business firm uses its inventory as collateral for a bank loan, how is the problem of storing and guarding the inventory accomplished for the bank?

14. What is meant by *trade credit*? Briefly describe some of the possible terms for trade credit.

15. What are the primary reasons for using trade credit for short-term financing?

16. Under what circumstances would a business secure its financing through a commercial finance company?

17. Describe how a factor differs from a commercial finance company in terms of accounts-receivable financing.

18. Why would a business use the services of a factor?

19. How does the Small Business Administration provide financing to businesses?

20. What is commercial paper, and how important is it as a source of financing?

21. Is commercial paper a reliable source of financing? Why or why not?

22. The cost of trade credit involving cash discounts as a form of short-term financing is _____.

23. What do commercial paper dealers distribute to investors?

24. For most fields of business, the basic source of short-term loan financing is _____.

25. Firms that wish to obtain short-term secured loans generally have two major current assets available as collateral in the form of _____.

26. The purchaser may deduct 2% from the purchase price if payment is made within 10 days; but if not paid within 10 days, the net amount of the purchase is due within 30 days. The sale is made on what terms?

27. Find the annualized cost of a commercial paper issue the has a $1,000,000 face value, matures in 180 days, has a placement fee of 1.5%, and an interest charge of 8.5% over the 6-month period it is outstanding.

28. If net working capital is negative, this means _____.

29. If a firm has positive net working capital, the current ratio is _____.

30. When short-term debt is replaced by new short-term debt as the old debt comes due, the process is known as _____.

31. In order to borrow $100,000 for a 10% loan on a discount loan basis, the firm will actually have to borrow _____.

32. In order to borrow $100,000 for a 5% loan on a discount loan basis with a 5% compensating balance, the firm will actually have to borrow

_____.

Applying This Chapter

1. Describe the effects of tightening money supplies on an aggressive short-term financing strategy. What type of financing strategy might be best-suited for periods of tight money supply?

2. Obtain a current issue of the Federal Reserve Bulletin, or review a copy from the Fed's Web site (www.federalreserve.gov) or the St. Louis Fed's Web site (www.stls.frb.gov), and determine the changes in the prime rate that have occurred since the end of 1998. Comment on any trends in the data.

3. Compute the effective cost of not taking the cash discount under the following trade credit terms:

   (a) 2/10 net 40

   (b) 2/10 net 50

   (c) 3/10 net 50

   (d) 2/20 net 40

4. Michael's Computers is evaluating proposals from two different factors that will provide receivables financing. Big Fee Factoring will finance the receivables at an APR of 8%, discounted, and with a fee of 4%. HighRate Factoring offers an APR of 14% (nondiscounted) with fees of 2%. The average term of either loan is expected to be 35 days. With an average receivables balance of $250,000, which proposal should Michael's accept?

5. Michael's Computers' local bank offers the firm a 12-month revolving credit agreement of $500,000. The APR of the revolver is 12% with a commitment fee of 0.5% on the unused portion. Over the course of a year, Michael's chief financial officer believes they will have an average balance of $280,000 on the revolving credit agreement, with a low of $50,000 and a high of $450,000. What is the annual effective cost of this proposed agreement?

6. Bank Two wants to attract Michael's Computers, Inc. to become a customer. Their sales force contacts Michael's and offers them line-of-credit financing. The credit line will be for $500,000 with a 1-month

"clean-up" period. The APR on borrowed funds is 11%. Bank Two will offer the line of credit if Michael's opens an account and maintains an average balance of $100,000 over the next 12 months. Ignoring compensating balances, Michael's CFO believes its financing needs will average $280,000 monthly over the next year with a low monthly need of $50,000 and a high need forecast of $450,000.

(a) Will the line of credit satisfy Michael's needs for short-term funds?

(b) How much money will Michael's draw-down from the credit line be during a low-use month?

(c) How much will Michael's need to borrow in a month before it maximizes its use of the line of credit?

(d) What is the average cost to Michael's of using the credit line for a year?

Obtaining Financing

You are the finance manager for a manufacturing facility that needs to buy a new piece of equipment to stay competitive. What are your options for financing sources? What factors go into the decision to obtain short-term versus long-term financing?

Line of Credit

You are the finance manager for a manufacturing facility that needs a line of credit to purchase new equipment and hire additional employees. What factors will the bank consider in their decision to grant the line of credit?

Inventory Loan

You are the financial manager for an automaker that needs financing. Do you recommend considering an inventory loan? Why or why not?

10

RISK AND RATE OF RETURN
Prudent Diversification

Starting Point

Go to www.wiley.com/college/Melicher to assess your knowledge of the basics of risks and returns.
Determine where you need to concentrate your effort.

What You'll Learn in This Chapter

▲ The historical rates of return and risk for different securities
▲ The value of historical data in predicting rates of return and risk
▲ The relationship between risk and return
▲ The three forms of market efficiency
▲ The definition and uses of a portfolio
▲ The capital asset pricing model (CAPM)
▲ The meaning of "beta" coefficients

After Studying This Chapter, You'll Be Able To

▲ Calculate the monthly return on a portfolio of securities
▲ Calculate a stock's variance, standard deviation, and coefficient of variation
▲ Examine how investors can improve their returns through diversification
▲ Examine what makes a market efficient
▲ Appraise the risk and returns of a portfolio
▲ Distinguish the difference between systematic and unsystematic risk

Goals and Outcomes

▲ Assess ways to measure risk for a portfolio of securities
▲ Compare and contrast a boom economy, normal conditions, and a recession
▲ Compare and contrast the risks and returns of large company stocks and small company stocks
▲ Evaluate a market and determine if it is a strong-form efficient market or a weak-form efficient market
▲ Predict the returns on a portfolio of securities
▲ Manage the combining of securities into portfolios to reduce the overall risk
▲ Assess the relationship between systematic risk and a portfolio's variability relative to the market portfolio

INTRODUCTION

In this chapter we will first learn how risk is measured relative to the average return for a single investment. We will also review historical data showing the risk-return relationship; we will see that higher-risk investments must compensate investors over time with higher expected returns. Having a good grasp of the concepts used by financial managers to manage investments and evaluate the risks and rates of returns on them is essential. This includes exposure to more complex mathematical equations and the calculations used to determine risk and rate of return. While these equations and calculations require more specific and advanced study, they are presented here to make you aware of the various ways managers evaluate financial information. This chapter also presents valuable insights on stock and bond portfolios and how diversification affects the income derived from them.

10.1 Historical Return and Risk for a Single Asset

Investors place their funds in stocks, bonds, and other investments to try to attain their financial goals. However, stock and bond market values rise and fall over time, based on what happens to interest rates, economic expectations, and other factors. Since no one can predict the future, the returns earned on investments are, for the most part, not known. Some may look back and see how different investments performed in the past and predict that future returns will be similar. Others do sophisticated economic and financial analyses in order to estimate future returns.

Figure 10-1 shows monthly prices for the stocks of two firms, Walgreens and Microsoft. Walgreens's stock price has trended mainly upward during this time frame, while Microsoft's stock prices have fluctuated.

Based on the information displayed in Figure 10-1, we can compute monthly returns on both of these stocks, taking their price changes and dividends into consideration. The monthly return is computed as follows:

Dollar return = Stock price at end of month − stock price at beginning of month + dividends.

For example, in 1 month, Walgreens's stock went from $33.63 per share at the beginning of the month to $34.31 at the end of the month. No dividends were paid that month. The dollar return is simply

$$\$34.31 - \$33.63 = \$0.68.$$

If a dividend were received, that amount would be added to the dollar return. For example, if a dividend of 4 cents had been received during the month, the dollar return would have been

$$\$34.31 - \$33.63 + \$0.04 = \$0.72.$$

Figure 10-1

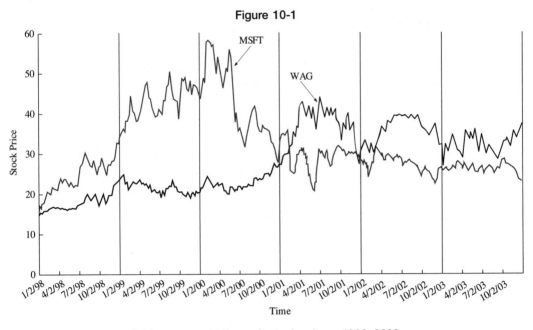

Walgreens and Microsoft stock prices, 1998–2003.

The formula to calculate the return as a percentage is

Percentage return = Dollar return/by stock price at the beginning of the month.

So, Walgreens's percentage return is

$$\$0.68/\$33.63 = 0.02022, \text{ or } 2.022\%.$$

With dividends, the percentage return is

$$\$0.72/\$33.63 = 0.02141, \text{ or } 2.141\%.$$

10.1.1 Arithmetic Average Annual Rates of Return

If historical data on a stock's returns are known, the analyst can easily compute historical average return and risk measures. One way to measure the risk of an asset is to examine the variability of its returns. For comparison, an analyst may want to determine the level of return and the variability in returns for these two stocks to see whether investors in the higher-risk stock earned a higher return over time to compensate or adequately reward them for the higher risk.

If R_t represents the stock's return for period, t, the **arithmetic average return,** or the sum of all the returns for the years divided by the number of years, $\bar{R}$, over n periods is calculated as follows:

$$\bar{R} = \sum_{t=1}^{n} [R_t]/n$$

The following is a list of annual rates of return over a 6-year period for Walgreens and Microsoft stock.

Year	Microsoft	Walgreens
2003	11.6%	3.0%
2002	−6.1	−21.6
2001	−17.4	58.1
2000	43.7	−62.8
1999	0.9	68.3
1998	92.9	111.5
Sum	125.6	156.5
Sum/6 years = Average Return	20.9	26.1

Performing this calculation in Excel is straightforward. Placing the annual returns in columns B and C, use the SUM function to add the Walgreens returns in cells B2 through B7 by typing "=SUM(B2:B7)" in cell B8. Then divide this sum by 6, the number of years observed, to compute the average Walgreens return by typing "=B8/6 in cell B9". Similar calculations for the Microsoft data are entered into column C.

◇	A	B	C
1	YEAR	WALGREEN	MICROSOFT
2	2003	11.6%	3.0%
3	2002	−6.1%	−21.0%
4	2001	−17.4%	58.1%
5	2000	43.7%	−62.8%
6	1999	0.9%	68.3%
7	1998	92.9%	111.5%
8	SUM	=SUM(B2:B7)	=SUM(C2:C7)
9	SUM/6=AVERAGE RETURN	=B8/6	=C8/6

Walgreens stock has an arithmetic average annual rate of return over these 6 years of 20.9%, whereas the average annual return for Microsoft stock over the same 6-year period was 26.1%. If we are willing to ignore risk as reflected in the variability of returns, an investment in Microsoft stock might be preferred. However, all investors do not have the same tolerance for risk associated with the wide swings possible in Microsoft's returns, so let's see how we might measure this variability in past returns.

10.1.2 Variance as a Measure of Risk

The historical risk of a stock can be measured by the variability of its returns in relation to this average. Some measures of this average are the

▲ variance;
▲ standard deviation or square root of the variance;
▲ coefficient of variation (CV) that measures the risk per unit of return.

All of these measures use deviations of periodic returns from the average return.

▲ A **deviation** is computed as a periodic return minus the average return.

The variance from a sampling of historical data is computed by summing the squared deviations and dividing by n − 1:

$$\sigma 2 = \sum_{t=1}^{n} (R_t - \overline{R})^2 / (n - 1)$$

$R_t - \overline{R}$, where $\overline{R}$ denoted the average arithmetic return over some time frame. Note that the sum of the deviations, $\Sigma\,(R_t - \overline{R})$, is always zero.

We can now find the historical variance in returns for Walgreens's and Microsoft's stocks over the past 6 years as shown in Table 10-1.

Squaring the deviations can make variance difficult to interpret. Therefore, analysts frequently prefer to use the **standard deviation,** which is simply the square root of the variance.

$$\sigma = \sqrt{\sigma^2}$$

The standard deviation formula gives units of measurement that match those of the return data. Taking the square root of the variance of 1,675.4 for Walgreens's stock gives a standard deviation of 40.9%. This compares to a standard deviation of 64.5% (i.e., the square root of 4,165.0) for Microsoft. Again, Microsoft has both a relatively higher average return (26.1% versus 20.9%) and standard deviation (64.5% versus 40.9%) when compared to Walgreens for the same time period.

The square root can also be found using a financial calculator with a square root key.

Financial Calculator Solution:

Walgreens stock:		Microsoft stock:
Inputs:	1675.4	4165.0
Press:	$\sqrt{}$	$\sqrt{}$
Solution:	40.9	64.5

Table 10-1: Finding the Variances for the Returns on Walgreens and Microsoft

Year	Walgreens		Microsoft	
	Return Difference From the Average (%)	Return Difference Squared	Return Difference From the Average (%)	Return Difference Squared
2003	$11.6\% - 20.9\% = -9.3\%$	$-9.3^2 = 86.49$	$3.0\% - 26.1\% = -23.1\%$	$-23.1^2 = 533.61$
2002	$-6.1\% - 20.9\% = -27.1\%$	$-27.1^2 = 734.41$	$-21.6\% - 26.1\% = -47.7\%$	$-47.7^2 = 2,275.29$
2001	$-17.4\% - 20.9\% = -38.3\%$	$-38.3^2 = 1,466.89$	$58.1\% - 26.1\% = 32.1\%$	$32.1^2 = 1,030.41$
2000	$43.7\% - 20.9\% = 22.8\%$	$22.8^2 = 519.84$	$-62.8\% - 26.1\% = -88.9\%$	$-88.9^2 = 7,903.21$
1999	$0.9\% - 20.9\% = -20.0\%$	$-20.0^2 = 400.00$	$68.3\% - 26.1\% = 42.3\%$	$42.3^2 = 1,789.29$
1998	$92.9\% - 20.9\% = 71.9\%$	$71.9^2 = 5,169.61$	$111.5\% - 26.1\% = 85.4\%$	$85.4^2 = 7,293.16$
SUM		$8,377.24\%^2$		$20,824.97\%^2$
Variance = Sum/(6 − 1) =		$1,675.4\%^2$		$4,165.0\%^2$

Spreadsheets can be used, too. Since we know the standard deviation is the square root of the variance, Excel's SQRT function can be used by keying in "=SQRT" (cell containing the variance). To make the calculation simpler, we can use the STDEV function. If Walgreens's returns are in cells B2 through B7, using =STDEV(B2:B7) in another cell computes the standard deviation.

Looking at historical annual returns on these stocks will tell us what their price range has been—namely, how low and how high each stock price has been. If an analyst believes the near future will be similar to the historical time period studied, calculating the standard deviation will help to give an investor an intuitive feel for the possible range of returns that can occur.

As shown in the Figure 10-2, if the underlying distribution of returns is continuous and approximately normal (that is, bell-shaped), then we expect 68% of actual periodic returns to fall within one standard deviation of the mean. About 95% of returns will fall within two standard deviations, and actual returns should fall within three standard deviations of the mean, $\bar{R}$. So, if the mean and standard deviation are known, an estimated range for expected returns over time can be estimated.

For Walgreens and Microsoft, this is probably not going to be the case. The returns of both of these stocks during the 1998–2003 time frame were well above what we can reasonably believe to occur over the long term. This is illustrated in Table 10-2, which shows the range of possible outcomes for these two stocks along with approximate probabilities of occurrence. Based on this table, we can say that 95% of the time, the annual return on Walgreens's stock will fall between –60.9% and +102.8% with an expected average annual return of 20.9%. For Microsoft, the annual return will fall within the range of –100% (total loss) and +155.2% about 95% percent of the time, and the expected average monthly return will be 26.1%.

One problem with using the standard deviation as a measure of risk is that we cannot tell which stock is riskier by looking at the standard deviation alone. For example, Walgreens stock returns have an annual standard deviation of 40.9% while Microsoft has an annual standard deviation of 64.5% a year.

Figure 10-2

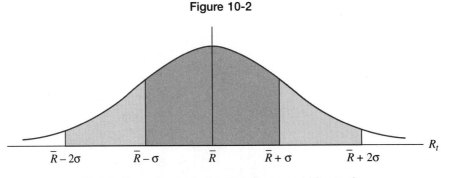

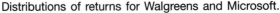

Distributions of returns for Walgreens and Microsoft.

Table 10-2: Finding the Variances for the Returns on Walgreens and Microsoft

Stock	Percent of Returns	Annual Return Estimates Downside (%)	Average (%)	Upside (%)
Walgreens	68	−20.0%	20.9%	69.1%
	95	−60.9	20.9	102.8
	99	−101.9 (total loss)	20.9	143.7
Microsoft	68	−38.4	26.1	90.6
	95	−103.0 (total loss)	26.1	155.2
	99	−167.5 (total loss)	26.1	219.7

Microsoft clearly has a higher standard deviation, but it also had a higher average annual return of 26.1% versus 20.9% for Walgreens. Which stock is riskier?

The coefficient of variation allows us to make comparisons because it controls for the size of the average.

▲ The **coefficient of variation (CV)** is a measure of risk per unit of return.

The coefficient of variation is computed as follows:

$$CV = \sigma/\overline{R}$$

FOR EXAMPLE

Investments

As you can see from the returns for Microsoft and Walgreens, returns can vary dramatically from one year to the next. This is why many stock ratings from financial analysts are based on 3, 5, or 10 years. Stock prices can vary dramatically from day-to-day as well, which is why many analysts advocate dollar-cost averaging. Dollar-cost averaging is investing a certain amount of money in the same stock on a routine basis such as every month. This way the risk is reduced over the long term. For example, if you buy 10 shares of a stock every month, you may buy shares for $50 one month and $40 the next. If you sell it at $45 per share, then you come out even.

A higher coefficient of variation indicates more risk per unit of return. A lower coefficient of variation indicates less risk per unit of return. For Walgreens, based on the information in the preceding table, the computation is as follows:

60.9 minus 20% = 40.9 divided by 20.9 average % = 1.96 units of risk for every unit of return. For Microsoft, the computation is 103.0 minus 38.4 = 64.5 divided by 26.1 = 2.47 units of risk per unit of return. Check the table to see where the numbers used in these computations were displayed. Based on the results of these calculations, Microsoft stock has a higher risk than Walgreens.

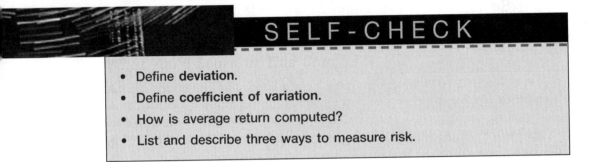

SELF-CHECK

- Define **deviation**.
- Define **coefficient of variation**.
- How is average return computed?
- List and describe three ways to measure risk.

10.2 Expected Measures of Return and Risk

The use of historical data to look backward is valuable for examining returns and performance over time. However, today's investment and business decisions must be made by looking forward, not backward. Future returns will depend upon decisions made today and by events that occur in the future.

A popular method to forecast future returns is to develop scenarios of future states of nature. A **state of nature** includes a set of economic trends and business conditions.

This is simply a method that tries to see into the future, because, in reality, the investor cannot control or predict what future states of nature will occur. One set of scenarios could be the following:

1. **Boom economy:** The domestic economy will grow at an above-average pace; inflation will increase slowly; interest rate trends will be slightly upward. Company sales will be assisted by a healthy export environment.
2. **Normal conditions:** The domestic economy will grow at a pace close to its long-run average. Inflation rates and interest rates will be relatively stable. No major disruptions in our export markets are expected.

3. **Recession:** The domestic economy will grow slowly, or maybe contract. Inflation will peak and start to decline; short-term interest rates will fall. Slow export markets will lead to lower levels of foreign sales.

Each of these three scenarios is a state of nature. The states of nature can be complicated or simple, few or many; but as a whole, they should include all reasonable (and maybe a few unreasonable) possible future environments. The three scenarios assumed inflation, interest rate, and a firm's exports will follow the trends in the overall domestic economy. This, of course, does not have to be the case. A more complex set of states of nature may include separate scenarios for the domestic economy, inflation, interest rates, exports, and any other variables deemed important by the investment analyst.

Once the possible states of nature are projected, the analyst must assign a probability, or a chance of occurrence, to each one. For the three scenarios, assume the first scenario of a growing economy has a probability (p1) of 0.30; the second scenario of normal conditions has a probability (p2) of 0.40; the third scenario, recession, has a probability (p3) of 0.30. In reality, these probabilities are developed from a combination of the analyst's experience, surveys of other analysts on their beliefs, economic and industry forecasts, monetary policy, and a review of what has happened in the past under similar conditions. There is no standard formula that can be used to determine these probability factors. The only rules are that each state of nature must have a non-negative probability assigned to it and that the probabilities of all the states of nature must total 1.00.

The analyst must also forecast the stock's return for the year under each state of nature. If the preceding three states of nature are being used, analysts might forecast a 20% return under good economic conditions, 10% in normal times, and −5% in a recession.

The expected return can now be found, using the following equation:

$$\text{Expected return } E(R) = \sum_{i=1}^{n} p_i R_i$$

The expected return E(R) is a weighted average of the different state of nature returns, where the weights are the probabilities of each state of nature occurring. Using the equation and the forecasted percentages, the computation would be

$$E(R) = (0.3)(20) + (0.4)(10) + (0.3)(-5) = 8.5\ \%$$

This number, or any other so calculated, represents the average return if the state of nature scenarios could be replicated many times under identical conditions. The process of computing expected returns from scenarios is not easy to apply practically. So, some analysts prefer to estimate expected returns from historical return data and forecasts.

Just as for historical data, measures of variance can be computed once the average or expected value is found. The variance is found by using the following equation:

$$\sigma^2 = \sum_{i=1}^{n} p_i[R_i - E(R)]^2$$

As with historical measures, the standard deviation is simply the square root of the variance. The coefficient of variation is the standard deviation divided by the expected return. The coefficient of variation is easily interpreted: it represents the risk per unit of expected return.

Let's compute the variance, standard deviation, and coefficient of variation for the stock return using the three scenarios developed earlier. The stock return forecast was 20% in an economic boom (30% probability), 10% in a normal economy (40% probability), and −5% in a recession (30% probability). The expected return was computed to be 8.5%. Using the preceding equation, the variance of the forecast is

$$\sigma^2 = (0.3)(20 - 8.5)^2 + (0.4)(10 - 8.5)^2 + (0.3)(-5 - 8.5)^2$$
$$= 39.675 + 0.90 + 54.675$$
$$= 95.25 \text{ percent squared}$$

The standard deviation will be the square root of this number, or 9.76%. The coefficient of variation is the standard deviation divided by the expected return, or 9.76/8.5 = 1.15.

Is it practical to develop states of nature, determine their expected probabilities, and estimate expected return and risk? Do investors really do these calculations? There is evidence that scenario analysis does have practical implications. Consider that when the Federal Reserve Board is expected to decide to act to change short-term interest rates, market watchers and investors anticipate what the Fed may do. Periodicals such as the *Wall Street Journal* and *USA Today* survey practitioners on their expectations of Fed action. One news article by E. S. Browning published by the *Wall Street Journal* (May 15, 2001, p. C1) presented this analysis prior to an expected interest rate cut by the Fed:

Scenario	Probability	Likely Market Response
No rate cut	Very unlikely	Stocks and bonds plunge
Quarter-point cut	Possible	Stocks and bonds fall
Half-point cut	Likely	Stocks and bonds could rise, at least initially
Three-quarter point cut, or more	Unlikely	Stocks and bonds surge

> ### FOR EXAMPLE
>
> **Interest Rates**
>
> In September 2004, Federal Reserve chairman Alan Greenspan increased the federal funds rate from 1.5 to 4.75%. The funds rate is the interest banks charge each other on overnight loans. On this news, the Dow Jones gained 40 points.

The market evidently anticipated the Fed's actions; that day the Fed announced it would attempt to reduce short-term rates by one-half point, which was the "likely" scenario. The stock market closed virtually unchanged; the Dow Jones Industrial Average closed down that day just 4.36 points (or 0.04% of the index's value) while the Nasdaq Composite Index closed up 3.66 points (0.18%). Another consideration is that while each individual investor may not compute a scenario analysis, the markets as a whole behaves as if they do. Expected changes, news, or announcements will generally have little effect on security prices. So if an investor follows the consensus set of beliefs, the investor will find it difficult to earn above-average returns, after adjusting for risk differences. In order to make above-average returns without undue risk, an investor must do analysis and determine if the consensus belief is incorrect and invest accordingly.

A more complex form of decision analysis than scenario analysis is called *simulation*. Rather than using a limited number of states of nature with specific values for, say, inflation, economic growth, and so on, simulation allows many different combinations of the important variables that may determine stock returns. After running the analysis several thousand times, the computer can calculate the average return from the simulation runs and the standard deviation of the returns. This technique is used by businesses for a variety of decisions involving uncertain revenues or expenses.

SELF-CHECK

- Define **state of nature**.
- Provide a state-of-nature scenario.
- How does computing expected return differ from finding a historical average return?
- Why must the probabilities of the various scenarios total 1.0?

10.3 Historical Returns and Risk of Different Assets

The value of an asset is the present value of the expected cash flows that arise from owning the asset. To compute a present value, we need to know the size and timing of expected future cash flows from an asset. We also must know the appropriate discount rate, or the required rate of return, at which to discount expected cash flows back to the present. The three components of the required rate of return are as follows:

▲ The real risk-free rate of return
▲ Inflation expectations
▲ A risk premium

The first two components are the same for all investments. Their combined effect is approximated by the yield on a short-term treasury bill. Expected returns differ as a result of different risk premiums, so financial professionals say that risk drives expected return. A low-risk investment will have a lower expected return than a high-risk investment. High-risk investments will have to offer investors higher expected returns in order to convince conservative people to place their savings at risk. Therefore, long-term treasury bonds will have to offer investors higher expected returns than treasury bills. Common stock, by virtue of its equity claim and low priority on company cash flows and assets, will have to offer investors a still larger expected return to compensate for its risk.

Evidence that high returns go hand in hand with high risk can be seen in Table 10-3, which reports the average annual returns and standard deviations for different types of investments. The return distributions for small-company common stocks and all common stocks have large standard deviations, indicating much more risk than the bond investments. However, investors who choose to undertake such risk earn high rewards over the long haul, since stock returns reward investors more than conservative bond investments.

Investors in small company stocks (the smallest 20% of those listed on the New York Stock Exchange) had an average annual return of 17.5%, but at a high level of risk: The standard deviation of the returns was over 33%. Recalling our interpretation of a standard deviation, and assuming future market conditions will be similar to those of the past 75 years, about two-thirds of the time the annual return from investing in small stocks should fall between −15.8% and +50.8%.

Large company stocks, as measured by the Standard & Poor's stock market index of 500 stocks, returned an average of 12.4% to investors with an annual standard deviation of 20.4%. Large company equities are less risky than those of small firms, so as expected we see a lower average return. The same is true for the international stock index; the level of its risk is close to that of large U.S.

Table 10-3: Historical Returns and Standard Deviations of Returns from Different Assets, 1926–2003

Asset	Average Annual Return	Standard Deviation
Small company stocks	17.5%	33.3%
Non-U.S. stocks (EAFE) (1970–2003)	13.0	22.8
Large company stocks	12.4	20.4
Long-term corporate bonds	6.2	8.6
Long-term government bonds	5.8	9.4
U.S. Treasury bills	3.8	3.2
Inflation rate	3.1	4.3

stocks and its return is comparable, too. The return and risk measures for long-term government bonds show that less risk does result in less return. Treasury bills' average annual return is the lowest in the table, as is the standard deviation of their returns over time.

The seeming oddity of long-term corporate bonds having higher returns and a lower standard deviation than long-term government bonds can be explained by digging deeper into how these measures were constructed. Historically, the government's bond issues have had longer terms to maturity than corporate bond issues. Longer time-to-maturity bonds have greater interest rate risk, so it is not surprising that the standard deviation of the government's long-term bonds is greater than those of the corporate bonds. We expect higher average return on the corporate bonds, since we know they have greater credit risk than treasury securities.

Although future returns and risk cannot be predicted precisely from past measures, the data in Table 10-3 does present information that investors find useful when considering the relative risks and rewards of different investment strategies.

Just because large company stocks have an arithmetic average return of 12.4% does not mean we necessarily should expect the stock market to rise by that amount each year. As the standard deviation of the annual returns indicates, 12.4% is the average return over a long time frame, during which there were substantial deviations—both positive and negative—from the average.

The behavior of the stock market in 2000–2002, particularly the technology sector, should remind us that market returns are not always positive. The S & P 500 stock market index lost over 9% in value during calendar year

FOR EXAMPLE

Diversify

During the late nineties until 2000, many investors ignored the longstanding finance maxim of diversifying one's investments. The stocks in technology, also called the "new economy," were generating such high returns that investors were investing all of their money in tech. These investors learned their lesson the hard way when the technology stocks posted heavy losses with many of the companies going under. Owning mutual funds or several stocks helps minimize risk and maximize returns.

2000, over 12% during 2001, and over 22% in 2002. The technology sector was very hard hit during this time, as bankruptcies and oversupply resulted in some sectors losing 60% or more in value in 2000, with losses continuing through 2002.

SELF-CHECK

- Explain what is meant by "risk drives expected return."
- How does Table 10-3 illustrate the concept that risk drives expected return?
- What are the three components of required rate of return?
- Why would investors diversify?

10.4 Efficient Capital Markets

Prices on securities change over the course of time because the prices are determined by the pattern of expected cash flows and a discount rate. Therefore, any change in price must reflect a change in expected cash flows, the discount rate, or both. Sometimes identifiable news can cause assets' prices to change. Unexpected good news may cause investors to view an asset as less risky or to expect increases in future cash flows. Either reaction leads to an increase in an asset's price. Unexpected bad news can cause an opposite reaction: The asset may be viewed as more risky or its future cash flows may be expected to fall. Either reaction results in a falling asset price.

An **efficient market** is a market in which prices adjust quickly after the arrival of new information and the price change reflects the economic value of the information, on average. If the market for Microsoft stock is efficient, there should be a quick price change shortly after any announcement of an unexpected event that affects sales, earnings, new products, or after an unexpected announcement by a major competitor. A quick movement in the price of a stock such as Microsoft should take no longer than several minutes. After this price adjustment, future price changes should appear to be random—that is, the initial price reaction to the news should, on average, fully reflect the effects of the news.

In an efficient market, only unexpected news or surprises should cause prices to move markedly up or down. Expected events should have no impact on asset prices, since investors' expectations would already be reflected in their trading patterns and the asset's price. If investors expected Microsoft to announce that earnings for the past year rose 10%, Microsoft's stock price should be at a level equal with that expectation. If Microsoft does indeed announce a 10% earnings increase, no significant price change should occur, as Microsoft's stock price already reflected that information. If, however, Microsoft announced an earnings increase of 20% or an earnings decline of 5%, the market would quickly adjust Microsoft's price in reaction to the unexpected news.

Every time Microsoft's stock price changes in reaction to new information, it should show no continuing tendency to rise or fall after the price adjustment. After new information hits the market and the price adjusts, no steady trend in either direction should persist.

Figure 10-3 shows how rapidly stock prices adjust, on average, to higher-than-expected earnings announcements and lower-than-expected earnings announcements. Market efficiency has increased, as the price reaction to earnings surprises was more rapid in the 1995–98 period than in the 1983–1989 period.

In an efficient market, it is difficult to consistently find stocks whose prices do not fairly reflect the present values of future expected cash flows. Prices will quickly change when the arrival of new information indicates that an upward or

Figure 10-3

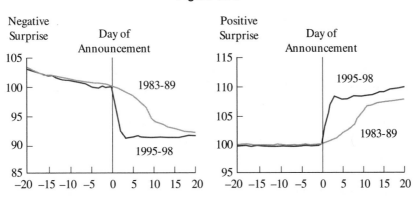

Stock market average price reaction to positive and negative earnings surprises.

downward revision in this present value is appropriate. The price adjustment occurs so rapidly that buy or sell orders placed after the announcement cannot, in the long run, result in risk-adjusted returns above the market's average return. An order to buy after the arrival of good news may result in large profits, but such a gain will occur only by chance, as will comparable losses. Stock price trends always return to their random ways after initially adjusting to the new information.

Efficient markets result from interactions among many market participants, all analyzing available information in pursuit of advantage. Also, the information flows they analyze must be random, both in timing and content (in an efficient market, no one can consistently predict tomorrow's news). The profit motive leads investors to try to buy low and sell high on the basis of new information and their interpretation of it. Hordes of investors analyzing all available information about the economy and individual firms quickly identify incorrectly priced stocks. Resulting trading pushes those stocks to their correct levels. This causes prices in an efficient market to move in a random walk.

▲ A **random walk** means that prices appear to fluctuate randomly over time, driven by the random arrival of new information.

Different assumptions about how much information is reflected in prices give rise to different types of market efficiency.

▲ A **strong-form efficient market** is a market in which prices reflect all public and private knowledge, including past and current information.

In such an efficient market, even corporate officers and other insiders cannot earn above-average, risk-adjusted profits from buying and selling stock. Even their detailed, exclusive information is already reflected in current stock prices.

The U.S. stock market appears to be a fairly good example of a semi-strong-form efficient market. News about the economy or individual companies appears to produce quick stock price changes without subsequent trends or price reversals.

▲ A **weak-form efficient market** is a market in which prices reflect all past information.

Such information includes last year's annual report, previous earnings announcements, and other past news. Some investors, called *chartists* or *technicians,* examine graphs of past price movements, number of shares bought and sold, and other figures to try to predict future price movements. A weak-form efficient market implies that such investors are wasting their time; they cannot earn above-average, risk-adjusted profits by projecting past trends in market variables.

Market efficiency has several important practical implications. First, for investors, efficient markets make it difficult to consistently "beat the market" by

FOR EXAMPLE

Returns and the Stock Index

During the decade of the 1990s, about two-thirds of professionally managed U.S. diversified stock mutual funds earned lower returns than the S & P 500 stock index. Indexers try to match the market's performance by placing funds in securities in the same proportion as their weight in their chosen index.

earning above-average returns after taking risk differences into account. Therefore, over time, more and more individual and institutional investors have chosen to "index"—that is, to invest in securities that comprise the market indexes (such as the Standard & Poor's 500 or Merrill Lynch's corporate bond index) rather than try to choose specific stocks or bonds.

SELF-CHECK

- Define **random walk.**
- What is an efficient market?
- If price trends are predictable, would that be an indication of an efficient or inefficient market?
- How does a strong-form efficient market differ from a weak-form efficient market?

10.5 Portfolio Returns and Risk

Although it is difficult for an investor to earn rates of return higher than risk-adjusted market returns, an investor can and should establish the amount of financial risk she or he is willing to accept. In section 10.1 we saw that investors received an arithmetic average annual rate of return of 20.9% on Walgreens's stock with a standard deviation of 40.9% over 6 years; the average return and risk achieved by investing in Microsoft over the same 6-year period was 26.1% and 64.5%, respectively.

Some investors may believe that Microsoft is too risky and that Walgreens is too conservative. These people could search for another stock that would have return-risk characteristics in between these two stocks, or they could invest a portion of their investment funds in both stocks. This choice is an example of building or forming a portfolio. A **portfolio** is any combination of financial assets or investments.

10.5.1 Expected Returns on a Portfolio

By investing half of their funds in Microsoft and the other half in Walgreens, the investors have diversified and have adjusted their risk to a level that is now acceptable to them. Study Table 10-4 to see the returns that would result from such an investment plan over a 6-year period.

10.5.2 Variance and Standard Deviation of Return on a Portfolio

The total risk of a portfolio can be measured by its variance or the standard deviation of its returns. Extending the concept of portfolio return, one might think that the variance of a portfolio is simply a weighted average of asset variances. Unfortunately, this is not always correct. To understand why, look at the time series of returns illustrated in the Figures 10-4 and 10-5, where we consider the relationship between airlines and oil companies. Airlines use tremendous amounts of oil products to keep their fleets flying. Oil lubricates the engines and flaps, and of course jet fuel is needed to power the planes. Energy costs are a major component of airline expenses. When oil prices are down, airline profitability generally rises; when energy prices rise, airlines generally have difficulty passing the higher costs on to consumers, so their profits fall.

Figure 10-4

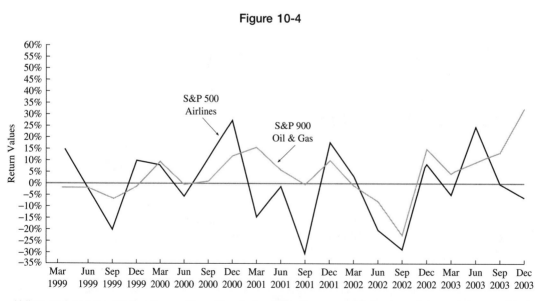

Airline and energy stock returns. Benefits of diversification—combining two risky assets may lead to lower portfolio risk.

Table 10-4: Portfolio Return Calculation Based on 50 Percent Investment in Walgreens and 50 Percent in Microsoft

Year	Walgreens Investment				Microsoft Investment				Weighted Return
	Percentage	×	Return	+	Percentage	×	Return	=	
2003	0.50	×	11.6%	+	0.50	×	3.0%	=	5.82% + 1.48% = 7.30%
2002	0.50	×	-6.1	+	0.50	×	-21.6	=	-3.07 + -10.79 = -13.90
2001	0.50	×	-17.4	+	0.50	×	58.1	=	-8.71 + 29.07 = 20.40
2000	0.50	×	43.7	+	0.50	×	-62.8	=	21.86 + -31.42 = -9.60
1999	0.50	×	0.9	+	0.50	×	68.3	=	0.44 + 34.17 = 34.60
1998	0.50	×	92.9	+	0.50	×	111.5	=	46.44 + 55.75 = 102.20

Sum of weighted returns = 141.00%

Portfolio average return = Sum/6 = 23.50%

Figure 10-5

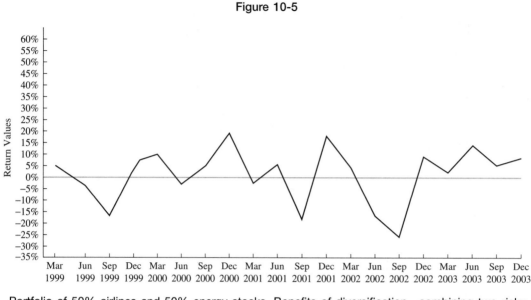

Portfolio of 50% airlines and 50% energy stocks. Benefits of diversification—combining two risky assets may lead to lower portfolio risk.

Just the opposite is true for energy firms: As oil prices rise, their profits rise because of the relatively fixed costs of oil production. When oil prices fall, so do the profits of oil firms. We expect the profits of oil firms and airlines to move opposite one another; when oil prices are rising, oil firms should enjoy higher profits while airlines suffer from higher expenses and lower prices. When energy prices fall, oil firm profits should decline and airlines should enjoy greater profitability. Since stock prices will be sensitive to company profits, the returns to oil and airline company stocks should be negatively related—that is, when one rises, the other falls. Therefore, investment funds spread between two such stocks can lead to lower portfolio risk.

FOR EXAMPLE

Asset Portfolio

Many people do not have the time and expertise needed to manage an asset portfolio. For many, acquiring the investment capital is difficult, too. This is why many small investors use investment companies. An investment company is a corporation that invests the pooled funds of savers. Many investment companies purchase the stocks and bonds of corporations. Others specialize in holding short-term commercial paper, bank CDs, and U.S. Treasury bills, and money market or mutual funds.

10.6 Diversification

Lower portfolio variability arises from the benefits of diversification. **Diversification** occurs when we invest in several different assets rather than just a single one.

The benefits of diversification are greatest when asset returns have negative correlations—that is, they tend to move in opposite directions.

▲ A **negative correlation** exists when two time series tend to move in opposite directions.

▲ A **positive correlation** exists when two stocks move in the same direction over time.

A look back on the returns for Walgreens and Microsoft stocks shows the impact of diversification even when the returns on two stocks generally move in the same direction over time. In this case, two stocks are said to have a positive correlation because their returns move together over time. Even so, the portfolio is less risky than investing in Microsoft alone because of its lower variability in annual returns over time.

The idea behind diversification is that at times some investments will do well while some are performing poorly and vice versa. Since it is difficult to forecast efficient markets, spreading funds across several different investments prevents investors from having a large exposure to any one investment. Another example of the benefits of diversification is found in Table 10-5.

Our time frame is 25 years; $10,000 invested over this time frame at an average annual rate of 7% gives us $54,274.33 in our account. However, let's examine what might happen if we divide our $10,000 initial investment into five different accounts, investing $2,000 in each one. Suppose one of the investments turns out to be a total failure and we lose the entire $2,000 invested. The second investment earns no return at all; 25 years later we still have $2,000 in that account. The third account earns a meager 5% annual average return over the 25 years. The fourth and fifth accounts perform better, one earning 10% and the other 12% on an average annual basis. Even though some accounts perform

Table 10-7: How to Calculate a Beta Coefficient or Measure of Systematic Risk

Month	Rates of Return S&P 500 X-axis	Microsoft Y-axis	Markets Returns Squared X^2	Product of the Returns $X \times Y$
1	−1.70%	−2.00%	2.89%	3.40%
2	−1.70	4.80	2.89	−8.16
3	−1.60	−6.00	2.56	9.60
4	1.20	−4.10	1.44	−4.92
5	1.70	1.00	2.89	1.70
6	5.10	6.50	26.01	33.15

Sum X = 3.00%   Sum Y = 0.20%   Sum X^2 = 38.68%   Sum XY = 34.77%

Estimating beta where n = 6 is the number of observations:

$$\beta = \frac{n\Sigma xy - (\Sigma x)(\Sigma y)}{n\Sigma x^2 - (\Sigma x)^2} = \frac{6(34.77) - (3.00)(0.20)}{6(38.68) - (3.0)(3.0)} = \frac{208.02}{223.08} = 0.93$$

SELF-CHECK

- Define capital asset pricing model *(CAPM)*.
- What is the market portfolio?
- What is the relationship between systematic risk and a portfolio's variability relative to the market portfolio?
- What is beta?

SUMMARY

Financial risk and return concepts are among the most mathematical and confusing to the first-time finance student, but they are vital to understanding financial markets, institutions, and management. In this chapter you learned how to better manage money in relation to risk and return for the company you work for and for your own personal investments. You have computed arithmetic averages, variances, and standard deviations using return data. You have also examined ways you can reduce financial risk and maximize return. These skills will help you in a variety of ways, including securing your retirement through investing.

KEY TERMS

Arithmetic average return	The sum of all the returns for the years divided by the number of years, R, over n periods
Beta (ß)	The measure of an asset's systematic risk.
Boom economy	The domestic economy will grow at an above-average pace; inflation will increase slowly; interest rate trends will be slightly upward.
Capital asset pricing model	States that the expected return on an asset depends upon its level of systematic risk.
Coefficient of variation (CV)	A measure of risk per unit of return.
Deviation	Computed as a periodic return minus the average return.
Diversification	Occurs when we invest in several different assets rather than just a single one.
Efficient market	A market in which prices adjust quickly after the arrival of new information and the price change reflects the economic value of the information, on average.
Market portfolio	Contains all risky assets and is the portfolio that truly eliminates all unsystematic risk.
Negative correlation	Exists when two time series tend to move in opposite directions.
Normal conditions	The domestic economy will grow at a pace close to its long-run average. Inflation rates and interest rates will be relatively stable.
Portfolio	Any combination of financial assets or investments.
Positive correlation	Exists when two stocks move in the same direction over time.
Random walk	Prices appear to fluctuate randomly over time, driven by the random arrival of new information.
Recession	The domestic economy will grow slowly, or maybe contract. Inflation will peak and start to decline; short-term interest rates will fall.
Standard deviation	Square root of the variance.
State of nature	Includes a set of economic trends and business conditions.

Strong-form efficient market	A market in which prices reflect all public and private knowledge, including past and current information.
Systematic risk	Risk that cannot be eliminated through diversification.
Unsystematic risk	Risk that is diversified away as assets are added to a portfolio is the firm- and industry-specific risk, or the "microeconomic" risk.
Weak-form efficient market	A market in which prices reflect all past information.

ASSESS YOUR UNDERSTANDING

Go to www.wiley.com/college/Melicher to evaluate your knowledge of the basics of risks and returns.

Measure your learning by comparing pre-test and post-test results.

Summary Questions

1. If standard deviation is used to measure the risk of stocks, one problem that arises is the inability to tell which stock is riskier by looking at the standard deviation alone. True or false?

2. Standard deviation is the square root of the variance. True or false?

3. The coefficient of variation is a measure of total return on a stock. True or false?

4. If a financial asset has a historical variance of 16%, then its standard deviation must be 4%. True or false?

5. Future returns and risk cannot be predicted precisely from past measures. True or false?

6. Which one of the following assets has historically had the highest average annual return?

   (a) Large company stocks

   (b) Long-term corporate bonds

   (c) Long-term government bonds

   (d) U.S. Treasury bills

7. A low-risk investment will have a lower required return than a high-risk investment. True or false?

8. In general, securities with higher historical standard deviations have provided higher returns. True or false?

9. A random walk means prices appear to fluctuate randomly over time, driven by the random arrival of new information. True or false?

10. In a strong-form efficient market, all public information, both past and current, is reflected in stock prices. True or false?

11. A weak-form efficient market is a market in which prices reflect all past information. True or false?

12. The total risk of a portfolio can be measured by its variance or the standard deviation of its returns. True or false?

13. The variance of a portfolio is simply a weighted average of asset variances. True or false?

14. The greatest level of risk reduction through diversification can be achieved when combining two securities whose returns are perfectly positively correlated. True or false?

15. Most diversifiable risk can be eliminated by creating a portfolio of around 30 stocks. True or false?

16. The only relevant risk for investors who hold diversified portfolios of securities is diversifiable risk. True or false?

17. Market risk or systematic risk is synonymous with diversifiable risk. True or false?

18. The linear relation between the returns on a stock and the returns on the market portfolio is called the
    (a) alpha.
    (b) beta.
    (c) covariance.
    (d) coefficient of variance.

19. A security with a beta greater than one suggests that the asset has more than average systematic risk. True or false?

Review Questions

1. How is a percentage return calculated?
2. What is meant by the *coefficient of variation*?
3. Describe the meaning of a *state of nature*.
4. How is the state of nature used to calculate risk?
5. What is diversification?
6. How do stocks with negative correlation help a portfolio?
7. What does the term *random walk* mean?
8. Explain what is meant by *market efficiency*.
9. What are the characteristics of an efficient market?
10. How does systematic risk differ from unsystematic risk?
11. Are there advantages to international diversification?
12. How is an arithmetic average return calculated?
13. What is the capital asset pricing model?
14. What is a semistrong efficient market?
15. What is a weak-form efficient market?
16. Can investors consistently receive large returns?
17. How does the market respond to an increase in the interest rate?
18. How does the market respond to a decrease in the interest rate?

19. What is a boom economy?
20. What are normal conditions in the economy?
21. Why are airlines and energy stocks in negative correlation to each other?
22. Explain the term *recession*.
23. How can investing in two different stocks reduce risk?
24. What is beta?
25. Why does beta interest investors?

Applying This Chapter

1. From the following information, compute the average annual return, the variance, standard deviation, and coefficient of variation for each asset.

Asset	Annual Returns
A	5%, 10%, 15%, 4%
B	−6%, 20%, 2%, −5%, 10%
C	12%, 15%, 17%
D	10%, −10%, 20%, −15%, 8%, −7%

2. Based upon your answers to question 1, which asset appears riskiest based on standard deviation? Based on coefficient variation?

3. Using the following information, compute the percentage returns for the following securities:

Price Today	Price 1 Year Ago	Dividends Received	Interest Received	Dollar Return = Change in Price + Income	Percentage Return = Dollar Return/Initial Price
Road Runner stock	$20.05	$18.67	$0.50	$1.88	10.07%
Wile E. Coyote stock	$33.42	$45.79	$1.10	−$11.27	−24.61%
Acme long-term bonds	$1,015.38	$991.78	$100.00	$123.60	12.46%
Acme short-term bonds	$996.63	$989.84	$45.75	$52.54	5.31%
Xlingshot stock	$5.43	$3.45	$0.02	$2.00	57.97%

4. Scenario analysis has many practical applications in addition to being used to forecast security returns. In this problem, scenario analysis is used to forecast an exchange rate. Jim Danday's forecast for the euro/dollar exchange rate depends upon what the U.S. Federal Reserve and European central bankers do to their country's money supply. Jim is considering the following scenarios and exchange rate forecasts:

Central Bank Behavior	Jim's Probability of Behavior Forecast	Jim's Exchange Rate
Euro banks increase MS growth; United States does not	.20	1.15 /$
Euro banks, United States maintain constant MS growth	.30	1.05 /$
United States increases MS growth; Euro banks do not	.35	0.95 /$
U.S., Euro banks increase MS growth	.15	0.85 /$

(a) What is Jim's expected exchange rate forecast?
(b) What is the variance of Jim's exchange rate forecast?
(c) What is the coefficient of variation of Jim's exchange rate forecast?

YOU TRY IT

Investing

You have $100,000 to invest. You have already invested $10,000 in Microsoft, which is up by 20%. How do you invest the rest of your money and why?

Returns

You have been with your company, a toy manufacturer, for 4 years. The first year, they had a return of 2%, the next year they had a return of 15%, the third year they had a return of 5%, and then this past year they had a return of a negative –1%. What is their average rate of return?

Risk

Does making monthly investments in a mutual fund maximize or minimize risk? How?

11

CAPITAL STRUCTURE AND THE COST OF CAPITAL
Balancing Debt and Equity

Starting Point

Go to www.wiley.com/college/Melicher to assess your knowledge of the basics of balancing debt and equity.
Determine where you need to concentrate your effort.

What You'll Learn in This Chapter

▲ How to estimate the cost of capital
▲ How to find a firm's weighted average cost of capital
▲ The relationship between growth potential, dividend policy, and capital structure
▲ The definition of EBIT/EPS analysis
▲ What comprises bankruptcy costs

After Studying This Chapter, You'll Be Able To

▲ Analyze the factors that affect capital structure
▲ Calculate the weighted average cost of capital
▲ Examine the need for restructuring capital
▲ Examine the measurable influences on growth
▲ Calculate a firm's degree of financial leverage
▲ Compare and contrast tangible and intangible assets

Goals and Outcomes

▲ Evaluate how EBIT analysis affects capital structure
▲ Evaluate the relationship between retained earnings and financing
▲ Assess a firm's target capital structure
▲ Assess the profitability of a firm
▲ Evaluate how an expected level of EBIT and its potential variability affects a firm's capital structure
▲ Evaluate how bankruptcy costs affect a firm's capital structure
▲ Assess the effects of financial leverage on earnings per share

INTRODUCTION

All areas of finance require good planning and organization. From the smallest individual investor to the largest of corporations, assets must be structured and handled in a way that provides maximum benefits to the owner and investors. We know that short-term and long-term financing is often necessary for growth and stability. Now we focus on how the assets acquired from this financing are controlled so that the cost of the capital does not reduce its effectiveness in the overall financial plan.

11.1 Capital Structure

Before financial managers can estimate the cost of capital, two important pieces of information must be gathered. First, the cost of each financing source must be determined. Second, they must determine the appropriate financing mix needed to fund the company. Once this information is obtained, managers can estimate the company's **weighted average cost of capital (WACC)**. WACC is the minimum required rate of return on a capital budget project.

The **capital structure** of a firm is its mix of debt and equity. The capital structure and the costs of each financing source can be combined to provide an estimate of the WACC. The interrelationship between a company's growth rate, dividend policy, and its capital structure decisions has a direct bearing on the projects it chooses that enable it to grow and prosper. Figure 11-1 illustrates capital structure based on its balance sheet.

11.1.1 Why Choose a Capital Structure?

A target capital structure is important, as it determines the proportion of debt and equity used to estimate a firm's **cost of capital**, or the minimum acceptable

Figure 11-1

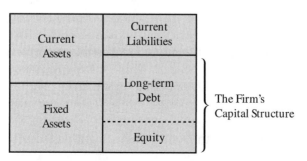

The balance sheet.

rate of return to a firm on a project. There is, however, a second, even more important reason. The firm's **optimum debt/equity mix,** or the proportionate use of debt or equity that minimizes the firm's cost of capital, in turn helps the firm to maximize shareholder wealth.

For example, suppose a firm expects cash flows of $20 million annually forever, or at least for the life of the company. In the world of finance, the period of time without an ending is referred to as *in perpetuity.* Each of the three capital structures shown in the following table has a different weighted average cost of capital. Also in the table the company's value is computed by dividing the expected cash flow by the firm's cost of capital under each capital structure. Capital Structure 2 minimizes the cost of capital at 8%, which in turn maximizes the value of the firm at $250 million.

	Capital Structure 1	Capital Structure 2	Capital Structure 3
Debt	25.0%	40.0%	70.0%
Equity	75.0%	60.0%	30.0%
Weighted Average Cost of Capital	10.0%	8.0%	12.5%

Firm value under

Capital Structure 1: $20 million/0.10 = $200 million

Capital Structure 2: $20 million/0.08 = $250 million

Capital Structure 3: $20 million/0.125 = $160 million

A nonoptimal capital structure with either too much or too little debt leads to higher financing costs, and the firm will have to reject some capital budgeting projects that could have increased shareholder wealth with the most favorable financing mix. Consider a firm that has a minimum cost of capital of 8%, but poor analysis leads management to choose a capital structure that results in a 10% cost of capital. It would probably reject an average-risk project that costs $100,000 and returns cash flows of $26,000 in years 1 through 5 at a 10% cost of capital where the net present value equals –$1,434. However, this same project would be acceptable at the minimum possible cost of capital of 8% and result in a net present value of $3,818. This example illustrates the difference that only two percentage points can make in structuring capital.

There is another, more intuitive way to see the importance of finding the best capital structure. A project's net present value (NPV) represents the increase in shareholders' wealth from undertaking a project. From section 5.5, we know there is an inverse relationship between value and discount rates (the "seesaw effect"). So it follows that a lower weighted average cost of capital

Figure 11-2

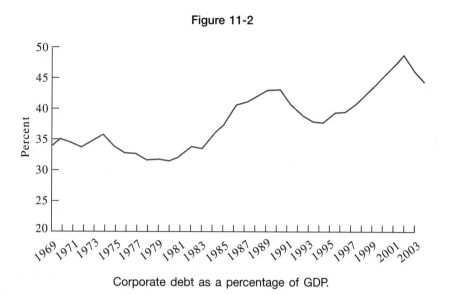

Corporate debt as a percentage of GDP.

(WACC) provides higher project net present values and results in higher levels of shareholder wealth.

11.1.2 Trends in Corporate Use of Debt

The ratio of long-term debt to GDP (gross domestic product), which measures the output of goods and services in our economy, grew during the 1960s for U.S. corporations until the mid-1970s, exceeding 35% only for limited occasions. But the relative use of debt then rose until 1989, peaking at nearly 45% of GDP. This is illustrated in Figure 11-2.

Many firms restructured themselves financially during the 1980s. Some did so in attempts to lower their cost of capital by taking advantage of the tax deductibility of interest by issuing debt to repurchase common stock, thereby increasing their debt-to-equity ratios. Other firms went private in the 1980s, fought off takeovers, or acquired other firms, financing the transactions with large amounts of debt. The surge in bankruptcies at the beginning of the 1990s shows the result of such excessive use of debt.

Into the early 1990s, the ratio of debt to economic activity fell as firms issued equity to strengthen their balance sheets and to reduce the probability of financial distress due to overborrowing. However, as the economy grew in the 1990s, so did the relative use of debt, until the economic slowdown in the early part of the new millennium started to reduce debt levels.

Figure 11-3 shows the relative use of debt to equity for different-sized firms in the latter part of the 1990s. Note that there is a fairly consistent pattern showing that smaller firms use relatively more debt than larger firms. This occurs because of the higher relative costs of equity for smaller firms as well as the better access to capital markets of the larger ones.

Figure 11-3

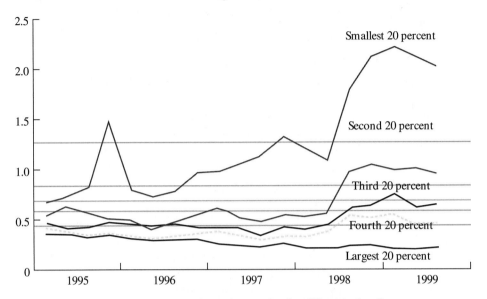

Ratios of debt to stock market equity for different-size firms.

FOR EXAMPLE

Enron: Hiding Debt

Enron is an energy company based in Houston, Texas, that declared bankruptcy in 2001. While it still exists on a small scale, it all but collapsed after it was revealed that Enron was hiding billions of dollars of corporate debt. In 2001, it was revealed that many of the losses and profits that Enron reported were the result of the special relationships it had with limited partnerships that it controlled. The result of this was that the losses were not reported on Enron's financial statements. On this news, the stock went from $90 a share to $0.30 a share. The employees were laid off, and many had their retirement tied up in Enron shares, so they lost their life savings. The collapse of Enron also brought the collapse of its accounting firm, Arthur Anderson. Arthur Anderson employees had shredded documents due to the Enron investigation. The firm had to surrender its accounting license. Eighty-five Arthur Anderson employees lost their jobs. Between the two companies, over 100,000 employees lost their jobs. Even more investors lost a substantial portion of their wealth as they were invested in these two stocks. Several executives have gone to jail and the trials are still going on.

SELF-CHECK

- What are the components of a firm's capital structure?
- What is the relationship between a firm's cost of capital and firm value?
- Have corporations been using a steady ratio of debt to equity over time?

11.2 Required Rate of Return and the Cost of Capital

Investors in a project expect to earn a return on their money. This expected return depends on current capital market conditions, such as levels of stock prices and interest rates and the overall risk of the project. The minimum acceptable rate of return of a project is the return that generates sufficient cash flow to pay investors their expected return.

To illustrate this, suppose a firm wants to spend $1,000 on an average-risk capital budgeting project, financing the investment by borrowing $600 and selling $400 worth of common stock. The firm must pay interest on the debt at a rate of 9%, while shareholders expect a 15% return on their investment. To compensate the firm's investors adequately, the project should generate an annual pretax expected cash flow equal to

Lender's interest + shareholders' return = annual expected cash flow.

In this case, this would be computed as follows:

$$0.09 \times \$600 = \$54$$
$$\underline{+.15 \times \$400 = \$60}$$
$$\$114$$

The project's minimum rate of return is then computed as follows:

Minimum cash flow divided by investment = minimum rate of return.

That is,

$$\frac{\$114}{\$1,000} = 11.4\%.$$

Thus, the required rate of return on a project represents a weighted average of lenders' and owners' return expectations. Since a cash flow or return to an investor represents a cash outflow or a cost to the firm, the minimum required rate of return is a weighted average of the firm's costs of various sources of capital. It is this number that should be used as a discount rate when evaluating a project's NPV. Required rate of return, cost of capital, and discount rate are different terms for the same concept.

11.2.1 Venture Capital

Venture capital is a good source of financing for the small business owner. **Venture capital** is money invested in start-ups and other risky ventures that have the potential for high returns.

Venture capitalists usually are members of partnerships that consist of a few general partners. The typical venture capital partnership manages between $50 million and $100 million in assets. The general approach for raising investment funds for a venture capital firm is to set up a venture capital fund and seek financial commitments from investors to contribute to it. Some venture capital funds are organized as a limited partnership in which the venture capitalist is the general partner and the other investors are limited partners. The general partner might invest 1% of the funds and the limited partners the remainder. Investors make an initial contribution and also commit to provide additional funds up to some stated maximum during the life of the fund, which is usually 10 years. Often there is an option to extend the fund for 2 or 3 more years. At the end of a fund's life, cash and securities are distributed to the investors.

Investors in venture capital partnerships are banks, insurance companies, corporations, individuals, foundations, endowments, and pension funds.

11.2.2 Cost of Capital

Relevant cash flows are incremental after-tax cash flows. To be consistent, these cash flows must be discounted using an incremental after-tax cost of capital. The firm's relevant cost of capital is computed from after-tax financing costs. Firms pay preferred and common stock dividends out of net income, so these expenses already represent after-tax costs to the firm. However, because debt interest is paid from pretax income, the cost of debt requires adjustment to an after-tax basis before computing the cost of capital.

A project's incremental cash flows must also be discounted at a cost of capital that represents the incremental or marginal cost to the firm of financing the project—that is, the cost of raising each additional dollar of capital. Thus, the cost of debt and equity that determines the cost of capital must come not from historical averages or past costs, but rather from projections of future costs. The firm's analysts need to evaluate investors' expected returns under likely market conditions, and then use these expected returns to compute the firm's marginal future cost of raising funds by each method.

Conceptually, the investors' required returns equal the firm's financing costs. The following sections use the valuation estimates for bonds and stocks to find the investors' required returns. We then adjust these required returns to reflect the company's after-tax cost of financing.

11.2.3 Cost of Debt

The firm's unadjusted cost of debt financing equals the yield to maturity on new debt issues, either a long-term bank loan or a bond issue. The yield to maturity represents the cost to the firm of borrowing funds in the current market environment. The firm's current financing costs determine its current cost of capital.

A company can determine its cost of debt by several methods.

▲ If the firm targets an "A" rating (or any other bond rating), a review of the yields to maturity on A-rated bonds in Standard & Poor's Bond Guide can provide an estimate of the firm's current borrowing costs. Several additional factors will affect the firm's specific borrowing costs, including covenants and features of the proposed bond issue as well as the number of years until the bond or loan matures or comes due. It is important to examine bonds whose ratings and characteristics resemble those the firm wants to match.

▲ The company can solicit the advice of investment bankers on the cost of issuing new debt.

▲ If the firm has debt currently trading, it can use public market prices and yields to estimate its current cost of debt. The publicly traded bond's yield to maturity can be found using the techniques for determining the internal rate of return on an investment.

▲ Finally, a firm can seek long-term debt financing from a bank or a consortium of banks. Preliminary discussions with the bankers will indicate the estimated interest rate the firm can expect to pay on its loans.

The yield estimate, however derived, is an estimate of the coupon rate on newly issued bonds (as we know that bonds are usually issued with prices close to their par value) or the interest rate on a loan. Interest is a pretax expense, so the interest estimate should be adjusted to reflect the tax shield provided by debt financing. If YTM (yield to maturity) is the pretax cost estimate, the after-tax estimate is YTM times $(1 - T)$, where T is the firm's marginal tax rate. The after-tax cost of debt, k_d, is

$$k_d = YTM\,(1 - T).$$

Assume that Global Manufacturing has a 40% marginal tax rate and it can issue debt with a 10% yield to maturity. Its after-tax cost of debt is 10% $(1 - 0.40) = 6\%$.

11.2.4 Cost of Preferred Stock

When issuing preferred stock, the firm will not receive the full price (P) per share. There will be a flotation (F_p) cost per share. Thus the cost to the firm of preferred stock financing (k_p) is

$$k_p = D_p/(P - F_p).$$

A firm wants to issue preferred stock that pays an annual dividend of $5 a share. The price of the stock is $55 per share, and the cost of floating a new issue will be $3 a share. So, the cost of preferred stock to this company is

$$k_p = D_p/(P - F_p)$$
$$\frac{\$5}{(\$55 - \$3)} = 0.0962, \text{ or } 9.62\%.$$

11.2.5 Cost of Common Equity

Unlike debt and preferred stock, cash flows from common equity are not fixed or known beforehand, and their risk is harder to evaluate. In addition, firms have two sources of common equity, retained earnings and new stock issues, and thus two costs of common equity. It may be clear that there is an explicit cost (dividends) associated with issuing new common equity. But even though the corporation pays no extra dividends to use retained earnings, they are not a free source of financing. We must consider the opportunity cost of using funds that could have been given to shareholders as dividends.

Retained earnings are the portion of net income that the firm does not distribute as dividends. As owners of the firm, common shareholders have a claim on all of its net income, but they receive only the amount that the board of directors declares as dividends. From the shareholders' perspective, the opportunity cost of retained earnings is the return the shareholders could earn by investing the funds in assets whose risk is similar to that of the corporation. If shareholders expect a 15% return on their investment in a firm's common stock and the firm could not invest its retained earnings to achieve a risk-adjusted 15% expected return, shareholders would be better off receiving 100% of its net income as dividends. That way they can reinvest the funds themselves in similar-risk assets that can provide a 15% expected return.

To maximize shareholder wealth, management must recognize that retained earnings have a cost. That cost is the return that shareholders expect from their investment in the firm. There are two methods of estimating the cost of retained earnings. One method uses the security market line. The security market line is the relationship between an investment's hurdle rate and its market risk. The security market line is often used in relation to the capital asset pricing model (CAPM). The CAPM formula takes into account the asset's sensitivity to nondiversifiable risk (also known as *systematic risk* or *market risk*), in a number often referred to as *beta* (β) in the financial industry. The security market line can provide an estimate of shareholder required return based on a stock's systematic risk. The security market line equation is as follows:

$$E(R_i) = RFR + \beta_i(R_{MKT} - RFR).$$

▲ ER_i = expected return on the capital asset.
▲ RFR = risk-free return.

▲ β_i = risk premium that is the product of a stock's systematic risk.

▲ R_{MKT} = market risk premium.

An estimate for the cost of retained earnings (k_{re}) is

$$k_{re} = E\,(R_i) = RFR + \beta_i\,(R_{MKT} - RFR).$$

The calculation of the security market line is explained using the following example: The current T-bill rate is 4.5%, and analysts estimate that the current market risk premium is slightly above its historical average at 9%. Analysts also estimate Global Manufacturing's beta to be 1.30. Global Manufacturing's cost of retained earnings using the SML approach is 4.5% + [(1.3) × (95)] = 16.2%.

The other method of estimating the cost of retained earnings is the constant growth model. Again, in a prior chapter we learned how to use this method to estimate a company's stock price. Rather than use the model to determine a price, however, we can substitute today's actual stock price to compute the shareholders' required rate of return, which represents the company's cost of retained earnings. The ratio D1/P represents the current income yield to shareholders from their investment. From the firm's perspective, this ratio represents the ratio of dividends it pays to its current market value. The growth rate represents shareholders' expected capital gain arising from dividend growth. From the firm's perspective, growth can be viewed as an opportunity cost of raising equity today. If a firm's growth rate is 8%, it expects to be able to sell its stock at a price that is 8% higher next year. The cost of equity is therefore the future price of the stock plus the dividends paid to stockholders.

Assume a firm has just paid a dividend of $2.50 a share, its stock price is $50 a share, and the expected growth rate of dividends is 6%. The current dividend of $2.50 must be multiplied by a factor to reflect the expected 6% growth for next year's dividend.

In this case, the calculation is as follows:

$$\text{Stock price} = \$50.00$$
$$\text{Dividend} = \underline{+\ 2.50}$$
$$\$52.50 \times 1.06 \text{ (growth rate)} = 55.65 - 50.00 = \underline{5.65 \text{ increase}} = 11.3\%.$$
$$50.\ \text{price}$$

The cost of using existing stock is 11.3%.

11.2.6 Cost of New Common Stock

To estimate the cost of new equity, we must modify the computation in section 11.2.5 to reflect the extra cost to the firm of issuing securities in the primary market. The costs of issuing stock, or flotation costs, include the accounting, legal, and printing costs of offering shares to the public as well as the commission or fees earned by the investment bankers who market the new securities to investors.

FOR EXAMPLE

Standard and Poor's Ratings

Standard and Poor's (S & P) is a division of McGraw-Hill that publishes financial analysis on stocks and bonds. They are one of the three major players in the industry. Moody's and Fitch are the other two credit-rating companies. The credit ratings these three organizations release have a profound effect upon companies and stock. On May 6, 2005, S & P declared the billions of dollars owed by General Motors and Ford to "junk" status. While Moody's and Fitch disagreed, this still affected the two companies. Many institutional investors had to shuffle their portfolio because some institutions are banned from dealing in junk or high-yield bonds because of their volatility and their greater risk. This also made it more difficult for GM and Ford to borrow money.

If new common stock is to be issued to finance the project and flotation costs are expected to be $4 per share, it increases the cost of the financing to 11.8%.

In an efficient market, the prices and interest rates reflect all known information as well as the market's expectations for the future. Financial managers cannot fight the market. If they feel their financing costs are too high, it is usually because the market perceives risk that the managers are ignoring. The efficient market ensures that financing costs are in line with the market's perception of firms' risks and expected returns.

SELF-CHECK

- What is the relationship between a project's cost of capital and its minimum required rate of return?
- Why is a weighted average cost used instead of a project's specific cost of financing to determine whether it should be accepted or rejected?
- How is a firm's after-tax cost of debt determined?
- How is a firm's cost of preferred stock calculated?
- Should retained earnings be considered a source of free financing to the firm?
- How can the cost of retained earnings be determined for a firm? The cost of new common equity?

11.3 Weighted Average Cost of Capital

We have seen how to compute the costs of the firms' basic capital structure components. Now we will combine the components to find the weighted average of the firm's financing costs.

▲ A firm's weighted average cost of capital (WACC) represents the minimum required rate of return on its capital budgeting projects.

The WACC is found by multiplying the marginal cost of each capital structure component: debt, preferred equity, and common equity by its appropriate weight and summing the terms:

$$\text{WACC} = w_d k_d + w_p k_p + w_e k_e$$

The weights of debt, preferred equity, and common equity in the firm's capital structure are given by w_d, w_p, and w_e, respectively. As the weighted average cost of capital covers all the firm's capital financing sources, the weights must sum to 1.0. The firm's cost of common equity, k_e, can reflect the cost of retained earnings, k_{re}, or the cost of new common stock, k_n, whichever is appropriate. Most firms rely on retained earnings to raise the common equity portion of their financial needs. If retained earnings are insufficient, they can issue common stock to meet the shortfall. In this case, k_n is substituted for the cost of common equity.

The weights in the last equation represent a specific intended financing mix. These target weights represent a mix of debt and equity that the firm will try to achieve or maintain over the planning process. As much as possible, the target weights should reflect the combination of debt and equity that management believes will minimize the firm's weighted average cost of capital. The firm should make an effort over time to move toward and maintain its target capital structure mix of debt and equity.

11.3.1 Measuring the Target Weights

As the firm moves toward a target capital structure, how will it know when it arrives? There are two ways to measure the mix of debt and equity in the firm's capital structure.

One method uses target weights based on the firm's book values, or balance sheet amounts, of debt and equity. The actual weight of debt in the firm's capital structure equals the book value of its debt divided by the book value of its assets. Similarly, the actual equity weight is the book value of its stockholders' equity divided by total assets. Once the target weights are determined, the firm can issue or repurchase appropriate quantities of debt and equity over time to move the balance sheet numbers toward the target weights.

A second method uses the market values of the firm's debt and equity to compare target and actual weights. The actual weight of debt in the firm's capital structure equals the market value of its debt divided by the market value of its assets. Similarly, the actual equity weight is the market value of the firm's stockholders' equity divided by the market value of its assets. Calculated in this way, bond and stock market price fluctuations, as well as new issues and security repurchases, can move the firm toward—or away from—its target.

Financial theory favors the second method as most appropriate. Current market values are used to compute the various costs of financing, so it is intuitive that market-based costs should be weighted by market-based weights. The basic capital structure of a firm may include debt, preferred equity, and common equity. In practice, calculating the cost of these components is sometimes complicated by the existence of mixed financing structures, such as convertible debt and other variations on straight debt, preferred equity, or common equity.

Let's compute the weighted average cost of capital for Global Manufacturing. Assume that Global Manufacturing has determined that its target capital structure should include one-third debt and two-thirds common equity. Global Manufacturing's current cost of debt is 6% and its current cost of retained earnings is 15%. What is Global Manufacturing's weighted average cost of capital, assuming that last year's operations generated sufficient retained earnings to finance this year's capital budget?

Since sufficient new retained earnings exist, Global Manufacturing will not need to issue shares to put its capital budget in operation. Thus, the cost of retained earnings will be used to estimate its weighted average cost of capital. The target capital structure is one-third debt and two-thirds common equity. Going back to the last equation, Global Manufacturing's weighted average cost of capital is

$$\text{WACC} = (1/3)(6\%) + (2/3)(15\%)$$
$$= 12\%.$$

Given current market conditions and Global Manufacturing's target capital structure weights, the firm should use a discount rate of 12% when computing the net present value for average risk projects.

To compare Global Manufacturing's current capital structure with its target capital structure, let's assume that Global Manufacturing has two bond issues outstanding. One is rated AA and has a yield to maturity of 8.8%; the other is rated A and yields 9.5%. The firm also has preferred stock and common stock outstanding. The following table shows the current market prices and the number of shares or bonds outstanding. How does Global Manufacturing's current capital structure compare to its target?

Security	Current Price	Number Outstanding
AA bonds	$1,050	10,000 bonds
A bonds	1,025	20,000 bonds
Preferred stock	40	250,000 shares
Common stock	50	700,000 shares

Based on this information, Global Manufacturing's target capital structure of one-third debt and two-thirds common equity does not leave any room for preferred stock. Evidently Global Manufacturing's management has decided not to raise funds in the future with new preferred stock issues. Using the given information, let's compute the market values of Global's securities and their current market value weights and then compare these figures to Global's target capital structure. A security market value is found by multiplying its market price by the number of bonds or shares currently outstanding; then each individual market value is divided by the total (i.e., $10.50 divided by $76 = .138$) to determine the market weight. Remember that the total market weight must equal 1.000.

The results of these computations are shown in the following table.

Security	Market Value ($ millions)	Market Weight
AA bonds	$10.50	0.138
A bonds	20.50	0.270
Preferred stock	10.00	0.132
Common stock	35.00	0.460
Total	$76.00	1.000

Presently, Global Manufacturing's capital structure is comprised of 41% debt, about 46% common equity, and about 13% preferred equity. To move toward its target capital structure, Global Manufacturing may want to issue common stock and use the proceeds to purchase outstanding preferred stock and bonds. There is no need for Global Manufacturing to restructure its finances immediately. The flotation costs and administrative fees of such a program would be prohibitive. Some movement toward the target capital structure would occur if Global Manufacturing could identify several positive-NPV projects. Barring a market downtrend, these projects would increase its market value of equity. Also, it could use future additions to retained earnings to repurchase some outstanding debt or preferred equity.

FOR EXAMPLE

Rate of Return

Surveys of U.S. firms find that most firms use after-tax weighted average costs of capital as their required rates of return for projects. Other methods include management-determined target returns or the cost of some specific source of funds. A survey of U.S.-based multinationals found that half of those companies use a single-firm-wide discount rate to evaluate projects, regardless of risk differences. The most popular method for estimating the cost of equity is the security market line approach; nearly 75% of firms use this method. Because of its assumption regarding growth, the constant dividend growth model is not used by many firms; only about 15% of firms in a 1999 survey used that method, about half the level found in a 1982 survey.

SELF-CHECK

- Define weighted average cost of capital (WACC).
- How is WACC computed?
- Should market value or book value weights be used to compare a firm's current capital structure to its target capital structure?

11.4 Making Capital Structure Decisions

Examining the various influences that affect a firm's capital structure is not an easy task. Unlike NPV or operating cash flow, there is no formula we can use to determine the proportions of debt and equity a firm should use to finance its assets. However, that does not mean it is impossible to do.

Financial theory and research on company behavior have given us a set of guidelines or principles by which to evaluate a firm's proper mix of debt and equity. It is simplified by referring only to debt and equity, with little distinction between the various types of debt and equity. The variations in debt and equity will be presented later in this chapter. For now, we'll examine the following inter-relationships affecting a firm's capital structure decisions:

▲ First is the firm's growth rate. All else equal, a firm with higher growth levels will need to tap the capital markets more frequently than a slow or no-growth firm.

Table 11-1: Debt Ratios, Selected Industries

Industry	Median* Ratio of Total Liabilities/Stockholders Equity
Air transportation	159.1%
Electric utilities	157.1%
Electronic computers	114.3%
Packaged frozen foods	176.5%
Retail drugstores	69.2%
Semiconductors	40.2%
Motor vehicles and passenger cars	150.8%
Stationery, office supplies	99.3%

▲ Second, given a firm's growth rate, the need for outside capital depends upon its return on assets and its dividend policy. Again, all else equal, a firm with a larger return on assets can rely more on retained earnings as a source of financing and will favor equity over debt financing. A firm with a large dividend payout will need more outside capital to finance growth.

Figure 11-3 showed how debt ratio—one indication of capital structure—can differ among different-sized firms. Table 11-1 shows median debt ratios for a number of industries to illustrate that capital structures also vary greatly among industries.

SELF-CHECK

- List two interrelationships affecting a firm's capital structure decisions.
- Retained earnings give firms what advantages?

11.5 Planning Growth Rates

A firm's growth is in part determined by management's strategy to acquire or maintain market share in a growing or stable market. But management's plans for future sales, asset, and financing growth are sometimes sidetracked because of the competitive struggle in the marketplace. Growth that is faster or slower than expected may occur.

11.5.1 Internal Growth Rate

A simple financial planning tool, the internal growth rate model is available to determine just how quickly a firm can grow without running short of cash. The **internal growth rate** measures how quickly a firm can increase its asset base over the next year without raising outside funds.

It does not measure divisional growth or break down total growth into domestic or international components. The internal growth rate gives a general, company-wide value.

It is equal to the ratio of the expected increase in retained earnings over the next year to the current asset base:

$$\frac{\text{Expected change in retained earnings}}{\text{Total assets}}$$

The internal growth rate makes the restrictive assumption that the firm will not pursue outside sources of financing. Should the firm grow at its internal growth rate, its retained earnings account will continually rise while its dollar amount of debt outstanding will remain constant. Therefore, the relative amount of debt in its capital structure declines over time, and the debt level will likely fall below its proportion in management's ideal financing mix.

11.5.2 Sustainable Growth Rate

Perhaps a more realistic assumption would be to allow management to borrow funds over time to maintain steady capital structure ratios. As the stockholder's equity account rises from new additions to retained earnings, the firm issues new debt to keep its debt-to-equity ratio constant over time.

This rate of growth is the sustainable growth rate. The **sustainable growth rate** measures how quickly the firm can grow when it uses both internal equity and debt financing to keep its capital structure constant over time.

11.5.3 Effects of Higher or Lower Growth Rates

The internal and sustainable growth rates are planning tools. Unfortunately, computations and estimates cannot make a firm grow by a certain prescribed amount. Changing global competition, political, and credit market conditions can cause actual growth to deviate from planned growth.

The internal and sustainable growth rate relationships suggest that there are three measurable influences on growth:

▲ **Dividend policy:** A reduction in the dividend payout ratio implies a higher retention rate and the ability for the firm to grow more quickly, if all else remains constant. A fast-growing firm may decide to maintain a low dividend payout in an effort to finance its rapid growth. More mature, slower-growing firms usually increase their dividend payout as growth opportunities diminish.

▲ **Profitability:** Higher returns on assets generate more net income, larger additions to retained earnings, and faster growth, when all else is held constant. (ROA = profit margin × total asset turnover). Management can attempt to change return on assets by influencing these factors should growth outpace or fall short of the planned rate.

▲ **Capital structure:** The equity multiplier is determined by the firm's financing policy. A firm that uses a larger amount of debt can support a higher sustainable growth rate, when all else remains constant. If actual growth exceeds the sustainable growth rate, a firm can finance the difference by taking on additional debt.

A fourth influence that is much harder to measure is management's preferences and beliefs about the use of external financing rather than relying solely on changes in retained earnings. Should actual growth differ from planned growth, one or more of these factors will have to be adjusted either to prevent financial difficulty or to absorb excess funds.

One or more of these variables must deviate from planned levels to accommodate a difference between planned and actual growth. If a firm's actual growth exceeds the planned rate, management will have to reduce its dividend payout, increase profitability, use more debt, or use a combination of these options. If growth slows, the firm will need to increase its dividend payout, reduce profitability, reduce its use of debt, or choose some combination of these alternatives.

11.5.4 The Role of Dividends and Retained Earnings

For a given growth strategy, a firm's dividend decision directly affects its capital structure decision. As you know, a firm's profits can be used in one of two ways: distributed as dividends or added to retained earnings. Findings from research shed some light on the role of dividends in corporate finance and how—and how not—to use retained earnings.

If a firm's dividends are too low from the perspective of an investor, they can sell some shares to generate extra cash. If an investor feels the dividend amount is too high, they can reinvest the excess back into the firm's shares. Whether the company issues a large or small dividend, the overall cash flows and earning power of the firm will not be changed. In a world without taxes and commissions, it will not matter whether dividends are paid or not. However, we live in a world with taxes, and many economies tax dividends more heavily than capital gains.

▲ **Dividends versus stock repurchases:** Although they are taxed more heavily than capital gains, investors like dividends. Many firms have a stable or constant dividend strategy or a dividend growth strategy. Dividends represent income that investors come to rely upon; unlike bond coupons, dividends may become a growing stream of income. Even though stock prices may fall in difficult economic times, dividends are a source of positive return to shareholders. During the past 75 years, stock dividends rose more than 2,250%, inflation rose over 870%, and treasury bill income rose about 80%. Dividends are commonly thought by investors to be a safe and growing source of return.

▲ **Dividends versus retained earnings:** The temptation to spend what cash we have is strong, for both the corporate executive and the shopper at the mall. Studies find that cash-rich firms destroy value—about 7 cents for every dollar of cash reserves held—because they seek acquisitions and projects that typically result in lower firm values. Managers sometimes overdiversify and bid too high for their acquisitions. Rather than having to raise capital in financial markets, such firms escape market discipline by relying on internal finance and on average make poor investment decisions.

▲ **Dividends as signals:** Dividends can be used by managers to signal or convey information to the markets about the firm's future prospects. Corporations do not usually decrease dividends unless absolutely necessary. Dividend changes, particularly increases, are usually permanent in nature, as firms don't want to add to investor risk by varying the dollar amount of dividends every year. This also means that managers won't commit to a dividend increase unless they feel it can be maintained on the basis of the firm's future cash inflows. Therefore, a dividend increase is a way of informing the market of management's confidence in the firm's future prospects.

The ability of the firm to grow is affected not only by management's strategy and by competitive conditions, but also by the firm's access to capital and levels of additions to retained earnings. Jointly, these influences of growth, dividend payout, and the amount of retained earnings determine the firm's need for outside capital.

FOR EXAMPLE

Dividend Policies

Research shows that dividends have evolved in some countries because of investor protection laws. In a study of dividend policies of firms in 33 countries, those countries with "common law" traditions with excellent investor protection, such as the United States and Great Britain, have dividend rates higher than countries with "civil law" traditions and weaker investor protection, such as in Latin America.

SELF-CHECK

- What does the internal growth rate measure?
- What does the sustainable growth rate measure?
- What causes the difference between them?
- List three measurable influences on a company's growth.

11.6 EBIT/EPS Analysis

As a first step in capital structure analysis, let's examine how different capital structures affect the earnings and risk of a firm in a simple world with no corporate income taxes. We will use a financial management tool called EBIT/EPS analysis. **EBIT/EPS analysis** allows managers to see how different capital structures affect the earnings and risk levels of their firms.

Specifically, EBIT/EPS analysis shows the graphical relationship between a firm's operating earnings, or earnings before interest and taxes (EBIT) and earnings per share (EPS). If we ignore taxes, these two quantities differ only by the firm's interest expense and by the fact that EPS is, of course, net income stated on a per-share basis. Examining scenarios with different EBIT levels can help managers see the effects of different capital structures on the firm's earnings per share.

Let's assume the Bennett Corporation is considering whether it should restructure its financing. As seen in Table 11-2, Bennett currently finances its $100 million in assets entirely with equity.

Under the proposed change, Bennett will issue $50 million in bonds and use this money to repurchase $50 million of its stock. If the stock's price is $25 a share, Bennett will repurchase 2 million shares of stock. Bennett expects to pay 10% interest on the new bonds, for an annual interest expense of $5 million.

Table 11-2: Current and Proposed Capital Structures for the Bennett Corporation

	Current	*Proposed*
Total assets	$100 million	$100 million
Debt	0 million	50 million
Equity	100 million	50 million
Common stock price	$25	$25
Number of shares	4,000,000	2,000,000
Interest rate	10%	10%

Assuming that Bennett's expected EBIT for next year is $12 million, let's see how the proposed restructuring may affect earnings per share. For simplicity, we ignore taxes in this example, so earnings per share (EPS) will be computed as EBIT less interest expense divided by the number of shares. As shown in Table 11-3, the scenario analysis assumes that Bennett's EBIT will be either $12 million, 50% lower ($6 million), or 50% higher ($18 million).

Continuing with this analysis of Bennett, Figure 11-4 graphs the EBIT/EPS combinations that result from the current and proposed capital structures. For lower EBIT levels, the current all-equity capital structure leads to higher earnings per share. At higher levels of EBIT, the proposed 50% equity, 50% debt capital structure results in higher levels of EPS.

11.6.1 Indifference Level

Figure 11-4 clearly shows that the EBIT/EPS lines cross. This means that, at some EBIT level, Bennett will be indifferent between the two capital structures because they result in the same earnings per share.

Table 11-3: Scenario Analysis with Current and Proposed Capital Structures

	Current No-Debt, 4 Million Shares (Millions Omitted)		
	EBIT 50%		*EBIT 50%*
	Below Expectations	*Expected*	*Above Expectations*
EBIT	$6.00	$12.00	$18.00
−I	0.00	0.00	0.00
NI	$6.00	$12.00	$18.00
EPS	$1.50	$3.00	$4.50

	Proposed −50% Debt (10% Coupon), 2 Million Shares (Millions Omitted)		
	EBIT 50%		*EBIT 50%*
	Below Expectations	*Expected*	*Above Expectations*
EBIT	$6.00	$12.00	$18.00
−I	5.00	5.00	5.00
NI	$1.00	$700	$1300
EPS	$0.50	$3.50	$6.50

Figure 11-4

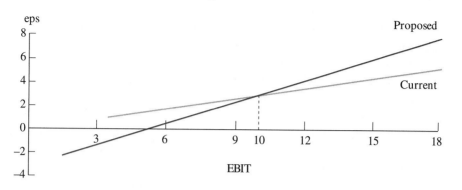

EBIT/EPS analysis Bennett Corporation.

Under Bennett's current capital structure, earnings per share is computed as (EBIT − $0 interest)/4 million shares. Under the proposed structure, earnings per share is calculated as (EBIT − $5 million interest)/2 million shares. To find the level of EBIT where the lines cross—that is, where the combination of earnings per share and EBIT are the same under each capital structure—we set these two earnings per share values equal to each other and solve for EBIT with this formula:

$$\frac{EBIT - 0}{4} = \frac{EBIT - 5}{2}$$

By doing so, we learn that the earnings per share under the two plans are the same when EBIT equals $10 million. When EBIT exceeds $10 million, the proposed, more highly leveraged capital structure will have the higher earnings per share. When EBIT is less than $10 million, the current, less-leveraged capital structure will have the higher earnings per share.

The indifference level of $10 million in EBIT did not occur by chance. It equals the firm's interest cost of 10% multiplied by its total assets ($100 million). In other words, if the firm can earn an operating return on assets (EBIT/TA) greater than its interest cost, leverage is beneficial in that it results in higher earnings per share. If the firm's operating return on assets is less than its 10% interest cost, leverage is expensive relative to the firm's earning ability and results in lower earnings per share. If Bennett strongly believes that EBIT will meet expectations at $12 million, the proposed capital structure change is attractive.

EBIT/EPS analysis has several practical implications. First, as you have just seen, it shows the ranges of EBIT where a firm may prefer one capital structure over another. The firm may decide to increase or decrease its financial leverage depending on whether its expected EBIT is above or below the indifference EBIT level. Second, EBIT is not constant over time; it will change, depending on sales growth, industry competitive conditions, and the firm's operating leverage.

Variations in EBIT will produce variations in earnings per share. Should the expected EBIT of the firm lie above the indifference EBIT level, the firm's managers need to consider potential variation of earnings in their EBIT forecast. Depending on its uncertainty, management may decide to use a more conservative financing strategy with less debt.

This shows one drawback of using EBIT/EPS analysis: It does not adequately capture the risk facing investors and how it affects shareholder wealth. We seek a capital structure that maximizes the value of the firm, not earnings per share. Although earnings per share may rise with financial leverage under certain values of EBIT, the value of earnings per share that maximizes firm value will likely be less than the maximum earnings per value. The firm's investors, both lenders and shareholders, consider the risk of cash flows when valuing investments.

Figure 11-5 shows the relationship among debt, earnings per share, and firm value. Because of the risk of excessive debt, the maximum firm value occurs at a lower debt ratio than that of maximum earnings per share.

Business risk for a company is measured by its variability in EBIT over time. Business risk is affected by several factors, including the business cycle, competitive pressures, and the firm's operating leverage or its level of fixed operating costs.

Figure 11-5

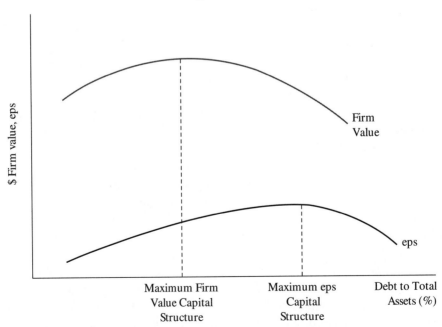

Firm value, earnings per share, and debt ratios.

FOR EXAMPLE

Business Risk

Business risk firms in the same industry will generally face the same business risks. Many financial managers confess that they examine their competitor's capital structures to help determine if their own financial strategies are appropriate. A firm's degree of operating leverage affects the amount of debt it can issue. Firms with highly variable EBIT can ill afford to issue large amounts of debt, as the combined effects of high business and financial risk may imperil the future of the firm. In general, greater EBIT variability reduces the firm's reliance on debt.

SELF-CHECK

- How is EBIT/EPS analysis useful to managers?
- How might the expected level of EBIT and its potential variability affect a firm's capital structure?
- Define business risk.

11.7 Combined Operating and Financial Leverage Effects

Business risk is often determined by the products the company sells and the production processes it uses. The effects of business risk are seen ultimately in the variability of operating income or EBIT over time.

Table 11-4 shows a simplified income statement. Because business risk is measured by variability in EBIT, line items that affect business risk appear on the top half of the income statement, between sales revenue and EBIT. This suggests a firm's business risk is affected by three major influences:

▲ Unit volume or quantity sold
▲ The relationship between selling price and variable costs
▲ The firm's fixed costs

11.7.1 Unit Volume Variability

Variability in the quantity sold of the firm's products or services will cause variation in sales revenue, variable costs, and EBIT. Fluctuating sales volumes can arise from a variety of factors, including pricing strategy from competitive products, new technologies or new products, customer impressions of product or service quality, and other factors affecting customer brand loyalty.

Table 11-4: Effects of Business Risk and Financial Risk on a Simplified Income Statement

Impact of Business Risk (Top Half of Income Statement)	Sales revenue (equals price × quantity sold) Less variable costs (such as labor and materials: equals variable cost per unit × quantity) Less fixed costs (such as rent and depreciation Expenses)
Impact of Financial Risk (Bottom Half of income statement)	Earnings before interest and taxes (operating income) Less interest expense (bank loans, bonds, other debt; a fixed expense as it is not dependent on sales

11.7.2 Price-Variable Cost Margin

Another factor affecting business risk is the firm's ability to maintain a constant, positive difference between price and per-unit variable costs. If the margin between price and cost fluctuates, the firm's operating income will fluctuate, too. Competitive pricing pressures, supply problems, labor union contracts, and other cost influences can cause the price-variable cost margin to vary over time, thus contributing to business risk.

11.7.3 Fixed Costs

The variability of sales or revenues over time is a basic operating risk. Furthermore, when fixed operating costs, such as rental payments, lease payments, contractual employee salaries, and general and administrative overhead expenses exist, they create operating leverage and increase business risk. Since fixed costs do not rise and fall along with sales revenues, fluctuating revenues lead to variability in operating income or EBIT.

When money is borrowed, financial leverage will be created as the firm will have a fixed financial obligation or interest to pay. Financial leverage affects the bottom half of a firm's income statement. A given percentage change in the firm's EBIT will produce a larger percentage change in the firm's net income or earnings per share. A small percentage change in EBIT may be levered or magnified into a larger percentage change in net income.

11.7.4 Degree of Financial Leverage

A company's financial risk reflects its interest expense. A direct method of computing a firm's degree of financial leverage (DFL) that avoids handling percentage changes in variables is presented in the following formula:

$$DFL = \frac{EBIT}{EBIT - 1} = \frac{EBIT}{EBT}$$

DFL equals the firm's earnings before interest and taxes (EBIT) divided by EBIT minus interest expense, or earnings before taxes (EBT).

11.7.5 Total Risk

Total earnings risk, or total variability in earnings per share, is the result of combining the effects of business risk and financial risk. As shown in Table 11-5, operating leverage and financial leverage combine to magnify a given percentage change in sales to a much greater percentage change in earnings.

A firm with less business risk may use more debt in its capital structure.

11.7.6 Other Factors Influencing Business Risk

Theories of financial researchers have shed light on the following additional influences on the capital structure decision:

Table 11-5: Effects of Leverage on the Income Statement

		Next Year	
	This Year	10% Sales Decrease	10% Sales Increase
Net sales	$700,000	$630,000	$770,000
Less: variable costs (60% of sales)	420,000	378,000	462,000
Less: fixed costs	200,000	200,000	200,000
Earnings before interest and taxes	80,000	52,000	108,000
Less: interest expenses	20,000	20,000	20,000
Income before taxes	60,000	32,000	88,000
Less: income taxes (30%)	18,000	9,600	26,400
Net income	$ 42,000	$ 22,400	$ 61,600
Percent change in operating income (EBIT)		−35.0%	+35.0%
Percent change in net income		−46.7%	+46.7%

> **FOR EXAMPLE**
>
> ### Tax and Nondebt Tax Shields
>
> Under current tax regulations, the debt interest reduction is a strong influence in favor of debt. The tax incentive for debt financing can diminish as a firm accumulates nondebt tax shields, such as depreciation expense, R & D, and large advertising outlays.

▲ **Taxes and nondebt tax shields:** Securities can reduce the adverse effects of price swings that might otherwise contribute to business risk. Bonds with coupons that rise and fall with changes in commodity prices, market interest rates, or foreign currencies can help mitigate the effects of EBIT variations on net income.

▲ **Interest:** Interest on debt is a tax-deductible expense, whereas stock dividends are not. Dividends are paid from after-tax dollars. This gives firms a tax incentive to use debt financing, but there are limits to the benefits of tax-deductible debt. Business risk leads to variations in EBIT over time, which can lead to uncertainty about the firm's ability to fully use future interest deductions. For example, if a firm has a negative or zero operating income, an interest deduction provides little help; it just makes the pretax losses larger.

▲ **Firms in lower tax brackets have less tax incentive to borrow than those in higher tax brackets:** In addition, firms have other tax-deductible expenses besides interest. Various cash and noncash expenses such as depreciation, research and development (R & D), and advertising expenses can reduce operating income. So, the tax deductibility of debt becomes less important to firms with large nondebt tax shields. Foreign tax credits, granted by the U.S. government to firms that pay taxes to foreign governments, also diminish the impact of the interest deduction.

SELF-CHECK

- What are the effects of financial leverage on earnings per share?
- What is the degree of financial leverage?
- As a firm's use of nondebt tax shields rises, how might its use of debt change?

11.8 Other Costs and Risks

The asset structure and the capital structure of a company are related because of the risks associated with agency costs and bankruptcy costs. **Agency costs** are the tangible and intangible expenses borne by shareholders because of the actual or potential self-serving actions of managers. Evidence shows that firms with tangible assets use more debt financing than companies with many intangible assets.

▲ **Tangible assets** are those such as railroad cars and automobiles that can be easily sold and used by other companies.

▲ **Intangible assets** include growth opportunities, the value of the firm's research and development efforts, and customer loyalty.

Agency costs and bankruptcy costs impose lighter burdens on financing for investments in tangible assets. It is much easier for a lender to monitor the use of tangible assets such as equipment and buildings. Well-developed accounting rules govern methods for tracking the values of such assets. Also, tangible assets can be sold and can maintain their value even in times of financial distress, whereas intangible assets may have value that only resides within the company.

Regardless of the type of assets a company owns, debt financing always carries a degree of risk because of the cost of the financing, interest and agency costs, and the possibility that the firm will be unable to repay the loan and have to seek relief in the bankruptcy courts.

11.8.1 Bankruptcy Costs

As the debt/ratio rises, or as earnings drop, a company will face higher and higher borrowing costs. That's because investors will insist on higher interest rates to compensate for additional risk.

A rational marketplace will evaluate the probability and associated costs of bankruptcy for a financially weak company.

Bankruptcy costs include legal and accounting fees, court costs, and the time and effort management must put forth to oversee the bankruptcy process. An efficient market will adjust the value of a company that has cash flow problems and is teetering on the brink of insolvency.

11.8.2 Agency Costs

To protect investments in debt instruments such as bonds, covenants may require the issuing firm to maintain a certain level of liquidity or may restrict future debt issues, future dividend payments or certain forms of financial restructuring. Agency costs may also take the form of specific expenses, such as audits.

Figure 11-6

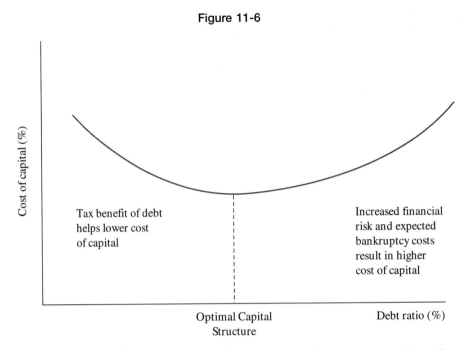

The static trade-off hypothesis: weighted average cost of capital versus debt ratio.

The cost to the company's shareholders of excessive covenants and interference with management decisions may cause firms to shy away from excessive debt in the U.S. In other words, the relationship between the level of agency costs and firm debt will look similar to that of bankruptcy costs and firm debt in Figure 11-6. This figure shows the joint effect of bankruptcy and agency costs has actually reduced the level of debt financing.

FOR EXAMPLE

Intangible Assets

For firms with large amounts of intangible assets, such as goodwill, customer loyalty, R & D, and growth opportunities, debt is less attractive as a financing alternative. This is because of the lack of collateral the firm has if it were to fault on their debt obligations. An example of an intangible asset is customer loyalty and goodwill. Firestone tires had both customer loyalty and a good company name and image until 2000 when defective tires caused an abnormally high rate of SUV accidents. The defective tires caused the SUVs to roll over.

SELF-CHECK

- What are tangible assets? Intangible assets?
- How do bankruptcy costs affect a firm's optimal capital structure?
- How to agency costs affect a firm's capital structure?

11.9 Debt and Equity

Today firms can choose among various types of security issues. Consequently, many companies have several layers of debt and several layers of equity on their balance sheets.

Debt can be made convertible to equity. Its maturity can be extended, or shortened, at the firm's option. Debt issues can be made senior or subordinate to other debt issues. Coupon interest rates can be fixed, float up and down along with other interest rates, or be indexed to a commodity price. Some bond issues do not even pay interest. Corporations can issue bonds in the United States or overseas. Bonds can be sold alone or with warrants attached that allow the bond investor to purchase shares of common stock at predetermined prices over time.

Equity variations also exist. Preferred stock has a claim on the corporation that is second to the bondholder claim but above the claim of the common stockholder. Preferred stock can pay dividends at a fixed or a variable rate.

Even types of common stock can differ. Firms can have different classes of common equity. Some classes can provide holders with higher levels of dividend income. Some may have superior voting rights.

All these variations of debt and equity give the firm valuable flexibility. All the choices available to financial managers can allow them to lower the cost of capital and increase the value of their company.

FOR EXAMPLE

Debt and Equity Decisions

A firm can minimize its financing costs by issuing debt when interest rates are near cyclical lows, especially if economists forecast rising rates in the future. It is the management team who make these decisions about financing. Some management teams may be more conservative and hesitant to issue debt, while others may be more aggressive and willing to increase the firm's financial leverage. Their judgment and expectations for the firm's financial future will affect the firm's capital structure.

SELF-CHECK

- Describe some differences that can exist among security issues.
- Why would firms issue bonds?

SUMMARY

The capital structure decision is a very difficult, but a very important, one for managers to make. An inappropriate mix of debt and equity can lead to higher financing costs for a firm, which will in turn cut shareholders' wealth. In this chapter, you used several tools that can be used to examine a firm's capital structure. You can now use EBIT analysis and explain how it affects capital structure. You can describe how to compute financial leverage. You can also determine what your company's tangible and intangible assets are.

KEY TERMS

Agency costs	Tangible and intangible expenses borne by shareholders because of the actual or potential self-servicing actions of managers.
Bankruptcy costs	Costs associated with financial distress, including legal and accounting fees, court costs, and the time and effort management must put forth to oversee the bankruptcy process.
Business risk	Variability in EBIT over time.
Capital structure	A firm's mix of debt and equity.
Cost of capital	The minimum acceptable rate of return to a firm on a project.
EBIT/EPS analysis	Allows managers to see how different capital structures affect the earnings and risk levels of their firms.
Intangible assets	Qualities of a company that cannot be easily sold or bought. For example, growth opportunities, the value of the firm's research and development efforts, and customer loyalty.
Internal growth rate	A measure of how quickly a firm can increase its asset base over the next year without raising outside funds.

Optimum debt/equity mix   The proportionate use of debt or equity that minimizes the firm's cost of capital in turn helps the firm to maximize shareholder wealth.

Sustainable growth rate   A measure of how quickly the firm can grow when it uses both internal equity and debt financing to keep its capital structure constant over time.

Tangible assets   Property such as railroad cars and automobiles that can be easily sold and used by other companies.

Venture capital   Money invested in start-ups and other risky ventures that have the potential for high returns.

Weighted average cost of capital (WACC)   Represents the minimum required rate of return on its capital budgeting projects.

ASSESS YOUR UNDERSTANDING

Go to www.wiley.com/college/Melicher to evaluate your knowledge of the basics of balancing debt and equity.
Measure your learning by comparing pre-test and post-test results

Summary Questions

1. A firm's capital structure is the mix of debt and equity used to finance its assets. True or false?
2. Firm value is calculated by adding expected cash flow to the firm's cost of capital under each capital structure. True or false?
3. The minimum required rate of return is a weighted average of the firm's cost of various sources of capital. True or false?
4. The cost of debt represents the minimum acceptable rate of return to a firm on a project of average risk. True or false?
5. The required return, the cost of capital, and the discount rate are actually three distinctively different concepts. True or false?
6. The weighted average cost of capital represents the minimum required rate of return on a capital-budgeting project and is found by multiplying the cost of each capital structure component by its appropriate weight and summing the terms. True or false?
7. The sustainable growth rate is the proportion of each dollar of earnings that is kept by the firm. True or false?
8. EBIT/EPS analysis allows managers to see how different capital structures affect the earnings levels of their firms. True or false?
9. EBIT/EPS analysis shows the ranges of EBIT where a firm may prefer one capital structure over another. True or false?
10. A firm's business risk is measured by its variability in EBIT over time. True or false?
11. A firm's business risk is affected by
    (a) the business cycle.
    (b) the firm's operating leverage.
    (c) competitive pressures.
    (d) all of the above.
12. The degree of financial leverage measures the sensitivity of _____ to changes in _____
    (a) net sales, EBIT.
    (b) EBIT, net sales.
    (c) EBIT, EPS.
    (d) EPS, EBIT.

Review Questions

1. What is a firm's capital structure?
2. Explain why determining a firm's optimum debt to equity mix is important.
3. What are some of the trends that have occurred in the corporate use of debt?
4. What does EBIT represent?
5. What is EPS?
6. How does EBIT/EPS analysis help a financial manager?
7. What does the term *indifference level* mean in relationship to EBIT/EPS analysis?
8. How can a company's business risk be measured?
9. How does operating leverage impact business risk?
10. How is financial leverage created?
11. How is the degree of financial leverage calculated?
12. Briefly explain the concepts of business risk, operating leverage, and financial leverage in terms of an income statement.
13. How do corporate control concerns affect a firm's capital structure?
14. What is the relationship between a firm's cost of capital and investor required rates of return?
15. What is the weighted average cost of capital?
16. Should book value weights or market value weights be used to evaluate a firm's current capital structure weights?
17. What is a tangible asset?
18. Give an example of an intangible asset.
19. What are some of the costs of bankruptcy?
20. What is the internal growth rate?
21. Why do shareholders like dividends?
22. What is venture capital?
23. Name some of the entities that invest in venture capital companies.

Applying This Chapter

1. A booming economy creates an unexpectedly high sales growth rate for a firm with a low internal growth rate. How can the firm respond to this unplanned sales increase?
2. Should book value weights or market value weights be used to evaluate a firm's current capital structure weights? Why?

3. How does management's strategies toward corporate growth and dividends affect its capital structure policy?

4. If a firm is eligible to receive tax credits, how might that affect its use of debt?

5. How do agency costs affect a firm's optimal capital structure? How can differences in agency costs explain capital structure differences across countries?

6. How do you expect the capital structures of two firms to differ if one is involved in steel production and the other does designs software to solve business problems?

7. AQ&Q has EBIT of $2 million, total assets of $10 million, stockholders' equity of $4 million, and pretax interest expense of 10%.

   (a) What is AQ&Q's indifference level of EBIT?

   (b) Given its current situation, might it benefit from increasing or decreasing its use of debt? Explain.

YOU TRY IT

Assets

Research the coffee company Starbucks. List their tangible and intangible assets.

Tax Credits

You are the financial manager for an environmental clean-up company. Because of the work your company does, you receive substantial tax credits. How might this affect your company's use of debt?

Microsoft and WACC

Use various Internet resources to estimate the weighted average cost of capital for Microsoft.

Venture Capitalist

You are a venture capitalist with $80 million to invest. What qualities, both financial and nonfinancial, do you look for in firms to invest in?

Internal Growth Rate

You are the financial manager for Microsoft. How do you figure out the internal growth rate?

12

STOCKS AND THE MARKETS
Trading Securities

Starting Point

Go to www.wiley.com/college/Melicher to assess your knowledge of the basics of securities trading.
Determine where you need to concentrate your effort.

What You'll Learn in This Chapter

▲ The role of stocks in the financial environment
▲ How stocks are traded on secondary markets such as the New York Stock Exchange
▲ The process of initial public offerings
▲ The growing importance of the over-the-counter (OTC) market and electronic communication networks (ECNs)
▲ The different kinds of brokerages
▲ Ethical issues related to securities trading

After Studying This Chapter, You'll Be Able To

▲ Categorize the regulatory mechanisms by which the securities exchanges and the over-the-counter markets are controlled
▲ Examine the processes and institutions used by businesses to distribute new securities to the investing public
▲ Illustrate how securities are traded among investors
▲ Distinguish influences that affect broker commissions

Goals and Outcomes

▲ Assess why foreign companies trade in the United States
▲ Compare and contrast the four types of preferred stock
▲ Assess how the New York Stock Exchange conducts day-to-day business
▲ Assess when to buy or sell stock
▲ Evaluate Initial Public Offerings
▲ Evaluate the direct and indirect costs of going public
▲ Examine the laws and ethics of insider trading

INTRODUCTION

The stock market is viewed by many investors as the road to riches, but it is a road that should be traveled cautiously. In recent years, the stock market has experienced significant ups and downs. Stock losses have reduced pension funds, put companies out of business, and made grown men cry. Yet, stocks remain a vital part of our financial system and our economy. Smart investments are the key to success in the market, and the more you know about stocks and how they are sold and traded, the more information you gather on the people and places that are part of the investment scene, the better your chances of making good, sound financial decisions.

12.1 Types of Common Stock

Corporations issue and sell shares of common stock as a means of raising addition capital. **Common stock** represents ownership shares in a corporation and may be divided into special groups, generally Class A and Class B.

▲ **Class A shares:** Class of common stock. They stock issues for trading from an Initial Public offering or if a company issues new stock at a later date.
▲ **Class B shares:** Class of common stock. A special category of stock usually retained by company founders at the time a company goes public. It carries certain rights not granted 10 stock available to the public.

When a corporation issues two kinds of stock, it often gives voting rights to Class B only. This is done to retain control of the business. Too many shareholders voting on business issues may lessen the amount of control exercised by the board of directors.

Except for voting, owners of Class A stock will usually have most of the other rights and privileges of common stockholders. Some government agencies, including the Securities and Exchange Commission (SEC), oppose issuing nonvoting stock shares. The New York Stock Exchange refuses to list the common stock of corporations that issue nonvoting classes of common stock.

Different stock classes may be created following an acquisition of one corporation by another. For example, General Motors' Class E shares and Class H shares were issued in the past to help finance GM's acquisition of Electronic Data Systems and Hughes Aircraft. The dividends on these shares were linked to the earnings of their respective subsidiary.

12.1.1 Foreign Securities

The growth in the market value of foreign securities has occurred because of general economic expansion, deregulation of exchange rates, and liberalization of regulations of equity markets. The integration of the world's markets is emphasized by the fact that many securities are listed on several markets.

The London Stock Exchange, for example, has over 500 foreign listings, of which about 200 are U.S. firms. The major U.S. stock markets, the NYSE, AMEX, and Nasdaq, trade about 600 foreign stocks. Foreign stocks can be traded in the United States if they are registered with the Securities and Exchange Commission.

Foreign companies trade in the United States for the same reason U.S. companies trade in their markets. It is a source of new funding and a way to finance assets overseas.

▲ **American depository receipts** (ADR) represent shares of common stock that trade on a foreign stock exchange.

These receipts can be traded on U.S. exchanges and are as negotiable as other securities. The ADRs are created when a broker purchases shares of a foreign company's stock in its local market. The shares are then delivered to a U.S. bank's custodial bank in that foreign country and the bank issues depository receipts. ADRs allow U.S. investors to buy stock in foreign companies without the problems of exchanging securities.

Investors and professional money managers have found it increasingly important to diversify their investments among the world's markets. Such diversification makes possible a broader search for investment values and can reduce the risk in investment portfolios.

As securities markets become more global, more and more foreign firms will seek to have their shares or ADRs listed on a U.S. exchange.

▲ **Global depository receipts** (GDR) represent shares of common stock that are listed on the London Stock Exchange.

U.S. investors can buy GDRs through a broker in the United States.

12.1.2 Rights and Privileges of Common Stockholders

Ownership gives common stockholders certain rights and privileges that bondholders do not have.

▲ **Shareholders vote to select the corporation's board of directors.** The board of directors, in turn, exercise general control over the company's business operations. In addition to voting for the board, common shareholders may also vote on major issues facing the firm, such as corporate charter changes and mergers.

▲ **The common shareholders have a claim on business profits,** but only those that remain after the holders of all other classes of debt and equity securities have received payments or returns. Also the corporation has the option of retaining some of the common shareholder's profits to finance modernization, expansion, and growth of the business.

Dividends on common stock may or may not be declared by the corporation's board of directors. A **dividend** is a payment to the owner of a share of corporation's stock, which represents the owner's portion of the corporation profits.

The dividend is typically a cash payment that allows shareholders to receive some income from their investment. To many investors, the appeal of common stock dividends is their potential to increase over time. As a firm achieves success, its profits should grow and the shareholders can expect to see the dollar amount of their dividends rise. Of course, success and growth are not guaranteed. A firm may experience poor earnings or losses, in which case shareholders bear the risk of smaller dividends or even the elimination of dividend payments until the firm's financial situation improves.

All in all, the common stockholders have the lowest standing when a business venture is liquidated or fails. All creditors, bondholders, and preferred stockholders must, as a rule, be paid in full before common stockholders receive any proceeds. In the event of a bankruptcy, it is rare that the proceeds of the asset sale satisfy the claims of all the creditors, so common stockholders usually receive little, if anything, from liquidation proceedings.

Obviously, the common stockholders lose the most when a business they have invested in fails. That is why it is important to study the market and get

---

Table 12-1: Elements of Common Stock

▲ Represents an ownership claim

▲ Board of directors oversees the firm on behalf of the shareholders and enforces the corporate charter

▲ Voting rights for board members and other important issues allowed by the corporate charter

▲ Lowest claim on assets and cash flow

▲ Par value is meaningless; many firms have very low or no-par stock

▲ Dividends: Received only if declared by the firm's board

    ▲ Are paid out from after-tax earnings and cash flow; they are not tax deductible

    ▲ Dividends are taxable when received by the shareholder and can vary over time

▲ Maturity: Never; stock remains in existence until firm goes bankrupt, merges with another firm, or is acquired by another firm

as much information as possible before purchasing the common stock of a corporation that does not have a proven record of success.

You must also be aware that the common stock of a corporation may be assigned a **par value,** or stated value, in the certificate of incorporation. However, that value usually has little bearing on the current price or book value of the stock. It is used mainly for accounting purposes and some legal needs.

SELF-CHECK

- Define **common stock** and distinguish between Class A and Class B.
- Explain what American depository receipts are and distinguish them from Global depository receipts.
- Lists two rights of being a common stockholder.
- In the event of a bankruptcy, list three parties who must be paid in full before common stockholders get any money?
- Discuss why foreign companies trade in the United States.

12.2 Preferred Stock

At this point we need to look at preferred stock and study the differences between it and common stock.

▲ **Preferred stock** is an equity security that has a preference, or senior claim, to the firm's earnings and assets.

FOR EXAMPLE

Dividends

A preferred stock may be a 9% preferred, meaning that its annual dividend participation is not to exceed 9% of its par or stated value. In such cases, unlike common stock, a preferred stock's par value does have important meaning. Often the holder of preferred stocks accepts a limited dividend amount as a fair exchange for the priority held in the earnings and assets of a company.

Unlike common stock, preferred stock generally carries a stated fixed dividend. This fixed dividend must be paid before common shareholders can receive any dividend at all. The fixed dividend on preferred stock is specified as either a percentage of par value or as a fixed number of dollars per year. In liquidation, the claims of the preferred shareholders are satisfied before common shareholders receive any proceeds.

In today's market, most preferred stock is cumulative, meaning that there is a provision for paying accumulated dividends to the preferred stockholders.

▲ **Cumulative preferred stock** requires that before dividends on common stock are paid, preferred dividends must be paid not only for the current period but also for all previous periods in which preferred dividends were not paid.

Unlike debt holders, the preferred stockholders cannot force the payment of their dividends. They may have to wait until earnings are adequate to pay dividends, but cumulative preferred stock offers some protection for periods during which dividends are not declared.

▲ **Noncumulative preferred stock** makes no provision for the accumulation of unpaid dividends.

The result may be that management is tempted to declare preferred dividends only when it appears that sufficient earnings are available to pay common stock dividends as well.

▲ **Callable preferred stock** gives the corporation the right to retire the preferred stock at its option.
▲ **Convertible preferred stock** has a special provision that makes it possible to convert the preferred stock into the common stock of the corporation. This is generally the stockholder's option.

The special features that preferred stock may have exist primarily to attract investors at times when distribution would otherwise be difficult. Preferred stock that is both cumulative and convertible is a popular choice for investors purchasing shares of stock in small firms with high growth potential.

The one tax advantage of preferred stock goes to corporate investors purchasing another firm's preferred stock. When one corporation buys preferred stock of another firm, 70% of the dividend income received by the corporation is exempt from taxes. Thus, for every $100 of dividend income, only $30 is taxable to an investing corporation.

Foreign firms who wish to issue preferred stock must do so in the United States. The U.S. security markets are the only public financial markets in which preferred stock is sold.

Table 12-2: Elements of Preferred Stock

▲ Does not represent an ownership claim

▲ No voting rights unless dividends are missed

▲ Claim on assets and cash flow lies between those of bondholders (specifically, subordinated debenture holders) and common shareholders

▲ Par value is meaningful, as it can determine the fixed annual dividend

▲ Dividends: Annual dividends are stated either as a dollar amount or as a percentage of par value

   ▲ Received only if declared by the firm's board

   ▲ Are paid out from after-tax earnings and cash flow; they are not tax deductible

   ▲ Dividends are taxable when received by the shareholder

   ▲ May be cumulative

▲ Maturity: Unless it has a callable or convertible feature, the stock never matures; it remains in existence until firm goes bankrupt, merges with another firm, or is acquired by another firm

SELF-CHECK

- Define **preferred stock** and explain how it is different from common stock.
- Identify four types of preferred stock and briefly describe each.

12.3 The New York Stock Exchange

An **organized securities exchange** is a location with a trading floor where all stock transactions take place. Organized exchanges in the United States include the New York Stock Exchange (NYSE) and the American Stock Exchange (AMEX), as well as several regional exchanges such as the Boston, Chicago, Cincinnati, Philadelphia, and Pacific Stock Exchanges.

Only the NYSE and AMEX, both located in New York City, may be considered truly national in scope, although the other exchanges trade both local and national stock issues, including dual-listed stocks, or those traded on more than one exchange.

The organized stock exchanges use the latest in electronic communications. This helps to ensure an internally efficient trading system, where orders are tracked and processed quickly. It also ensures that prices on the different exchanges are identical, so a trader cannot purchase a security on one exchange at one price while selling it on another, at a different, lower price, to realize a quick profit.

The relative importance of the New York Stock Exchange, sometimes called the "Big Board," makes it the one to study when learning about typical stock transactions.

12.3.1 Structure of the New York Stock Exchange

Like all the stock exchanges, the objective of the New York Stock Exchange (NYSE) is to provide a convenient meeting place where buyers and sellers of securities may conduct business. In addition, the NYSE provides facilities for the settlement of transactions, establishes rules for the trading processes and the activities of its members, provides publicity for the transactions, and establishes standards for the corporations that have securities trading on the exchange.

The New York Stock Exchange is a voluntary association of 1,366 members. Membership seats are considered quite valuable. In order to purchase a seat, it is necessary to negotiate with other exchange members who may be willing to sell their memberships. Since members' earnings are related to trading activity, seat prices typically rise and fall along with trading volume.

A seat on the New York Stock Exchange sold for a recent-history low price of $250,000 in 1990. With trading volume rising in the 1990s, seats have consistently sold for over $1 million. In 2005, 450 of the 2,780 firms listed on the NYSE were foreign firms. Trading volume was $20.6 trillion, and the market value of all the shares listed on the exchange was $17.8 trillion.

There are three basic types of members: floor brokers, registered traders, and specialists.

- ▲ **Floor brokers** fall into one of two categories: **house brokers** and **independent brokers.** House brokers are the largest group of members on the NYSE. The key function of house brokers is to act as agents who carry out customers' orders for security purchases and sales. In return, the broker receives a commission for the service. When trading volume is particularly heavy, house brokers may ask an independent broker to help them handle their orders.

- ▲ **Registered traders** are individuals who purchase a seat on the exchange to buy and sell stocks for their own account. Since they do their own trading, they do not pay any commissions. They may also be on retainer from a brokerage house, often a regional firm that does not have their own seat on the exchange.

- ▲ **Specialists,** or assigned dealers, have the responsibility of making a market for an assigned security.

Seven specialist firms collectively own 480 seats. Each stock is assigned to a specialist, who has a trading post on the exchange floor. All trades in a specialist's assigned stock need to take place at the specialist's post.

As a market maker, the specialist maintains an inventory of the assigned security and stands ready to buy or sell to maintain a fair and orderly market. That means they must be ready to purchase shares of their assigned stock when there are many sellers, and they must be willing to sell shares when traders want to buy.

Exchange regulations require the specialist to maintain an orderly market, meaning that trading prices should not change by more than a few cents. Since stocks are traded in decimals, the smallest difference in price can be 1 cent. The specialist maintains bid-and-asked prices for the security, and the margin between the two prices represents the specialist's gross profit.

▲ The **bid price** is the price the buyer is willing to pay for the securities.
▲ The **ask price** is the price at which the owner is willing to sell the securities.

If the current bid price from brokers is $50.00 and the current ask price is $50.05, the specialist may enter a bid of $50.02 or $50.03 or a lower ask price in order to lower the spread and maintain market order. The spread is the difference between the offer price and the price paid by the investment bank. The lower the spread, the more likely an investor's buy order will be accepted.

A penny may not seem like much, but an extra penny per share profit on the billion shares traded each day on the NYSE can add up to a sizable amount. Specialist firms have been accused of placing their own interests above that of their customers.

As with all aspects of trade and finance, oversight is needed. The Securities Exchange Act of 1934 established the Securities and Exchange Commission (SEC) and gave it authority over the securities markets. All brokers and dealers doing business in the organized markets must register with the SEC.

In 2004, the NYSE and SEC fined five specialist firms $240 million for not maintaining an orderly and fair market. They traded ahead of customer orders. It was also discovered that specialist firms were advocating one company over another to investors unfairly. During this time, it also came to light that some brokerage companies overcharged large-scale investors. The NYSE also received sanctions from the Securities and Exchange Commission and was forced to add staff and funds to increase its oversight of regulations and trading.

12.3.2 Changes in the Structure of the Stock Market

In an effort to increase the technological and informational efficiency of the stock market, the SEC has actively promoted major changes in the structure of stock market activities and institutions.

Many of the changes proposed have met with resistance from existing interests, especially the NYSE, which fears the effect such changes will have on their particular role in market activities. The NYSE's fears stem from the possible loss of trading on the exchange. However, many of the SEC's recommendations have been adopted, and many more will be instituted in due time.

One important change relates to electronic technology. Since the technology is now at hand to link organized exchanges and OTC markets electronically, the SEC would like to see the stock market take the form of one giant trading floor, all at the command of the broker. The broker would be able to tell which market has the best quote on each stock by punching buttons on the quotation machine.

Bid and asked prices on covered stocks would be available in all markets. Nasdaq is now offering "dual-listing" to NYSE firms, meaning that NYSE-listed stocks can choose to have their shares listed on Nasdaq.

Opponents offer strong arguments against the plan. They claim that many existing market institutions will be destroyed and that costs for the investor will rise.

Despite the opposition, electronic trading is occurring; Nasdaq has an electronic European exchange that it hopes will be the forerunner of an all-European exchange. Another European electronic exchange, Virt-X, is a joint effort of the Swiss exchange and London's Tradepoint trading platform. Both systems work to give investors swift trade execution and the best price available. For quicker trades, some will give the advantage to an electronic market. For the best price (lowest price for buyers, highest price for sellers), some argue that NYSE's specialists can intervene to offer better prices to traders. For clearing large trades, the advantage goes to the NYSE; it has more trading volume and offers greater liquidity for handling large transactions.

Highly automated securities exchanges now exist in the major money-center cities of the world, permitting trading on a global basis. Because of varying time zones, trading is now possible 24 hours a day.

SELF-CHECK

- Define *organized securities exchange* and list two examples.
- Briefly describe the role of the NYSE's floor brokers, registered traders, and specialists.
- Define **bid price** and **ask price**.
- List at least one pro and one con of electronic trading.

12.4 Stock Transactions

Investors can buy and sell stock in a number of different ways. In order to trade, they need to contact a stock brokerage firm where they can set up an account. The investor can then specify the type of order to be placed as well as the number of shares to be traded in specific firms.

12.4.1 Market Order

A **market order** is an order for immediate purchase or sale at the best possible price. The brokerage firm that receives an order to trade shares of stock listed on the New York Stock Exchange at the best price possible transmits the order to its New York office, where the order is transmitted to its commission broker on the floor of the exchange.

12.4.2 Limit Order

Sometimes investors only want to buy or sell if a stock is selling for a specific price. A **limit order** is an order in which the maximum buying price (limit buy) or the minimum selling price (limit sell) is specified by the investor.

If a commission broker has a limit buy order at 50 from an investor and other brokers have ask prices higher than 50, the order cannot be filled at that moment. The broker will wait until a price of 50 or less becomes available.

Usually any limit order that is not quite close to the current market price is turned over to the specialist, who places it in his or her central limit order book. The specialist will make the trade for the commission broker when the price comes within the limit.

Of course, if the price of the stock progresses upward rather than downward, the buy order will not be completed (and vice versa for sell limit orders). Limit orders may be placed to expire at the end of 1 day, 1 week, 1 month, or on a good-until-canceled basis.

12.4.3 Stop-Loss Order

A **stop-loss order** is an order to sell stock at the market price when the price of the stock falls to a specified level. The stockholder may protect gains or limit losses due to a fall in the price of the stock by placing a stop-loss order at a price a few points below the current market price.

12.4.4 Short Sale

A **short sale** is sale of securities that the seller does not own. An investor will want to short a stock if he/she feels the price will decline in the future. Shares of the stock are borrowed by the broker and sold in the stock market. In the event that a price decline does occur, the short seller covers the resulting short position by buying enough stock to repay the lender.

> ### FOR EXAMPLE
>
> #### Stop-Loss Order
>
> An investor who has paid $50 for shares of stock may place a stop-loss order at a price of $45. If the price does fall to $45, the commission broker sells the shares for as high a price as possible. This order does not guarantee a price of $45 to the seller, since by the time the stock is actually sold, a rapidly declining stock price may have fallen to well below $45. On the other hand, if the stock price does not reach the specified price, the order will not be executed. These orders can be used to protect profits. If the stock increases in price after its purchase, the investor can cancel the old stop-loss order and issue a new one at a higher price.

If any dividends are paid during the time the stock is shorted, the short seller must pay the dividends owed on the borrowed shares.

Because short sales have an important effect on the market, the SEC regulates them closely. Heavy short sale trades can place undue pressure on a firm's stock price. Among the restrictions on short sales is one relating to selling only on an uptick. This means that a short sale can take place only when the last change in the market price of the stock from transaction to transaction was an increase. For example, if the most recent transaction prices were 19.95, 19.95, 20.00, 20.00, 20.00, the short sale would be allowed as the last price change was an increase. A short sale would not be allowed if the most recent transactions prices were, for example, 20.07, 20.01, 20.00 or 20.10, 20.00, 20.00, since the most recent price change was a decrease.

In addition, both the Federal Reserve System and New York Stock Exchange regulations require the short seller to maintain a margin or deposit of at least 50% of the price of the stock with the broker. Loans of stock are callable on 24 hours' notice. The term *callable* means that corporations can retire the stock.

12.4.5 Buying on Margin

Buying on margin means the investor borrows money and invests it along with his own funds in securities. The securities so purchased become collateral for the loan. The margin is the minimum percentage of the purchase price that the investor must pay in cash. In other words, margin is the ratio of the investor's equity (own money) to the market value of the security. In order to buy on margin, the investor must have a margin account with the brokerage firm, which in turn arranges the necessary financing with banks.

Margin trading is risky; it magnifies the profits as well as the losses from investment positions. Should the value of the securities used as collateral in a margin trade begin to decline, the investor may receive a margin call from the brokerage firm.

FOR EXAMPLE

Buying on Margin

Assume an investor borrows $20,000 and combines it with $30,000 of his own money to purchase $50,000 worth of stocks. His initial margin is 60% ($30,000 of his own money divided by the $50,000 value of the securities). Should the market value of his stock rise 10% to $55,000, the value of his equity rises to $35,000: This increase in value to $35,000 represents a gain of 16.7% ($5,000/$30,000). A 10% rise in the stock's value increased the value of the investor's position by 16.7% because of the use of margin.

The investor will face a choice of either closing out the position or investing additional cash to increase the position's equity or margin. If the market price of the pledged securities continues to decline and the investor fails to provide the new margin amount, the brokerage house will sell the securities. Under current Federal Reserve regulations, investors must have an initial margin of at least 50% when entering into a margined trade. The minimum maintenance margin to which the position can fall is 25% before the broker will have to close out the position. Depending upon the individual investor's creditworthiness, a brokerage firm can impose more stringent margin requirements.

The combination of falling prices, margin calls, and sales of securities can develop into a downward spiral for securities prices. This kind of spiral played an important role in the stock market crash of 1929. At that time, there was no regulatory restraint on margin sales and, in fact, margins of only 10% were common.

Also before the current regulation, settlement of the transactions did not have to take place until 5 days after the trade. Today, the "T + 3" requirement means funds for sales or purchases of stock must be presented to the stockbroker within 3 days of the transaction. Plans are under way for a 1-day (T-1) settlement requirement, and hopes exist for an all-electronic process that would make settlement immediate.

12.4.6 Program Trading

Around 1975, stocks began to be traded not only individually, but also in packages or programs. **Program trading** is a technique for trading stocks as a group rather than individually. It is the trading for a group of at least 15 different stocks with a value of at least $1 million.

At first, program trades were simply trades of any portfolio of stocks held by an equity manager who wanted to change the portfolio's composition for any number of reasons. An equity manager is someone who chooses which stock, and how much of it, should be in a portfolio. For example, mutual funds have equity managers who choose which companies should be represented in the fund and what percentage of the funds should be invested in those companies.

Today the portfolios traded in package form are often made up of the stocks included in a stock index, such as the Standard & Poor's 500. In 2003, nearly 40% of all NYSE trading volume was program trades, but it was not unusual for that percentage to rise to 50% or more during times of unstable market prices.

Program traders use computers to keep track of prices in the different markets and to give an execution signal when appropriate. At the moment the signal is given, the orders for the stocks are sent directly to the NYSE trading floor to be carried out by the proper specialist. While the use of computers allows trades to be accomplished more quickly, it can cause problems if price movements trigger simultaneous sales orders by a number of large program traders. This can result in a serious plunge in market prices. Therefore, efforts have been made to control some aspects of program trading by limiting its use on days when the Dow Jones Industrial Average rises or falls more than 200 points. The **Dow Jones Industrial Average** is an average of 30 well-known companies chosen by the editors of the *Wall Street Journal*. These companies represent trends in the stock market. This limit is reset quarterly based on the level of the Industrial Average.

12.4.7 Record Keeping

When a trade takes place, the information is sent to a central computer system that then sends the information to display screens across the nation. This consolidated report includes all transactions on the NYSE as well as those on the regional exchanges and other markets trading NYSE-listed stocks.

Trades can be for a round lot of 100 shares or an odd lot, a trade of less than 100 shares. The details of the purchase transaction are also sent to the central office of the exchange and then to the brokerage office where the order was originally placed. Trade information is also sent to the registrar of the company whose shares were traded. The company needs this information so new certificates can be issued in either the name of the investor or the brokerage firm.

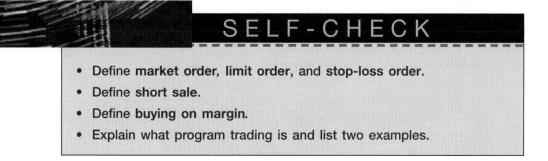

SELF-CHECK

- Define **market order, limit order, and stop-loss order.**
- Define **short sale.**
- Define **buying on margin.**
- Explain what **program trading** is and list two examples.

12.5 Initial Public Offerings (IPOs)

An **initial public offering (IPO)** is a sale of securities to the investing public, or a sale of securities to a small group of private investors. Most of the larger investment banking firms engage in originating securities. As an originator, the investment bank seeks to identify firms that may benefit from a public offering, which is a sale of securities to the investing public, or a private placement, which is a sale of securities to a small group of private investors.

The Securities and Exchange Commission (SEC) regulates the public offering process. The private placement process has fewer regulations, but the securities can only be sold to investors who meet certain SEC-regulated guidelines for wealth and investment knowledge.

The investment bank makes a detailed study, called *due diligence,* of the corporation. The investment bank uses this information to determine the best way of raising the needed funds for the corporation. The investment banker will recommend the types, terms, and offering price of securities that should be sold. He or she also aids the corporation in preparing the registration and informational materials required by the Securities and Exchange Commission. If due diligence goes well, then the company will have an initial public offering. A company would do this to raise money for long-term growth and for the prestige of being publicly traded.

One of the most important and carefully regulated pieces of information is the prospectus. It details the issuer's finances and must be provided to each buyer of the stock shares. Another big consideration for an initial offering is when to go public. There are times when the public is more interested in specific industries or in companies that are developing certain technologies. Firms that go public in "hot" IPO markets—when investors are anxious to buy new issues and prices are bid up, sometimes to two or three times their initial offering price—are likely to receive better prices for their shares than if they go public in a "cold" market when investors are less receptive to new stock issues.

12.5.1 Underwriting

Investment bankers not only help sell securities to the investing public, but they also sometimes assume the risk arising from the possibility that such securities may not be purchased by investors. This occurs when the investment banker enters into an **underwriting agreement** with the issuing corporation. The **terms of an underwriting agreement** provide that securities are purchased at a predetermined or "firm commitment" price by the underwriters, who then sell them to investors at the offer price. Figure 2-1 illustrates this.

The difference between the offer price and the price paid by the investment bank is called a *spread.* The **spread** is revenue to the investment bank and is intended to cover the bank's expenses and to provide a profit from its underwriting activities.

Figure 12-1

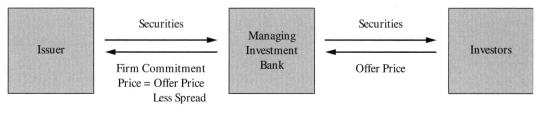

Diagram of a firm commitment underwriting.

The issuer has virtually no price risk in a firm commitment offering once the offer price is set. The issuer receives the proceeds from the stock sale immediately and can spend the money on the purposes outlined in the prospectus. Under this type of agreement, the investment bank carries, or underwrites, the risk of fluctuating stock prices and the possibility of loss and/or a smaller spread than expected. However, the practice of underpricing the stocks or first-day price increases for IPOs is common and reduces the banks risk on a firm commitment agreement.

Another means of offering securities is called *best-effort selling*.

▲ A **best-effort agreement** is one in which investment bankers try to sell the securities of the issuing corporation, but they assume no risk for a possible failure of the sale or the flotation.

▲ The **flotation** is the cost of the IPO.

The investment bankers are paid a fee or commission for those securities they sell. The best-effort agreement is typically used when the investment bankers anticipate that there may be some difficulty in selling the securities and they are unwilling to assume the underwriting risk. From the perspective of investors, an investment bank putting its money at risk with a firm commitment underwriting agreement is preferable. Investors should view a best-effort offering with some concern. If the investment banker is not willing to support the firm's security sale, why should other investors?

Companies that are already public and wish to raise additional funds have several choices. They can sell additional securities by using the underwriting process, as previously discussed. They can also choose to use shelf registration, sell securities to a private party, have a rights offering, or seek competitive bids.

12.5.2 Shelf Registration

The Securities and Exchange Commission's Rule 415 allows firms to register security issues (both debt and equity) and then "put them on the shelf" for sale any time over the next 2 years. Once registered, the securities can be offered for sale by submitting a short statement to the SEC whenever the firm needs the funds or market conditions are attractive. The shelf registration process saves issuers both time and money. There is no cost or penalty for registering shelf securities and then not issuing them. Filing fees are relatively low, and the firm can take some securities from the shelf and sell them immediately through one underwriter and then sell more later with another underwriter.

Not every firm can use shelf registration. Firms must meet certain size, credit quality, and ethics requirements:

▲ The market value of the firm's common stock must be at least $150 million.

▲ It must have made no defaults on its debt in the previous 3 years.

▲ The firm's debt must be investment grade.

▲ The firm must not have been found guilty of violating the Securities Exchange Act of 1934 in the previous 3 years.

12.5.3 Selling Stocks to Private Investors

A publicly held firm can choose to sell securities in a private placement. To keep current shareholders from suspecting any "sweetheart deals," privately placed equity is typically sold at a slight premium to the stock's current market price.

Private equity sales may occur if the firm is the rumored or actual target of a hostile takeover. Management may try to stall the takeover or stop it by selling a large block of voting stock to an investor or syndicate that seems friendlier. Occasionally news stories contain articles of rumored deals involving firms in financial difficulty that are seeking equity infusions to keep them afloat.

Private placements may also fulfill a need for an emergency infusion of equity. Since the shares are not being sold in a public offering, the private placement avoids SEC registration and subsequent publicity. However, other SEC regulations must be followed in a private sale. The firm must disclose the sale after it occurs, and the private investors must meet SEC requirements as "accredited investors." Basically, accredited investors are those who are considered knowledgeable enough or sufficiently strong enough financially to invest without the

---

FOR EXAMPLE

Business Angels: Who Are They?

Business angels are private investors who provide start-up capital for small businesses. Angels, although wealthy individuals, seldom invest more than $100,000 in a firm. The annual investment in the angel market is estimated to be $20 billion. In addition to providing financing, angels provide valuable advice and sometimes help with the preparation of business plans.

protection provided by the SEC's registration process. Accredited investors can include wealthy individuals with investment experience as well as financial institutions, such as insurance companies and pension funds.

12.5.4 Rights Offerings

Under the charters of some corporations, if additional shares of common stock, or any security that may be converted to common stock, are to be issued, the securities must be offered for sale first to the existing common stockholders—that is, the existing shareholders have the first rights to purchase newly issued securities.

The purpose of this regulation is to permit existing stockholders to maintain their proportional share of ownership. Once popular in the United States, rights offerings among public corporations became infrequent during the 1980s and 1990s, although they are still used among privately held firms.

12.5.5 Competitive Bidding

State, local, and federal government issues, as well as those of governmental agencies, usually require competitive bidding by investment bankers before underwriting agreements are awarded. This is also the case for debt and equity securities issued by some public utilities.

Occasionally, large financially strong firms will announce that they are seeking competitive bids on a new security offering. In these cases, the issuer decides upon the size of issue and the type of security that it wishes to sell. Then it invites the investment banking houses to offer bids for handling the securities. The investment banking group offering the highest price for the securities, while also providing information showing it will be able to carry through a successful flotation, will usually be awarded the contract.

A great deal of disagreement has existed about the relative advantages and disadvantages of competitive bidding by investment banking houses. Investment bankers strongly contend that the continuing advice they give is essential to an economical and efficient distribution of an issuer's primary market securities. Others contend that competitive bidding enables corporations to sell their securities at higher prices.

A variation of competitive bidding—which usually occurs when issuers seek bids solely from investment banking firms—is the **Dutch auction bidding process,** which allows smaller firms and individual investors to purchase securities.

The U.S. Treasury uses a Dutch auction and some IPOs use the Dutch auction, too. Most notable was the Google stock public offering in 2004. The process begins when the issuer and its investment banks determine a price range for the stock. After setting up an account with one of the underwriters, investors place bid prices for the number of shares they want to purchase via Internet, fax, or telephone. Bidders can place bids outside the price range if they believe demand will be high (higher bid price) or weak (lower bid price) than expected by underwriters. At the close of the bidding period, the underwriters determine the highest bid, or clearing price, at which all the offered shares are sold.

12.5.6 Selling Retail

To assist the underwriting and best-effort process, the majority of large investment banking houses maintain "retail" outlets throughout the nation. **Retail selling** is selling to individual investors. There are also many independent retail brokerage outlets not large or financially strong enough to engage in major originating and underwriting functions. These independents may be able to assist the major investment banks in selling new issues. Like the underwriters, they depend upon the resale of securities at a price above their cost to cover expenses and provide profit from operations.

A few of the large investment banking houses do not sell to individuals. Rather, they confine their activities entirely to originating, underwriting, and selling securities to institutional investors. **Institutional investors** are large investors such as insurance companies, pension funds, investment companies, and other large financial institutions.

Regulatory authorities permit announcements of security offerings to be placed in newspapers and other publications. These announcements, called *tombstones*, are very restricted in wording and must not seem to be soliciting sales.

Note that the tombstone in Figure 12-2 is careful to point out that "this is neither an offer to sell nor a solicitation of an offer to buy any of these securities." The word *tombstone* apparently derives from the small amount of information it provides and the large amount of white space it features. Boston Chicken was seeking to sell 10.35 million shares of common stock at an offer price of $34.50 a share.

The underwriters are shown on the bottom of the announcement. The investment bank or banks chosen to originate and handle a flotation are called the *lead bankers*. In Boston Market tombstone, the two firms listed at the top, Merrill Lynch and Alex Brown, are the lead bankers. These lead bankers formed a syndicate of several investment banking firms to participate in the underwriting and distribution of the issue. Syndicate members are listed under the lead bankers, in alphabetical order, in the tombstone ad.

The period after a new issue is initially sold to the public is called the *aftermarket*. This period may vary from a few hours to several weeks. During this period, the members of the syndicate may not sell the securities for less than the offering price.

Investors who decide to sell their newly purchased securities may depress the market price temporarily, so the syndicate steps in to buy back the securities in order to prevent a larger price drop. This is called *market stabilization*.

Figure 12-2

This announcement is under no circumstances to be construed as an offer to sell or as a solicitation of an offer to buy any of these securities. The offering is made only by the Prospectus.

New Issue

December 5, 1995

10,350,000 Shares

Boston Chicken, Inc.

Common Stock

Price $34.50 Per Share

Copies of the Prospectus may be obtained from any State or jurisdiction in which this announcement is circulated from only such of the undersigned or other dealers or brokers as may lawfully offer these securities in such State or jurisdiction.

Merrill Lynch & Co.		Alex. Brown & Sons Incorporated
Dean Witter Reynolds Inc.	A.G. Edwards & Sons, Inc.	Goldman, Sachs & Co.
Montgomery Securities	Morgan Stanley & Co. Incorporated	Oppenheimer & Co., Inc.
Piper Jaffray Inc.	Prudential Securities Incorporated	Schroder Wertheim & Co.
Smith Barney Inc.		Nesbitt Burns Securities Inc.
Arnhold and S. Bleichroeder, Inc.	J. C. Bradford & Co.	Equitable Securities Corporation
EVEREN Securities, Inc.	Hanifen, Imhoff Inc.	Interstate/Johnson Lane Corporation
Janney Montgomery Scott Inc.	Edward D. Jones & Co.	Ladenburg, Thalmann & Co. Inc.
Legg Mason Wood Walker Incorporated	Principal Financial Securities, Inc.	Pryor, McClendon, Counts & Co., Inc.
Rauscher Pierce Refsnes, Inc.	Wessels, Arnold & Henderson, L.L.C.	Wheat First Butcher Singer

Sample tombstone announcement.

Although the Securities Exchange Act of 1934 prohibits manipulation of this sort by all others, underwriters are permitted to buy shares if the market price falls below the offering price. If market stabilization is allowed for a particular issue, it must be stipulated in the prospectus. If part of an issue remains unsold after a period of time, for example 30 days, members may leave the syndicate and sell their securities at whatever price the market will allow.

The lead underwriter decides when the syndicate is to break up, freeing members to sell at the prevailing market price. As an example of underwriting risk, at times the lead banker is left holding many more shares of an offering than it would like.

SELF-CHECK

- Explain what an initial public offering is and indicate the kind of companies that usually handle such transactions.
- Distinguish between a firm commitment underwriting agreement and a best-effort underwriting agreement.
- Define **spread** and **flotation**.
- Explain what retail selling is and how it differs from selling to institutional investors.

12.6 Direct and Indirect Costs of Going Public

One of the drawbacks of going public is its cost. The issuing firm faces direct out-of-pocket costs for accountants' and lawyers' fees, printing expenses, and filing fees. In addition, the firm faces two additional costs, which together represent the difference between the market value of the firm's shares in the aftermarket and the actual proceeds the firm receives from the underwriters. The first of these costs is the spread, as discussed earlier. The second cost, *underpricing,* represents the difference between the aftermarket stock price and the offering price.

▲ **Underpricing** represents money left on the table, or money the firm could have received had the initial offer price been set higher and more accurately estimated the aftermarket value of the stock.

Studies of IPOs in the United States find that firms' IPOs are underpriced more if it is a smaller stock issue, issued by a technology firm, if the firm has benefited from venture capital financing, and if the issue's underwriters are more prestigious.

Direct costs, the spread, and underpricing are the flotation costs of an IPO. The flotation costs of an issue depend upon a number of factors, including the

FOR EXAMPLE

Underpricing

Assume a firm raises $15 million by selling 1 million shares at an offer price of $15. By the close of trading on the first day, the firm's stock price is $20. Had the securities originally been offered at $20, the firm might have received an additional $5 million for the stock. Some would argue that the firm left $5 million "on the table," financing it could have received had the stock not been underpriced. Or to view this another way, if the offer price had been $20, the firm could have raised $15 million by selling only 750,000 shares.

size of the offering, the issuing firm's earnings, its industry, and the condition of the stock market. The flotation costs, relative to the amount raised, are usually lower for a firm commitment offering rather than a best-efforts offering.

SELF-CHECK

- Define **underpricing.**
- List all the costs of going public.

12.7 Trading Securities—Secondary Securities Markets

The primary market is where securities are first issued and sold in an offering to investors. Any trading of the securities thereafter occurs in the secondary market.

The **secondary markets** provide liquidity to investors who wish to sell securities. Selling securities to investors would be difficult if investors had no easy way to profit from their holdings or no way to sell them for cash. Investors often want to shift their assets into different securities and different markets. Secondary markets provide pricing information, thus providing a means to evaluate a firm's management and for management to determine how investors are interpreting its actions.

The secondary market for securities has two components:

▲ **Organized security exchanges,** which have physical trading floors such as the NYSE trading floor on Wall Street.
▲ **Over-the-counter (OTC) markets,** which are networks of independent dealers and agents who communicate and trade electronically rather than on a trading floor.

The New York Stock Exchange is the prime example of an organized exchange, whereas the Nasdaq is an over-the-counter market.

If a firm's stock prices fall in the secondary market, the stockholders often place pressure on the company's management. In addition, when such a firm seeks new capital, it will have to provide a higher expected return to investors. The position of a firm's management becomes increasingly vulnerable as business deteriorates. Ultimately the firm's directors may replace management, or the firm may be a target of a takeover attempt.

To qualify for listing its security, a corporation must meet certain requirements regarding profitability, total value of outstanding stock, or stockholder's equity. Over time, the NYSE revamped its listing standards in an attempt to attract more high-growth firms (which had been favoring the Nasdaq over-the-counter market for listings) and more foreign companies. The new standards are listed in Table 12-3.

Table 12-3: New York Stock Exchange Listing Requirements

NYSE, U.S. Firms	NYSE, Non-U.S. Firms
Number of shareholders, trading volume, and market value:	III. Revenues of $75 million for the past year and an average market capitalization (number of shares 3 stock price) of $750 million
I. a) 2,000 owners of 100 shares and average monthly trading volume in the past 6 months 100,000 shares; or	
b) 2,200 total shareholders and average monthly trading volume in the past 6 months of 100,000 shares; or	
c) 500 shareholders with average monthly trading volume over the past year of 1,000,000 shares	
II. 1.1 million shares outstanding	
III. Market value: $100 million ($60 million for IPOs)	
Earnings, cash flow, and revenues:	
I. Pretax earnings of $10.0 million in past three years, with $2.0 millon in each of the two preceding years; or	
II. Positive operating cash flow in each of last three years with a cumulative total of $25 million for these years; or	

The corporation also pays a fee for the privilege of being listed. The original listing fee ranges from $150,000 to $250,000. Continuing annual fees range from $35,000 to $500,000, depending on the number of outstanding shares.

The acceptance of the security by the exchange for listing on the Big Board does not constitute endorsement of its quality. The American Stock Exchange and all of the regional exchanges permit unlisted trading privileges as well as listed trading privileges.

For unlisted securities, the exchange itself (instead of the issuing corporation) recommends the securities for trading privileges. The SEC must approve unlisted trading privileges. The securities of approximately 1,000 corporations carry unlisted trading privileges on the nation's stock exchanges.

12.7.1 Over-the-Counter Market

In addition to the organized exchanges, the other major secondary market for securities trading is the over-the-counter market or OTC. The largest OTC market is the Nasdaq system; "Nasdaq" stands for National Association of Securities Dealers Automated Quotation system. Although it trades more than twice as many issues as the NYSE, the OTC is comprised mainly of stocks of smaller firms, although companies such as Intel, Microsoft, Novell, and Apple Computer are listed on it.

There are several differences between the organized exchanges and the OTC market.

Organized Exchanges	Over-the-Counter (OTC) Market
Has a central trading location floor	Telecommunications network linking brokers and dealers that trade OTC stocks
Has specialists that make markets and control trading in listed stocks	Does not have any specialists; OTC dealers buy and sell from their own account to the public, other dealers
Stocks from primarily larger firms	Stocks from primarily smaller firms
	Trades more than twice as many issues as the NYSE

In a sense, OTC markets operate in the manner of any merchant. They have an inventory, comprised of the securities in which they specialize, that they hope to sell at a price enough above their purchase price to make a profit.

The OTC markets contend that theirs is a competitive system, with multiple dealers making a market in a company's stock.

To trade in an OTC stock, an investor contacts his broker, who then checks a computer listing of dealers for that particular stock. After determining which dealer has the highest bid price or lowest ask price, the broker contacts the dealer to confirm the price and to execute the transaction.

The OTC market is regulated by the Maloney Act of 1938. This act amended the Securities Exchange Act of 1934 to extend SEC control to the OTC market. The law created the legal basis for OTC brokers and dealers to form national self-regulating trade associations. This was one instance where business itself requested government regulation. It stemmed from the fact that honest dealers in the investment field had little protection against bad publicity resulting from the unscrupulous practices of a few OTC dealers. Under this provision, one association, the National Association of Security Dealers (NASD), has been formed. All rules adopted by NASD must be reported to the SEC. The SEC has the authority to take away any powers of the NASD.

The NASD has established a lengthy set of rules and regulations intended to ensure fair practices and responsibility on the part of the association's members. Any broker or dealer engaged in OTC activities is eligible to become a member of the NASD as long as he or she can prove a record of responsible operation and the broker or dealer is willing to accept the NASD code of ethics.

12.7.2 Third and Fourth Security Markets

It should not be surprising that an activity as broad as the security market would give rise to special arrangements. Despite their names, the third and fourth markets are two additional types of secondary markets that have evolved over time.

▲ The **third market** is for large blocks of listed shares and operates outside the confines of the organized exchanges. In the third market, blocks of stock (units of 10,000 shares) are traded OTC.

The participants in the third market are large institutions, such as mutual funds, insurance companies, and pension funds, that often need to trade large blocks of shares. Brokers assist the institutions in the third market by bringing buyers and sellers together and, in return, receive a fee.

▲ The **fourth market** is comprised of **electronic communications networks,** or **ECNs,** which are computerized trading systems that automatically match buy and sell orders at specified prices.

Certain large institutional investors arrange purchases and sales of securities among themselves without the benefit of a broker or dealer. They subscribe to an electronic network in which offers to buy or sell are made known to other subscribers. The offers are made in code, and institutions wishing to accept a buy or sell offer know the identity of the other party only upon acceptance of the offer. A fee is paid to the network provider when the trade is completed. Those who support fourth-market trading argue that transfers are often quicker and more economical, but the confidentiality is also an important feature to many firms.

SELF-CHECK

- Define **secondary market** and list two such markets.
- Give an example of an organized security exchange and an over-the-counter market.
- Explain what the third market and fourth market are and give examples of each.

12.8 A Word on Commissions

It costs money to trade securities. About the only market participants who don't pay commissions are the exchange specialists and registered traders on the NYSE and dealers in OTC stocks.

Stock commissions vary from brokerage firm to brokerage firm.

▲ **Full-service brokerages** not only assist your trades but also have research staffs that analyze firms and make recommendations on which stocks to buy or sell.

Their analysts write research reports that are available to the firm's brokerage customers. Examples of full-service brokerages include Merrill Lynch, A. G. Edwards, and Morgan Stanley.

▲ **Discount brokerages** simply execute customers' stock transactions without offering recommendations or doing research for customers. Also referred to as *deep-discount brokerages*.

Investors who do not desire or need the extra services of a full-service broker use discounters. The average discount investor makes his or her own investment decisions and wishes to trade at the lowest possible costs. Examples of discount brokerages include Brown and Company, Charles Schwab, Muriel Siebert, and Olde Discount.

A recent innovation that is shaking up the traditional stock brokerage industry is the deep-discount broker and Internet trading. With low overhead costs and offers of basic services, stock trading on some Internet-based brokerages are quite inexpensive, even compared to discount brokers. Falling commissions and ease of access make **online trading** attractive to those who make their own investment decisions.

Commissions on security trades depend upon several additional factors. Commissions generally are lower on more liquid securities—that is, those that are more actively traded or securities with a popular secondary market. Commissions are higher for smaller trades that involve fewer shares or lower-priced shares. Many brokerages charge a minimum commission that may make small trades relatively costly. They also charge a transaction fee to cover their costs of processing the trade. Others assess fees if your account is inactive for a year. So, even if you don't trade, you still pay the broker some fees. As with so many other things in life, a wise investor will shop around for the brokerage firm and broker that best meets his or her particular needs.

It is possible to buy shares of some companies without going through a stockbroker. Some firms sell their shares directly to the public; this is called **direct investing.** Other firms allow shareholders to add to their stock holdings through **dividend reinvestment plans;** as the name implies, the shareholder's dividends are used to purchase shares (including partial or fractional shares) of the corporation.

SELF-CHECK

- **Explain the difference between full-service brokerage firms and discount brokerages.**
- **Define direct investing and dividend reinvestment plans.**

12.9 Security Market Indexes

The Dow Jones Industrial Average or Standard & Poor's 500 Stock Index are announced and published every day. The 30 stocks that are part of the Dow Jones Industrial Average are listed in the Table 12-4. You are probably familiar with most of their names.

Market indexes are useful for keeping track of trends in the market. A **market index** is a list of companies that are believed to represent the stock market. If the index increases in value, then the economy is said to be doing well. An example of a market index is the Dow Jones Industrial Average.

Table 12-4: Stocks in the Dow Jones Industrial Average (as of March 2006)

3M	Alcoa Inc.
Altria Group Inc.	American Express Company
American International Group, Inc.	AT&T Inc.
Boeing Co.	Caterpillar Inc.
Citigroup, Inc.	E.I. du Pont de Nemours and Company
ExxonMobil Corporation	General Electric Company
General Motors Corporation	Hewlett-Packard Co.
Honeywell Intl Inc.	Intel Corporation
International Business Machines	Johnson & Johnson
JPMorgan & Chase & Co	McDonald's Corporation
Merck & Co., Inc.	Microsoft Corporation
Pfizer Inc.	The Coca-Cola Company
The Home Depot, Inc.	United Technologies Corporation
Verizon Communications	Wal-Mart Stores, Inc.
Walt Disney Company (The) (Holding Company)	The Procter & Gamble Company

The NYSE index tracks all stocks listed in the NYSE. The S & P 400 industrials summarizes the activity in 400 stocks of industrial firms. Dow Jones indexes various industries such as banks, autos, chemicals, retail, just to name a few.

Market indexes exist for many different countries' securities markets, including a variety of both stock and bond market indexes. There are many ways in which an index can be constructed and computed.

SELF-CHECK

- Explain what a market index is and list two examples.
- Name two stocks on the Dow Jones Industrial Average and what services or goods they offer.

12.10 Inside Information and Other Ethical Issues

The capital markets are successful in allocating capital because of their integrity. Should investors lose confidence in the fairness of the capital markets, all will lose; investors lose an attractive means for investing funds and issuers lose access to low-cost public capital.

Some people who deal in securities and have access to private information about mergers, new security offerings, or earnings announcements may be tempted to take advantage of this information when trading in the stock market. **Insider trading** is the illegal practice of buying and selling stocks based on information that is known only by corporate information and that is not available to the public.

In the United States, taking advantage of private "inside" information is thought to be unfair to other investors. These factors, combined with the ease with which inside information can be used, explain why insider trading is not allowed under provisions of the Securities Exchange Act of 1934.

The frantic efforts of large firms to control insider trading is understandable in light of the damage that can occur to their reputations. It is also understandable that the SEC has resorted to very strong efforts to resolve the question that continues to exist with respect to a meaningful and fair definition of insider information. After all, it is the investing public without access to this information that pays the price for insider information abuses.

Another breach of investor confidence can occur via churning. **Churning** is when a broker constantly buys and sells securities from a client's portfolio in an effort to generate commissions.

Rather than making decisions that are in the client's best interest, frequent commission-generating trades may be made by brokers with selfish motives. There are some times when frequent trading may be appropriate, but it should occur only within the clients' investing guidelines and with the clients' interests at heart. Ethics and integrity are at the center of fair and well-functioning financial markets.

FOR EXAMPLE

Investment Scandal

In 2003, several investment banking firms were fined for ethical lapses. Evidence showed stock analysts, whose stock recommendations should be unbiased, were sometimes rewarded for writing favorable reports to attract investment banking clients.

SELF-CHECK

- Define **insider trading** and name the law under which it is prohibited.
- Explain **churning**.

SUMMARY

The stock market is the engine of the U.S. and world economies. Companies sell stock to receive funds for continued growth. Investors purchase stocks to receive a return on their investment. In this chapter you learned how stocks are traded. You examined the way the sale of stocks is regulated. You determined what factors should go into all investing decisions. You also learned the positive and negative aspects of going public. This knowledge will help you in your professional role as you guide companies in investments, and it will help you in your personal life as you look to receive healthy returns on your investments.

KEY TERMS

American depository receipts (ADR)	Represent shares of common stock that trade on a foreign stock exchange.
Ask price	The price at which the owner is willing to sell the securities.
Best-effort agreement	One in which investment bankers try to sell the securities of the issuing corporation, but they assume no risk for a possible failure of the sale or the flotation.
Bid price	The price the buyer is willing to pay for the securities.
Business angels	Private investors who provide start-up capital for small businesses.
Buying on margin	Means the investor borrows money and invests it along with his own funds in securities.
Callable preferred stock	Gives the corporation the right to retire the preferred stock at its option.
Churning	When a broker constantly buys and sells securities from a client's portfolio in an effort to generate commissions.

Class A shares	Class of common stock. The stock issues for trading from an Initial public offering or if a company issues new stock at a later date.
Class B shares	Class of common stock. A special category of stock usually retained by company founders at the time a company goes public. It carries certain rights not granted to stock available to the public.
Common shareholders claim on business profits	Available only to those that remain after the holders of all other classes of debt and equity securities have received payments or returns.
Common stock	Represents ownership shares in a corporation.
Convertible preferred stock	Has a special provision that makes it possible to convert the preferred stock into the common stock of the corporation. This is generally the stockholder's option.
Cumulative preferred stock	Requires that before dividends on common stock are paid, preferred dividends must be paid not only for the current period but also for all previous periods in which preferred dividends were not paid.
Direct investing	Firms sell their shares directly to the public.
Discount brokerages	Simply execute customer's stock transactions without offering recommendations or doing research for customers.
Dividend	A payment to the owner of a share of corporation's stock; represents the owner's portion of the corporation profits.
Dividend reinvestment plans	Shareholder's dividends are used to purchase shares (including partial or fractional shares) of the corporation.
Dow Jones Industrial Average	An average of 30 well-known companies chosen by the editors of the *Wall Street Journal*. These companies represent trends in the stock market.
Dutch auction bidding process	A variation of competitive bidding that allows smaller firms and individual investors to purchase securities.
Electronic communications networks (ECN)	Computerized trading systems that automatically match buy and sell orders at specified prices.
Floor brokers	Fall into one of two categories: house brokers and independent brokers.

Flotation	The cost of the IPO.
Fourth market	A type of secondary market that is comprised of electronic communications networks, or ECNs, which are computerized trading systems that automatically match buy and sell orders at specified prices.
Full-service brokerages	Execute trades and also have research staffs that analyze firms and make recommendations on which stocks to buy or sell.
Global depository receipts (GDR)	Represent shares of common stock that are listed on the London Stock Exchange.
House brokers	Act as agents who carry out customers' orders for security purchases and sales.
Independent brokers	May be asked by house brokers to help them handle their orders.
Initial public offering (IPO)	A sale of securities to the investing public.
Insider trading	Illegal practice of buying and selling stocks based on information that is known only by corporate information and that is not available to the public.
Institutional investors	Large investors such as insurance companies, pension funds, investment companies, and other large financial institutions.
Limit order	An order in which the maximum buying price (limit buy) or the minimum selling price (limit sell) is specified by the investor.
Market index	List of companies that are believed to represent the stock market. If the index increases in value, then the economy is said to be doing well. An example of a market index is the Dow Jones Industrial Average.
Market order	An order for immediate purchase or sale at the best possible price.
Noncumulative preferred stock	Makes no provision for the accumulation of unpaid dividends.
Online trading	Buying and selling securities such as stocks over the Internet.
Organized securities exchange	A location with a trading floor where all stock transactions take place.
Over-the-counter (OTC)	Networks of independent dealers and agents

markets	who communicate and trade electronically rather than on a trading floor.
Par value	Stated value; usually has little bearing on the current price or book value of the stock. It is used mainly for accounting purposes and some legal needs.
Preferred stock	An equity security that has a preference, or senior claim, to the firm's earnings and assets.
Program trading	A technique for trading stocks as a group rather than individually.
Registered traders	Individuals who purchase a seat on the exchange to buy and sell stocks for their own account.
Retail selling	Selling to individual investors.
Secondary markets	The primary market is where securities are first issued and sold in an offering to investors. Any trading of the securities thereafter occurs in the secondary market. Secondary markets provide liquidity to investors who wish to sell securities.
Short sale	A sale of securities that the seller does not own. An investor will want to short a stock if he/she feels the price will decline in the future.
Specialists	Assigned dealers, who have the responsibility of making a market for an assigned security.
Spread	The difference between the offer price and the price paid by the investment bank.
Stop-loss order	An order to sell stock at the market price when the price of the stock falls to a specified level.
Terms of an underwriting agreement	Provides that securities are purchased at a predetermined or "firm commitment" price by the underwriters, who then sell them to investors at the offer price.
Third market	A type of secondary market that is for large blocks of listed shares and operates outside the confines of organized exchanges.
Underpricing	Represents the difference between the aftermarket stock price and the offering price.
Underwriting agreement	An agreement in which investment bankers assume the risk arising from the possibility that securities may not be purchased by investors.

ASSESS YOUR UNDERSTANDING

Go to www.wiley.com/college/Melicher to evaluate your knowledge of the basics of securities trading.
Measure your learning by comparing pre-test and post-test results.

Summary Questions

1. The common stockholders have the lowest standing when a business venture is liquidated. True or false?
2. The par value of a common stock is the liquidation value or base price that a stockholder receives per share when the firm files for bankruptcy. True or false?
3. Shareholders of common stock
   (a) can vote to select the corporation's board of directors.
   (b) have a preferred claim on business profits.
   (c) can demand a dividend payment.
   (d) have a higher standing than bondholders when a business venture is liquidated.
4. American depository receipts are receipts that represent foreign shares to U.S. investors. True or false?
5. A global depository receipt is traded on the American Stock Exchange. True or false?
6. Preferred stock is an equity security that has a senior claim to the firm's earnings and assets over bonds. True or false?
7. Callable preferred stock gives the corporation the right to retire the preferred stock at its option. True or false?
8. The par value of a preferred stock is meaningful in that it is often used to determine the fixed annual dividend. True or false?
9. Convertible preferred stock has a special provision that makes it possible to convert it to common stock of the corporation, generally at the stockholder's option. True or false?
10. Preferred stock can have what following characteristic?
    (a) Cumulative
    (b) Noncumulative
    (c) Convertible
    (d) All of the above
11. Which of the following types of stocks have the lowest risk to shareholders?
    (a) Common stock
    (b) Cumulative preferred stock

(c) Noncumulative preferred stock

(d) Callable preferred stock

12. Floor brokers act as agents to execute customers' orders for securities purchases and sales. True or false?

13. Specialists are assigned dealers who have the responsibility of making a market in an assigned security. True or false?

14. The price for which the owner is willing to sell the security is called the
   (a) bid price.
   (b) spread.
   (c) ask price.
   (d) limit price.

15. Independent brokers who handle the commission broker's overflow are called
   (a) specialists.
   (b) registered traders.
   (c) floor brokers.
   (d) all the above.

16. A person who facilitates market transactions by selling (buying) when other investors wish to buy (sell) is called a
   (a) registered trader.
   (b) floor broker.
   (c) market maker.
   (d) commission broker.

17. A limit order is an order to sell stock at the market price when the price of the stock falls to a specified level. True or false?

18. A market order is an order for immediate purchase or sale at the best possible price. True or false?

19. The maintenance margin is the minimum margin to which an investment may fall before a margin call is placed. True or false?

20. Program trading is a technique for trading stocks as a group rather than individually, defined as a minimum of at least 15 different stocks with a minimum value of $1 million. True or false?

21. If a limit order is not quite close to the current market price and is turned over to the specialist, it is placed into a
   (a) central limit order book.
   (b) market order book.
   (c) short sale book.
   (d) None of the above

22. Sales of securities that the seller does not own is called a
    (a) stop-loss order.
    (b) short sale.
    (c) limit order.
    (d) maintenance margin.

23. An order to sell stock at the market price when the price of the stock falls to a specified level is called a
    (a) limit order.
    (b) market order.
    (c) short sale.
    (d) stop-loss order.

24. If you borrowed money from your broker to purchase securities and the value falls, you may receive a
    (a) maintenance margin call.
    (b) margin call.
    (c) limit order call.
    (d) specialist call.

25. The maximum buying price or the minimum selling price specified by the investor is called a
    (a) stop-loss order.
    (b) market order.
    (c) short sale.
    (d) limit order.

26. The advantage, and potential disadvantage, of buying on margin is
    (a) larger profit.
    (b) greater leverage.
    (c) deductible loss.
    (d) nontaxable capital gain.

27. The Federal Reserve System and the New York Stock Exchange regulations currently require the short seller to have an initial margin of at least _____ of the price of the stock.
    (a) 10%
    (b) 25%
    (c) 30%
    (d) 50%

28. Under a best-effort agreement, investment bankers try to sell the securities of the issuing corporation, but they assume no risk for a possible failure of the flotation. True or false?

29. Shelf registration allows firms to register only debt issues with the SEC and have them available to sell for 2 years. True or false?

30. All firms can use shelf registration, which saves issuers both time and money. True or false?

31. The flotation costs of an initial public offering are comprised solely of direct costs and the spread. True or false?

32. IPO underpricing occurs only in the United States. True or false?

33. Firm commitment flotation costs are typically lower than those of best efforts. True or false?

34. The prospectus is a contract outlining the duties, responsibilities, and fees between the issuing firm and its underwriter. True or false?

35. An underwriting agreement is a contract in which the investment banker agrees to buy securities at a predetermined price and then resell them to investors. True or false?

36. The aftermarket is a period of time during which members of an underwriting syndicate may not sell the securities for less than the initial offering price. True or false?

37. If there were no secondary markets for trading between investors, there would be no primary market for the initial sale of securities. True or false?

38. A Dutch auction is an offering process in which investors bid on the price and quantity of securities they wish to purchase. True or false?

39. Underpricing represents the difference between the aftermarket par value and the offering price. True or false?

40. The fourth market is a market for large blocks of listed stocks that operate outside the confines of the organized exchanges. True or false?

41. Over-the-counter markets are organized exchanges for trading securities such as the American Stock Exchange. True or false?

42. Organized securities exchanges include the New York Stock Exchange, the American Stock Exchange, and Nasdaq. True or false?

43. Trades between large institutional investors that take place without the benefits of brokers or dealers occur in the
    (a) primary market.
    (b) secondary market.
    (c) third market.
    (d) fourth market.

44. The market for large blocks of listed stocks that operates outside the confines of the organized exchanges is called the
    (a) primary market.
    (b) secondary market.

(c) third market.

(d) fourth market.

45. An over-the-counter market trade occurs in the

(a) primary market.

(b) secondary market.

(c) third market.

(d) fourth market.

46. Existing securities are traded in the primary market. True or false?

47. Discount brokers assist your trades and also have research staffs that analyze firms and make recommendations on which stocks to buy or sell. True or false?

48. You can avoid paying commissions to trade securities if you

(a) use the Internet to trade online

(b) use the services of a discount broker.

(c) trade before 9:00 a.m. or after 4:30 p.m.

(d) None of the above

49. Commissions are generally higher for more liquid securities than for less liquid securities. True or false?

50. Market indexes should never be used for tracking trends in the market. True or false?

51. The Dow Jones Industrial Average index summarizes the activity in 400 stocks of industrial firms. True or false?

52. The growth in the market value of foreign securities has occurred because of general economic expansion, increased regulation of exchange rates, and tightening of regulations of equity markets. True or false?

53. Foreign stocks can be traded in the United States if they are registered with the Securities and Exchange Commission. True or false?

54. Churning happens when a broker makes a recommendation to a client to reinvest (or churn) dividend payments for the purchase of new shares of stock. True or false?

55. Insider trading regulation is provided for under the Securities Exchange Act of 1934. True or false?

56. The SEC's definition of "insiders" is limited to corporate personnel. True or false?

57. The NYSE has embraced the move toward electronic trading because its members believe it will result in better prices than using NYSE specialists. True or false?

58. With electronic trading, bid and asked prices on covered stocks would be available in all markets. True or false?

Review Questions

1. Common stock represents ownership shares in a corporation. Briefly describe the types of risk faced by investors of common stock. Compare them to the risks associated with preferred stock.

2. When a corporation divides its common stock into Class A and Class B, it typically gives voting rights only to Class B shareholders. What is the reason for restricting voting rights to only one class of common stockholders?

3. When can foreign stocks be traded in the United States?

    (a) Because global depository receipts are listed on the London Stock Exchange, U.S. investors cannot buy GDRs through a broker in the United States.

    (b) Foreign stocks can be traded in the United States if they are registered with the Securities and Exchange Commission.

    (c) The fourth market is a market for large blocks of listed stocks that operate outside the confines of the organized exchanges.

    (d) All of the above statements are correct.

4. Preferred stock is an equity security that has a preference, or senior claim, to the firm's earnings and assets. Describe two ways in which the fixed dividend on preferred stock is specified.

5. In what markets can preferred stock be sold?

    (a) The par value of a common stock or preferred stock is not important.

    (b) A convertible preferred stock gives the corporation the right to retire the preferred stock at its option.

    (c) The U.S. security markets are the only public financial markets in which preferred stock can be sold.

    (d) The fixed preferred stock dividend is a tax-deductible expense.

6. What are some of the characteristics of an organized securities exchange?

7. What does a floor broker do?

    (a) Because a specialist is given the monopoly power to make a market on a particular stock, all trades must pass through the specialist.

    (b) A specialist can also perform the function of a commission broker.

    (c) A floor broker acts as an agent to execute customer's orders for securities purchases and sales.

    (d) Each of the above statements is false.

8. Why is there a difference between bid and ask prices at some point in time for a specific security?

9. Describe the differences among the following three types of orders: market, limit, and stop loss.

10. What is meant by a short sale?

11. If an investor feels the price of a stock will decline in the future, which trade should the investor undertake?

    (a) Market order

    (b) Buy on margin

    (c) Limit order

    (d) Short sale

12. Describe the meaning of buying on margin.

13. What is meant by *program trading*?

14. How can existing firms that are already public raise additional funds?

    (a) Sell additional securities by using the underwriting process

    (b) Sell securities to a private party

    (c) Seek competitive bid

    (d) All of the above

    (e) None of the above

15. Why do corporations employ investment bankers?

16. Discuss how investment bankers assume risk in the process of marketing securities of corporations. How do investment bankers try to minimize these risks?

17. What is not a cost to the issuing firm of going public with an initial stock offering?

    (a) Direct costs (legal fees, accounting fees, etc.)

    (b) Underwriter's spread

    (c) Overpricing

    (d) Underpricing

18. How does trading OTC differ from trading at the NYSE?

19. How do the third and fourth markets differ from the NYSE?

20. Discuss why someone would pay a higher commission at a full-service brokerage when they could trade the same stocks for a lower commission using a discount brokerage.

21. Identify and describe two ways it is possible to buy shares of some companies without going through a stockbroker.

22. Name five companies that are part of the Dow Jones Industrial Average.

23. Money managers and investors recommend investing in foreign securities for what reasons?

    (a) Such diversification makes possible a broader search for investment values

    (b) Such diversification can greatly diminish an investor's tax burden

(c) Such diversification can reduce the risk in investment portfolios

(d) b and c

(e) a and c

24. Investors often charge brokers with the task of buying and selling securities for them. When is such buying and selling considered churning?

25. Why is it illegal to trade on insider information?

26. Describe some recent innovations in securities markets.

27. What are the advantages of having a specialist-based trading system? An electronic trading system?

Applying This Chapter

1. A company issues common stocks with a par value of $30 per share. You want to buy 10 shares of this stock. Can you determine the approximate cost of purchasing these shares based on the information provided?

2. Common stocks and preferred stocks are both equity securities issued by corporations. If part of your investment strategy is to earn income through dividend payments, which type of stock should you purchase?

3. Specialists, or assigned dealers, have the responsibility of making a market for an assigned security. How do specialists turn a profit?

4. You paid $10 for shares of ABC Corporation, and the current price is $18. You think that the stock will continue to rise in price, but you also want to protect your profits should they take a turn for the worse. What kind of order can you place to help protect your profits?

5. If the initial margin requirement is 50% and you have $5,000 in your brokerage account, how much in additional securities may you buy on margin?

6. Your company is looking for an investment banking firm to handle your firm's initial public offering. Your company must have a guaranteed return of $1,000,000 or it's not worth it to your company to go public. What kind of underwriting agreement should you seek?

7. Your company went public and offered shares for $10. Later that same day, the aftermarket price of the stock shot up to $30. What percentage of this increase in price did your company get?

8. Your company is a large institutional investor that wants to sell 10,000 shares of stock in a company. You don't want potential buyers to know your identity until after the sale is complete. What type of secondary securities market should you use?

9. Commissions vary widely among brokerage firms. What are some factors that influence the commission on a stock trade with a broker?

10. Market indexes are useful for keeping track of trends in the market. Track the Dow Jones Industrial Average over a 5-day period and describe the trend.

11. Investment in foreign shares by U.S. investors may be facilitated through the use of American depository receipts, or ADRs. The ADR index was developed by the Bank or New York. Go to the index at www.adrbny.com and list the top performing stocks for the day. What countries are they from?

12. You are a high-level employee of a publicly owned pharmaceutical company. You read in the newspaper that the FDA has just given final approval for one of your company's highly anticipated new drugs. You call your broker and ask him to buy 100 shares of your company, in anticipation of it increasing in value. Is this an example of insider trading? If so, why? If not, why not?

13. In an effort to increase the technological and informational efficiency of the stock market, the SEC has actively promoted major changes in the structure of stock market activities and institutions. List one recent innovation in securities markets.

YOU TRY IT

Price Quotes

Get stock price quotes online and learn more about stock investing at www.fool.com and finance.yahoo.com. Try the investment calculators at these sites.

Dutch Auctions

Go to www.openipo.com to visit a site of an investment bank (W.R. Hambrecht & Co.) that uses Dutch auctions in initial public offerings.

Market Indexes

Studying the indexes and becoming familiar with the stocks each reports will give you a better understanding of how they are structured and computed.

13

DISTRIBUTIONS TO STOCKHOLDERS
Growth Rates and Changes

Starting Point

Go to www.wiley.com/college/Melicher to assess your knowledge of the basics of stock growth and change.
Determine where you need to concentrate your effort.

What You'll Learn in This Chapter

▲ How income from stocks is distributed
▲ The difference between dividends and capital gains
▲ How to estimate future stock dividends
▲ The importance of evaluating dividend stability
▲ Explain stock options, restricted stock, tracking stock, and dividend reinvestment plans
▲ The role of stock options and restricted stock in employee incentive programs
▲ The reasons firm's issue stocks splits and reverse splits
▲ The benefits of dividend reinvestment plans

After Studying This Chapter, You'll Be Able To

▲ Examine the tax implications of dividends and capital gains
▲ Appraise the factors that affect corporate profits
▲ Calculate the value of all future stock dividends
▲ Analyze a stock's price quote

Goals and Outcomes

▲ Compare and contrast dividends, capital gains, and capital losses
▲ Analyze how stock changes help the market grow
▲ Evaluate the benefits of dividend reinvestment plans
▲ Assess the components of a stock quote
▲ Evaluate the factors that affect corporation profits
▲ Estimate the future dividends of constant growth stocks

INTRODUCTION

The income derived from trading stocks is distributed either as dividends or capital gains. While investors want to purchase stocks that have the potential of earning the highest returns, they must also consider how the income will affect their tax liability. With this in mind, financial planners analyze stocks to determine their expected rate of return, as well as the stability and growth potential of the stock and the issuing corporations. Now that you have studied the creation and trading of securities, the next step is learning about how stocks generate income and how that income flows through the financial system.

13.1 Dividends versus Capital Gains

There are two ways you can earn money in the stock market: by receiving dividends and realizing capital gains.

▲ **Dividends:** payments that represent the owner's portion of the corporation's stock. They may be paid monthly, quarterly, or annually, or in some cases not at all, depending on the profits earned by the issuing corporation.

Shareholders are eligible to receive dividends for as long as they own the stock.

▲ **Capital gains** are realized only when the stock is sold for a profit. Capital gains do not need to be held for any length of time to be considered a capital gain; the investors just have to pay capital gains on stock held for a year or longer.

▲ **Capital losses** are realized if the sale price of the stock is lower than the purchase price.

Of course, financial managers watch the markets carefully because part of their responsibility is to keep their clients from suffering losses on securities.

For investors, the major difference in receiving income from dividends rather than capital gains is the way income is viewed by the Internal Revenue Service. Dividends are considered ordinary income to individuals and corporations, and are added to profits or used to reduce losses. Capital gains and losses are treated differently and depending on how long the stocks have been held can be reported as long-term capital gains or short-term capital gains. Special tax rates and certain reductions in the gain or loss are also built into our tax system.

There is much to learn about our federal income tax system and how it

---

FOR EXAMPLE

Capital Gains Tax

Capital gains tax can be levied on the profits made from tax and home sales. However, if you have held a stock longer than 1 year, the capital gain is not subject to income tax but rather the lower capital gains tax. For a house, a single person would have to make in excess of $250,000 in profit before it was taxed and for married people that increases to $500,000.

---

capital gains and losses are not taxable until a sale takes place, and the income or loss from the sale is not considered ordinary income.

If you are wondering how an individual knows how to categorize income at the end of the tax year, the answer is simple: Brokers and managers of mutual funds and pension funds issue statements to investors that contain all the information needed for tax purposes.

SELF-CHECK

- Distinguish between dividends and capital gains.
- Define **capital losses**.
- Explain how the IRS categorizes the two types of payments.

13.2 Estimating Future Dividends

The principle for determining an appropriate stock price is the same as that for determining a bond price: find the present value of future expected cash flows. Common and preferred stocks are generally assumed to have endless lives. For stock, dividend payments may vary over time, so determining an appropriate rate at which to calculate future dividends is difficult. However, it is believed the value of all future dividends should equal a stock's current price.

It may seem strange to consider the stock price as the present value of all future dividends. Investors generally buy stock with the intention of selling it at some future time ranging from a few hours to 30 years or longer. Despite the length of any one investor's time frame, the current price of any dividend-paying common stock should equal the present value of all future dividends.

Even if a corporation currently pays no dividends and has no plans to pay dividends in the future, the value of this company's stock will not be zero. Just because a company does not post a profit does not mean that the company is

If dots (...) appear in the Net Chg column, it would indicate that the closing price was unchanged from the previous trading day. Dots (...) will appear in the dividend yield column for some stocks. This indicates that the firm did not pay dividends in the previous 12 months. Lack of a number under the PE column indicates a firm with a negative net income.

SELF-CHECK

- List three elements of a stock quote and explain each.
- What is a penny stock?

13.6 Tracking Stocks

Although the practice actually started in the mid-1980s with General Motors' acquisitions of ElectronicData Systems (EDS) and Hughes Aircraft, tracking stocks gained popularity in the late 1990s and early 2000s. A **tracking stock** is issued by the parent company to track a subsidiary rather than the entire firm.

When GM acquired EDS and Hughes Aircraft, it offered stock for the firm's shareholders that would be driven by the fortunes of each new subsidiary rather than GM as a whole. Investment bankers and corporate executives rediscovered this idea a few years ago as a way to separate, on paper, the fortunes of a "hot" subsidiary from its sluggish parent company.

Shares can be sold and capital raised to help the subsidiary fund grow in an area such as the Internet or wireless communications. But unlike common stock, the tracking shares have no ownership claim on the subsidiary; the parent company (and the parent's shareholders) retains all ownership in it. Tracking stock is thus very different from the case of a **spinoff**, where the parent sells the subsidiary to another firm or in a public offering and the new owners truly do own the firm. Since the parent retains ownership, the tracking stock merely cuts the pieces of the firm's pie differently; it does not increase the size of the pie. In other words, the value of the tracking stock plus the firm's stock after the tracking stock has been issued should closely reflect the pretracking stock value of the entire firm.

Although tracking stocks may have some claim on the division's cash flow, the parent company still has control over where the cash goes. Some have claimed tracking stocks are a way to give incentives to managers in the subsidiaries, as they can get paid in tracking shares or receive options on the tracking stock of a "successful" subsidiary rather than in the stodgy parent.

FOR EXAMPLE

Tracking Stocks

Firms that have issued tracking stock include AT&T, Cendant, Disney, DuPont, and Dow Jones. Some studies have shown that the performance of tracking stocks has lagged that of the parent firms. One reason for this is that the subsidiary is still very much a part of the firm. Therefore, there is no reason to expect that an investor will be getting more value out of the same company merely by buying tracking shares.

SELF-CHECK

- Explain what a tracking stock is and discuss why a company would issue them.
- Describe how tracking stocks differ from spinoffs.

13.7 Evaluating the Corporation

A company's profits are determined by the following factors:

▲ Sales revenues
▲ Expenses
▲ Taxes

In addition, the financial system and the economic environment provide necessary information when evaluating a corporations' profit-making ability. That's because the company's cash flow and the outlook for their stock is affected by the global economy and our domestic economy. Growth overseas and at home will affect demand for the firm's products and will affect its costs, too.

13.7.1 Competition

Tight competition means it will be difficult to raise prices to increase sales revenue or profitability. Factors like customer service, product innovation, and using technology to the fullest extent in the manufacturing and sales process may reduce profits by increasing expenses if the features do not generate sufficient sales.

Competition may come from similar firms and other company's vying for the same consumer dollars. This is especially true in the entertainment industry where theaters, music venues, and sports events are all trying to attract the ticket-buying public. Both trucking firms and railroads compete for freight transportation; cable and satellite firms compete in the home television market.

Slower sales or higher expenses can harm a firm's ability to pay its bond interest or stock dividends or to reinvest in its future growth. Besides affecting cash flows, reduced profits alter an investor's required rate of return. Market changes can also influence the level of interest rates and required returns.

The most attractive firms for investing will be firms with a competitive advantage over their rivals. They may offer a high-quality product, or be the low-cost producer, or be innovators in the use of technology, or offer the best customer support. Whatever the source of the advantage, if they can build and maintain their advantage over time, they will reap above-normal profits and be attractive investments.

13.7.2 Overseas Influences

Two main overseas influences also have an effect on U.S. companies.

▲ **Health of foreign economies:** Growth in foreign economies will increase the demand for U.S. exports. Similarly, sluggish foreign demand will harm overseas sales and hurt the financial position of firms doing business overseas.

▲ **Exchange rates:** An adjustment in exchange rates over time leads to higher or lower U.S. dollar cash flows from overseas sales, more competitively priced import goods, or changing input costs. In other words, exchange rates affect profitability by influencing sales, price competition, and expenses. Exchange rates also affect the level of domestic interest rates.

The possibility of a weaker U.S. dollar can lead to higher U.S. interest rates. To attract capital, U.S. rates will have to rise to compensate foreign investors for expected currency losses because of the weaker dollar. Conversely, a stronger dollar can result in lower U.S. interest rates.

13.7.3 U.S. Disposable Income

On the home front, individuals can spend only what they have or what their future earning capacity will allow them to borrow. Consumption spending—that is, purchasing items such as food, cars, clothes, and computers—comprises about two-thirds of gross domestic product in the United States. Generally, higher disposable incomes (income after taxes) lead to higher levels of consumption spending. Higher levels of spending mean inventories are reduced and companies need to produce more and hire additional workers to meet sales demand. Corporations will spend to obtain supplies and workers based upon expectations of future demand. Similarly, they will invest in additional plant and equipment based upon expected future sales and income.

Economic growth results in higher levels of consumer spending and corporate investment, which in turn stimulates job growth and additional demand. Slow or negative growth can lead to layoffs, pessimistic expectations, and

FOR EXAMPLE

Recent Stock Trends

Beginning in 2001, after the September 11, 2001, terrorist attacks, government spending in the military sectors has increased, leading companies that make military equipment to post profits. Also, companies that specialize in security systems and chemical-detection equipment have also done well.

reduced consumer and corporate spending. These effects will directly influence company profits and cash flows.

Economic conditions affect required returns, too. Investors will be more optimistic in good economic times and more willing to accept lower-risk premiums on bond and stock investments. In poor economic times, credit spreads will rise as investors want to place their funds in safer investments.

13.7.4 Government Spending

Governments shape the domestic economy by government spending and taxation decisions and monetary policy. In addition, these decisions may affect consumer disposable income and the level of interest rates and inflation expectations; therefore, they will affect the valuation of the bond and stock markets.

Some industry sectors are sensitive to changes in consumer spending. Sales by auto manufacturers, computer firms, and other manufacturers of high-priced items will rise and fall by greater amounts over the business cycle than food or pharmaceutical firms. Changes in interest rates affect some industries more than others, too: banks and the housing industry are sensitive to changes in interest rates more than, say, book and music publishers or restaurants.

13.7.5 Changes in Supply

Changes in the cost and availability of raw materials, labor, and energy can adversely affect a firm's competitive place in the market. The influences of competition and supply ultimately affect a firm's profitability and investors' perceptions of the firm's risk. This, in turn, will affect its bond and stock prices.

SELF-CHECK

- List the three factors that determine a company's profits.
- List five things to consider when evaluating a company's profit-making ability and briefly explain each.
- Define **health of foreign companies**.

13.8 Stock Options

A corporation's managers can make or break the company. That is why assessing the managerial staff is important in evaluating the company's growth and earnings potential. It's imperative to have managers who will make decisions that will further the company's goals and increase its profit margin.

For several years, stock options were used as a method to keep managers focused on the good of the company. A **stock option** allows managers to purchase, at a future time, a stated number of the firm's shares at a specific price.

If the firm's stock price rises, the value of the shares, and therefore the managers' wealth, also rises. This was supposed to make managers aware that decisions that detracted from the best interest of shareholders would affect them as well by making the stock options less valuable. However, stock option plans are subject to several criticisms.

One is the past practice (since corrected by a revised accounting standard) of not reflecting the difference between market price and the (low) stock option price in the company's income statement. New regulations now stipulate it must be shown on the income statement as an expense.

Another problem with stock options is that managers, regardless of their managerial skill, may be able to receive huge bonuses if economic conditions create a rising stock market. When the stock market falls, not all managers are financially harmed as some firms chose to revalue their stock options at lower prices.

Finally, stock options were blamed for some of the ethical lapses of managers in the late 1990s. Accounting decisions to push up a firm's earnings can result in sharp stock price changes and a windfall for managers who cash in their options.

Some companies still offer stock options to their employees, but with the new accounting regulations, it has become less of a problem in the markets.

13.8.1 Restricted Stock

Restricted stock is gaining popularity as a way to align managers' interests with those of shareholders without the unfavorable aspects connected to stock options. **Restricted stock** is given to employees, but they cannot sell the shares until it

---

FOR EXAMPLE

Enron

While executives of the ill-fated energy company Enron were telling employees that they should be buying more stock because it was a "good deal" and would post a profit, they were selling their options and cashing out when stock was at a high. Employees who kept buying stock and held on to it lost all of their money as well as their jobs when Enron collapsed. The stock went from $90.00 a share to .30 a share.

vests. This means that it is held under the company's control for a set period of time, usually 3 to 5 years.

Employees who leave the firm before the stock vests lose their restricted shares. Under some company plans, top managers forfeit restricted shares if the firm has poor financial performance or if they miss financial targets.

Restricted stock's time to vest is typically longer than that of shorter-term stock options, and it has less potential for a large return. Another benefit of this plan is the fact that stock options can become worthless if the stock price does not rise sufficiently, while restricted shares will retain some value as long as the firm doesn't go bankrupt. In addition, holders receive dividends of restricted shares, even before they vest.

13.8.2 Stock Splits

Companies sometimes offer stock splits, which help the company raise additional revenue. A **stock split** occurs when a publicly held corporation decides to make a change in the number of outstanding shares issued to stockholders.

There are two important things to remember regarding stock splits:

1. The split can either decrease or increase the number of shares.

In most instances the stock split increases the number of shares issued. For example, a two-for-one split doubles the total shares. If you are a stockholder and own 50 shares of ABC Company's stock, you will own 100 shares after the two-for-one split. Assume one share of stock was worth $30 before the split, so the split makes each share now worth $15. However, the overall value has not changed: 50 shares of stock at $30 each is worth $1,500, and 100 shares of stock now valued at $15 each is still worth $1,500.

2. A split does not change the overall value of the stock.

The total value of the stock does not change with the split because the value of the company has not changed. It still has the same assets and liabilities it had before the split. One way of thinking is that the lower price per share of the stock may attract more investors, and eventually, as more people try to acquire the stock, the price will rise. If and when that happens, the original stockholder will benefit because they now own more shares that are valued at the new higher market price.

Stockholders will receive additional shares of stock after the split. Although a two-for-one split is the most common, the split can be higher or lower. A two-for-one split is a 100% split, doubling the number of shares. In a 50% split, each stockholder receives one additional share for every two owned before the split. Other splits such as 5 to 1 and 10 to 1 are possible. Occasionally, a fractional number of shares are involved in a split. Usually, the company will round up the shares to a whole number.

> ### FOR EXAMPLE
>
> #### Stock Split
>
> Net Money In Inc., a patent technology company, issued 250 shares of stock to each of its employees. A year later, the company declared a 10-to-1 split. Each employee then received a stock certificate for 2,500 shares of Net Money In stock.

A **reverse split** reduces the number of shares each stockholder owns. Again the total value of the stock does not change with the split, but the price per share does increase. In this instance, if you own 50 shares of ABC stock before the split valued at $5 each, after the split you own 25 shares valued at $10 each. The total value of the stock remains $250.

Reverse splits don't seem practical because they don't lower the price of the stock and make it more attractive to investors, but they serve a purpose for the corporation. Companies do reverse splits when they want the per-share price of their stock to increase. This is especially true of the so-called penny stocks that do not have the prestige in the market that the higher-priced stocks enjoy.

Although the value of the stock does not need to be assessed until the stock is sold, it's a good idea to recalculate it after the split and keep a record of it. The capital gain or loss that is triggered when the stock is sold can be long-term or short-term, depending on the amount of time that has passed since the original stock purchase before the split. More detail on the tax consequences of selling stock and other assets will be presented in the accounting chapters.

SELF-CHECK

- Define **stock option.**
- List three criticisms of stock option plans that lead to increased regulations.
- Define **restricted stock** and explain how it differs from stock options.
- Explain what a stock split is.
- Define **reverse split** and discuss why a company might do one.

13.9 Dividend Reinvestment Plans

Dividend reinvestment plans offer the investor with limited funds a way to buy stocks in small amounts over time. They allow the brokers and agents that run these plans to use the dividends on stockholders' stocks to purchase more stock.

These plans are not usually for investors who want to accumulate stocks quickly, as the key words with these plans are *patience* and *perseverance*. However, a reinvestment plan can work for any size investor. Over the long run, the reinvestment plan should garner more income for the investor than a regular savings account when interest rates on savings are on the low side. Investors can also add cash contributions to the plans, enabling them to buy more stocks at a faster rate.

Another advantage to these plans is that some companies offer discounts on the stock purchases, providing the investor with an instant return. Be aware, however, that the discounted stock purchases may only apply to purchases made with the dividends realized from the stocks currently held.

FOR EXAMPLE

Dividend Reinvestment Plans

The dividends do not have to equal the price of a share of stock to be reinvested. For example, a company may post dividends of $2.00 when a share of stock is $40.00. A dividend reinvestment plan will automatically reinvest the $2.00 for an additional 1/20th of a share of stock.

SELF-CHECK

- Explain what a dividend reinvestment plan is.
- Describe the kind of investor who might be interested in dividend reinvestment plans.

SUMMARY

As a financial manager, you want to make your company attractive to investors. As an investor, you need to understand how income from stocks is generated. This chapter helped you accomplish both goals. You analyzed how stock changes affect the market. You determined the factors that affect corporation profits. And you learned investment strategies that will serve you well.

KEY TERMS

52 WEEKS HI and LO	Present the high and low stock prices for the previous 52 weeks.
Capital gains	Are realized only when the stock is sold.
Capital losses	Are realized if the sale price of the stock is lower than the purchase price.
CLOSE	Indicates the stock's current price.
Constant growth stocks	Stocks from corporations that are stable and profitable.
DIV	Lists the 12-month dividend paid by the firm.
Dividend reinvestment plans	Allow the brokers and agents that run these plans to use the dividends on stockholders' stocks to purchase more stock.
Dividends	Payments that represent the owner's portion of the corporation's stock. They may be paid monthly, quarterly, or annually, or in some cases not at all, depending on the profits earned by the issuing corporation.
Exchange rates	An adjustment in exchange rates over time leads to higher or lower U.S. dollar cash flows from overseas sales, more competitively priced import goods, or changing input costs.
Health of foreign economies	Growth in foreign economies will increase the demand for U.S. exports. Similarly, sluggish foreign demand will harm overseas sales and hurt the financial position of firms doing business overseas.
NET CHG	Gives the change in price from the previous day's close.
PE	Gives the price/earnings ratio of the stock. This value is computed by dividing the firm's latest annual earnings per share into its current stock price.
Rate of return	The percentage of profit earned from an investment.
Restricted stock	Given to employees but they cannot sell the shares until it vests.
Reverse split	Reduces the number of shares each stockholder owns.

Spinoff	Where the parent sells the subsidiary to another firm or in a public offering and the new owners truly do own the firm.
Stock option	Allows the purchase at a future time a stated number of the firm's shares at a specific price.
Stock quotes	Appear in major newspapers or Web sites and provide a summary of the stock's performance.
Stock split	Occurs when a publicly held corporation decides to make a change in the number of outstanding shares issued to stockholders.
SYM	Gives the trading symbol, or ticker, an abbreviation of three letters or less that identifies reports of all transactions in the stock on the stock market for the day.
Tracking stock	Issued by the parent company to track a subsidiary rather than the entire firm.
VOL (000s)	Tells how many shares of the company's stock were traded, in hundreds.
YLD %	Gives the dividend yield of the stock.
YTD % CHG	Shows the year-to-date change in price for a stock.

ASSESS YOUR UNDERSTANDING

Go to www.wiley.com/college/Melicher to evaluate your knowledge of the basics of stock growth and change.
Measure your learning by comparing pre-test and post-test results.

Summary Questions

1. Dividends are not treated as regular income by the IRS. True or false?
2. A capital loss results when the sale price of the stock is higher than the purchase price. True or false?
3. For common stock, the value of all future dividends should equal
   (a) the stock's current price.
   (b) the stock's initial offering price.
   (c) the current dividend times the age of the stock.
   (d) none of the above.
4. For a common stock owned by a corporation that currently pays no dividends and has no plans to pay dividends, the value of the stock is
   (a) zero.
   (b) worth the per-share liquidation value of its assets.
   (c) worth the value of all future dividends.
   (d) none of the above.
5. To finance rapid growth, young firms often pay a large percentage of their profit in dividends. True or false?
6. When evaluating the stability of a corporation's dividends, you should
   (a) review the company's financial statements.
   (b) attend board meetings.
   (c) review the corporation's dividend policy.
   (d) All of the above
7. If you are investing in stocks with the hope of receiving increasing dividends over time, then you should invest in
   (a) preferred stocks.
   (b) cumulative preferred stocks.
   (c) constant growth stocks.
   (d) none of the above.
8. Constant growth stocks are stocks from young, rapidly growing corporations. True or false?
9. The dollar return on a stock is the total of all received dividends on the stock, minus the capital gain. True or false?

10. In a stock quote, the YTD % CHG column shows the
    (a) dividend yield of the stock.
    (b) year-to-date change in price for the stock.
    (c) stock's current price.
    (d) price/earnings ratio of the stock.

11. A typical stock quote lists the high and low price for the previous year. True or false?

12. In a stock quote, which column indicates the stock's current price?
    (a) PRICE
    (b) $
    (c) CLOSE
    (d) YLD %

13. A spinoff stock is issued by the parent company to track a subsidiary rather than the entire firm. True or false?

14. Unlike common stock, tracking shares
    (a) have no ownership claim on the subsidiary.
    (b) do not pay dividends.
    (c) have ownership claim on the parent company.
    (d) None of the above

15. In general, research has shown that the performance of tracking stocks has exceeded that of parent company stocks. True of false?

16. A company's profits are determined by sales revenues, expenses, and taxes. True or false?

17. When evaluating a corporation's profit-making ability, you should consider
    (a) the firm's position in the competitive marketplace.
    (b) the health of U.S. and foreign economies.
    (c) changes in the cost of raw materials, labor, and energy.
    (d) all of the above.

18. A stock option allows managers to purchase, at a future time, an unlimited number of the firm's shares at a specific price. True or false?

19. Severe criticism of stock option plans has led the SEC to ban them. True or false?

20. Stock options can become worthless if the stock price does not rise sufficiently. True or false?

21. An employee must be vested for a certain period of time before they can sell their restricted stock. True or false?

22. Unlike stock options, restricted shares will retain some value as long as the firm doesn't go bankrupt. True or false?

23. A stock split occurs when a publicly held corporation splits itself into two new companies. True or false?

24. Stock splits
    (a) can either decrease or increase the number of shares.
    (b) do not change the overall value of the stock.
    (c) All of the above
    (d) None of the above

25. Dividend reinvestment plans are ideal for the
    (a) investor with limited funds to buy stocks in small amounts over time.
    (b) small investor who wants to accumulate stocks quickly.
    (c) investor who wants to reinvest their dividends in other company's stocks.
    (d) None of the above

Review Questions

1. If you buy a stock for $13 per share and you sell it 2 years later for $20 dollars per share, what type of loss or gain do you have and in what amount?
    (a) Capital loss of $7 per share
    (b) Dividend payment of $7 per share per year
    (c) Capital gain of $7 per share
    (d) Tax deduction of $7 per share

2. If a 10-year-old stock is currently selling for $120, what is the estimated value of all future dividends?
    (a) $12
    (b) $1,200
    (c) $120
    (d) None of the above

3. An investor can expect a firm's dividends to remain constant and possibly grow in the future if which conditions apply?
    (a) Profits have risen steadily
    (b) New products have been added and introduced to the public
    (c) Liabilities have been reduced
    (d) Expenses are being monitored and controlled
    (e) All of the above

4. Assume the growth rate of a company's stock is 10% and the company is retaining 5% of those profits and paying shareholders an additional 5% per year in dividends. The current dividend per share is $20. At the end of 3 years, by how much is the dividend expected to increase?

   (a) $23.15

   (b) $3.15

   (c) $3

   (d) None of the above

5. Briefly explain why even the most complicated of calculations cannot guarantee total accuracy in valuing any stock.

6. The stock that you bought for $10 is currently worth $45, and you have received $5 in total dividends. If you were to sell the stock today, what would be the percentage of return?

   (a) 50%

   (b) 40%

   (c) 28%

   (d) 25%

7. Interpret each column of the following stock price quote. In addition, what is Sizzler's approximate earnings per share? What was the stock's closing price the previous day?

YTD % CHG	52 weeks Hi	Lo	Stock	Sym	Div	YLD %	PE	VOL 100s	Last	Net CHG
+17.3	7.13	5.00	Sizzlr	SZ	16	2.7	25	844	6	0.25

8. Suppose McDonald's created a new subsidiary named Little Fry and issued tracking stocks for the new subsidiary. The pretracking stock value of McDonald's stock was $35 per share. The value of the parent company's stock after issuing the tracking stock falls to $25. What is the approximate value of the new tracking stock?

   (a) $35

   (b) $25

   (c) $60

   (d) $10

9. Is industry competition good or bad if you are looking for attractive stock investments?

10. Briefly explain how an upper-level manager might manipulate a stock's price to inappropriately make money on stock options.

11. Briefly explain how an employee can earn money on restricted stock without even cashing it in.

12. If you are a stockholder and own 30 shares of IBM stock, you will own ____ after a two-for-one split. Assume one share of stock was worth $20 before the split, so the split makes each share now worth ____.
    (a) 60, $10
    (b) 15, $40
    (c) 45, $30
    (d) 30, $20

13. Explain why a dividend reinvestment program is beneficial to investors with limited income.

Applying This Chapter

1. You want to invest in stocks that won't increase your annual tax burden until you sell them. What kind of stocks should you consider, and why?

2. A stock's price is generally considered to be the present value of all future dividends. However, your investment strategy involves selling stocks within a few days of buying them. How do you calculate the value of such stocks?

3. Give examples of firms you believe have been successful over time because they are industry leaders in quality, they are the low-cost producer, they are innovative, and they offer superior customer service.

4. There are a number of calculations that can be done to estimate future dividends for a stock that is considered to be a constant growth stock. Go to www.investopedia.com and use their online calculator to determine the growth rate of your favorite stock.

5. Using a current stock price quote, determine how much in dividend payments you would have received over the past year if you owned 100 shares of Coca-Cola stock. If you sold the stocks today, how much would you get for those stocks?

6. If you own shares of Company A and the firm creates a new subsidiary, Company A1, for which it issues tracking stocks, do you retain ownership rights or do those go to the owners of the tracking stock?

7. Energy prices are forecast to go higher. How would this affect your decision to purchase the stocks of (a) ExxonMobil, (b) American Airlines, (c) Ford, (d) Archer Daniels Midland, a food processor?

8. You are given an option to purchase 100 shares of your company's stock at $10 a share. Currently, your company's stock is selling for $8 a share. Is now a good time to take advantage of this option? Why or why not?

9. Discuss some ways managers with stock options can make self-serving decisions. Explain how restricted stocks can eliminate those problems.

10. If a stock split does not change the overall value of a stock, why do firms split stocks?

Reporting Dividends

Review Schedule A of the 1040 individual tax return to see the instructions given for reporting dividends on a personal tax return.

Stock Quotes

Review for yourself the 52-week ranges of different stocks from a current issue of the *Wall Street Journal.*

Stock prices are quoted in dollars and cents, so 42.75 represents $42.75 per share.

Incentive Programs

Assume you are a manager and have a choice between a stock option program or a restricted stock program. Which would you prefer, and why?

14

ANNUITIES, BONDS, FUTURES, AND OPTIONS
Other Financial Investments

Starting Point

Go to www.wiley.com/college/Melicher to assess your knowledge of the basics of other types of financial investments.
Determine where you need to concentrate your effort.

What You'll Learn in This Chapter

▲ The role of annuities and bonds in the financial environment
▲ The different categories of bonds and their investment risks
▲ Bond investment strategies
▲ How bonds work in the global marketplace
▲ The role of futures and options in the financial environment

After Studying This Chapter, You'll Be Able To

▲ Analyze the long-term benefits of an annuity
▲ Appraise a bond's coupon, par value, and maturity date
▲ Compare straight, convertible, callable, putable, and extendable bonds
▲ Examine the financial risks of holding bonds, including the seesaw effect
▲ Compare and contrast the fixed and variable annuities
▲ Interpret bond ratings

Goals and Outcomes

▲ Assess why bond returns are lower than stock returns on average
▲ Assess how asset securitization works
▲ Choose bond investments with the lowest amount of risk and the highest returns
▲ Assess the pros and cons of investing in annuities
▲ Assess the ladder strategy of investing in bonds
▲ Design a portfolio that includes annuities, bonds, futures, and options
▲ Assess when a firm would purchase mortgage bonds and equipment trust certificates

INTRODUCTION

The financial investments presented in this chapter may have familiar names. They may already be a part of your personal financial plan or your retirement plan. Compared to trading stocks, these investments can provide a safer way to build a good financial base. However, that doesn't mean they are risk-free, so it is important to understand what they are and how they can help investors and consumers accumulate more money.

14.1 Annuities

Annuities are financial contracts with insurance companies that have a series of equal payments that occur over a number of time periods. There are two types of annuities: fixed and variable. Both of these categories have options built in that must be considered before deciding if this investment will be advantageous.

▲ **Fixed annuities** earn a guaranteed rate of interest for a specified time period.

The time period is set for 1 year or more. When the time period expires, it can be renewed, but the interest rate may change. The big difference between a certificate of deposit and an annuity is that funds in an annuity are not insured by the Federal Deposit Insurance Corporation but are secured by the financial position of the insurance company where it was purchased.

▲ **Variable annuities** offer a variety of funding options, such as stocks, bonds, and money market accounts.

However, the return on a variable annuity is not guaranteed because it relies on the performance of the underlying investments. Some variable annuities guarantee the principle and interest.

Annuities can be purchased in one of two ways:

▲ A **single-payment annuity** involves one lump sum payment with no provision for funds to be added at a later date.
▲ A **flexible-payment annuity** is one in which contributions can be made anytime for any amounts.

Deferred annuities are available for those who wish to use this financial tool to accumulate retirement funds. Like an individual retirement account (IRA), you can deposit funds into the annuity and the tax on the income it earns is postponed until you withdraw the money. It is believed that when a person hits

---

FOR EXAMPLE

Charitable Contribution

Money donated to a church organization was invested in an annuity with no payment structure and kept there for several years earning a modest amount of income. However, withdrawing funds from this annuity took several days and was subject to fees. The church group finally decided that it would be easier to use the funds to open a savings account where the money would be immediately accessible when needed.

---

retirement age, he/she will be in a lower tax bracket, minimizing the tax liability on the withdrawn funds.

With an **immediate annuity**, income payments are steady and dependable. It can be set up for any time period and provide a lifetime of income if you so desire. The income is based on the amount of your contribution, the interest rate, and your age. When selecting the amount of your income payments, you should take economic conditions such as inflation into account.

The annuity can be set up for you personally or for someone else you wish to name as a beneficiary. On lifetime annuities, you can modify the terms to suit your needs and those of your heirs.

SELF-CHECK

- Define **annuities** and explain the difference between single-payment and flexible-payment annuities.
- Define **fixed annuities** and compare them to certificates of deposit; explain the primary difference.
- Briefly explain the purpose of deferred-payment annuities.

14.2 Bonds

Long-term funds are obtained by issuing corporate stocks, but most of the annual funds raised by corporations come from corporate bond sales. In fact, corporate bonds accounted for approximately 88% of total new security issues from 1997 to 2002. A **bond** is a debt agreement that a corporation or government agency issues when it wants to borrow money for more than 10 years. The issuer agrees to pay back the lender at a specified maturity date, with interest.

Firms issue more bonds than stocks for two basic reasons. First, it is cheaper to borrow than to raise equity financing. Second, bonds and other loans have a maturity date; when they expire or come due, new bonds can be issued and sold to repay maturing ones. Securities, on the other hand, never mature. Firms can only repurchase their outstanding stock, or the shares of one firm may be merged or acquired by another firm.

Holders of debt capital have certain rights and privileges not extended to those holding common shares of the corporation's stock. A debt holder may force the firm to abide by the terms of the debt contract even if the result is reorganization or bankruptcy of the firm. The periodic interest payments due the holders of debt securities must be paid or else the creditors can force the firm into bankruptcy. Table 14-1 summarizes the important characteristics of bonds.

As noted in Table 14-1, most bonds are issued with a maturity date. The **maturity date** is the date when the issuer is obligated to pay the bond's principal (par value or face value) to bondholders.

In the United States, par value is usually $1,000 for corporate bonds. All but zero-coupon bonds issue pay interest. This interest is called *coupon payments*. If a bond has an 8% coupon and a par value of $1,000, it pays annual interest

Table 14-1: Common Elements of Bonds

Represent borrowed funds
Contractual agreement between a borrower and lender (indenture)
Senior claim on assets and cash flow
No voting rights
Par value
Having a bond rating improves the issue's marketability to investors
Covenants
Interest: Tax-deductible to the issuing firm
Usually fixed over the issue's life but can be variable as the indenture
Allows coupon rate on new issues affected by market interest rates and bond rating
Maturity: Usually fixed, can be affected by convertibility, call and put provisions, sinking fund, extendibility features in the indenture
Security: Can have senior claim on specific assets pledged in case of default or can be unsecured (debenture or subordinated [junior claim] debenture)

of $80. The par value is the same as the face value. A bond with a 10% coupon would pay interest of $100 per year.

Eurobonds, bonds issued in Europe, pay a single annual coupon interest payment. In the United States, bonds pay interest semiannually; an 8% coupon will pay interest of $40 every 6 months during the life of the bond.

Since bondholders have the legal status of creditors, they have priority claims on the firm's cash flows and assets. This means that bondholders must receive their interest payments before the firm's stockholders receive their dividends. In case of bankruptcy, the debt holders must receive the funds owed to them before funds are distributed to the company's owners. Because of this first claim on a firm's cash flow and assets, a bond is a safer investment than an equity holding of stock. However, as discussed in Section 2.7.1, the trade-off for less risk is a lower amount of return on the investment.

The interest payments creditors receive are usually considerably less over a period of years than the returns received by shareholders. Also, as long as the corporation meets its contractual obligations, the creditors have little influence over its management and control.

Long-term corporate bond or debt securities fall into two categories:

▲ **Secured obligations:** Loans backed by collateral.
▲ **Unsecured obligations:** Loan that is a claim against a borrower's assets.

A single firm can have many types of debt contracts outstanding. Although ownership of many shares of stock may be covered by a single stock certificate, the bondholder has a separate agreement for each bond owned.

Bonds can be either registered or bearer bonds.

▲ **Registered bonds** include the bondholders' names, and interest payments are sent directly to the bondholders.
▲ **Bearer bonds** have coupons that are literally "clipped" from the side of the bond certificate and presented, like a check, to a bank for payment. With a bearer bond, the issuer does not know who is receiving the interest payments.

Regulations in the United States prevent the issuing of bearer bonds because of the possibility that investors may evade income taxes on the clipped coupons. However, bearer bonds are still common in foreign markets. A **perpetuity** is a bond without a maturity date. Its owners and heirs receive interest payments for as long as the company exists.

Following registration with the Securities Exchange Commission, bonds can be sold in the public market and traded by investors. There is also a private market where bonds can be sold in a private placement to qualified investors, typically institutional investors, such as insurance companies and wealthy individuals.

The U.S. Treasury has a Treasury Direct program to sell treasury securities to individual investors, but the main holders of treasury bonds are large institutions. Pension funds and insurance companies hold bonds for investment purposes while investment banks often purchase bonds and then resell them to smaller investors. Corporate bond sales are mainly intended for the large institutional investor who can purchase millions of dollars of bonds at a time. However, in recent years, innovative firms like IBM, UPS, Caterpillar, and GE Capital initiated programs to sell $1,000 par value bonds directly to the individual investor. These bonds are called *SmartNotes, medium-term notes,* or *direct-access notes.* These sale programs target small investors who have thousands rather than millions to invest in bonds.

14.2.1 Bond Covenants

Bond covenants are rules or regulations. They are often included in trust indentures. A bond covenant imposes restrictions of the firm. The **trust indenture** is an extensive document and includes in great detail the various provisions and covenants of the loan arrangement. A trustee represents the bondholders to ensure the bond issuer abides by the indenture's provisions. In essence, the agreement is a contract between the bondholders and the issuing firm. The indenture details the par value of the issue, its maturity date, and coupon rate. A bond indenture may also include covenants. Bond covenants impose restrictions or extra duties on the firm.

Covenants can include stipulations that the firm must maintain a minimum level of net working capital, keep pledged assets in good working order, and send audited financial statements to bondholders. Others include restrictions on the amount of the firm's debt, its dividend payments, the amount and type of additional covenants it may undertake, and asset sales. All of these are designed to protect the bondholder's investment in the company.

Bonds have value, first, because of the corporation's ability to pay coupon interest and, second, because of the value of the assets or collateral backing the bonds in case of default. Without proper covenant protection, the value of a bond can decline sharply if a firm's liquidity and assets depreciate or if its debt begins to exceed its equity. Some provisions affect the firm's financing costs, since bonds giving greater protection to the investor can be sold with lower coupon rates. The issuing corporation must decide if the restrictions and duties in the covenants are worth the access to lower-cost funds.

The covenants are important to bondholders. Holders of RJR-Nabisco bonds owned high-quality, A-rated bonds prior to the firm's takeover in 1988 by a leveraged buyout. After the buyout, large quantities of new debt were assumed.

FOR EXAMPLE

Special Covenant

Some bonds allow the investor to force the firm to redeem them if the credit rating falls below a certain level; others, such as Deutsche Telekom's $14.5 billion issue in 2000, increase the coupon rate (in this case by 50 basis points or 0.50 percentage points) if the bond rating falls below an "A" rating. We discuss bond ratings in the next section.

RJR-Nabisco's original bonds were given a lower rating and fell by 17% in value. Lawsuits by disgruntled bondholders against the takeover were unsuccessful. The courts decided that the bondholders should have sought protection against such increases in the firm's debt load by seeking appropriate covenant language before investing, rather than running to the courts after the fact to correct their mistake. Covenants are the best way for bondholders to protect themselves against suspicious management actions or decisions.

14.2.2 Bond Ratings

Most bond issuers purchase bond ratings from one or more agencies such as Standard & Poor's (S & P), Moody's, or Fitch. **Bond ratings** assess both the collateral underlying the bonds as well as the ability of the issuer to make timely payments of interest and principal. Examples of bond rating categories are listed in Figure 14-1.

For a one-time fee of approximately $25,000, the rater examines the credit quality of the firm, the indenture provisions, covenants, and the expected trends of firm and industry operations. From its analysis and discussions with management, the agency assigns a bond rating that indicates the likelihood of default on the bond issue. The rating agency also agrees to reexamine the bond's risks on a continuing basis. For example, should the financial position of the firm weaken or strengthen, S & P may place the issue on its Credit Watch list. Shortly thereafter, S & P will either downgrade, upgrade, or reaffirm the original rating.

Despite the initial cost and the issuer's concern of a lower-than-expected rating, a bond rating makes it much easier to sell the bonds to the public. The rating acts as a signal to the market that an independent agency has examined the qualities of the issuer and the bond itself and has determined that the credit risk of the bond justifies the published rating.

A bond that is not rated is likely to find a cool reception from investors. This is because investors tend to think the issuing company is trying to hide something that would result in a lower rating. Certain types of investors, such as pension funds and insurance companies, have restrictions that prohibit them from purchasing unrated bonds.

Figure 14-1

MOODY'S	STANDARD & POORS	FITCH	
Aaa	AAA	AAA	Best quality, least credit risk
Aa1	AA+	AA+	High quality, slightly more risk than a top-rated bond
Aa2	AA	AA	
Aa3	AA−	AA−	
A1	A+	A+	Upper-medium grade, possible future credit quality difficulties
A2	A	A	
A3	A−	A−	
Baa1	BBB+	BBB+	Medium-quality bonds
Baa2	BBB	BBB	
Baa3	BBB−		
Ba1	BB+	BB+	Speculative issues, greater credit risk
Ba2	BB	BB	
Ba3	BB−	BB	
B1	B+	B+	Very speculative, likelihood of future default
B2	B	B	
B3	B−	B−	
Caa	CCC	CCC	Highly speculative, either in default or high likelihood of going into default
Ca	CC	CC	
C	C	C	
	D	DDD	
		DD	
		D	

Examples of bond-rating categories.

14.3 Bondholder Security

A bond's security or collateral provisions also affect its rating. Bonds with junior or unsecured claims (claims without the backing of collateral) receive lower bond ratings, leading investors to demand higher yields to compensate for the higher risk. It is possible for bond issues of a single firm to have different bond ratings if their security provisions differ.

In addition to its traditional credit quality ratings, Standard & Poor's has also instituted "r" ratings. An *r* attached to an issue's credit-quality rating (such as AAAr or AAr) signifies that the price instability of the issue is expected to be especially high. This happens when bonds have special provisions that make their prices especially sensitive to interest rate, commodity, or exchange rate trends.

To examine bondholder security, let's first look at the type of bond that relates to home mortgages, which is something you are probably familiar with. **Mortgage bonds,** despite their name, are not secured by home mortgages. Rather, they are secured by specific property pledged by the firm. As a rule, the mortgage applies only to real estate, buildings, and other assets classified as real property. For a corporation that issues bonds to expand its plant facilities, the mortgage usually includes only a legal claim on the facilities to be constructed.

When a parcel of real estate has more than one mortgage lien against it, the first mortgage filed and recorded at the appropriate government office has priority. Any other bonds subsequently recorded are known by the order in which they are filed, such as second or third mortgage bonds. Because first mortgage bonds have priority with respect to asset distribution if the business fails, they generally provide a lower yield to investors than the later liens. An **equipment trust certificate** is a type of mortgage bond that gives the bondholder a claim to specific "rolling stock" (movable assets) such as railroad cars or airplanes.

The serial numbers of the items of rolling stock are listed in the bond indenture, and the collateral is periodically examined by the trustee to ensure its proper maintenance and repair.

There are two basic types of mortgage bonds:

▲ A **closed-end mortgage bond** does not permit future bond issues to be secured by any of the assets pledged as security under the closed-end issue.

▲ An **open-end mortgage bond** is one that allows the same assets to be used as security in future bond issues.

As a rule, open-end mortgages usually stipulate that any additional real property acquired by the company automatically becomes a part of the property secured under the mortgage. This provides added protection to the lender.

▲ **Debenture bonds** are unsecured obligations and depend on the general credit strength of the corporation for their security.

They represent no pledge of property; their holders are classed as general creditors of the corporation equal with the holders of promissory notes and trade creditors. Debenture bonds are used by governmental bodies and by many industrial and utility corporations.

The riskiest type of bond is a subordinated debenture.

▲ **Subordinated debentures,** as the name implies, means that the claims of these bondholders are subordinate to the claims of debenture holders.

Most bonds with low bond ratings, sometimes called *junk bonds* or *high-yield bonds*, are subordinated debentures.

Another bond market innovation is "asset securitization." **Asset securitization** refers to bonds that have coupon and principal payments that are paid from another existing cash flow source. Suppose a mortgage lender with a number of previously issued mortgages has a steady cash flow stream coming from those loans. By selling bonds that use that cash flow source as collateral, the mortgage banker can receive funds today rather than waiting for the mortgages to be paid off over time. Principal and interest on the newly issued bonds will be paid by homeowners' mortgage payments. Essentially, the mortgage payments will "pass through" the original mortgage lender to the investor who purchased the mortgage-backed securities. Not all the interest payments are passed on, however, as the mortgage lender charges a servicing fee for collecting the mortgage payments and distributing them to the bondholders.

Securitization allows the original lender to reduce its risk exposure, as any homeowner defaults are now a risk borne by the new investor. In addition, this makes it possible for the lender to receive new funds, which then form the basis for new loans and new issues of mortgage-backed securities.

FOR EXAMPLE

Securitization

Music artists who collect royalties from past recordings have taken advantage of securitization. In 1997, British rock star David Bowie initiated this trend by offering a $55 million bond deal in which royalty rights from his past recordings were pooled and sold to investors. Interest on the bonds is paid by the royalty cash flow generated by record, compact disk, tape sales, and radio air playtime.

Many other cash flow sources are open to securitization. Payments flowing in from credit card receivables and auto loans have been packaged as bonds and sold to investors. The cash flow source used for securitization doesn't necessarily have to be debt-related.

Other variations include offering bonds backed by pools of insurance contracts. Interest on such bonds is paid from the policy premiums of the contract holders. Many times, however, these bonds have provisions for future payoffs that could be affected by the catastrophic claims from natural disasters like hurricanes and earthquakes.

SELF-CHECK

- Explain what a bond rating is and why junior or unsecured bonds typically offer higher yields.
- Indicate what secures mortgage bonds, equipment trust certificates, and debenture bonds.
- Distinguish between a closed-ended and open-ended mortgage bond.
- Explain what subordinated debenture bonds are and give two other names for them.

14.4 Other Types of Bonds

U.S firms routinely issue bonds with 10- to 30-year maturities, while the European market rarely extends a bond's maturity longer than 10 years. However, as European firms are starting to access the capital markets more and rely on bank debt less for their longer-term financing needs, the terms of their bonds may become more in line with the U.S. bond terms.

14.4.1 Straight and Convertible Bonds

Two types of bonds are straight and convertible bonds.

▲ A **straight bond** is issued with a preset maturity date. That is the date the final interest payment is made and the bond's par value is paid to investors, but a number of provisions can be built into a bond that affect its final maturity.

▲ A **convertible bond** can be changed, or converted, at the investor's option, into a specified number of shares of the issuer's common stock.

The convertible bond has a built-in conversion ratio that is usually set to make conversion unattractive. If the firm meets with success, however, its stock price will rise and the bond's price will be affected by its conversion value (the stock price times the conversion ratio) rather than just its value as a straight bond.

Assume that a firm has just issued a $1,000 par value convertible bond. Its conversion ratio is 30, and the stock currently sells for $25 a share. The conversion value of the bond is 30 × $25/share or $750. This is substantially lower than the issue value of the bond, so it makes sense to keep the bond as is. Should the stock's price rise to $40, the bond's conversion value will be 30 × $40/share or $1,200. At this point, the investor may decide to use the conversion feature to increase the value of his/her investment. Some corporations offer convertible bonds as a way to attract investors during time when the stock market is in a slump. Convertible bonds provide an opportunity for the company to raise funds immediately instead of waiting for the stock market to recover.

14.4.2 Callable Bonds

The issuing corporation can redeem **callable bonds** prior to maturity, if a decline in interest rates makes it attractive for the firm to issue lower-coupon debt to replace high-coupon debt. A firm with cash from successful marketing efforts or a recent stock issue also may decide to retire its callable debt. Most callable bonds carry a provision that requires the investor to be paid the par value of the bond plus a call premium of 1 year's interest. Thus, to call a 12% coupon, $1,000 par value bond, an issuer must pay the bondholder $1,120. Despite receiving the call price and the premium, investors are not pleased when their bonds are called away because the call usually comes after a substantial decline in interest rates.

The call eliminates their high coupon payments and makes it necessary to reinvest the call proceeds in bonds that have lower interest rates and consequently offer lower yields.

In order to attract investors to callable bonds, they must initially offer higher coupons or yields than noncallable bonds of similar credit quality and maturity. Many indentures specify a call deferment period immediately after the bond issue during which the bonds cannot be called.

14.4.3 Putable Bonds

Putable bonds (sometimes called *retractable bonds*) allow investors to force the issuer to redeem them prior to maturity. Indenture terms differ as to the circumstances when an investor can "put" the bond to the issuer prior to the maturity date and receive its par value. Some bond issues can be put only on certain dates. Some can be put to the issuer in case of a bond rating downgrade. The put option allows the investor to receive the full face value of the bond, plus accrued interest. Since this protection is valuable, investors pay for it in the form of a lower coupon rate.

14.4.4 Extendable Bonds

Extendable notes have their coupons reset every 2 or 3 years to reflect the current interest rate and any changes in the firm's credit quality. At each reset, the investor may accept the new coupon rate (and thus effectively extend the maturity of the investment) or put the bonds back to the firm. An indenture may require the firm to retire the bond issue over time through payments to a sinking fund. A **sinking fund** requires the issuer to retire specified portions of the bond issue over time.

This provides for an orderly and steady retirement of debt over time instead of paying the entire amount at maturity. Sinking funds are more common in bonds issued by firms with lower credit ratings. A higher-quality issuer may have only a small annual sinking fund obligation due to a perceived ability to repay investor's principal at maturity.

14.4.5 Inflation-Adjusted Bonds

Although most bonds pay a fixed coupon rate, some bonds have coupon payments that vary over time. **Inflation-adjusted bonds** are bonds where the principal value of the bond is adjusted every 6 months to keep pace with the consumer price index. The bond's coupon rate is then applied to the new principal value.

The bond's indenture may tie coupon payments to an underlying market interest rate so that the interest payment will always be a certain level above or will be a specified percentage of a market interest rate, such as the 10-year treasury note rate.

SELF-CHECK

- Briefly describe each of the following types of bonds: straight, convertible, callable, putable, and extendable.
- Explain what a sinking fund is and when it is used.
- What are the different maturity time periods for U.S. and European bonds?

14.5 Bond Income and Strategies

A typical bond will pay a fixed amount of interest each year over the bond's life. U.S. bonds pay interest semiannually, whereas Eurobonds pay interest annually. One of the risks associated with bonds is called the *seesaw effect*. The **seesaw effect** means that lower interest rates cause bond prices to rise, and higher interest rates result in lower bond prices (see Figure 14-2).

This means the yield curve shifts up and down over time and sometimes it twists. The twist is caused when short-term rates rise while long-term rates are stable or falling, or when long-term rates rise while short-term rates are stable or falling. To avoid having their holdings hit by sudden fluctuations in interest rates, some investors employ a ladder strategy. A **ladder strategy** invests an equal amount of money in bonds with a wide range of long and short-term maturities, so interest rate cycles will average out.

In times of declining interest rates, bonds may be sold at a discount and are called **discount bonds.** This gives the investor an opportunity to offset the bond's lower income potential with up-front savings, and at maturity the investor will receive the face value of the bond. On the other hand, when interest rates are higher, bonds may be sold at a price higher than their par value. These bonds are called **premium bonds** because the investor is paying a higher price up front but should make it up with the higher yield of the bond. Zero coupon bonds pay no interest over the life of the bond. The investor buys the bond at a deep discount from its par value; the return to the investor over time is the difference between the purchase price and the bond's par value plus interest when it matures. A drawback to these investors is that the IRS assumes interest is paid over the life of the bond so the investor must pay tax on interest he or she doesn't receive. Because of these tax implications, zero coupon bonds are best suited for tax-exempt investment accounts such as IRAs or tax-exempt investment organizations such as pension funds.

A large risk faced by bond investors is an unexpected change in inflation. An unexpected increase in inflation can cause lower returns to an investor as the bond's fixed interest rate does not adjust to varying inflation. In 1997, the

Figure 14-2

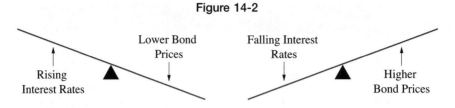

Relationship between current interest rates and bond prices: the seesaw effect.

U.S. Treasury offered an innovation to investors in U.S. debt: inflation-protected treasury notes. Issued in $1,000 minimum denominations, the principal value of the notes changed in accordance with changes in the consumer price index (CPI). **Treasury inflation protected securities (TIPS)** work as follows: Interest payments are computed based upon the inflation-adjusted principal value. In times of rising consumer prices, both the principal value and interest payments rise along with inflation. Should the CPI fall, the principal amount is reduced accordingly.

A drawback to this method of adjusting to inflation is once again the way IRS views it. Although the principal is not paid until the note matures, the IRS considers the year-by-year change in principal as taxable income in the year in which the change in value is made. Like the zero coupon bonds, TIPS work well for tax-exempt organizations.

In 1998, to make the inflation protection more affordable to smaller investors, the U.S. Treasury announced plans to offer inflation-protected U.S. savings bonds. In addition, several corporations, such as Merrill Lynch, Morgan Stanley, Household International, Fannie Mae, and Sallie May, have issued inflation-protected bonds. Some banks have followed suit by offering inflation-protected certificates of deposit.

All the many variations in bonds are designed to meet the needs of different types of investors. Some bond issuers reduce borrowing costs by offering lenders better collateral; others want to maintain flexibility (or they have no collateral to offer), so they issue debentures and pay higher interest rates.

FOR EXAMPLE

Inflation–Protected Bond

Assume an inflation-indexed note with a $1,000 par value is sold at a 3% interest rate. If inflation over the next year is 4%, the principal value rises to $1,000 plus 4%, or $1,040. The annual interest payment will be 3% of $1,040, or $31.20. With 4% inflation, the principal rises by 4% ($1,000 to $1,040) as well as the interest ($30 to $31.20).

SELF-CHECK

- Describe the seesaw effect as it relates to bonds.
- Explain the ladder strategy of investing in bonds.
- Distinguish between premium bonds and discount bonds.
- Describe how treasury inflation protected securities protect investors against unexpected increases in inflation.

14.6 Global Bond Market

Increasingly, the international bond market is ignoring national boundaries. A growing number of debt issues are being sold globally. In 1989, the World Bank was the first issuer of global bonds. **Global bonds** are bonds that are usually denominated in U.S. dollars and marketed globally.

As they are marketed globally, their offering sizes typically exceed $1 billion. In addition to the World Bank, issuers include the governments of Finland and Italy and corporations such as Deutsche Telekom ($14.5 billion raised), Ford Motor Credit ($8.6 billion), Tecnost International Finance ($8.3 billion), AT&T ($8 billion), WorldCom ($6.1 billion), and Wal-Mart ($5.8 billion).

Many U.S. corporations have issued Eurodollar bonds. **Eurodollar bonds** are dollar-denominated bonds that are sold outside the United States. Because of this, they escape review by the SEC, somewhat reducing the expense of issuing the bonds. Eurodollar bonds usually have fixed coupons with annual coupon payments. Most mature in 5 to 10 years, so they are not normally used by firms that want to issue long-term debt.

Most Eurodollar bonds are debentures. This is not a major concern to investors, as only the largest, financially strongest firms have access to the Eurobond market. Investors do care that the bonds are sold in bearer form, because investors can remain anonymous and evade taxes on coupon income. Some researchers believe that this is the main reason that Eurodollar bond interest rates are low relative to U.S. rates.

U.S. firms aren't the only issuers of securities outside their national borders. Foreign firms can issue securities in the United States if they follow U.S. security registration procedures. **Yankee bonds** are U.S. dollar-denominated bonds that are issued in the United States by a foreign issuer.

Japanese firms often find it necessary to issue bonds outside their national borders. This is another type of Yankee bond. Regulations and a requirement for mandatory bank guarantees on publicly traded debt in Japan limit the market for Japanese domestic debt issues to only the largest blue-chip firms. While Eurodollar bonds typically mature in 5 to 10 years, Yankees may have maturities as long as 30 years. Some issuers find the longer maturities of Yankees attractive to meet long-term financing needs. Nonetheless, the Eurobond is becoming a strong competitor to the U.S. dollar for firms that want to raise funds in a currency that has broad appeal to many investors.

SELF-CHECK

- List the characteristics of Eurodollar bonds and explain why they are attractive to investors.
- List the characteristics of Yankee bonds and explain why they are attractive to investors.
- Name three companies that issue global bonds.

14.7 Reading Bond Quotes

Figure 14-3 shows a bond quote taken from the *Wall Street Journal*. Becoming familiar with bond quotes will help you understand their value and allow you to compare them with other investment opportunities.

Figure 14-3 contains a bond quote for a bond issued by Ford Motor Credit, the subsidiary of Ford Motor Company that raises funds to finance car loans and leases.

The ticker symbol (F) refers to Ford's common stock; in stock trading, ticker symbols are used as a shorthand notation rather than full company names. The Ford Credit bond has a coupon rate of 7.000%. If its par value is $1,000, as are most corporate bonds, then Ford Credit pays interest of 7% of $1,000, or $0.0700 \times 1,000 = \$70.00$ per year or $35.00 every 6 months. The bond matures on October 1, 2013.

The "Last Price" reports the closing price of the bond, expressed as a percentage of par value. Since its par value is $1,000, a closing price 105.296% of par gives a value for the bond of $1,052.96.

Figure 14-3

COMPANY (TICKER)	COUPON	MATURITY	LAST PRICE	LAST YIELD	EST. SPREAD	UST	EST. $ VOL (000S)
Ford Motor Credit (F)	7.000	Oct. 1,2013	105.296	6.252	236	10	270,068

Sample bond quotation.

A commonly used term that is simple to compute is the *current yield of a bond*. The **current yield** of a bond is calculated by dividing the annual coupon interest by the current price.

The Ford Credit bond's current yield is $70.00/$1,052.96 = 6.65%. The current yield does not adequately represent the return on a bond investment because it considers income return only and ignores price changes.

The yield to maturity is a better measure of investor return on a bond and is shown by the "Last Yield." **Yield to maturity** represents an estimate of the investor's return on the bond if it was purchased today and held to maturity.

We calculate the yield to maturity using the bond's coupon, par value, last price, and time to maturity.

SELF-CHECK

- Explain how the current yield of a bond is calculated.
- List three elements found on a bond quote and explain each.

14.8 Futures and Options

Derivative securities are a type of financial vehicle that are gaining widespread use among institutional investors and corporate managers. The value of a derivative security is determined by, or derived from, the value of another investment vehicle. Futures and options are the two financial properties that are used most frequently to back a derivative security.

▲ A **futures contract** represents an obligation to buy or sell an asset at a specified price by a certain date.

▲ An **options contract** gives the owner of the contract the option of buying or selling a particular good at a specified price on or before a certain expiration date.

The big difference between these two contracts is that a futures contract represents an obligation to carry through a transaction, while an option contract represents a choice and does not obligate the owner of the contract to actually conclude the transaction. Both contracts are used to lock in prices and reduce the risk of inflation.

There are always times when it may be advantageous to enter into a transaction now with the promise that the exchange of asset and money will take place at a future time. Such an exchange allows a transaction price to be determined today for a trade that will not occur until a mutually agreed upon future date.

As an example, in June a wheat farmer may want to lock in the price at which he can sell his harvest in September. That way, his profits will not be affected by price swings in the wheat market between now and harvest.

The option contract gives the owner a choice in whether or not to complete the deal on or before the specified expiration date. Option contracts are quite popular in the real estate industry. A common option agreement may give a real estate developer an opportunity to purchase a parcel of land at a fixed price some time before the end of the year. In exchange for holding the property at that price, the owner receives a nonrefundable option fee when the contract is signed. Usually the option fee is deducted from the price of the land if the developer exercises his option and purchases the land. If the developer decides not to buy the property, the owner keeps the option fee and is free to sell the property to another buyer.

Future and option contracts can be written on almost any kind of asset. Therefore, over time, derivatives securities have filled an important place in the economy and our financial environment. These contracts also help to bring additional information into the market and are attractive because they are less costly in terms of commissions and required investment dollars.

The prudent use of derivatives to hedge, or reduce risk, is similar to the concept of insurance. For example, auto insurance is used as a way to avoid the large dollar expenses that might result from a car accident. Policyholders pay an upfront premium to buy a certain level of protection for a limited amount of time. Derivatives can protect investors from the risk of a substantial increase in the cost of an asset.

Investing in futures in the hopes that big profits can be realized can be a risky investment strategy. Speculators are not hedging an underlying investment; they are looking for a price increase that will allow them to reap cash benefits. The complexity of some futures has resulted in some investors undertaking risks that they had not contemplated. In recent years, firms such as Barings PLC, Gibson Greetings, Metallgesellschaft, Procter and Gamble, and several municipalities and colleges have suffered large losses and even bankruptcy because of inappropriate speculation in the derivatives markets.

14.8.1 Exchange-Traded Futures

Exchange-traded futures are standardized as to terms and conditions, such as quality and quantity of the underlying asset and expiration dates. For example, corn delivered under a futures contract must meet certain moisture-content standards. This standardization allows futures to be bought and sold, just as common stocks are bought and sold in secondary markets. Someone purchasing (selling) a futures contract can counteract their obligation by selling (purchasing) the identical type of contract. This is called a *reversing trade*.

Today, futures contracts are traded not only on agricultural goods and precious metals, but also on oil, stock indexes, interest rates, and currencies.

One of the risks of investing in a futures contract is the creditworthiness of the entity on the other side of the transaction. However, exchange-traded futures have little credit or default risk. Purchasers and sellers of futures are required to deposit funds in a margin account with the exchange's clearing corporation or clearinghouse. The initial margin requirement is usually 3 to 6% of the price of the contract. Funds are added to or subtracted from the margin account daily, reflecting that day's price changes in the futures contract. At the end of each trading day, a special exchange committee determines an approximate closing price, called the *settlement price*. Futures are cash-settled every day through this process, known as *marking to the market*. As is the case with common stocks, should a margin account become too low, the investor must place additional funds in the margin account or have his/her position closed.

Rather than buying or selling futures from a specific investor, the exchange becomes the counterparty to all transactions. Should an investor default, the exchange covers any losses, but the daily settling of accounts through marking to the market and margin requirements help to prevent an investor's losses from growing indefinitely.

14.8.2 Exchange-Traded Options

Options for stock can also be created and sold in the organized exchange markets. This is known as a **call option.** The call option is the contract for the purchase of a security within a specified time and place. The price for the option is called the *option premium.* The following example shows the value in a call option. Assume that there is an option to buy 100 shares of ABC Company stock at $20.00 per share within the next 30 days. The option premium is $5.00 per share, which is paid up front when the option is purchased. At the end of the option period, ABC Company's stock is $35.00 per share. The investor would exercise the option and buy the stock at $20.00 per share, giving the investor a total cash outlay of $2,500. However, the investor can then turn around and sell the stock for the current market price of $35.00 a share and realize a quick profit of $1,000.

The growth in the volume of outstanding derivatives has increased dramatically in the last few decades. In 1986, one estimate was that $2 trillion in value was traded; this rose to nearly $10 trillion in 1991, over $40 trillion on a worldwide basis by the end of 1995, and $207 trillion at year-end 2003.

SELF-CHECK

- Define **derivative securities.**
- Explain the difference between future contracts and options contracts.
- Indicate where call options are traded and briefly explain them.

SUMMARY

Stock and debt offerings are major sources of long-term funds for businesses. Bonds offer investors a fixed income flow and priority in terms of liquidation. Bonds can be secured by corporate assets or can be unsecured. Bonds can be sold overseas by I.S. issuers; non-U.S. firms can issue bonds in the United States, as long as SEC requirements are fulfilled. In this chapter, you also learned about annuities and futures. With your knowledge of bonds, futures, and annuities, you can create a comprehensive investing strategy.

KEY TERMS

Asset securitization	Bonds that have coupon and principal payments that are paid from another existing cash flow source.
Bearer bonds	Coupons that are literally "clipped" from the side of the bond certificate and presented, like a check, to a bank for payment. With a bearer bond, the issuer does not know who is receiving the interest payments.
Bond	A debt agreement that a corporation or government agency issues when it wants to borrow money for more than 10 years. The issuer agrees to pay back the lender at a specified maturity date, with interest.
Bond covenants	Rules or regulations imposing restrictions on the firm; they are often included in trust indentures.
Bond ratings	Assesses both the collateral underlying the bonds as well as the ability of the issuer to make timely payments of interest and principal.
Callable bonds	Can be redeemed by the issuing corporation prior to maturity.
Call option	Contract for the purchase of a security within a specified time and at a specified price.
Closed-end mortgage bond	Does not permit future bond issues to be secured by any of the assets pledged as security under the closed-end issue.
Convertible bond	Can be changed, or converted, at the investor's option, into a specified number of shares of the issuer's common stock.

Current yield	Calculated by dividing the annual coupon interest by the current price.
Debenture bonds	Unsecured obligations that depend on the general credit strength of the corporation for their security.
Deferred annuities	Available for those who wish to use this financial tool to accumulate retirement funds. Tax on the income it earns is postponed until the money is withdrawn.
Derivative securities	A type of financial vehicle that is gaining widespread use among institutional investors and corporate managers.
Discount bonds	In times of declining interest rates, bonds may be sold at a discount.
Equipment trust certificate	A type of mortgage bond that gives the bondholder a claim to specific "rolling stock" (movable assets) such as railroad cars or airplanes.
Eurodollar bonds	Dollar-denominated bonds that are sold outside the United States.
Exchange-traded futures	Standardized as to terms and conditions, such as quality and quantity of the underlying asset and expiration dates.
Extendable notes	Have their coupons reset every 2 or 3 years to reflect the current interest rate and any changes in the firm's credit quality.
Fixed annuities	Earn a guaranteed rate of interest for a specified time period.
Flexible-payment annuity	One in which contributions can be made any time for any amount.
Futures contract	Represents an obligation to buy or sell an asset at a specified price by a certain date.
Global bonds	Usually are denominated in U.S. dollars.
Immediate annuity	Income payments are steady and dependable. It can be set up for any time period and provide a lifetime of income if so desired. The income is based on the amount of the contribution, the interest rate, and the person's age.
Inflation-adjusted bonds	Bonds where the principal value of the bond is adjusted every 6 months to keep pace with the consumer price index. The bond's coupon rate is then applied to the new principal value.

Ladder strategy	Invests an equal amount of money in bonds with a wide range of long and short-term maturities, so interest rate cycles will average out.
Maturity date	The date when the issuer is obligated to pay the bond's principal (par value or face value) to bondholders.
Mortgage bonds	Are not secured by home mortgages. Rather, they are secured by specific property pledged by the firm.
Open-end mortgage bond	Allows the same assets to be used as security in future bond issues.
Options contract	Gives the owner of the contract the option of buying or selling a particular good at a specified price on or before a certain expiration date.
Perpetuity bond	A bond without a maturity date. Its owners and heirs receive interest payments for as long as the company exists.
Premium bonds	When interest rates are higher, bonds may be sold at a price higher than their par value.
Putable bonds	Retractable bonds that allow investors to force the issuer to redeem them prior to maturity.
Registered bonds	Include the bondholders' names, and interest payments are sent directly to the bondholders.
Secured obligations	Specific property is pledged as collateral for the obligation.
Seesaw effect	Means that lower interest rates cause bond prices to rise and higher interest rates result in lower bond prices.
Single-payment annuity	Involves one lump sum payment with no provision for funds to be added at a later date.
Sinking fund	Requires the issuer to retire specified portions of the bond issue over time.
Straight bond	Issued with a preset maturity date. That date the final interest payment is made and the bond's par value is paid to investors.
Subordinated debentures	The claims of these bondholders are subordinate to the claims of debenture holders.
Treasury inflation protected securities (TIPS)	Both the principal value and interest payments rise and fall along with inflation.

Trust indenture	An extensive document that includes in great detail the various provisions and covenants of the loan arrangement.
Unsecured obligations	Represents a general claim against the assets of issuer.
Variable annuity	Offers a variety of funding options, such as stocks, bonds, and money market accounts.
Yankee bonds	U.S. dollar-denominated bonds that are issued in the United States by a foreign issuer.
Yield to maturity	Represents an estimate of the investor's return on the bond if it was purchased today and held to maturity.

ASSESS YOUR UNDERSTANDING

Go to www.wiley.com/college/Melicher to evaluate your knowledge of the basics of other types of financial investments.

Measure your learning by comparing pre-test and post-test results.

Summary Questions

1. An annuity is a series of equal payments that occur over a number of time periods. True or false?

2. With a variable annuity, the return is guaranteed because it relies on the performance of underlying investments. True or false?

3. Bondholders have priority claims over equity holders to a firm's assets and cash flows. True or false?

4. Corporate bonds are not as risky as common stocks; as a result, corporate bonds always lower returns to investors than do common stock. True or false?

5. Bearer bonds are more prevalent within the United States. True or false?

6. Bond covenants are the best way for bondholders to protect themselves against dubious management actions. True or false?

7. Covenants in a bond indenture may impose restrictions on a firm. True or false?

8. Bonds rated higher than CCC by Standard & Poor and Fitch are considered to be investment grade issues.

9. Mortgage bonds are secured by home mortgages. True or false?

10. A closed-end mortgage bond is one that allows the same assets to be used as security in future bond issues. True or false?

11. The claims of collateralized bondholders are junior to the claims of debenture holders. True or false?

12. A convertible bond can be converted, at the issuing firm's option, into a specific number of shares of the issuer's common stock. True or false?

13. Callable bonds can be redeemed prior to maturity by the firm. True or false?

14. Putable bonds allow investors to force the issuer to redeem them prior to maturity. True or false?

15. Many convertible bonds possess a call-deferment period, which is a specified period of time after the issue during which the bonds cannot be called. True or false?

16. Many putable bonds possess a call-deferment period, which is a specified period of time after the issue during which the bonds cannot be called. True or false?

17. A bond that can be changed into a specified number of shares of the issuer's common stock is called a
    (a) retractable bond.
    (b) convertible bond.
    (c) callable bond.
    (d) collateralized bond.

18. A bond that allows investors to force the issuer to redeem the bond prior to maturity is called a
    (a) convertible bond.
    (b) callable bond.
    (c) debenture bond.
    (d) putable bond.

19. A sinking fund
    (a) is a special fund set up to pay off the creditors of bankrupt firms.
    (b) requires specific approval by the firm's board of directors.
    (c) requires the issuer to retire a bond issue incrementally over time.
    (d) None of the above

20. In actual practice, most corporate bonds pay interest
    (a) annually.
    (b) semiannually.
    (c) quarterly.
    (d) monthly.

21. Zero coupon bonds are not suited for tax-exempt accounts such as IRAs or pension funds. True or false?

22. Inflation-protected treasury notes have a principal value that changes in accordance with the consumer price index (CPI). True or false?

23. Eurodollar bonds are dollar-denominated bonds that are sold outside the United States. True or false?

24. All Eurodollar bonds must be approved by the Securities and Exchange Commission. True or false?

25. Yankee bonds are an example of Eurodollar bonds. True or false?

26. Yankee bonds are U.S. dollar-denominated bonds that are issued in the United States by a foreign issuer. True or false?

27. Global bonds usually are denominated in U.S. dollars and have offering sizes that typically exceed $1 billion. True or false?

28. The current yield of a bond is calculated by dividing the annual coupon interest by the current price. True or false?

29. A bond's yield to maturity is calculated using the bond's
    (a) coupon.
    (b) par value.

(c) last price and time to maturity.

(d) All of the above

(e) None of the above

30. A futures contract represents an obligation to buy or sell an asset at a specified price by a certain date. True or false?

31. An options contract gives the owner of the contract the option of buying or selling a particular good at a specified price on or before a certain expiration date. True or false?

32. Investing in futures with the aim of realizing large profits is a conservative investment strategy. True or false?

Review Questions

1. What is the income on an immediate annuity based on?
   (a) The amount of your contribution
   (b) Your age
   (c) The interest rate
   (d) All of the above

2. Deferred annuities are often used to accumulate retirement funds. Briefly explain why the tax-deferred feature of these funds will minimize the eventual tax liability.

3. Name an advantage of owning debt securities. The periodic interest payments must be paid to the holders or the holders can force the firm into bankruptcy.

4. Corporate and treasury bonds are mainly intended for large institutional investors who can purchase millions of dollars of bonds at a time. However, certain types of programs have been introduced to make bonds available to small investors. Describe how a small investor might purchase both a U.S. Treasury bond and a corporate bond.

5. A trust indenture includes the various provisions and covenants of the loan arrangement. List three details that always appear on a trust indenture.

6. Name the factors that may affect a bond rating.
   (a) Security provisions
   (b) Indenture provisions
   (c) Expected trends of industry operations
   (d) All of the above
   (e) None of the above

7. Which types of bonds have the lowest risk?

   (a) Closed-end mortgage bond

   (b) Subordinated debenture

   (c) Open-end mortgage bond

   (d) All of the above would have the same risk.

8. Securitization involves issuing bonds whose coupon and principal payments are paid from another existing cash flow source. List three cash flow sources that are open to securitization.

9. What is meant by the following terms: *convertible bonds, callable bonds,* and *putable bonds*?

10. Although most bonds pay a fixed coupon rate, some bonds have coupon payments that vary over time. Briefly explain how inflation-adjusted bonds are structured so as to always account for changes in inflation.

11. The seesaw effect means that lower interest rates cause bond prices to rise and higher interest rates result in lower bond prices. The seesaw effect causes the yield curve to shift up and down over time and sometimes even twist. Describe the conditions that result in a twisting yield curve.

12. Name two reasons why investors would choose bonds over stocks despite the fact that bonds present a lower rate of return.

13. Zero coupon bonds pay no interest over the life of the bond. How does an investor make money on them?

14. Most Eurodollar bonds are sold in bearer form. Explain why this is important to many investors.

15. What kind of global bond would be of interest to firms wanting to issue long-term debt?

16. What is meant by the "yield to maturity" on a bond? How does it differ from the current yield?

17. The initial margin requirement of futures contracts is usually 3 to 6% of the price of the contract. How do margin accounts help minimize credit and default risk?

Applying This Chapter

1. Given two bonds identical in all respects except one pays coupons annually and the other pays coupons semiannually, which one will have the higher price? Why?

2. Although corporate bonds usually entail less risk than stocks, they are not risk-free. Briefly describe the types of bonds that can be issued to provide a high degree of bondholder security.

3. You have a 10% coupon, $1,000 per value callable bond. When interest rates drop to 4%, the issuing corporation calls the bond. What will you be paid?

4. You plan to invest $10,000 in bonds and want to employ a ladder strategy to minimize the effect of sudden fluctuations in interest rates. Look at current bond offerings online and list 10 bonds that will fit this strategy.

5. Go to www.treasurydirect.gov and find out when the U.S. Treasury will issue the next 30-year treasury bond.

6. On Thursday, the following bond price quotation appears in the newspaper. Interpret each item that appears in the quote and compute its current yield.

Company (Ticker)	Coupon	Mat.	Last Price	Last Yield	EST Spread	EST UST	$VOL (000s)
Wal-Mart Stores							
WMT	4.550	May 1, 2013	99.270	4.649	47	10	66,830

7. Perusing the corporate bond quotations, you write down some summary information:

Company (Ticker)	Coupon	Mat.	Last Price	Last Yield	EST Spread	EST UST	$VOL (000's)
Wal-Mart Stores							
WMT	4.550	10 years	99.270	4.649	47	10	66,830
Wal-Mart Stores							
WMT	4.125	8 years	99.554	4.200	2	10	50,320
Liberty Media							
L	5.700	10 years	102.750	5.314	112	10	26,045
Ford Motor Credit							
F	7.250	8 years	107.407	6.012	183	10	22,863

(a) Which company is the riskiest? Why?

(b) Which bond has the highest default risk? Why?

(c) Why would Wal-Mart have two bonds trading at different yields?

8. Suppose you purchase an option to buy 1,000 shares of Acme Oil Company stock at $50 per share within the next 30 days. You pay an option premium of $7 per share. At the end of 30 days, Acme Oil company stock has risen to $60.

   (a) If you exercise your option and buy the stock at $60 per share, how much is your total cash outlay?

   (b) If you turn around and sell the stock for the current market price, what is your profit?

Raising Money

You work for a firm that needs to raise money quickly. The firm is stable and does over $500 million annually in revenue. What types of bonds do you urge the firm to issue and why?

Design a Portfolio

You have a million dollars to invest, and you want to build a portfolio that is a mix of 40% low-risk investments and 60% medium-high risk invetments. You have to decide how much to put in different types of bonds, annuities, and derivateive securities. Write a paper on how you decide to invest your money and why.

Futures and Options Online

The Web sites of futures and options exchanges offer visitors the chance to see time-delayed quotes. See, for example, the Chicago Mercantile Exchange (www.cme.com), Chicago Board of Trade (www.cbot.com), and the Chicago Board Options Exchange (www.cboe.com).

15

INTERNATIONAL TRADE AND FINANCE
The Global Economy

Starting Point

Go to www.wiley.com/college/Melicher to assess your knowledge of the
basics of the global economy.
Determine where you need to concentrate your effort

What You'll Learn in This Chapter

▲ How the international monetary system operates
▲ The factors that affect currency exchange rates
▲ The organization of foreign exchange markets
▲ How to work toward balance in international transactions
▲ The impact of a strong or weak dollar on international transactions

After Studying This Chapter, You'll Be Able To

▲ Compare and contrast the gold standard with flexible exchange rates
▲ Analyze the factors that led to the development of the European Union
▲ Differentiate between economic and political risk when investing overseas
▲ Distinguish how the Fed works in conjunction with other governments
▲ Examine the impact a weak dollar has on the international economy
▲ Examine how international trade is financed

Goals and Outcomes

▲ Assess the efforts undertaken to achieve economic unification of Europe
▲ Assess how the development of the European Union has affected international finance
▲ Assess recent developments in the U.S. balance of payments
▲ Examine how the world banking systems facilitate financing of sales by exporters and purchases by importers
▲ Assess factors that affect currency exchange rates and lead to a stronger currency
▲ Evaluate when and under what conditions people should invest overseas

INTRODUCTION

You are most likely already aware of how important foreign markets are to the U.S. economy. Financial managers must constantly look for ways to increase shareholder wealth and therefore must study and understand how trade with other countries opens a new avenue of investments and opportunities. With the advent of electronic banking and transfers, the financial world has been able to work with foreign markets quickly and efficiently, making foreign trade more accessible to all investors. Most people agree that it is in the best interests of worldwide economic growth and productivity for countries to work together in facilitating international trade and the flow of financial capital.

15.1 International Monetary System

When viewed in a global context, the responsibilities of the U.S. monetary system become more complex. The **international monetary system** is a system of institutions and mechanisms to foster world trade, manage the flow of financial capital, and determine currency exchange rates.

15.1.1 Development of International Finance

International finance probably began about 5,000 years ago when Babylonian cities rose to importance as centers of trading between the Mediterranean Sea and civilizations in the East. Gold was used for transactions and became a store of value when the pharaohs ruled Egypt. Centers of international finance shifted to the Roman Empire and Rome around 100 BC and to the Greek city of Athens around 500 BC.

It appears that whenever international trade developed, financial institutions came into existence and international bankers followed. Instruments and documents similar to those in use today were designed to control movement of cargo, insure against losses, satisfy government requirements, and transfer funds. Financial centers shifted to the northern European cities during the 1500s, and in more recent years to London, New York, and Tokyo.

Today, international trade takes place and international claims are settled around the clock. It is no longer necessary to have a physical center, such as a city, in which to carry out international financial operations.

15.1.2 How the International Monetary System Evolved

Prior to the start of World War I in 1914, the international monetary system

Back then, an ounce of gold might be worth 20 U.S. dollars, or $1 would be worth one-twentieth (or 0.05) of an ounce of gold. At the same time, an ounce of gold might be worth five French francs (FF). Since $20 could be converted into 1 ounce of gold that could then be used to purchase five FF, the exchange rate between the dollar and franc would be 4 to 1.

By the end of the 1800s, most countries had adopted the gold standard. However, coinciding with the start of World War I, most countries went off the gold standard. For example, the Federal Reserve Act of 1913 provided for the issuance of Federal Reserve Notes, called fiat money because they were not backed by either gold or silver. Our government decreed the notes to be "legal tender" for purposes of making payments and discharging public and private debts. Fiat money has value that is based solely on confidence in the U.S. government's being able to achieve economic growth and maintain price stability. Most foreign governments also moved to monetary systems based on fiat money.

A major criticism of the gold standard was that as the volume of world trade increases over the years, the supply of "new" gold would fail to keep pace. Therefore, without some form of supplementary international money, the result would be international deflation. A second criticism of the gold standard was a lack of an international organization to monitor and report whether countries were deviating from the standard when it was in their own best interests.

During the interwar period from 1915 through 1944, which encompassed World War I, the period in between, and World War II, an attempt was made to go back on to the gold standard. Many nations returned to the gold standard during the 1920s only to go off it again in the early 1930s because of financial crises associated with the Great Depression. A series of bank failures and continued outflow of gold caused the United States to abandon the gold standard in 1933.

In 1944, authorities from all major nations met in Bretton Woods, New Hampshire, to formulate a postwar international monetary system.

▲ The **International Monetary Fund (IMF)** was created to promote world trade through monitoring and maintaining fixed exchange rates and by making loans to countries facing balance of trade and payments problems.

▲ The **International Bank for Reconstruction and Development,** or World Bank, was created to help economic growth in developing countries.

The most significant development of the conference was the exchange rate agreement commonly called the Bretton Woods System.

▲ The **Breton Woods System** is an international monetary system in which individual currencies are tied to gold through the U.S. dollar via fixed or pegged exchange rates.

One ounce of gold was set to equal $35. Each participating country's currency was then set at a "par" or fixed value in relation to the U.S. dollar.

Countries adopting the Bretton Woods system could hold their reserves either in gold or U.S. dollars because the dollar was the only currency on the gold standard. This eliminated one of the criticisms associated with all currencies being on a gold standard system in which world economic growth was restricted to the rate of increase in new gold production, since gold was the only monetary reserve. Since the Bretton Woods System allowed for the holding of both gold and U.S. dollars as foreign exchange reserves, this new monetary system allowed for less restrictive world economic growth. The negative side of the Bretton Woods system was that the U.S. government had to produce balance-of-payments deficits—that is, its spending was greater than its reserves, so that foreign exchange reserves would grow.

Unfortunately, by the 1960s the value of the U.S. gold stock was less than the amount of foreign holdings of dollars. This, of course, caused concern about the viability of the Bretton Woods system. To help keep the system operating, in 1970 the International Monetary Fund (IMF) created a new reserve asset called Special Drawing Rights. **Special Drawing Rights (SDRs)** are a reserve asset created by the IMF consisting of a basket or portfolio of currencies that could be used to make international payments.

At first the SDR was a weighted average of 16 currencies. At the beginning of the 1980s, the SDR basket was reduced to include only 5 major currencies. At that time, the SDR basket included the U.S. dollar (45% weight), the euro (29% weight), the Japanese yen (15% weight), and the British pound (11% weight).

Beginning in March 1973, major currencies were allowed to "float" against one another. By the mid-1970s, gold was abandoned as a reserve asset and IMF members accepted a system of **flexible exchange rates,** a system in which currency exchange rates are determined by supply and demand. This is still in use today.

A primary objection to flexible exchange rates is the possibility of wide swings in response to changes in supply and demand, with a resulting uncertainty in world trade. Evidence indicates that exchange rates indeed have been much more volatile since the collapse of the Bretton Woods system in the 1970s compared to when the system was in place.

Today, a large number of countries allow their currencies to float against others. Included are Australia, Japan, Canada, the United States, and the United Kingdom. The European Monetary Union also allows the euro to float freely. In contrast, India, China, and Russia use managed floating systems involving active government intervention. China, for example, pegs its currency to the dollar, with adjustments being related to monetary targets. Thus, the current exchange rate system is a composite of flexible or floating exchange rates, managed floating exchange rates, and pegged exchange rates.

FOR EXAMPLE

Deflation

Although not talked about as much as inflation is, deflation can also affect an economy. Deflation is the decrease in the money supply. As the money supply can be difficult to measure, it can also be measured as a decrease in the general price level. Deflation is the opposite of inflation. Japan experienced a period of deflation in the early 1990s. There were several reasons for this. One reason is that asset prices fell in both real estate and equities. When assets decrease in value, the money supply shrinks. Also there were many insolvent companies. Banks lent money to companies that invested in real estate. When real estate values dropped, these loans could not be paid. Many banks then, in turn, became insolvent. The Japanese people then decided it was unsafe for them to put their money in the banks so they bought gold or treasury bills, which led to less money in the banks for economic growth and lending.

SELF-CHECK

- When did international finance begin?
- What does being on a gold standard mean?
- What was the Breton Woods System of exchange rates?
- What exchange rate system is in use today?

15.2 European Unification

Efforts to unify the countries of Europe have resulted in a common currency for 12 of the countries and major changes in the international monetary system. The **European Union (EU)** was established to promote trade and economic development among European countries.

Economic integration was to be achieved by eliminating barriers that previously restricted the flow of labor, goods, and financial capital between countries. The European Union's history can be traced back to a treaty that established the European Economic Community (EEC) in 1957. The EEC became the European Community (EC) in 1978, and the EC became the EU in 1994.

In late 1991, members of the European Community met in Maastricht, Netherlands, to prepare, sign, and later ratify the Maastricht Treaty, which provided for economic convergence, the fixing of member country exchange rates, and the introduction of the euro as the common currency at the beginning of 1999. By 1995, the 15 EU members were Austria, Belgium, Denmark, Finland, France, Germany, Greece, Ireland, Italy, Luxembourg, Netherlands, Portugal, Spain, Sweden, and the United Kingdom. In May 2004, the European Union grew to a total of 25 members with the addition of Cyprus, the Czech Republic, Estonia, Hungary, Latvia, Lithuania, Malta, Poland, Slovakia, and Slovenia.

15.2.1 European Monetary Union

The **European Monetary Union (EMU)** is the 12-member organization of the EU that, by ratifying the Maastricht Treaty, agreed to have overall monetary policy set by the European Central Bank (ECB) and adopted the euro as their common currency.

Of the original 15 EU members, Denmark, Sweden, and the United Kingdom chose not to join the EMU. None of the 10 new members of the EU qualify for EMU status because they do not comply with the standards for budget deficits and government debt relative to gross domestic product.

15.2.2 The Euro

On January 1, 1999, the official currency of the European Monetary Union members became the euro. The **euro** is the official currency of the countries in the European Monetary Union.

The paper currency consists of seven denominations from 5 to 500. Coins were designed and minted separately. At the beginning of 2002, individual EMU

FOR EXAMPLE

Euro Choices

Although the countries in the Eurozone all have one currency, they still exert some control over the printing of money. For example, some countries do not print the 500 and 200 euro note, but these notes are legal tender throughout the Eurozone. Finland decided not to mint or circulate 1-cent and 2-cent coins, except in small numbers for collectors. All cash transactions in Finland ending in 1, 2, 6, or 7 cents are rounded down, and those ending in 3, 4, 8, or 9 cents are rounded up. Despite this convention, the 1-cent and 2-cent coins are still legal tender in Finland.

countries' currencies began being phased out; only the euro coin and currency were legal tender by July 2002.

SELF-CHECK

- What is the **European Union?**
- What is the **European Monetary Union?**
- What is a **euro?**

15.3 Currency Exchange Markets and Rates

We usually think of a market as a specific place or institution, but this is not always so. **Currency exchange markets,** also called *foreign exchange markets,* are electronic markets where banks and institutional traders buy and sell various currencies on behalf of businesses, other clients, and themselves.

The major financial centers of the world are connected electronically so that when an individual or firm engaged in a foreign transaction deals with a local bank, that individual or firm is, in effect, dealing with the exchange markets of the world. Transactions throughout the world may be completed in only a few minutes by virtue of the effective communications network serving the various financial institutions, including central banks of every nation.

15.3.1 Exchange Rate Quotations

Table 15-1 shows the currency exchange rates for a variety of foreign currencies relative to the U.S. dollar on July 1, 2004. A **currency exchange rate** indicates the value of one currency relative to another currency.

Currency exchange rates are stated in two basic ways: the direct quotation method and the indirect quotation method.

▲ The **direct quotation method** indicates the value of one unit of a foreign currency in terms of a home country's currency.

Note that Table 15-1 shows that the "U.S. dollar equivalent" of one euro was $1.2167. In other words, it took $1.2167 to buy one euro.

▲ The **indirect quotation method** indicates the amount of units of a foreign currency needed to purchase one unit of the home country's currency.

By again turning to Table 15-1 we see that in July 2004, it takes 0.8219 euros to purchase one U.S. dollar.

Table 15-1: Selected Foreign Exchange Rates, July 1, 2004

Country	Currency	U.S. Dollar Equivalent (Direct Method)	Currency Per U.S. Dollar (Indirect Method)
Australia	Dollar	0.705600	1.4172
Canada	Dollar	0.751000	1.3316
China	Renminbi	0.120800	8.2781
Denmark	Krone	0.163700	6.1087
India	Rupee	0.021830	45.8090
Japan	Yen	0.009235	108.2800
Mexico	Peso	0.086700	11.5354
Russia	Ruble	0.034450	29.0280
Singapore	Dollar	0.583400	1.7141
South Africa	Rand	0.161700	6.1843
Sweden	Krona	0.132700	7.5358
Switzerland	Franc	0.800600	1.2491
United Kingdom	Pound	1.820300	0.5494
European Monetary Union	Euro	1.216700	0.8219

Sources: www.Reuters.com, money.cnn.com, and other sources.

Table 15-1 also shows the value of other major currencies in U.S. dollar terms on July 1, 2004. An Australia dollar was worth $0.7056, a United Kingdom (British) pound $1.8203, a Swiss franc $0.8006, and a Japanese yen about $0.0092. The corresponding indirect quotations in units relative to one U.S. dollar were Australia dollar = 1.4172, United Kingdom pound = 0.5494, Swiss franc = 1.2491, and Japanese yen = 108.28.

It is worth noting that electronic and newspaper exchange rate quotes are for large unit transfers within the currency exchange markets. Consequently, individuals buying foreign currencies would not get exactly the same ratio shown on the table. The currency exchange prices for an individual always favor the seller, who makes a margin of profit.

The balance in the foreign account of a U.S. bank is subject to constant drain as the bank sells foreign currency claims to individuals who import goods or obtain services from other countries. These banks may reestablish a given deposit level in their correspondent banks either through selling dollar claims in the foreign countries concerned or by buying claims from another dealer in the foreign exchange.

15.3.2 Factors That Affect Currency Exchange Rates

Each currency exchange rate shown in Table 15-1 is said to be a *spot exchange rate*.

 A **spot exchange rate** is the rate being quoted for the immediate delivery of the currency.

Actually, it is common practice to have up to 2 days for delivery after the trade date. It is also possible to enter into a contract for the purchase or sale of a currency where delivery will take place at a future date. In this case, the negotiated exchange rate is referred to as a *forward exchange rate*.

 A **forward exchange rate** is the rate for the purchase or sale of a currency where delivery will take place at a future date.

The supply and demand relationship involving two currencies is said to be in balance or equilibrium at the current or spot exchange rate. Demand for a foreign currency derives from the demand for that country's goods, services, and financial assets. U.S. consumers and investors demand a variety of British goods, services, and financial assets, most of which must be paid for in British pounds. The supply of pounds comes from British demand for U.S. goods, services, and financial assets. A change in the relative demand for British pounds versus U.S. dollars will cause the spot exchange rate to change. Currency exchange rates also depend on relative inflation rates, relative interest rates, and political and economic risks.

A change in the demand for one country's financial assets relative to another country's financial assets also will cause the currency exchange rate between the two countries to change to a new equilibrium price. For example, a nation with a relatively strong stock market will attract investors who seek out the highest returns on their investment funds, much as a nation with a higher relative economic growth rate attracts capital investments. If the stock market in the United States is expected to perform poorly compared to the stock market in Britain, investors will switch or move their debt investments denominated in U.S. dollars into pound-denominated debt investments. This increased demand for British pounds relative to U.S. dollars will cause the pound's dollar value to increase.

Now let's turn our attention to what happens if changes occur in relative nominal (observed) interest rates and inflation rates between two countries. For government debt securities, the nominal interest rate is composed of a "real rate"

FOR EXAMPLE

Indirect Quotation Equation

If you want to determine the indirect quotation yourself, you can do so. The equation you need is as follows:

Indirect quotation (foreign currency units) = 1 divided by $\overline{\text{direct quotation}}$ (home currency value)

Let's use the euro at a value of $1.2167 for this calculation. You would have

Indirect quotation = 1 divided by $1.2167 = 0.8210 euros.

plus an inflation expectation. So, the higher or lower the inflation rate, the higher or lower will be the nominal interest rate. A nation with a relatively lower inflation rate will have a relatively stronger currency.

SELF-CHECK

- What are **currency exchange markets**?
- What is the difference between the direct and indirect quotation methods for stating currency exchange rates?
- What is a **spot exchange rate**? A **forward exchange rate**?
- What factors determine currency exchange rates?

15.4 Investing Overseas

People living in the United States are affected by international finance in at least two ways. First, the growth or recession of overseas economies affects jobs in the United States. If foreign economies go into recession (as the Japanese and other Asian economies did in the mid- to late 1990s) there will be less export demand for U.S. goods and services. So, a worker's personal financial status can be imperiled by a layoff or reduced working hours.

The second effect on individuals is perhaps less apparent. It is the effect of foreign investors on U.S. financial markets and interest rates. Stock and bond prices are affected, as is any other price, by supply and demand. Foreign inflows of capital into U.S. financial markets can help raise U.S. stock and bond prices, giving U.S. investors better returns on their own investment. Of course, money can flow out, too. If foreign investors sell their U.S. security holdings, this can lead to lower security prices and lower, even negative, returns to U.S. investors.

```
  FOR EXAMPLE
```

Weak Dollar

Suppose interest rates in Japan are 4% and economists predict the U.S. dollar will fall in value against the yen by 3% in the next year. That means Japanese investors will not find U.S. bonds attractive unless their interest rate is at least 4% (the Japanese interest rate) + 3% (the expected loss of the U.S. dollar), or 7%. If the dollar is expected to fall by 5%, U.S. interest rates will have to be 9% (4% + 5%) to attract Japanese investors. A falling or weaker dollar puts upward pressure on interest rates throughout the U.S. economy.

Pessimism about the strength of the U.S. dollar can even lead to higher U.S. interest rates on everything from treasury bills to home mortgages.

The following risks affect the value of currency in the nations of the world.

▲ **Political risk** is the risk associated with the possibility that a national government might confiscate or expropriate assets held by foreigners.

A nation with relatively lower political risk will generally have a relatively stronger currency.

▲ **Economic risk** is the risk associated with the possibility of slow or negative economic growth, as well as variability in economic growth.

A nation that has a higher economic growth rate, along with growth stability, will generally have a stronger currency and will attract more capital inflows compared to a nation growing more slowly.

The currency exchange rate is subject to appreciation or depreciation, depending on the economic conditions of the country issuing it. Be aware that currency exchange rates can change on a daily basis and should be checked frequently.

SELF-CHECK

- Define **political risk** and **economic risk**.
- List two ways that people living in the United States are affected by international finance.

15.5 Arbitrage

Arbitrage is the simultaneous purchasing of commodities, securities, or bills of exchange in one market and selling them in another where the price is higher.

In international exchange, variations in quotations between countries at any time are quickly brought into alignment through the arbitrage activities of international financiers. If the exchange rate in New York was reported at £1 = $1.61 and in London the rate was quoted at £1 = $1.60, alert international arbitrageurs would simultaneously sell claims to British pounds in New York at the rate of $1.61 and have London correspondents sell claims on U.S. dollars in London at the rate of $1.60 for each pound sterling. Of course, such arbitrage is only profitable when dealing in large sums. If an arbitrageur, under these circumstances, sold a claim on £100 million in New York, $161 million would be received. The corresponding sale of claims on American dollars in London would be at the rate of £100 million for $160 million. Hence, a profit of $1 million would be realized on the transaction. A quotation differential of as little as one-sixteenth of one cent may be sufficient to encourage arbitrage activities.

The ultimate effect of large-scale arbitrage activities on exchange rates is the elimination of the variation between the two markets. The sale of large amounts of claims to American dollars in London would drive the price for pounds sterling up, and in New York the sale of claims to pounds sterling would force the exchange rate down.

SELF-CHECK

- What is arbitrage?
- What is the relationship between exchange rates and arbitrage?

15.6 Exchange Rate Developments for the U.S. Dollar

The dollar continues to be an important currency for international commercial and financial transactions. Because of this, both the United States and the rest of the world benefit from a strong and stable U.S. dollar. Its strength and stability depend directly on the ability of the United States to pursue noninflationary economic policies. In the late 1960s and the 1970s, the United States failed to meet this objective. Continuing high inflation led to a dollar crisis in 1978, which threatened the stability of international financial markets.

Figure 15-1 shows the strength of the dollar relative to an index of major currencies that trade widely outside the U.S. for the years 1980 through 2003. As

Figure 15-1

(Index, March 1973 = 100)

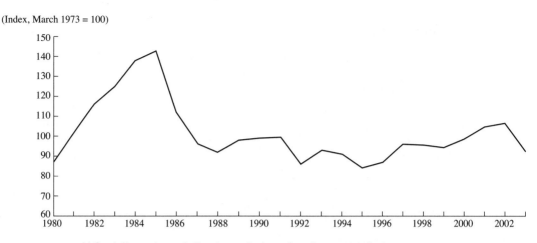

U.S. dollar value relative to an index of major currencies.

inflation was brought under control in the early 1980s and economic growth accelerated after the 1981–1982 recession, the dollar rose against other major currencies until it reached record highs in 1985.

Higher economic growth and relatively lower inflation rates lead to a stronger currency. These economic developments, coupled with a favorable political climate, caused the value of the dollar to rise sharply. However, the renewed strength of the dollar contributed to a worsening of the trade imbalance because import prices were effectively reduced while exported U.S. goods became less cost competitive.

Beginning in 1985, U.S. economic growth slowed relative to economic growth in other developed countries. Also, the belief that the U.S. government wanted the dollar to decline on a relative basis so as to reduce the trade deficit contributed to a decline in the desirability of holding dollars. This resulted in a major shift toward holding more foreign assets and fewer U.S. assets. As a consequence, the dollar's value declined by 1987 to levels below those in place when flexible exchange rates were reestablished in 1973. Since 1987, the value of the dollar in international exchange has continued to fluctuate, but within a fairly narrow range compared to the 1980–1987 period.

A stronger dollar leads to concern about the deficit in our trade balance, but at the same time it offers hope of lower inflation. A stronger dollar results in more imports of foreign merchandise since it requires fewer dollars for purchase. Just as a U.S. tourist abroad finds it cheaper to travel when the dollar is strong, importers find prices lower when their dollars increase in relative strength. When the dollar weakens, inflation may follow, countered by a reduced balance of trade deficit.

FOR EXAMPLE

Trade Deficit

Economists differ on whether a trade deficit is inherently good or bad. Some economists contend that the trade deficit is one part of the economic picture and must be taken into consideration with other factors when looking at a country's economy. The United States has posted a trade deficit since the 1970s. The 2005 deficit in goods and services set a new record. The trade deficit has resulted in or represents a decline in American manufacturing, a rise in imports from countries with growing economies such as China, and a fairly strong dollar relative to other countries.

SELF-CHECK

- Briefly describe the potential impact of a stronger dollar on the U.S. economy.
- Briefly describe the potential impact of a weaker dollar on the U.S. economy.

15.7 Conducting Business Internationally

Firms that have foreign sales must be concerned with the stability of the governments and changing values of currency in the countries in which they do business. They must also pay attention to commodity price changes and other uncertainties related to monetary systems.

Large firms usually have special departments that handle international transactions. These firms may engage in foreign exchange speculation as opportunities arise, but risk reduction is their primary goal. Among the possible actions of skilled foreign exchange specialists are hedging, adjusting accounts receivable and payable procedures, cash management, and borrowing and lending activities. Existing or anticipated variations in the value of the foreign currencies guide all of these actions. A seller with a claim for payment within 90 days may anticipate a possible decline in the currency value of his customer's country. The seller can hedge by entering into a futures contract for the delivery of that currency at the existing exchange rate on the day of the contract. By so doing, a loss in the collection process is offset by a gain in the delivery process 90 days in the future. The fee for the futures contract becomes a cost of the transaction.

Large multinational companies enjoy special opportunities for risk reduction and speculation since they can move cash balances from one country to another as monetary conditions warrant. If a decline in the value of a particular currency is expected, cash in the branch in that country may be moved back to the United States. Or, a firm may borrow funds in a foreign market and move them immediately to the United States or another country with the expectation of repaying the loan at a reduced exchange rate. This is speculation rather than a risk-reduction activity.

An expected decline in a currency may lead to an attempt to accelerate collection of accounts receivable, with funds transferred quickly to another country. Payments on accounts payable may be delayed in the expectation of a decline in exchange rates. If, on the other hand, a foreign currency is expected to increase in relative value, the preceding actions would be reversed.

New career opportunities have developed with the increasing importance of multinational financial management. Some corporations maintain special departments to study foreign business activities and their prospective profitability. These departments analyze governmental attitudes, tax rates, and duties and determine how foreign operations are to be financed. In addition, almost constant attention must be given to day-to-day changes in the exchange rates to protect bank balances and other investments.

The concept of acceptable ethical behavior differs across cultures and countries. In some developing countries it seems to be acceptable for government officials and others to request side payments and bribes from foreign companies in return for being able to do business in these countries. The **Foreign Corrupt Practices Act (FCPA)** prohibits U.S. firms from bribing foreign officials.

For violators of the FCPA, the U.S. Justice Department may impose monetary penalties, and criminal proceedings may be brought against violators. Government

FOR EXAMPLE

HealthSouth

In 2004, two former HealthSouth Corporation executives were indicted for conspiracy in a bribery scheme involving a Saudi Arabian hospital. An attempt was made to conceal the bribery by setting up a bogus consulting contract for the director general of the Saudi foundation that owned the hospital. The former HealthSouth executives were indicted after a Justice Department investigation alleged that they had violated the U.S. Travel Act by using interstate commerce when making the bribes and the FCPA by falsely reflecting the bogus bribe payments as legitimate consulting expenses on HealthSouth's financial statements.

actions may result in lost reputations and firm values. Titan Corporation had its proposed 2004 sale to Lockheed Martin Corporation fall apart because it could not promptly resolve a bribery investigation brought by the Justice Department.

When conducting business activities in certain foreign countries, business executives are sometimes faced with extortion demands by organized criminals. Most of us would agree that extortion payments are morally wrong, and paying organized criminals is not much different from paying corrupt government officials.

SELF-CHECK

- What actions can firms that have foreign sales take to reduce foreign exchange risk?
- Briefly explain the purpose of the Foreign Corrupt Practices Act.
- What are the possible effects of a decline in currency?

15.8 Financing International Trade

A substantial financial burden of any industrial firm is the process of manufacturing. When a U.S. manufacturer exports goods to distant places such as India or Australia, funds are tied up not only for the manufacturing period, but also for a lengthy period of transportation. To reduce costs, manufacturers may require the foreign importer to pay for the goods as soon as they are on the way to their destination. In this way, the financial burden is transferred to the importer.

If the exporter has confidence in foreign customers and is in a financial position to sell to them on open-book account, which is a credit account, then sales arrangements should operate very much as in domestic trade, subject, of course, to the more complex nature of any international transaction.

15.8.1 Sight and Time Drafts

As an alternative to shipping merchandise on open-account financing, the exporter may use a collection draft.

▲ A **draft** or **bill of exchange** is an unconditional written order, signed by the party drawing it, requiring the party to whom it is addressed to pay a certain sum of money to orderer or to bearer.

A draft may require immediate payment by the importer upon its presentation, or it may require only acceptance on the part of the importer, providing for payment at a specified future time.

▲ A **sight draft** is a financial instrument requiring immediate payment.

▲ A **time draft** is a financial instrument requiring payment at a later date.

A draft may require remittance, or payment, in the currency of the country of the exporter or of the importer, depending on the transaction's terms. An example of a sight draft form is shown in Figure 15-2.

Drafts may be either documentary or clean.

▲ A **clean draft** is one that is not accompanied by any special documents and is generally used when the exporter has confidence in the importer's ability to meet the draft when presented

▲ A **documentary draft** is accompanied by an order bill of lading along with other papers such as insurance receipts, certificates of sanitation, and consular invoices.

The **order bill of lading** represents the written acceptance of goods for shipment by a transportation company and the terms under which the goods are to be transported to their destination.

In addition, the order bill of lading carries title to the merchandise being shipped, and only its holder may claim the merchandise from the transportation company. An example of an order bill of lading is shown in Figure 15-3.

15.8.2 Bank Assistance in the Collection of Drafts

An importer will generally try to avoid paying for a purchase before the goods are actually shipped because several days or perhaps weeks may elapse before the goods arrive. However, the exporter is often unwilling to send the draft and documents directly to the importer and usually works through a commercial bank.

Figure 15-2

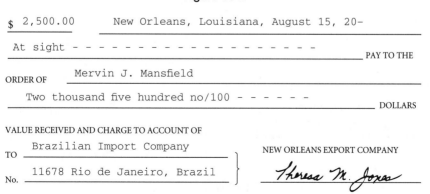

Sight draft or bill of exchange.

Figure 15-3

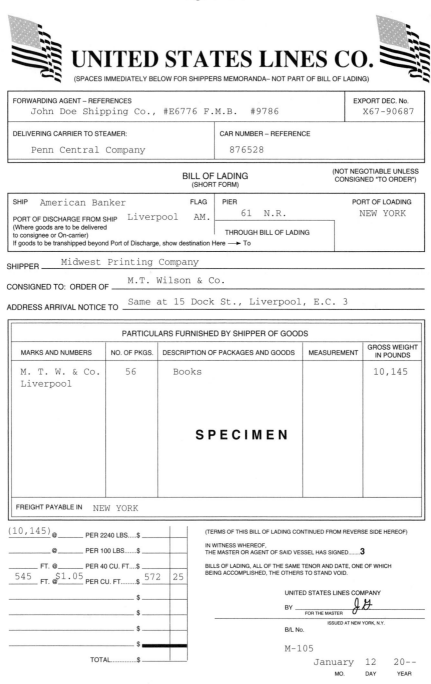

Order bill of lading.

A New York exporter dealing with an importer in Portugal with whom there has been little experience may ship goods on the basis of a documentary draft that has been deposited for collection with the local bank. That bank, following the specific instructions regarding the manner of collection, forwards the draft and the accompanying documents to its correspondent bank in Lisbon. The correspondent bank holds the documents until payment is made in the case of a sight draft, or until acceptance is obtained if a time draft is used. When collection is made on a sight draft, it is remitted to the exporter.

15.8.3 Financing through the Exporter's Bank

It is important to recognize that throughout the preceding transaction, the banking system only provided a service to the exporter and in no way financed the transaction itself. The exporter's bank, however, may offer financing assistance by allowing the exporter to borrow against the security of a documentary draft. Such loans have the financial strength of both the exporter and the importer to support them, since documents for taking possession of the merchandise are released only after the importer has accepted the draft.

The amount that the exporter can borrow is less than the face amount of the draft and depends mainly on the credit standing of both the exporter and the importer. When the exporter is financially strong enough to offer suitable protection to the bank, a substantial percentage of the draft may be advanced even though the importer may not be known to the exporter's bank. In other cases, the advance may be based on the importer's financial strength.

The character of the goods shipped also has an important bearing on the amount advanced, since the goods offer collateral security for the loan. Goods that are not breakable or perishable are preferred as collateral, as are goods for which there is a ready market rather than goods with a very limited market.

15.8.4 Financing by the Importer

Like the exporter, the importer may also arrange payment for goods without access to bank credit. When an order is placed, payment in full may be made or a partial payment offered. The partial payment gives some protection to both the exporter and the importer. It protects the exporter against rejection of the goods. It also gives the importer some bargaining power in the event the merchandise is damaged in shipment or does not meet specifications.

When the importer is required to make full payment with an order but wants some protection in the transaction, payment is sent to a bank in the exporter's country. The bank is instructed not to release payment until certain documents are presented to the bank to prove shipment of the goods according to the terms of the transaction. The bank, of course, charges a fee for this service.

15.8.5 Financing through the Importer's Bank

In foreign trade, because of language barriers and the difficulty in obtaining credit information about companies in foreign countries, the use of the bankers' acceptance is common. The bankers' acceptance is a draft drawn on and accepted by a bank rather than the importing firm. An example of a bankers' acceptance is shown in Figure 15-4.

The importer must make arrangements with the bank in advance. The exporter must know before shipment is made whether or not the bank in question has agreed to accept the draft. This arrangement is facilitated by the use of a commercial letter of credit, a bank's written statement to an individual or firm guaranteeing acceptance and payment of a draft up to a specified sum if the draft is presented according to the terms of the letter. An example of a letter of credit is shown in Figure 15-5.

Assume the owner of a small exclusive shop in Chicago wishes to import expensive perfumes from Paris. Although the shop is well known locally, its financial reputation is not known widely enough to permit it to purchase from foreign exporters on the basis of an open-book account or drafts drawn on the firm. Under these circumstances, the firm would substitute the bank's credit for its own through the use of a letter of credit.

Upon application by the firm, the bank issues the letter if it is entirely satisfied that its customer is in a satisfactory financial condition. The letter of credit is addressed to the French exporter of perfumes. The exporter, upon receipt of the commercial letter of credit, would not be concerned about making the shipment. Although the exporter may not have heard of the Chicago firm, the bank issuing the commercial letter of credit may be known to the exporter or to his bank. International bank directories provide bank credit information. The French exporter then ships the perfumes and at the same time draws a draft in

Figure 15-4

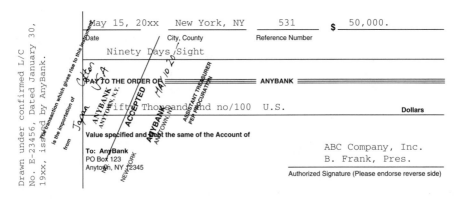

Bankers' acceptance.

Figure 15-5

| Irrevocable Commercial
Letter Of Credit | AnyBank
P.O. Box 123
Anytown, New York 12345 | **AnyBank** | Cable Address:
AnyBank | Letter Of Credit
Division |

May 2, 20-- $50,000.

Drafts drawn hereunder must be marked
*Drawn under AnyBank Anytown
L/C Ref.   E-23456   *and indicate the date hereof

ABC Company, Inc.

B. Frank, President

Gentlemen:
We hereby authorize you to draw on   AnyBank, Anytown

by order of   J. R. Doe & Company, New York, N.Y.

and for account of   J. R. Doe & Company

up to an aggregate amount of   Fifty Thousand Dollars U.S. Currency

available by your drafts at 90 days sight, for full invoice value, in duplicate
accompanied by   Commercial Invoice in triplicate . . .
                 Consular Invoice in duplicate . . .
                 Full set of onboard Bills of Lading to order of AnyBank,
Anytown, marked Notify J. R. Doe & Company, New York,N.Y., and bearing
a separate onboard endorsement signed by the Master and also marked
freight collect at port of destination . . . .

Relating to shipment of Cotton.

. . . Any charges for negotiation of the draft(s) are for your account.
. . . Marine and war risk insurance covered by buyers.

Drafts must be drawn and negotiated not later than   October 2, 20--

The amounts thereof must be endorsed on this Letter Of Credit.
We hereby agree with the drawers, endorsers, and bonafide holders of all drafts drawn under and in compliance
with the terms of this credit, that such drafts will be duly honored upon presentation to the drawee.
This letter of credit is subject to the Uniform Customs and Practice for Documentary Credits (1974 Revision) International Chamber Of Commerce Publication No. 290.

Yours very truly,

D. E. Price

D. E. Price
Vice President
Authorized Signature

Irrevocable letter of credit.

the appropriate amount on the bank that issued the letter of credit. The draft and the other papers required by the commercial letter of credit are presented to the exporter's bank. The bank sends the draft and the accompanying documents to its New York correspondent, who forwards them to the importer's bank in Chicago.

The importer's bank thoroughly inspects the papers that accompany the draft to make sure that all provisions of the letter of credit have been met. If the bank is satisfied, the draft is accepted and the appropriate bank officials sign it. The accepted draft, now a bankers' acceptance, may be held until maturity by the accepting bank or returned to the exporter on request. If the acceptance is returned to the exporter, it may be held until maturity and sent to the accepting bank for settlement or it may be sold to other investors. An active market for bankers' acceptances exists in the world's money centers.

After having accepted the draft, the Chicago bank notifies its customer that it has the shipping documents and that arrangements should be made to take them over. As the shop sells the perfume, it builds up its bank account with daily deposits until they are sufficient to retire the acceptance. The bank can then meet its obligation on the acceptance without having advanced its other funds at any time.

In releasing shipping documents to a customer, some banks prefer to establish an agency arrangement between the firm and the bank whereby the bank retains title to the merchandise. The instrument that provides for this is called a *trust receipt*.

Should the business fail, the bank would not be in the position of an ordinary creditor trying to establish its claim on the business assets. Rather, it could repossess, or take back, the goods and place them with another agent for sale since title had never been transferred to the customer. As the merchandise is sold under a trust receipt arrangement, the business must deposit the proceeds with the bank until the total amount of the acceptance is reached.

The bankers' acceptance and the commercial letter of credit involve four principal parties: the importer, the importer's bank, the exporter, and the exporter's bank. Each benefits to a substantial degree through this arrangement. The importer benefits by securing adequate credit. The importer's bank benefits because it receives a fee for issuing the commercial letter of credit and for the other services provided in connection with it. The exporter benefits by being assured that payment will be made for the shipment of merchandise. Finally, the exporter's bank benefits if it discounts the acceptance, since it receives a high-grade credit instrument with a definite, short-term maturity. Acceptances held by commercial banks provide a low, but certain, yield, and banks can liquidate them quickly if funds are needed for other purposes.

15.8.6 Bankers' Acceptances

The board of governors of the Federal Reserve System authorizes member banks to accept drafts that arise in the course of certain types of international transactions. These include the import and export of goods, the shipment of goods between foreign countries, and the storage of highly marketable staple goods in any foreign country. A **bankers' acceptance** is a promise of future payment issued by a firm and guaranteed by a bank.

> ### FOR EXAMPLE
>
> **Wachovia and Banker's Acceptance Financing**
>
> Wachovia offers a banker's acceptance to support customer's short-term (6 months or less) trade transactions. In many cases, this is less expensive than traditional trade financing methods.

The maturity of bankers' acceptances arising out of international transactions may not exceed 6 months. This authority to engage in bankers' acceptance financing is intended to encourage banks to participate in financing international trade and to strengthen the U.S. dollar abroad.

Bankers' acceptances are used to finance international transactions on a wide variety of items, including coffee, wool, rubber, cocoa, metals and ores, crude oil, jute, and automobiles. Because of the growth of international trade in general and the increasing competition in foreign markets, bankers' acceptances have become increasingly important. Exporters have had to offer more liberal terms on their sales to compete effectively. The bankers' acceptance permits them to do so without undue risk.

The cost of financing an international transaction with the bankers' acceptance involves not only the interest cost involved in the exporter's discounting the acceptance but also the commission charge of the importer's accepting bank.

Foreign central banks and commercial banks regard bankers' acceptances as attractive short-term commitments. In recent years, foreign banks have held more than half of all dollar-denominated bankers' acceptances, with most of the remainder held by domestic banks. Nonfinancial corporations have played only a small role as investors in acceptances. Relatively few firms deal in bankers' acceptances. These dealers arrange nearly simultaneous exchanges of purchases and sales.

SELF-CHECK

- What is meant by a **draft** or **bill or exchange**?
- What is an order bill of lading?
- What is meant by a commercial letter of credit?
- What is a trust receipt?
- What are bankers' acceptances and how are they used?

15.9 Other Aids to International Trade

The Export-Import Bank was authorized in 1934 and became an independent agency of the government in 1945. The bank's purpose is to help finance and facilitate exports and imports between the United States and other countries. It is the only U.S. agency engaged solely in financing foreign trade.

The Export-Import Bank is a government-owned corporation with capital of $1 billion in nonvoting stock paid in by the U.S. Treasury. It may borrow from the Treasury on a revolving basis and sell short-term discount promissory notes. It pays interest on these loans and dividends on the capital stock. In performing its function, the bank makes long-term loans to private enterprises and governments abroad to finance the purchase of U.S. equipment, goods, and services. The Export-Import Bank also aids substantially in the economic development of foreign countries by giving emergency credits to assist them in maintaining their level of U.S. imports during temporary balance-of-payments difficulties. In addition, the bank finances or guarantees the payment of medium-term commercial export credit extended by exporters and, in partnership with private insurance companies, offers short- and medium-term credit insurance. It lends and guarantees only where repayment is reasonably assured and avoids competition with sources of private capital.

Another aid to international trade is the **traveler's letter of credit.** This is issued by a bank in one country and addressed to a list of foreign banks authorizing them to cash checks or purchase drafts presented by the bearer.

A firm's buyer who is traveling abroad may not know in advance from which individuals or firms purchases will be made. The buyer could carry U.S. currency, but this involves possible physical loss of the money and sometimes a substantial discount for its conversion into the local currency. A traveler's letter of credit is a convenient and safer method for travelers who need large amounts of foreign currency.

FOR EXAMPLE

Traveler's Checks

Traveler's checks are offered by banks, express companies, and other agencies in the United States. They are issued in denominations of $10, $20, $50, and $100. These checks, usually purchased by someone before leaving for a foreign country, promise to pay on demand the even amounts indicated on the face of the checks. The use of traveler's checks is widespread and offers several advantages to the traveler. The traveler has protection if they are lost or stolen, and they are usually sold for their face value plus 1%. This eliminates a traveler's exposure to changing exchange rates.

These banks are usually correspondents of the issuing bank. When a bank issues a letter of credit, it sends a copy of the signature of the person to whom the letter is issued to each of its correspondent banks. Therefore, when the person holding the letter of credit appears at one of the banks, his or her signature is already on file and can be compared.

As with a commercial letter of credit, a maximum amount is stated in the document. In order to guarantee that the individual with the letter of credit does not exceed the amount of the credit, each bank to which the letter is presented enters on it the amount of the draft it has honored.

SELF-CHECK

- **What is the Export-Import Bank, and what does it do?**
- **What is a traveler's letter of credit and how is it used internationally?**

15.10 Balance in International Trade

No nation is a world unto itself, nor can a nation pursue whatever policies it desires without regard to other nations. Policy makers of all economies must recognize the interdependence of their actions in attempting to maintain a balance in international transactions.

The nations of the world try to achieve international financial equilibrium by maintaining a balance in the exchange of goods and services. International trade benefits all countries involved. Consumers benefit by getting lower-cost goods. Producers benefit by expanding their market. Well over one-tenth of the U.S. national income comes from selling goods in foreign markets, and many of our needs are met through imports.

Export sales are a source of income to domestic producers. Imports divert spending to foreign producers and therefore represent a loss of potential income to domestic producers. However, when the two are in balance, there is no net effect on total income in the economy. However, an increase in exports over imports tends to expand an economy, while an excess of imports tends to contract the economy.

Since producers, consumers, and investors in different countries use different currencies, the international financial system requires a mechanism for establishing values or exchange rates amount countries. Under the system of flexible exchange rates that began in 1973, rates are determined in the actual process of exchange by supply and demand in the foreign exchange market. This system reduces the impact of international financial transactions on domestic money supplies. However, changes in the exchange rates still affect imports and exports and can affect domestic production, incomes, and prices. International financial markets strongly influence domestic interest rates, so our monetary polices must always involve international considerations.

The **U.S. balance of payments** is a summary of all economic transactions with the rest of the world. It includes foreign investment, private and government grants, U.S. military spending overseas, and many other items besides the buying and selling of goods and services. The most important element of the balance of payments is the balance of trade. The **balance of trade** is the net value of a country's exports of goods and services compared to its imports.

Factors that impact international trade balances include the exchange value of the U.S. dollar, inflation rates, and economic growth. A stronger U.S. economy means that more will be spent on imports, while a weaker foreign economy means that less will be spent on U.S. exports. A weaker exchange rate where the nominal rate is adjusted for inflation difference makes for a weaker U.S. dollar that lowers the cost of U.S. goods relative to foreign goods.

Figure 15-6 depicts U.S. international transactions from 1993 through late 2003. The balance on goods for 1993 was about $35 billion per quarter. This deficit of imports over exports continued to grow until it reached a quarterly rate of nearly $120 billion by the end of 2000.

▲ The **current account balance** shows the flow of income in and out of the U.S. during a specific period.

▲ The **capital account balance** includes all foreign private and government investment in the United States netted against U.S. investments in foreign countries.

Deficits or surpluses in the current account must be offset by changes in the capital account. This is accomplished by a change in the relationship between foreign private and government investment in the United States relative to the U.S. investment in foreign countries.

From an international monetary management perspective, U.S. government ownership of foreign assets is of special interest. Under the current system of flexible exchange rates, a country's central bank does not have to redeem its

FOR EXAMPLE

Linked Economies

Domestic economies are linked to one another in a worldwide economic growth and financial system. The United States has played a leading role in the development and growth of that system. This is, in part, because the dollar is widely held as the medium of international exchange. Therefore, U.S. monetary policy has especially significant effects on the world economy.

Figure 15-6

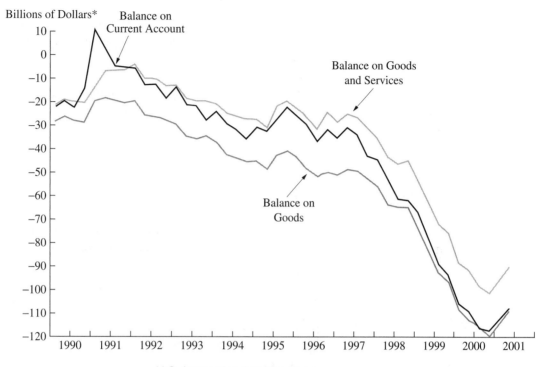

U.S. international transactions.

Source: Economic Indicators, Council of Economic Advisers (April 2004).
*Seasonally adjusted.

currency. However, it may try to control its exchange rate by entering the foreign exchange market to buy or sell that currency, thus adding to demand and supply. Intervention by central banks in the flexible exchange rate system is called a *managed float*.

Under a pure flexible system in which central banks do not enter the foreign exchange market at all, there would be no change in the official government ownership of foreign assets.

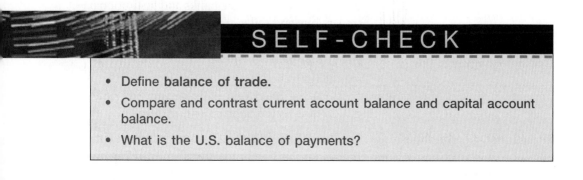

SELF-CHECK

- Define **balance of trade**.
- Compare and contrast current account balance and capital account balance.
- What is the U.S. balance of payments?

SUMMARY

In this chapter, you examined the development of international finance and learned about the evolution of the international monetary system as it evolved from a gold standard system to a system of flexible exchange rates. You can now describe the organization of foreign exchange markets. You can also explain how currency exchange rates are quoted. In addition, you understand the basics of foreign trade and how to work toward balance in international transactions. All of these skills will help you lead your company in carrying out international transactions.

KEY TERMS

Arbitrage	The simultaneous purchasing of commodities, securities, or bills of exchange in one market and selling them in another where the price is higher.
Balance of trade	The net value of a country's exports of goods and services compared to its imports.
Bankers' acceptance	A promise of future payment issued by a firm and guaranteed by a bank.
Breton Woods System	An international monetary system in which individual currencies are tied to gold through the U.S. dollar via fixed or pegged exchange rates.
Capital account balance	Includes all foreign private and government investment in the United States netted against U.S. investments in foreign countries.
Clean draft	Draft that is not accompanied by any special documents and is generally used when the exporter has confidence in the importer's ability to meet the draft when presented.
Currency exchange markets	Also called *foreign exchange markets,* these are electronic markets where banks and institutional traders buy and sell various currencies on behalf of businesses, other clients, and themselves.
Currency exchange rate	Indicates the value of one currency relative to another currency.
Current account balance	Shows the flow of income in and out of the U.S. during a specific period.
Direct quotation method	Indicates the value of one unit of a foreign currency in terms of a home country's currency.

Documentary draft	Accompanied by an order bill of lading along with other papers such as insurance receipts, certificates of sanitation, and consular invoices.
Draft or **bill of exchange**	An unconditional written order, signed by the party drawing it, requiring the party to whom it is addressed to pay a certain sum of money to orderer or to bearer.
Economic risk	The risk associated with the possibility of slow or negative economic growth, as well as variability in economic growth.
Euro	The official currency of the countries in the European Monetary Union.
European Monetary Union (EMU)	The 12-member organization of the EU that, by ratifying the Maastricht Treaty, agreed to have overall monetary policy set by the European Central Bank (ECB) and adopted the euro as their common currency.
European Union (EU)	Established to promote trade and economic development among European countries.
Flexible exchange rates	A system in which currency exchange rates are determined by supply and demand.
Foreign Corrupt Practices Act (FCPA)	Prohibits U.S. firms from bribing foreign officials.
Forward exchange rate	The rate for the purchase or sale of a currency where delivery will take place at a future date.
Gold standard	A monetary system in which the currency is convertible into gold at fixed exchange rates.
Indirect quotation method	Indicates the amount of units of a foreign currency needed to purchase one unit of the home country's currency.
International Bank for Reconstruction and Development, or **World Bank**	Created to help economic growth in developing countries.
International Monetary Fund (IMF)	Created to promote world trade through monitoring and maintaining fixed exchange rates and by making loans to countries facing balance of trade and payments problems.
International monetary system	Is a system of institutions and mechanisms to foster world trade, manage the flow of financial capital, and determine currency exchange rates.

Order bill of lading	Represents the written acceptance of goods for shipment by a transportation company and the terms under which the goods are to be transported to their destination.
Political risk	The risk associated with the possibility that a national government might confiscate or expropriate assets held by foreigners.
Sight draft	A financial instrument requiring immediate payment.
Special Drawing Rights (SDRs)	Are a reserve asset created by the IMF consisting of a basket or portfolio of currencies that could be used to make international payments.
Spot exchange rate	The rate being quoted for the immediate delivery of the currency.
Time draft	A financial instrument requiring payment at a later date.
Traveler's letter of credit	Issued by a bank in one country and addressed to a list of foreign banks authorizing them to cash checks or purchase drafts presented by the bearer.
U.S. balance of payments	A summary of all economic transactions with the rest of the world. It includes foreign investment, private, and government grants; U.S. military spending overseas; and many other items besides the buying and selling of goods and services.

ASSESS YOUR UNDERSTANDING

Go to www.wiley.com/college/Melicher to evaluate your knowledge of the basics of the global economy.
Measure your learning by comparing pre-test and post-test results.

Summary Questions

1. The United Nations operates a world central bank that provides a world monetary unit to accommodate commerce across national boundaries. True or false?

2. Prior to the start of World War I, the international monetary system operated mostly under a gold standard in which the currencies of major countries were convertible into gold at fixed exchange rates. True or false?

3. The International Monetary Fund (IMF) was created to control the excessive growth and inflation of developing nations. True or false?

4. A flexible exchange rate system in which currency exchange rates are determined by supply and demand has been in place since the Bretton Woods Agreement in 1944. True or false?

5. The European Monetary Union (EMU) is an organization of 12 European countries that agreed to have a common overall monetary policy and the euro as their common currency. True or false?

6. The euro is the official currency of the European Monetary Union. True or false?

7. An indirect exchange rate quotation is simply the reciprocal of a direct exchange rate quotation. True or false?

8. The exchange rate is the rate at which a given unit of foreign currency is quoted in terms of
   (a) commodity prices.
   (b) the domestic currency.
   (c) the foreign currency.
   (d) gold.

9. The price that an individual must pay when purchasing claims to foreign exchange
   (a) is always higher than the basic quotation rate.
   (b) is readily available in financial publications.
   (c) is relatively constant from day to day.
   (d) varies widely among sources of foreign exchange.

10. Slow economic growth in investments in another country would be an example of political risk. True or false?

11. The effect of arbitrage activities in foreign exchange markets is to
    (a) create disparity among the rates of various currencies.
    (b) eliminate or reduce rate quotation differentials.
    (c) hinder the otherwise smooth functioning of the exchange markets.
    (d) create wide swings in quotations from period to period.

12. A stronger U.S. dollar generally
    (a) results in more imports of foreign merchandise.
    (b) leads to concern about worsening trade deficits.
    (c) results in lower domestic inflation.
    (d) All of the above

13. The banker's sight draft provides an exchange rate that is lower than either the banker's time draft or cable rate. True or false?

14. The order bill of lading represents the written acceptance of goods for shipment by a transportation company and the terms under which the goods are to be transported to their destination. True or false?

15. A trust receipt is an instrument through which a bank retains title to goods until they are paid for. True or false?

16. The bankers' acceptance and the documentary draft involve four principal parties: the importer, the importer's bank, the exporter, and the exporter's bank. True or false?

17. A purchasing agent for a domestic art gallery touring foreign countries for possible acquisitions might find it convenient to have
    (a) travelers' checks.
    (b) a commercial letter of credit.
    (c) regular checkbook drafts.
    (d) a traveler's letter of credit.

18. The Export-Import Bank
    (a) makes loans and offers guarantees to foreign exporters to the United States.
    (b) may offer emergency credits to assist other countries to maintain their level of imports from the United States.
    (c) makes loans or offers guarantees when the soundness of the transaction is in doubt.
    (d) makes loans to domestic exporters to encourage foreign trade.

19. The _____ includes ALL international transactions.
    (a) balance of trade
    (b) balance of payments
    (c) current account balance
    (d) capital account balance

Review Questions

1. What is the purpose of an international monetary system?
2. What is meant by the statement that the international monetary system has operated mostly under a "gold standard"?
3. What are the major criticisms associated with being on a gold standard?
4. Describe the Bretton Woods system for setting currency exchange rates.
5. What is meant by "special drawing rights" and how are they used to foster world trade?
6. What is meant by an international monetary system based on "flexible exchange rates"?
7. Describe the international monetary system currently in use.
8. What is the European Union (EU)?
9. Who are the current members of the EU?
10. What is the European Monetary Union (EMU)?
11. How does the EU differ from the EMU?
12. Who are the current members of the EMU?
13. What is the euro?
14. What are currency or foreign exchange markets?
15. Explain the role of supply and demand in establishing exchange rates between countries.
16. Describe the activities and economic role of the arbitrageur in international finance.
17. What is a sight draft?
18. Describe the various ways by which an exporter may finance an international shipment of goods.
19. How do commercial banks assist the exporter in collecting drafts?
20. How do importers protect themselves against improper delivery of goods when they are required to make payment as they place an order?
21. What is a letter of credit?
22. How do banks ensure that a letter of credit is not overdrawn?
23. What are the costs involved in connection with financing exports through bankers' acceptances?
24. How are the current balance account and the capital balance account adjusted for changes?

Applying This Chapter

1. You are the owner of a business that has offices and production facilities in several foreign countries. Your product is sold in all of these countries,

and you maintain bank accounts in the cities in which you have offices. At present you have short-term notes outstanding at most of the banks with which you maintain deposits. This borrowing is to support seasonal production activity. One of the countries in which you have offices is now strongly rumored to be on the point of a devaluation, or lowering, of their currency relative to that of the rest of the world. What actions might this rumor cause you to take?

2. Explain the concept of "balance" as it relates to a nation's balance of payments.

3. As an exporter of relatively expensive electronic equipment, you have a substantial investment in the merchandise that you ship. Your foreign importers are typically small- or medium-size firms without a long history of operations. Although your terms of sales require payment upon receipt of the merchandise, you are concerned about the possible problem of nonpayment and the need to reclaim merchandise that you have shipped. How might the banking system assist and protect you in this situation?

4. As an importer of merchandise, you depend upon the sale of the merchandise for funds to make payment. Although customary terms of sale are 90 days for this type of merchandise, you are not well known to foreign suppliers because of your recent entry into business. Furthermore, your suppliers require almost immediate payment to meet their own expenses of operations. How might the banking systems of the exporter and importer accommodate your situation?

5. As a speculator in the financial markets, you notice that for the last few minutes Swiss francs are being quoted in New York at a price of $0.5849 and in Frankfurt at $0.5851.

   (a) Assuming that you have access to international trading facilities, what action might you take?

   (b) What would be the effect of your actions and those of other speculators on these exchange rates?

6. You manage the cash for a large multinational industrial enterprise. As a result of credit sales on 90-day payment terms, you have a large claim against a customer in Madrid. You have heard rumors of the possible devaluation of the Spanish peseta. What actions, if any, can you take to protect your firm against the consequences of a prospective devaluation?

7. Assume, as the loan officer of a commercial bank, that one of your customers has asked for a "commercial letter of credit" to enable his firm to import a supply of well-known French wines. This customer has a long record of commercial success yet has large outstanding debts to other creditors. In what way might you accommodate the customer and at the same time establish protection for your bank?

8. Assume you are the international vice president of a small U.S.-based manufacturing corporation. You are trying to expand your business in several developing countries. You are also aware that some business practices are considered to be "acceptable" in these countries but not necessarily in the United States. How would your react to the following situations?

(a) You met yesterday with a government official from one of the countries you would like to make sales in. He said that he could speed up the process for acquiring the necessary licenses for conducting business in his country if you would pay him for his time and effort. What would you do?

(b) You are trying to make a major sale of your firm's products to the government of a foreign country. You have identified the key decision maker. You are considering offering the official a monetary payment if she would recommend buying your firm's products. What would you do?

(c) Your firm has a local office in a developing country where you are trying to increase business opportunities. Representatives from a local crime syndicate have approached you and have offered to provide "local security" in exchange for a monthly payment to them. What would you do?

YOU TRY IT

Exchange Rate

Find the current exchange rate for the dollar. How many dollars currently equals one euro?

Ethics

You are the financial manager for a manufacturing facility in the United States. Your boss sends you to Russia to scout out locations for a manufacturing plant. You find very inexpensive property. The labor costs in Russia are so low that it will save your company $1 billion per year. The Russian officials, however, want a kickback of $10,000. What do you do?

Global Economies

For the entire year, the nation's balance of trade with other nations has been in a substantial deficit position, yet, as always, the overall balance of payments will be in "balance." Describe the various factors that accomplish this overall balance, in spite of the deficit in the balance of trade.

Banker's Acceptance

In what situations would you use a banker's acceptance?

APPENDIX A

Table 1: Future Value of $1 (FVIF)

Year	1%	2%	3%	4%	5%	6%	7%	8%	9%
1	1.010	1.020	1.030	1.040	1.050	1.060	1.070	1.080	1.090
2	1.020	1.040	1.061	1.082	1.102	1.124	1.145	1.166	1.188
3	1.030	1.061	1.093	1.125	1.158	1.191	1.225	1.260	1.295
4	1.041	1.082	1.126	1.170	1.216	1.262	1.311	1.360	1.412
5	1.051	1.104	1.159	1.217	1.276	1.338	1.403	1.469	1.539
6	1.062	1.126	1.194	1.265	1.340	1.419	1.501	1.587	1.677
7	1.072	1.149	1.230	1.316	1.407	1.504	1.606	1.714	1.828
8	1.083	1.172	1.267	1.369	1.477	1.594	1.718	1.851	1.993
9	1.094	1.195	1.305	1.423	1.551	1.689	1.838	1.999	2.172
10	1.105	1.219	1.344	1.480	1.629	1.791	1.967	2.159	2.367
11	1.116	1.243	1.384	1.539	1.710	1.898	2.105	2.332	2.580
12	1.127	1.268	1.426	1.601	1.796	2.012	2.252	2.518	2.813
13	1.138	1.294	1.469	1.665	1.886	2.113	2.410	2.720	3.066
14	1.149	1.319	1.513	1.732	1.980	2.261	2.579	2.937	3.342
15	1.161	1.346	1.558	1.801	2.079	2.397	2.759	3.172	3.642
16	1.173	1.373	1.605	1.873	2.183	2.540	2.952	3.426	3.970
17	1.184	1.400	1.653	1.948	2.292	2.693	3.159	3.700	4.328
18	1.196	1.428	1.702	2.026	2.407	2.854	3.380	3.996	4.717
19	1.208	1.457	1.754	2.107	2.527	3.026	3.617	4.316	5.142
20	1.220	1.486	1.806	2.191	2.653	3.207	3.870	4.661	5.604
25	1.282	1.641	2.094	2.666	3.386	4.292	5.427	6.848	8.623
30	1.348	1.811	2.427	3.243	4.322	5.743	7.612	10.063	13.268

(Continues)

Note: The basic equation for finding the future value interest factor (FVIF) is:

$$FVIF_{r,n} = (1 + r)_n$$

where r is the interest rate and n is the number of periods in years.

Future Value of $1 (FVIF) *(Continued)*

10%	12%	14%	15%	16%	18%	20%	25%	30%
1.100	1.120	1.140	1.150	1.160	1.180	1.200	1.250	1.300
1.210	1.254	1.300	1.322	1.346	1.392	1.440	1.563	1.690
1.331	1.405	1.482	1.521	1.561	1.643	1.728	1.953	2.197
1.464	1.574	1.689	1.749	1.811	1.939	2.074	2.441	2.856
1.611	1.762	1.925	2.011	2.100	2.288	2.488	3.052	3.713
1.772	1.974	2.195	2.313	2.436	2.700	2.986	3.815	4.827
1.949	2.211	2.502	2.660	2.826	3.185	3.583	4.768	6.276
2.144	2.476	2.853	3.059	3.278	3.759	4.300	5.960	8.157
2.358	2.773	3.252	3.518	3.803	4.435	5.160	7.451	10.604
2.594	3.106	3.707	4.046	4.411	5.234	6.192	9.313	13.786
2.853	3.479	4.226	4.652	5.117	6.176	7.430	11.642	17.922
3.138	3.896	4.818	5.350	5.936	7.288	8.916	14.552	23.298
3.452	4.363	5.492	6.153	6.886	8.599	10.699	18.190	30.288
3.797	4.887	6.261	7.076	7.988	10.147	12.839	22.737	39.374
4.177	5.474	7.138	8.137	9.266	11.974	15.407	28.422	51.186
4.595	6.130	8.137	9.358	10.748	14.129	18.488	35.527	66.542
5.054	6.866	9.276	10.761	12.468	16.672	22.186	44.409	86.504
5.560	7.690	10.575	12.375	14.463	19.673	26.623	55.511	112.460
6.116	8.613	12.056	14.232	16.777	23.214	31.948	69.389	146.190
6.728	9.646	13.743	16.367	19.461	27.393	38.338	86.736	190.050
10.835	17.000	26.462	32.919	40.874	62.669	95.396	264.700	705.640
17.449	29.960	50.950	66.212	85.850	143.371	237.376	807.790	2,620.000

Table 2: Present Value of $1 (PVIF)

Year	1%	2%	3%	4%	5%	6%	7%	8%	9%	10%
1	0.990	0.980	0.971	0.962	0.952	0.943	0.935	0.926	0.917	0.909
2	0.980	0.961	0.943	0.925	0.907	0.890	0.873	0.857	0.842	0.826
3	0.971	0.942	0.915	0.889	0.864	0.840	0.816	0.794	0.772	0.751
4	0.961	0.924	0.888	0.855	0.823	0.792	0.763	0.735	0.708	0.683
5	0.951	0.906	0.863	0.822	0.784	0.747	0.713	0.681	0.650	0.621
6	0.942	0.888	0.837	0.790	0.746	0.705	0.666	0.630	0.596	0.564
7	0.933	0.871	0.813	0.760	0.711	0.665	0.623	0.583	0.547	0.513
8	0.923	0.853	0.789	0.731	0.677	0.627	0.582	0.540	0.502	0.467
9	0.914	0.837	0.766	0.703	0.645	0.592	0.544	0.500	0.460	0.424
10	0.905	0.820	0.744	0.676	0.614	0.558	0.508	0.463	0.422	0.386
11	0.896	0.804	0.722	0.650	0.585	0.527	0.475	0.429	0.388	0.350
12	0.887	0.788	0.701	0.625	0.557	0.497	0.444	0.397	0.356	0.319
13	0.879	0.773	0.681	0.601	0.530	0.469	0.415	0.368	0.326	0.290
14	0.870	0.758	0.661	0.577	0.505	0.442	0.388	0.340	0.299	0.263
15	0.861	0.743	0.642	0.555	0.481	0.417	0.362	0.315	0.275	0.239
16	0.853	0.728	0.623	0.534	0.458	0.394	0.339	0.292	0.252	0.218
17	0.844	0.714	0.605	0.513	0.436	0.391	0.317	0.270	0.231	0.198
18	0.836	0.700	0.587	0.494	0.416	0.350	0.296	0.250	0.212	0.180
19	0.828	0.686	0.570	0.475	0.396	0.331	0.276	0.232	0.194	0.164
20	0.820	0.673	0.554	0.456	0.377	0.312	0.258	0.215	0.178	0.149
25	0.780	0.610	0.478	0.375	0.295	0.233	0.184	0.146	0.116	0.092
30	0.742	0.552	0.412	0.308	0.231	0.174	0.131	0.099	0.075	0.057

(Continues)

Note: The basic equation for finding the present value interest factor (PVIF) is:

$$PVIF_{r,n} = \frac{1}{(1 + r)_n}$$

where r is the interest or discount rate and n is the number of periods in years

Present Value of $1 (PVIF) *(Continued)*

12%	14%	15%	16%	18%	20%	25%	30%
0.893	0.877	0.870	0.862	0.847	0.833	0.800	0.769
0.797	0.769	0.756	0.743	0.718	0.694	0.640	0.592
0.712	0.675	0.658	0.641	0.609	0.579	0.512	0.455
0.636	0.592	0.572	0.552	0.516	0.482	0.410	0.350
0.567	0.519	0.497	0.476	0.437	0.402	0.328	0.269
0.507	0.456	0.432	0.410	0.370	0.335	0.262	0.207
0.452	0.400	0.376	0.354	0.314	0.279	0.210	0.159
0.404	0.351	0.327	0.305	0.266	0.233	0.168	0.123
0.361	0.308	0.284	0.263	0.225	0.194	0.134	0.094
0.322	0.270	0.247	0.227	0.191	0.162	0.107	0.073
0.287	0.237	0.215	0.195	0.162	0.135	0.086	0.056
0.257	0.208	0.187	0.168	0.137	0.112	0.069	0.043
0.229	0.182	0.163	0.145	0.116	0.093	0.055	0.033
0.205	0.160	0.141	0.125	0.099	0.078	0.044	0.025
0.183	0.140	0.123	0.108	0.084	0.065	0.035	0.020
0.163	0.123	0.107	0.093	0.071	0.054	0.028	0.015
0.146	0.108	0.093	0.080	0.060	0.045	0.023	0.012
0.130	0.095	0.081	0.069	0.051	0.038	0.018	0.009
0.116	0.083	0.070	0.060	0.043	0.031	0.014	0.007
0.104	0.073	0.061	0.051	0.037	0.026	0.012	0.005
0.059	0.038	0.030	0.024	0.016	0.010	0.004	0.001
0.033	0.020	0.015	0.012	0.007	0.004	0.001	0.000

Table 3: Future Value of a $1 Ordinary Annuity (FVIFA)

Year	1%	2%	3%	4%	5%	6%	7%	8%
1	1.000	1.000	1.000	1.000	1.000	1.000	1.000	1.000
2	2.010	2.020	2.030	2.040	2.050	2.060	2.070	2.080
3	3.030	3.060	3.091	3.122	3.152	3.184	3.215	3.246
4	4.060	4.122	4.184	4.246	4.310	4.375	4.440	4.506
5	5.101	5.204	5.309	5.416	5.526	5.637	5.751	5.867
6	6.152	6.308	6.468	6.633	6.802	6.975	7.153	7.336
7	7.214	7.434	7.662	7.898	8.142	8.394	8.654	8.923
8	8.286	8.583	8.892	9.214	9.549	9.897	10.260	10.637
9	9.369	9.755	10.159	10.583	11.027	11.491	11.978	12.488
10	10.462	10.950	11.464	12.006	12.578	13.181	13.816	14.487
11	11.567	12.169	12.808	13.486	14.207	14.972	15.784	16.645
12	12.683	13.412	14.192	15.026	15.917	16.870	17.888	18.977
13	13.809	14.680	15.618	16.627	17.713	18.882	20.141	21.495
14	14.947	15.974	17.086	18.292	19.599	21.015	22.550	24.215
15	16.097	17.293	18.599	20.024	21.579	23.276	25.129	27.152
16	17.258	18.639	20.157	21.825	23.657	25.673	27.888	30.324
17	18.430	20.012	21.762	23.698	25.840	28.213	30.840	33.750
18	19.615	21.412	23.414	25.645	28.132	30.906	33.999	37.450
19	20.811	22.841	25.117	27.671	30.539	33.760	37.379	41.466
20	22.019	24.297	26.870	29.778	33.066	36.786	40.995	45.762
25	28.243	32.030	36.459	41.646	47.727	54.865	63.249	73.106
30	34.785	40.568	47.575	56.805	66.439	79.058	94.461	113.283

(Continues)

Note: the basic equation for finding the future value interest factor of an ordinary annuity (FVIFA) is:

$$FVIFAr,n = \sum_{t=1}^{n}(1 + r)^{n-t} = \frac{(1 + r)^n - 1}{r}$$

where r is the interest rate and n is the number of periods in years.
Future Value of a $1 Annuity Due (FVIFAD)
The future value interest factor of an annuity due (FVIFAD) may be found by using the following formula to convert FVIFA values found in Table 3:

$$FVIFAD_{r,n} = FVIFA_{r,n}(1 + r)$$

where r is the interest rate and n is the number of periods in years.

Future Value of a $1 Ordinary Annuity (FVIFA) *(Continued)*

9%	10%	12%	14%	16%	18%	20%	25%	30%
1.000	1.000	1.000	1.000	1.000	1.000	1.000	1.000	1.000
2.090	2.100	2.120	2.140	2.160	2.180	2.200	2.250	2.300
3.278	3.310	3.374	3.440	3.506	3.572	3.640	3.813	3.990
4.573	4.641	4.779	4.921	5.066	5.215	5.368	5.766	6.187
5.985	6.105	6.353	6.610	6.877	7.154	7.442	8.207	9.043
7.523	7.716	8.115	8.536	8.977	9.442	9.930	11.259	12.756
9.200	9.487	10.089	10.730	11.414	12.142	12.916	15.073	17.583
11.028	11.436	12.300	13.233	14.240	15.327	16.499	19.842	23.858
13.021	13.579	14.776	16.085	17.518	19.086	20.799	25.802	32.015
15.193	15.937	17.549	19.337	21.321	23.521	25.959	33.253	42.619
17.560	18.531	20.655	23.044	25.733	28.755	32.150	42.566	56.405
20.141	21.384	24.133	27.271	30.850	34.931	39.580	54.208	74.327
22.953	24.523	28.029	32.089	36.786	42.219	48.497	68.760	97.625
26.019	27.975	32.393	37.581	43.672	50.818	59.196	86.949	127.910
29.361	31.772	37.280	43.842	51.660	60.965	72.035	109.690	167.290
33.003	35.950	42.753	50.980	60.925	72.939	87.442	138.110	218.470
36.974	40.545	48.884	59.118	71.673	87.068	105.931	173.640	285.010
41.301	45.599	55.750	68.394	84.141	103.740	128.117	218.050	371.520
46.018	51.159	63.440	78.969	98.603	123.414	154.740	273.560	483.970
51.160	57.275	72.052	91.025	115.380	146.628	186.688	342.950	630.170
84.701	98.347	133.334	181.871	249.214	342.603	471.981	1,054.800	2,348.800
136.308	164.494	241.333	356.787	530.312	790.948	1,181.882	3,227.200	8,730.000

Table 4: Present Value of a $1 Ordinary Annuity (PVIFA)

Year	1%	2%	3%	4%	5%	6%	7%	8%	9%	10%
1	0.990	0.980	0.971	0.962	0.952	0.943	0.935	0.926	0.917	0.909
2	1.970	1.942	1.913	1.886	1.859	1.833	1.808	1.783	1.759	1.736
3	2.941	2.884	2.829	2.775	2.723	2.673	2.624	2.577	2.531	2.487
4	3.902	3.808	3.717	3.630	3.546	3.465	3.387	3.312	3.240	3.170
5	4.853	4.713	4.580	4.452	4.329	4.212	4.100	3.993	3.890	3.791
6	5.795	5.601	5.417	5.242	5.076	4.917	4.767	4.623	4.486	4.355
7	6.728	6.472	6.230	6.002	5.786	5.582	5.389	5.206	5.033	4.868
8	7.652	7.325	7.020	6.733	6.463	6.210	5.971	5.747	5.535	5.335
9	8.566	8.162	7.786	7.435	7.108	6.802	6.515	6.247	5.995	5.759
10	9.471	8.983	8.530	8.111	7.722	7.360	7.024	6.710	6.418	6.145
11	10.368	9.787	9.253	8.760	8.306	7.887	7.499	7.139	6.805	6.495
12	11.255	10.575	9.954	9.385	8.863	8.384	7.943	7.536	7.161	6.814
13	12.134	11.348	10.635	9.986	9.394	8.853	8.358	7.904	7.487	7.103
14	13.004	12.106	11.296	10.563	9.899	9.295	8.745	8.244	7.786	7.367
15	13.865	12.849	11.938	11.118	10.380	9.712	9.108	8.559	8.061	7.606
16	14.718	13.578	12.561	11.652	10.838	10.106	9.447	8.851	8.313	7.824
17	15.562	14.292	13.166	12.166	11.274	10.477	9.763	9.122	8.544	8.022
18	16.398	14.992	13.754	12.659	11.690	10.828	10.059	9.372	8.756	8.201
19	17.226	15.678	14.324	13.134	12.085	11.158	10.336	9.604	8.950	8.365
20	18.046	16.351	14.877	13.590	12.462	11.470	10.594	9.818	9.129	8.514
25	22.023	19.523	17.413	15.622	14.094	12.783	11.654	10.675	9.823	9.077
30	25.808	22.397	19.600	17.292	15.372	13.765	12.409	11.258	10.274	9.427

(Continues)

Note: The basic equation for finding the present value interest factor of an ordinary annuity (PVIFA) is:

$$PVIFA_{r,n} = \sum_{t=1}^{n} \frac{1}{(1 + r)^t} = \frac{1 - \dfrac{1}{(1 + r)^n}}{r}$$

where r is the interest or discount rate and n is the number of periods in years.
Present Value of a $1 Annuity Due (PVIFAD)
The present value interest factor of an annuity due (PVIFAD) may be found by using the following formula to convert PVIFA values found in Table 4:

$$PVIFAD_{r,n} + PVIFA_{r,n}(1 + r)$$

where r is the interest or discount rate and n is the number of periods in years.

Present Value of a $1 Ordinary Annuity (PVIFA) *(Continued)*

12%	14%	16%	18%	20%	25%	30%
0.893	0.877	0.862	0.847	0.833	0.800	0.769
1.690	1.647	1.605	1.566	1.528	1.440	1.361
2.402	2.322	2.246	2.174	2.106	1.952	1.816
3.037	2.914	2.798	2.690	2.589	2.362	2.166
3.605	3.433	3.274	3.127	2.991	2.689	2.436
4.111	3.889	3.685	3.498	3.326	2.951	2.643
4.564	4.288	4.039	3.812	3.605	3.161	2.802
4.968	4.639	4.344	4.078	3.837	3.329	2.925
5.328	4.946	4.607	4.303	4.031	3.463	3.019
5.650	5.216	4.833	4.494	4.193	3.571	3.092
5.938	5.453	5.029	4.656	4.327	3.656	3.147
6.194	5.660	5.197	4.793	4.439	3.725	3.190
6.424	5.842	5.342	4.910	4.533	3.780	3.223
6.628	6.002	5.468	5.008	4.611	3.824	3.249
6.811	6.142	5.575	5.092	4.675	3.859	3.268
6.974	6.265	5.668	5.162	4.730	3.887	3.283
7.120	5.373	5.749	4.222	4.775	3.910	3.295
7.250	6.467	5.818	5.273	4.812	3.928	3.304
7.366	6.550	5.877	5.316	4.843	3.942	3.311
7.469	6.623	5.929	5.353	4.870	3.954	3.316
7.843	6.873	6.097	5.467	4.948	3.985	3.329
8.055	7.003	6.177	5.517	4.979	3.995	3.332

GLOSSARY

52 WEEKS HI and **LO**   Present the high and low stock prices for the previous 52 weeks.

Adjustable-rate mortgage (ARM)   Interest rates on these home loans rise and fall in line with a specified government rate, usually a treasury security.

Advance factoring   Form of factoring where the factor pays the firm for its receivables before the account due date.

Agency costs   Tangible and intangible expenses borne by shareholders because of the actual or potential self-servicing actions of managers.

Aggressive approach   When all current assets, both temporary and permanent, are financed with short-term financing.

American depository receipts (ADR)   Represent shares of common stock that trade on a foreign stock exchange.

Amortized loan   Loan that is repaid in equal payments over a specified time period.

Annual reports   Contain descriptive information on operating and financial performance during the past year, a discussion of current and future business opportunities, and financial statements that provide a record of financial performance.

Annual straight-line depreciation   Expense is computed by dividing the asset's cost by an estimate of its useful life.

Annuity   A series of equal payments (receipts) that occur over a number of time periods.

Annuity due   Exists when the equal periodic payments occur at the beginning of each period.

Arbitrage   The simultaneous purchasing of commodities, securities, or bills of exchange in one market and selling them in another where the price is higher.

Arithmetic average return   The sum of all the returns for the years divided by the number of years, R, over n periods

Ask price   The price at which the owner is willing to sell the securities.

Asset-management ratios   Measure that indicates the extent to which assets are used to support sales.

Assets   Cash, inventory, accounts receivable, fixed assets, and investments.

Asset securitization   Bonds that have coupon and principal payments that are paid from another existing cash flow source.

Average collection period   Measure that indicates how long it takes a company to collect its accounts receivables. It is calculated by taking the year-end accounts receivable divided by the average net sales per day.

Average payment period   Measure that includes all of a company's financial obligations and how long, in terms of days, it will take the company to fulfill their obligations. It is computed by dividing the year-end accounts payable amount by the firm's average cost of goods sold per day.

Average tax rate   Determined by dividing the total tax amount by the total taxable income.

Balance of trade   The net value of a country's exports of goods and services compared to its imports.

Balance sheet   A statement of a company's financial position as of a particular date, usually at the end of the quarter or year.

Bankers' acceptance   A promise of future payment issued by a firm and guaranteed by a bank.

Bankruptcy costs   Costs associated with financial distress, including legal and accounting fees, court costs, and the time and effort management must put forth to oversee the bankruptcy process.

Base case   A firm's after-tax cash flows without a new project.

Bearer bonds   Coupons that are literally "clipped" from the side of the bond certificate and presented, like a check, to a bank for payment. With a bearer bond, the issuer does not know who is receiving the interest payments.

Best-effort agreement   One in which investment bankers try to sell the securities of the issuing corporation, but they assume no risk for a possible failure of the sale or the flotation.

Beta (β)   The measure of an asset's systematic risk.

Bid price   The price the buyer is willing to pay for the securities.

Blanket inventory lien   A claim against a customer's inventory when individual items are indistinguishable, as may be the case with grain or clothing items.

Bond   A debt agreement that a corporation or government agency issues when it wants to borrow money for more than 10 years. The issuer agrees to pay back the lender at a specified maturity date, with interest.

Bond covenants   Rules or regulations imposing restrictions on the firm; they are often included in trust indentures.

Bond ratings   Assesses both the collateral underlying the bonds as well as the ability of the issuer to make timely payments of interest and principal.

Boom economy   The domestic economy will grow at an above-average pace; inflation will increase slowly; interest rate trends will be slightly upward.

Break-even analysis   Financial technique used to estimate how many units of product must be sold in order for the firm to break even or have a zero profit.

Breton Woods System   An international monetary system in which individual currencies are tied to gold through the U.S. dollar via fixed or pegged exchange rates.

Brokerage firms   Firms that assist individuals who want to purchase new stock issues or who want to sell previously purchased securities.

Business angels   Private investors who provide start-up capital for small businesses.

Business risk   Variability in EBIT over time.

Buying on margin   Means the investor borrows money and invests it along with his own funds in securities.

Callable bonds   Can be redeemed by the issuing corporation prior to maturity.

Callable preferred stock   Gives the corporation the right to retire the preferred stock at its option.

Call option   Contract for the purchase of a security within a specified time and at a specified price.

Cannibalization   Occurs when a project robs cash flow from the firm's existing lines of business.

Capacity   The ability to pay bills and often involves an examination of liquidity ratios.

Capital   The adequacy of owners' equity relative to existing liabilities as the underlying support for creditworthiness.

Capital account balance   Includes all foreign private and government investment in the United States netted against U.S. investments in foreign countries.

Capital asset pricing model   States that the expected return on an asset depends upon its level of systematic risk.

Capital budgeting   The process of identifying, evaluating, and implementing a company's investment opportunities.

Capital formation   The expansion of capital or capital goods through savings, which leads to investment.

Capital gains   Are realized only when the stock is sold.

Capital losses   Are realized if the sale price of the stock is lower than the purchase price.

Capital markets   Markets that include debt securities with maturities longer than 1 year and equity securities.

Capital structure   A firm's mix of debt and equity.

Cash budget   The cash inflows and cash outflows of a firm over a specific time frame.

Cash conversion cycle   The time it takes to collect money from the company's customers and use those funds to pay its suppliers.

Central bank   A government-established organization responsible for supervising and regulating the banking system and for creating and regulating the money supply.

Change the discount rate   The interest rate charged by Federal Reserve Banks to depository institutions.

Change the reserve requirements   The portions of deposits that banks must maintain either in their own vaults or on deposit at a Federal Reserve Bank.

Character   The ethical quality of the applicant and his/her willingness to pay bills on time and is best judged by reviewing the past credit history for the company or person.

Checks   Document used to withdraw, deposit, or transfer money from a bank account. Also referred to as *drafts*.

Churning   When a broker constantly buys and sells securities from a client's portfolio in an effort to generate commissions.

Class A shares   Class of common stock. The stock issues for trading from an Initial Public offering or if a company issues new stock at a later date.

Class B shares   Class of common stock. A special category of stock usually retained by company founders at the time a company goes public. It carries certain rights not granted to stock available to the Public. For example, only owners of Class B stock can vote.

Clean draft   Draft that is not accompanied by any special documents and is generally used when the exporter has confidence in the importer's ability to meet the draft when presented.

CLOSE   Indicates the stock's current price.

Closed-end mortgage bond   Does not permit future bond issues to be secured by any of the assets pledged as security under the closed-end issue.

Coefficient of variation (CV)   A measure of risk per unit of return.

Collateral   Assets that secure credit.

Collection float   The time between when a payer sends payment and the funds are credited to the payee's bank account.

Commercial banks   Financial institutions that collects deposits from individuals and lends those funds to businesses and individuals.

Commercial finance company   An organization without a bank charter that advances funds to businesses by (1) discounting accounts receivable, (2) making loans secured by chattel mortgages on machinery or liens on inventory, or (3) financing deferred-payment sales of commercial and industrial equipment.

Commercial paper   A short-term unsecured promissory note issued by a corporation with a high credit rating.

Commercial paper   A short-term promissory note backed solely by the credit quality of the issuer; there is no security or collateral behind them.

Common shareholders claim on business profits   Available only to those that remain after the holders of all other classes of debt and equity securities have received payments or returns.

Common-size financial statements   Express balance sheet numbers as a percentage of total assets and income statement numbers as a percentage of revenue.

Common stock   Represents ownership shares in a corporation.

Compensating balance   Ten to 20% of outstanding unsecured loans must be kept on deposit by the business.

Competitive advantage   The reason that customers are willing to purchase one company's products or services rather than another firm's.

Compounding   An arithmetic process whereby an initial value increases or grows at a compound interest rate over time to reach a value in the future.

Compound interest   Process where an initial value earns interest on interest in addition to interest on the principal or initial investment.

Conditions   The current economic climate and state of the business cycle. They are an important consideration in assessing whether the applicant can meet credit obligations.

Constant growth stocks   Stocks from corporations that are stable and profitable.

Consumer Advisory Council   Group composed of representatives from depository institutions and their customers. The council provides advice relating to consumer issues.

Contractual savings organizations   Organizations that collect premiums and contributions from participants and provide retirement benefits and insurance against major financial losses.

Convertible bond   Can be changed, or converted, at the investor's option, into a specified number of shares of the issuer's common stock.

Convertible preferred stock   Has a special provision that makes it possible to convert the preferred stock into the common stock of the corporation. This is generally the stockholder's option.

Corporate bonds   Bonds issued by corporations and are typically issued with 5- to 20-year maturities.

Cost of capital   Project's required rate of return.

Cost of capital   The minimum acceptable rate of return to a firm on a project.

Cost-volume-profit analysis   Financial technique used by managers for financial planning to estimate the firm's operating profits at different levels of unit sales.

Credit bureaus   Firms that obtain credit information about business firms and individuals.

Credit money   Money backed by the creditworthiness of the issuer; can be used instead of physical money.

Credit unions   Banks that focus on working with consumers and provide loans to individuals seeking to purchase items such as automobiles and houses.

Cross-section analysis   Financial technique that uses ratios to compare different companies at the same point in time.

Cumulative preferred stock   Requires that before dividends on common stock are paid, preferred dividends must be paid not only for the current period but also for all previous periods in which preferred dividends were not paid.

Currency   U.S. physical money in the form of coins and paper currency.

Currency exchange markets   Also called *foreign exchange markets*; electronic markets where banks and institutional traders buy and sell various currencies on behalf of businesses, other clients, and themselves.

Currency exchange rate   Indicates the value of one currency relative to another currency.

Current account balance   Shows the flow of income in and out of the United States during a specific period.

Current ratio   Measure of a company's ability to pay off its short-term debt as it comes due.

Current yield   Calculated by dividing the annual coupon interest by the current price.

Debenture bonds   Unsecured obligations that depend on the general credit strength of the corporation for their security.

Debt securities   Obligations to repay borrowed funds. Federal, state, and local governments can issue debt securities, while business corporations and financial institutions can issue both debt and equity securities.

Default risk premium   Indicates compensation for the possibility that the borrower will not pay interest and/or repay principal according to the loan agreement.

Deferred annuities   Available for those who wish to use this financial tool to accumulate retirement funds. Tax on the income it earns is postponed until the money is withdrawn.

Demand deposit   A type of deposit money that gets its name from the fact that the owner of a deposit account may demand that all or a portion of the amount in his or her account be transferred to another individual or organization.

Deposit money   A special type of credit money. It is backed by the good credit of the depository institution that issued the deposit.

Depreciation tax shield   Represents the tax savings due to depreciation of fixed assets. It equals the amount of the depreciation expense multiplied by the firm's tax rate.

Derivative securities   Financial contracts that derive their values from underlying securities or from other related financial assets; gaining widespread use among institutional investors and corporate managers.

Derivatives markets   Markets that facilitate the purchase and sale of derivative securities.

Development   Stage that requires estimating relevant cash inflows and outflows. It also involves discussing the pros and cons of each project. Development sometimes requires asking what the strategic impact will be of not doing the project.

Deviation   Computed as a periodic return minus the average return.

Direct investing   Firms sell their shares directly to the public.

Direct quotation method   Indicates the value of one unit of a foreign currency in terms of a home country's currency.

Disbursement float   The time between when a payer sends payment and when the funds are deducted from the payer's bank account.

Discount bonds   In times of declining interest rates, bonds may be sold at a discount.

Discount brokerages   Simply execute customer's stock transactions without offering recommendations or doing research for customers.

Discounted loan   Loan in which the borrower receives the principal less the interest at the time the loan is made.

Discounting   An arithmetic process whereby a future value decreases at a compound interest rate over time to reach a present value.

DIV   Lists the 12-month dividend paid by the firm.

Diversification   Occurs when we invest in several different assets rather than just a single one.

Dividend   A payment to the owner of a share of corporation's stock; represents the owner's portion of the corporation profits.

Dividend   Payments that represent the owner's portion of the corporation's stock. They may be paid monthly, quarterly, or annually, or in some cases not at all, depending on the profits earned by the issuing corporation.

Dividend reinvestment plans   Shareholder's dividends are used to purchase shares (including partial or fractional shares) of the corporation.

Dividend reinvestment plans   Allow the brokers and agents that run these plans to use the dividends on stockholders' stocks to purchase more stock.

Documentary draft   Accompanied by an order bill of lading along with other papers such as insurance receipts, certificates of sanitation, and consular invoices.

Dow Jones Industrial Average   An average of 30 well-known companies chosen by the editors of the *Wall Street Journal*. These companies represent trends in the stock market.

Draft or **bill of exchange**   An unconditional written order, signed by the party drawing it, requiring the party to whom it is addressed to pay a certain sum of money to orderer or to bearer.

Du Pont analysis   The technique of breaking down return on total assets and return on equity into their component parts.

Dutch auction bidding process   A variation of competitive bidding that allows smaller firms and individual investors to purchase securities.

EBIT/EPS analysis   Allows managers to see how different capital structures affect the earnings and risk levels of their firms.

Economic risk   The risk associated with the possibility of slow or negative economic growth, as well as variability in economic growth.

Efficient market   A market in which prices adjust quickly after the arrival of new information, and the price change reflects the economic value of the information, on average.

Electronic communications networks (ECN)   Computerized trading systems that automatically match buy and sell orders at specified prices.

Electronic funds transfers (ETFs)   Money that is transferred through the Internet.

Enhancement   Reflects an increase in the cash flows of the firm's other products that occur because of a new project.

Equipment trust certificate   A type of mortgage bond that gives the bondholder a claim to specific "rolling stock" (movable assets) such as railroad cars or airplanes.

Equity   Funds supplied by the owners and represents their residual claim on the firm.

Equity multiplier ratio   Measure of a company's financial leverage. Measure is determined by dividing total assets by total stockholders' equity. The higher the rate, the more the company is using debt to finance its asset base.

Equity securities   Ownership rights in businesses and institutions.

Euro   The official currency of the countries in the European Monetary Union.

Eurobonds   Bonds denominated in U.S. dollars that are sold to investors located in a country outside the United States.

Eurodollar bonds   Dollar-denominated bonds that are sold outside the United States.

European commercial paper (Euro CP) market   A market that offers advantages to commercial paper issuers just as the Eurodollar bond market offers advantages over the U.S. bond market. There is no SEC regulation of the Euro CP market, so commercial paper maturities are generally a little longer and interest costs lower.

European Monetary Union (EMU)   The 12-member organization of the EU that, by ratifying the Maastricht Treaty, agreed to have overall monetary policy set by the European Central Bank (ECB) and adopted the euro as their common currency.

European Union (EU)   Established to promote trade and economic development among European countries.

Exchange rates   An adjustment in exchange rates over time leads to higher or lower U.S. dollar cash flows from overseas sales, more competitively priced import goods, or changing input costs.

Exchange-traded futures   Are standardized as to terms and conditions, such as quality and quantity of the underlying asset and expiration dates.

Exit or abandonment option   If initial results from a multistage project are poor, managers can save the firm's value by reducing the size of the initial project or by pulling the plug and stopping the project completely to stop further value-diminishing investments.

Expectations theory   Belief that the shape of a yield curve reflects investor expectations about future inflation rates.

Extendable notes   Have their coupons reset every 2 or 3 years to reflect the current interest rate and any changes in the firm's credit quality.

Factor   Engages in accounts-receivable financing for business; purchases the accounts receivable outright and assumes all credit risks.

Factors of production   Land, capital, and labor needed to operate a business.

Fair Credit Billing Act   Sets up a procedure for the prompt correction of errors on a revolving charge account and prevents damage to credit ratings while a dispute is being settled.

Fair Credit Opportunity Act   Act that prohibits discrimination in the granting of credit on the basis of sex, marital status, race, color, religion, national origin, age, or receipt of public assistance.

Fair Credit Reporting Act   Act that sets a procedure for correcting mistakes on credit records and requires that records be used only for legitimate business purposes.

Federal Advisory Council   Group that provides advice and general information on banking-related issues to the board of governors.

Federal Deposit Insurance Corporation (FDIC)   Organization set up in 1933 to protect deposits in banks.

Federal Open Market Committee (FOMC)   Along with the five Reserve Bank presidents, the board manages our nation's money supply. FOMC meets eight times a year in Washington, D.C., to discuss the outlook for the U.S. economy and monetary policy.

Federal Reserve System (Fed)   The central bank of the United States and is responsible for setting monetary policy and regulating the banking system.

Field warehouse   An enterprise that has the means to establish a warehouse on the grounds of the borrowing business establishment.

Finance   The study of how individuals, institutions, governments, and businesses acquire, spend, and manage money and other financial assets.

Finance companies   Companies that loan money to individuals and businesses. Their loan requirements are not as stringent. However, finance companies traditionally charge higher interest rates on the loans they make.

Finance firms   Institutions that provide loans directly to consumers and businesses, as well as help borrowers obtain mortgage loans on real property.

Financial assets   Debt instruments, equity securities, and other financial contracts that are backed by real assets. Examples include mortgages and auto loans.

Financial institutions   Institutions that support capital formation either by channeling savings into investment in physical assets or by fostering direct investments by individuals in financial institutions and businesses.

Financial-leverage ratios   Measure that indicates the extent to which borrowed or debt funds are used to finance assets.

Financial management   Process that encompasses the people and companies who are responsible for financial planning, asset management, and fund-raising decisions. The goal of the management professional is to protect and increase the value of investments and businesses

Financial markets   Markets that work with institutions to facilitate the transfer of financial assets among individuals, institutions, businesses, and governments.

Financial system   A network of financial institutions that match one person's savings with another person's investment.

Fixed annuities   Earn a guaranteed rate of interest for a specified time period.

Fixed-assets-turnover ratio   Measure of how efficiently a company uses its fixed assets to generate sales. It is computed by dividing net sales by the fixed assets.

Fixed capital   A firm's fixed assets, which include plant, equipment, and property.

Fixed-charge-coverage ratio   Measure that indicates the ability of a firm to meet its contractual obligations for interest, leases, and debt principal repayments out of its operating income.

Flexibility option   Flexibility adds value; a work disruption in a plant in one country can allow the firm to shift production to another plant elsewhere.

Flexible exchange rates   A system in which currency exchange rates are determined by supply and demand.

Flexible-payment annuity   One in which contributions can be made anytime for any amounts.

Float   The time between sending out payments and having them actually be charged to the bank account.

Floor brokers   Fall into one of two categories: house brokers and independent brokers.

Flotation   The cost of the IPO.

Follow-up   Decisions need to be reviewed periodically with a follow-up analysis to determine whether they are meeting expectations. If disappointing results occur, it is sometimes necessary to terminate or abandon a new undertaking.

Foreign bonds   Bonds issued by a corporation or government that are valued in the currency of the country where it is sold.

Foreign Corrupt Practices Act (FCPA)   Prohibits U.S. firms from bribing foreign officials.

Forward exchange rate   The rate for the purchase or sale of a currency where delivery will take place at a future date.

Fourth market   A type of secondary market that is comprised of electronic communications networks, or ECNs, which are computerized trading systems that automatically match buy and sell orders at specified prices.

Full-bodied money   The metal content in gold and silver coins is worth the same as the face values of the coins.

Full-service brokerages   Execute trades and also have research staffs that analyze firms and make recommendations on which stocks to buy or sell.

Futures contract   Represents an obligation to buy or sell an asset at a specified price by a certain date.

Future value of a savings amount or investment   Value of a savings amount or investment at a specified time or date in the future.

Generally accepted accounting principles (GAAP)   A set of guidelines as to the form and manner in which accounting information should be presented.

Global bonds   Usually are denominated in U.S. dollars.

Global depository receipts (GDR)   Represent shares of common stock that are listed on the London Stock Exchange.

Gold standard   A monetary system in which the currencies is convertible into gold at fixed exchange rates.

Gross domestic product (GDP)   The measure of the output of goods and services in the economy.

Growth opportunities option   Investing may create as-yet-unforeseen opportunities that would not be available if the firm doesn't undertake the project.

Health of foreign economies   Growth in foreign economies will increase the demand for U.S. exports. Similarly, sluggish foreign demand will harm overseas sales and hurt the financial position of firms doing business overseas.

House brokers   Act as agents who carry out customers' orders for security purchases and sales.

Identification   Stage that involves finding potential capital investment opportunities and identifying whether a project involves a replacement decision and/or additional financing.

Immediate annuity   Income payments are steady and dependable. It can be set up for any time period and provide a lifetime of income if so desired. The income is based on the amount of the contribution, the interest rate, and the person's age.

Implementation   Stage where projects that are accepted must be executed in a timely manner.

Income statement   Reports the revenues generated and expenses incurred by the firm over an accounting period.

Incremental after-tax cash flows   Represent the difference between the firm's after-tax cash flows with a new project and the firm's base case, or after-tax cash flows without the project.

Independent brokers   May be asked by house brokers to help them handle their orders.

Independent projects   Projects that are not in direct competition with one another.

Indirect quotation method   Indicates the amount of units of a foreign currency needed to purchase one unit of the home country's currency.

Industry comparative analysis   Financial technique used to compare a firm's ratios against average ratios for other companies in the same industry.

Inflation   A rise in the price of goods. Simply stated, it means that a dollar buys less.

Inflation-adjusted bonds   Bonds where the principal value of the bond is adjusted every 6 months to keep pace with the consumer price index. The bond's coupon rate is then applied to the new principal value.

Inflation premium   The average inflation rate expected over the life of the instrument.

Information efficient   All information is available to the public—for example, when the prices of securities reflect all the information available to the public. When new information becomes available, prices can change quickly to reflect that information.

Initial public offering (IPO)   A sale of securities to the investing public.

Insider trading   Illegal practice of buying and selling stocks based on information that is known only by corporate information and that is not available to the public.

Institutional investors   Large investors such as insurance companies, pension funds, investment companies, and other large financial institutions.

Insurance companies   Companies that provide financial protection to individuals and businesses for life, property, liability, and health. Policyholders pay premiums to insurance companies that are then invested or withdrawn to pay claims.

Intangible assets   Qualities of a company that cannot be easily sold or bought. For example, growth opportunities, the value of the firm's research and development efforts, and customer loyalty.

Interest   The cost of money. For banks and other financial institutions, the cost of money is the interest they pay on savings accounts. For consumers, the cost of money is the interest they pay on loans and credit card accounts.

Interest coverage   Measures the ability of the firm to service all debts. It is calculated by dividing the firm's operating income or earnings before interest and taxes (EBIT) by the annual interest expense. It is commonly referred to as **times-interest-earned ratio.**

Interest rate   A price that equates the demand for and supply of loanable funds.

Internal growth rate   A measure of how quickly a firm can increase its asset base over the next year without raising outside funds.

Internal rate of return (IRR)   Method finds the return that causes the net present value to be zero. That is the point in the project when the present value of the cash flows equals the project's initial investment.

International Bank for Reconstruction and Development, or World Bank   Created to help economic growth in developing countries.

International Monetary Fund (IMF)   Created to promote world trade through monitoring and maintaining fixed exchange rates and by making loans to countries facing balance of trade and payments problems.

International monetary system   A system of institutions and mechanisms to foster world trade, manage the flow of financial capital, and determine currency exchange rates.

International money markets   The markets where debt securities with maturities of 1 year or less are traded in foreign currency.

Inventory-turnover ratio   Measures the number of times in a year that a company replaces its inventory. It is computed by dividing the cost of goods sold by total inventory.

Investment banking firms   Firms that sell or market new securities issued by businesses to individual and institutional investors.

Investment companies   Companies that sell shares in their firms to individuals and others and invest the proceeds in corporate and government securities.

Investments   The outlay of money for an income or a profit.

Just-in-time (JIT) inventory control system   a system where there are enough materials in inventory to cover needs for a short time, but not more inventory than is needed for short-term needs.

Ladder strategy   Invests an equal amount of money in bonds with a wide range of long- and short-term maturities, so interest rate cycles will average out.

Learning option   Successful introduction of a product may lead managers to expand a product or innovation more quickly than initially proposed to take advantage of consumer interest and to gain production experience, lock up distribution channels, and to shut competitors out of the market.

Level production plan   Schedule where the same amount of raw material is purchased and the same amount of finished product is manufactured every month.

Liabilities   The debts of a business.

Limit order   An order in which the maximum buying price (limit buy) or the minimum selling price (limit sell) is specified by the investor.

Line of credit   The loan limit that the bank establishes for each of its business customers.

Liquidity preference theory   Belief that investors or debt instrument holders prefer to invest short term so they have greater liquidity and less maturity or interest rate risk.

Liquidity premium   Is the compensation for those financial debt instruments that cannot be easily converted to cash at prices close to their estimated fair market values.

Liquidity ratios   Measures that indicate the ability to meet short-term obligations to creditors as they mature or come due.

Loanable funds theory   Belief that interest rates are a function of the supply and demand for funds earmarked for loans.

Loan amortization schedule   Worksheet that shows the breakdown of each payment between interest and principal, as well as the remaining balance after each payment.

M1 money supply   Supply of currency, travelers' checks, demand deposits, and other checkable deposits at depository institutions.

M2 money supply   Includes M1 plus financial assets that can be quickly turned into cash.

M3 money supply   Includes M2 plus large time deposits (over $100,000) and institutional money market mutual funds (with minimal initial investments of $50,000).

Marginal tax rate   The rate paid on the last dollar of income.

Market Index   List of companies that are believed to represent the stock market. If the index increases in value, then the economy is said to be doing well. An example of a market index is the Dow Jones Industrial Average.

Market order   An order for immediate purchase or sale at the best possible price.

Market portfolio   Contains all risky assets and is the portfolio that truly eliminates all unsystematic risk.

Market segmentation theory   Belief that securities of different maturities are not perfect substitutes for each other.

Market value of an investment   The present value of future cash flows to be received from the investment.

Market-value ratios   Measure that indicates the willingness of investors to value a firm in the marketplace relative to financial statement values.

Maturity date   The date when the issuer is obligated to pay the bond's principal (par value or face value) to bondholders.

Maturity factoring   A form of factoring where the firm selling its accounts receivable is paid on the normal collection date or net due date of the account.

Maturity-matching approach   The financial manager tries to match the term of the loan to the life of the asset it is financing.

Maturity risk premium   The added return expected by lenders or investors because of interest rate risk on instruments with longer maturities.

Modified accelerated cost recovery system (MACRS)   Depreciates assets by an accelerated method.

MOGS   Missions, objectives, goals, and strategies for a firm. A firm makes decisions and designs projects around MOGS.

Monetary policy   Refers to the actions of the Federal Reserve that influence the amount of money and credit in the U.S. economy. That, in turn largely determines interest rates and the performance of our economy.

Monetary system   A network of institutions that regulate financial transaction types, the supply of money, and economic agents.

Money   Anything that is commonly accepted as payment.

Money market mutual funds (MMMFs)   Issue shares to customers and invest the proceeds in highly liquid, very-short-maturity, interest-bearing debt instruments called *money market investments*.

Money markets   The markets where debt securities with maturities of 1 year or less are traded.

Mortgage banking firms   Companies that originate real estate mortgages by bringing together borrowers and investors. Also referred to as *mortgage companies*.

Mortgage bonds   Are not secured by home mortgages. Rather, they are secured by specific property pledged by the firm.

Municipal bonds   Long-term debt securities issued by state or local governments.

Mutually exclusive projects   Selecting one project that precludes others from being undertaken.

National Credit Union Administration (NCUA)   Supervises and regulates credit unions.

Negative correlation Exists when two time series tend to move in opposite directions.

Negotiable certificates of deposit Short-term debt instrument issued by depository institutions to individual or institutional depositors. Also known as *negotiable CDs*.

Net benefit The present value of an investment project's cash flows minus its cost.

NET CHG Gives the change in price from the previous day's close.

Net loss Total expenses are greater than total revenue.

Net present value Net present value = present value of cash flows − cost of the project.

Net profit Total revenue is greater than total expenses.

Net profit margin A widely used measure of a company's profitability; calculated as the firm's net income after taxes divided by net sales.

Net return on total assets Firm's net income divided by total assets. Commonly referred to as the *return on total assets*.

Net working capital Measure of a firm's liquidity. The measure is the firm's current assets minus current liabilities.

Nominal interest rate The rate that we observe in the marketplace. The nominal interest rate includes a premium for expected inflation.

Noncumulative preferred stock Makes no provision for the accumulation of unpaid dividends.

Nonprofit corporation Does not pay taxes unless their income rises above the level set by the IRS. Even then, the tax rate is reduced.

Normal conditions The domestic economy will grow at a pace close to its long-run average. Inflation rates and interest rates will be relatively stable.

Office of Thrift Supervision (OTS) Oversees S & Ls and other savings institutions.

Online trading Buying and selling securities such as stocks over the Internet.

Open-end mortgage bond Allows the same assets to be used as security in future bond issues.

Open market operations The buying and selling of U.S. government securities. *Open market* refers to the fact that the Fed doesn't decide which security dealers to do business with on a specific day.

Operating cycle The time between receiving raw materials and collecting the cash from credit sales posted to accounts receivables.

Operating profit margin Indicates the profits of the company before interest, and taxes are deducted from a firm's operations. It is calculated on the firm's earnings before interest and taxes divided by net sales.

Operating return on assets Earnings before interest and taxes divided by total assets.

Opportunity cost The cost of passing up the next best alternative.

Optimum debt/equity mix   The proportionate use of debt or equity that minimizes the firm's cost of capital, in turn helps the firm to maximize shareholder wealth.

Options contract   Gives the owner of the contract the option of buying or selling a particular good at a specified price on or before a certain expiration date.

Order bill of lading   Represents the written acceptance of goods for shipment by a transportation company and the terms under which the goods are to be transported to their destination.

Ordinary annuity   A series of equal payments (receipts) that occur at the end of each time period.

Organized securities exchange   A location with a trading floor where all stock transactions take place.

Other checkable deposits   Twenty-four percent of M1, includes automatic transfer service (ATS) accounts and negotiable order of withdrawal (NOW) accounts at depository institutions.

Over-the-counter (OTC) markets   Networks of independent dealers and agents who communicate and trade electronically rather than on a trading floor.

Partnership   A form of business organization involving two or more people who own a business operated for profits.

Par value   Or, stated value, usually has little bearing on the current price or book value of the stock. It is used mainly for accounting purposes and some legal needs.

PE   Gives the price/earnings ratio of the stock. This value is computed by dividing the firm's latest annual earnings per share into its current stock price.

Pension funds   Funds composed of contributions from employees and/or their employers who invest the proceeds on behalf of the employees.

Perpetuity bond   A bond without a maturity date. Its owners and heirs receive interest payments for as long as the company exists.

Physical money   The coin and paper currency used to pay debts and expenses and purchase goods and services.

Pledge   A way of obtaining a short-term loan by using accounts receivable as collateral.

Political risk   The risk associated with the possibility that a national government might confiscate or expropriate assets held by foreigners.

Portals   Specialized and secure Web sites through which clients can access order and account information.

Portfolio   Any combination of financial assets or investments.

Positive correlation   Exists when two stocks move in the same direction over time.

Preauthorized checks   Regular (typically monthly) deductions by a vendor from a customer's checking account.

Precautionary motives   Demands for funds that may be caused by unpredictable events, such as delays in production or in the collection of receivables.

Preferred stock   An equity security that has a preference, or senior claim, to the firm's earnings and assets.

Premium bonds   When interest rates are higher, bonds may be sold at a price higher than their par value.

Present value   The present value of all cash flows for the life of the project less the cost of the initial investment.

Present value of savings or investment   Current value or amount of savings or investment.

Price/earnings ratio   The market price of the firm's common stock divided by its annual earnings per share. Also referred to as the *P/E ratio*.

Price-to-book-value ratio   Measures the market's value of the firm relative to balance sheet equity.

Primary securities markets   Markets that facilitate the sales of initial offerings of debt and equity securities to the public.

Prime interest rate   The rate that banks charge each other. The rate charged consumers and businesses is always higher and is determined by various factors.

Prime rate   The interest rate the bank charges its most creditworthy customers.

Profitability Index (PI) method   Method computes the ratio between the present values of the inflows and outflows.

Profitability ratios   Measure that indicates the firm's ability to generate returns on its sales, assets, and equity.

Program trading   A technique for trading stocks as a group rather than individually.

Putable bonds   Or, retractable bonds allow investors to force the issuer to redeem them prior to maturity.

Quick ratio   Used to gauge a firm's liquidity. The measure is computed by dividing the sum of cash, marketable securities, and accounts receivable by the current liabilities. Also referred to as the **acid-test ratio.**

Random walk   Prices appear to fluctuate randomly over time, driven by the random arrival of new information.

Rate of return   The percentage of profit earned from an investment.

Ratio analysis   Financial technique that involves dividing various financial statement numbers into one another.

Real assets   Property, including the direct ownership of land, buildings or homes, equipment, inventories, durable goods, and even precious metals.

Real rate of interest   The interest rate on a risk-free financial debt instrument when no inflation is expected.

Real-option analysis   Evaluates investments by recognizing the sources of flexibility that can enhance a project's value.

Receivables turnover   Measure of how effectively a firm extends credit and collects debts. It is computed by dividing annual sales, preferably credit sales, by the year-end accounts receivable.

Recession   The domestic economy will grow slowly, or maybe contract. Inflation will peak and start to decline; short-term interest rates will fall.

Registered bonds   Include the bondholders' names, and interest payments are sent directly to the bondholders.

Registered traders   Individuals who purchase a seat on the exchange to buy and sell stocks for their own account.

Regular corporation   Pays tax on its profits.

Repurchase agreement   A way of making a loan. The lender buys an asset, usually securities, from the borrower, thus providing funds to the borrower. The borrower repays by buying back the asset at a prearranged time and price.

Restricted stock   Given to employees, but they cannot sell the shares until it vests.

Retail selling   Selling to individual investors.

Retained earnings   The amount that the company keeps to improve or expand business operations.

Return on equity   Measures the return that shareholders earned on their equity invested in the firm.

Reverse split   Reduces the number of shares each stockholder owns.

Revolving credit agreement   A commitment in the form of a standby agreement for a guaranteed line of credit.

Risk-adjusted discount rate (RADR)   Adjusts the required rate of return at which the analyst discounts a project's cash flows.

Risk-free rate of interest   Combines the real rate of interest and the inflation premium, which in the United States is represented by U.S. Treasury debt instruments or securities.

Rule of 72   Shortcut method used to approximate the time required for an investment to double in value. This method is applied by dividing the interest rate into the number 72 to determine the number of years it will take for an investment to double in value.

Savings and loans   Banks that lend to both businesses and individuals.

Savings banks   Banks that focus on working with consumers and provide loans to individuals seeking to purchase items such as automobiles and houses. Fulfills the same purpose as credit unions.

Secondary markets   The primary market is where securities are first issued and sold in an offering to investors. Any trading of the securities thereafter occurs in the secondary market. Secondary markets provide liquidity to investors who wish to sell securities.

Secondary securities markets   They facilitate the transfer of previously issued securities from existing investors to new investors. Security transactions or transfers typically take place on organized security exchanges or in the electronic over-the-counter market.

Secured lending   Lending with some collateral or security backing the loan that can be claimed or sold by the lender if the borrower defaults. Also called **asset-based lending**.

Secured loan Specific property is pledged as collateral for the loan.

Secured obligations Specific property is pledged as collateral for the obligation.

Securities firms Firms that accept and invest individual savings and also facilitate the sale and transfer of securities between investors.

Securities markets Physical locations or electronic forums where debt and equity securities are sold and traded.

Seesaw effect Means that lower interest rates cause bond prices to rise and higher interest rates result in lower bond prices.

Selection Stage that involves applying the appropriate capital budgeting techniques to determine the financial feasibility of the project, which will help the company make a final decision to accept or reject the project.

Short sale A sale of securities that the seller does not own. An investor will want to short a stock if he/she feels the price will decline in the future.

Sight draft A financial instrument requiring immediate payment.

Simple interest Interest earned only on the principal amount of the investment.

Single-payment annuity Involves one lump sum payment with no provision for funds to be added at a later date.

Sinking fund Requires the issuer to retire specified portions of the bond issue over time.

Small Business Administration Organization that was established by the federal government to provide financial assistance to small firms that are unable to obtain loans through private channels on reasonable terms.

Sole proprietorship A business venture that is owned by a single individual who personally receives all profits and assumes all responsibility for the debts and losses of the business.

Special drawing rights (SDRs) Are a reserve asset created by the IMF consisting of a basket or portfolio of currencies that could be used to make international payments.

Specialists Assigned dealers, have the responsibility of making a market for an assigned security.

Speculative motives Demands for funds to take advantage of unusual cash discounts for needed materials.

Spinoff Where the parent sells the subsidiary to another firm or in a public offering and the new owners truly do own the firm.

Spot exchange rate The rate being quoted for the immediate delivery of the currency.

Spread The difference between the offer price and the price paid by the investment bank.

Stand-alone principle Ensures that analysis focuses on the project's own cash flows, without regard to the cash flows produced by the firm's other activities.

Standard deviation Square root of the variance.

Standard of value A function of money that occurs when prices and debts are stated in terms of the monetary value.

Statement of cash flows Provides a summary of the cash sources that come into the company and the cash that goes out of the company during a specified accounting period.

State of nature Includes a set of economic trends and business conditions.

Stock option Allows the purchase at a future time of a stated number of the firm's shares at a specific price.

Stock quotes Appear in major newspapers or Web sites and provide a summary of the stock's performance.

Stock split Occurs when a publicly held corporation decides to make a change in the number of outstanding shares issued to stockholders.

Stop-loss order An order to sell stock at the market price when the price of the stock falls to a specified level.

Store of value Money held for some period of time before it is spent.

Straight bond Issued with a preset maturity date. That date the final interest payment is made and the bond's par value is paid to investors.

Strong-form efficient market A market in which prices reflect all public and private knowledge, including past and current information.

Subordinated debentures The claims of these bondholders are subordinate to the claims of debenture holders.

Sunk cost A project-related expense that does not depend on whether or not the project is undertaken.

Sustainable growth rate A measure of how quickly the firm can grow when it uses both internal equity and debt financing to keep its capital structure constant over time.

SYM Gives the trading symbol, or ticker, an abbreviation of three letters or less that identifies reports of all transactions in the stock on the stock market for the day.

Systematic risk Risk that cannot be eliminated through diversification.

Tangible assets Property that can be easily sold and used by other companies such as railroad cars and automobiles.

Terms of an underwriting agreement Provides that securities are purchased at a predetermined or "firm commitment" price by the underwriters, who then sell them to investors at the offer price.

Third market A type of secondary market that is for large blocks of listed shares and operates outside the confines of organized exchanges.

Thrift institutions Institutions, including savings and loan associations, savings banks, and credit unions, accumulate individual savings and provide credit primarily to individuals.

Thrift Institutions Advisory Council Consists of members from savings and loans associations, savings banks, and credit unions and provides advice on issues that directly affect thrift institutions.

Time draft   A financial instrument requiring payment at a later date.

Total-assets-turnover ratio   Measure of how efficiently a company uses its assets to generate sales. Measure that is computed by dividing net sales by the company's total assets.

Total-debt-to-equity ratio   Measure that shows a firm's total debt in relation to the total dollar amount owners have invested in the firm.

Tracking stock   Issued by the parent company to track a subsidiary rather than the entire firm.

Trade credit   Credit that is extended on purchases to a firm's customers; Accounts receivable together with longer-term notes receivable taken by manufacturers, wholesalers, jobbers, and other businesses that sell products or services to businesses.

Transactions motives   Demands for holding cash is that cash is needed to conduct day-to-day operations.

Travelers' checks   Offered by banks and other organizations are a promise to pay on demand the face amounts of the checks.

Traveler's letter of credit   Issued by a bank in one country and addressed to a list of foreign banks authorizing them to cash checks or purchase drafts presented by the bearer.

Treasury bills   Short-term debt obligations issued by the U.S. federal government to meet its short-term borrowing needs when imbalances exist between tax revenues and government expenditures.

Treasury bonds   Long-term debt securities issued by the U.S. federal government.

Treasury Inflation Protected Securities (TIPS)   Both the principal value and interest payments rise and fall along with inflation.

Trend analysis   Measure that uses ratios to evaluate a firm's performance over time. Also referred to as **time-series analysis.**

Trust indenture   An extensive document that includes in great detail the various provisions and covenants of the loan arrangement.

Trust receipt   A lien against specific items in inventory.

Truth-in-Lending   A section of the Consumer Credit Protection Act that requires disclosure of the finance charges and the annual percentage rate of credit along with certain other costs and terms to allow consumers to compare the cost of credit from different sources.

Underpricing   Represents the difference between the aftermarket stock price and the offering price.

Underwriting agreement   An agreement in which investment bankers assume the risk arising from the possibility that securities may not be purchased by investors.

Unit of account   A way to measure prices.

Unsecured obligations   Represents a general claim against the assets of the issuer.

Unsystematic risk   Risk that is diversified away as assets are added to a portfolio is the firm- and industry-specific risk, or the "microeconomic" risk.

U.S. balance of payments   A summary of all economic transactions with the rest of the world. It includes foreign investment, private and government grants, U.S. military spending overseas, and many other items besides the buying and selling of goods and services.

Usury   The act of lending money at an excessively high interest rate.

Variable annuity   Offers a variety of funding options, such as stocks, bonds, and money market accounts.

Velocity of money   The rate of circulation of the money supply.

VOL (000s)   Tells how many shares of the company's stock were traded, in hundreds.

Waiting-to-invest option   Rather than begin a project this year, there may be value in waiting until next year in order to better evaluate changing technology, input prices, or conditions in their own product market.

Warehouse receipt   Placing inventory in a bonded warehouse for safekeeping; items are removed as they are paid for.

Weak-form efficient market   A market in which prices reflect all past information.

Weighted average cost of capital (WACC)   Represents the minimum required rate of return on its capital budgeting projects.

Working capital   A firm's current assets as shown on the balance sheet and includes cash in the bank accounts, marketable securities, inventory, and accounts receivable.

Yankee bonds   U.S. dollar-denominated bonds that are issued in the United States by a foreign issuer.

Yield curve   Reflects the profits realized on securities of similar default risk. It represents a particular point in time, and the interest rates should reflect yields for the remaining time to maturity. U.S. government securities provide the best basis for constructing yield.

Yield to maturity   Represents an estimate of the investor's return on the bond if it was purchased today and held to maturity.

YLD %   Gives the dividend yield of the stock.

YTD % CHG   Shows the year-to-date change in price for a stock.

A